Canadian Corrections

THIRD EDITION

CURT T. GRIFFITHS

SIMON FRASER UNIVERSITY

NELSON EDUCATION

Canadian Corrections, Third Edition

by Curt T. Griffiths

Associate Vice President, Editorial Director:
Evelyn Veitch

Editor-in-Chief, Higher Education:
Anne Williams

Senior Acquisitions Editor:
Lenore Taylor-Atkins

Senior Marketing Manager:
David Tonen

Developmental Editor:
Mark Grzeskowiak

Photo Researcher:
Joanne Tang

Permissions Coordinator:
Joanne Tang

Content Production Manager:
Susan Ure

Production Service:
Macmillan Publishing Solutions

Copy Editor:
Matthew Kudelka

Proofreader:
Barbara Storey

Indexer:
Maura Brown

Production Coordinator:
Ferial Suleman

Design Director:
Ken Phipps

Managing Designer:
Franca Amore

Interior Design:
Tammy Gay

Cover Design:
Peter Papayanakis

Cover Image:
"Future so Defined"—Osnat Tzadok HYPERLINK "http://www.OsnatFineArt.com" www.OsnatFineArt.com

Compositor:
Macmillan Publishing Solutions

Printer:
Webcom

Printed and bound in Canada
3 4 5 13 12 11

For more information contact Nelson Education Ltd., 1120 Birchmount Road, Toronto, Ontario, M1K 5G4. Or you can visit our Internet site at http://www.nelson.com

Library and Archives Canada Cataloguing in Publication

Griffiths, Curt T. (Curt Taylor), 1948-

Canadian corrections / Curt T. Griffiths. – 3rd ed.

Includes bibliographical references and index.

ISBN 978-0-17-647336-5

1. Corrections–Canada–Textbooks. I. Title.

HV9507.G75
2009 364.60971 C2009-900436-4

ISBN-13: 978-0-17-647336-5
ISBN-10: 0-17-647336-X

To my mentors—

Dr. Gordon W. Browder

and

Dr. Robert W. Balch

and

To Dr. William J. Griffiths (Will), M.D., Ph.D.

my brother, my hero

CONTENTS

CHAPTER 6 DOING TIME: THE INMATES 204

LIST OF BOXES

LIST OF FIGURES

LIST OF TABLES

LIST OF "AT ISSUE" FEATURES

PREFACE

This text is designed to provide a comprehensive overview of corrections in Canada. It attempts to capture the dynamics of corrections in this country and to explore the unique attributes of the Canadian correctional enterprise. The materials presented in this text are descriptive and analytical. In writing this text, I have endeavoured to present the materials in a way that will stimulate your thinking about corrections and capture the intensity of the issues surrounding the response to criminal offenders by systems of corrections.

The public, criminal justice and corrections personnel, and offenders have expressed a considerable amount of frustration, anger, and disappointment with the response to criminal offenders and the operations of correctional systems in Canada over the past 200 years. It often appears that, despite the expenditure of considerable time, effort, and money, we are no further ahead in our quest to find successful strategies for preventing and correcting criminal behaviour. Given the pessimism that often surrounds corrections, it would have been quite easy to write a text that focused only on the failures, of which there have been enough to fill volumes. However, to have done so would have been to tell only part of the story. In recent years there have been some exciting initiatives in corrections, many of which hold great promise.

This text avoids the doom and gloom that so often characterizes discussion of corrections. It describes community-based and institutional programs and, as well, includes the latest research findings. No doubt the text may raise more questions for you than it answers. This is the nature of scholarly inquiry and of any study of corrections.

It is also important to keep in mind that corrections systems have been given a very difficult role to play: to sanction offenders while providing programs and services that are designed to reduce the likelihood that the offender will return to a life of crime. The response of correctional systems to offenders in carrying out this mandate has ranged from the brutal to the humane. Nearly always, it has been controversial.

Correctional institutions continue to be beset by violence and the health-related challenges of HIV/AIDS, Hepatitis, and an aging inmate population are among the more significant health-related challenges confronting systems of corrections. For correctional officers and inmates, correctional institutions continue to be unsafe places to work and live. The breakdown of the traditional inmate code of conduct has created more unpredictability and a considerable amount of violence, much of it related to the illicit drug trade, continues as a feature of daily life in correctional institutions.

On the treatment side, Canada continues to be a world leader in the development of effective correctional programs, and there has been success in implementing programs for Aboriginal offenders and for female offenders. The research evidence is substantial that correctional treatment programs, if properly implemented, can reduce the rates of re-offending. The release and reentry of offenders into the community remain areas of concern, with increasing scrutiny of parole board decision making and efforts to meet the needs of—and to manage the risk posed by—special categories of offenders, including sex offenders.

New features of the third edition of *Canadian Corrections*:

- Updated research findings
- "Perspectives" of correctional personnel and inmates at the beginning of each chapter
- Discussion of new challenges to Canadian corrections, including Aboriginal gangs
- Key Points Review and Key Term Questions at the end of each chapter to assist students
- "At Issue" topics at the end of each chapter to facilitate discussion of critical issues in contemporary Canadian corrections, including "Should the federal and provincial/territorial governments initiate/expand harm reduction programs in prisons?", "Should inmates have the right to reduce treatment?", "Should section 745 of the Criminal Code—the faint hope clause—be removed from the Criminal Code?", and "Should Inmates Have the Full Benefit of the Charter of Rights and Freedoms?"
- Extensive coverage of the findings and recommendations of the Correctional Service of Canada Review Panel
- Expanded coverage of offenders' and inmates perceptions of and experiences in the corrections system

Every attempt has been made to make this text student friendly and to ensure that the text compliments the well-taught corrections course. Learning objectives are set out at the beginning of each chapter, along with a list of key terms. Boxes highlight specific programs, research findings and important issues. "Hot" topics in corrections are presented in At Issue boxes at the end of each chapter, as well as questions for review and key term questions. There is also a Glossary at the end of the text that contains the key terms from all of the chapters.

The reader will note that the text has not been written within any one theoretical framework. It is my view that Canadian corrections is best studied from a perspective that combines description with critical analyses of key issues and concepts. There is no one theoretical or conceptual framework within which materials on corrections can neatly fit. Rather, the text should be viewed as only one resource in the study of corrections. It should be supplemented both by information from local jurisdictions and regions and by any additional theoretical/conceptual materials that instructors may want to introduce.

There are, no doubt, issues that have not been adequately addressed in the text. Should you wish to offer comments on any aspect of the book or have suggestions on how it can be improved in future editions, you can reach me by e-mail at griffith@sfu.ca.

Curt Taylor Griffiths, Ph.D.
Simon Fraser University
Burnaby, B.C.

ACKNOWLEDGMENTS

There are many persons who contributed, directly and indirectly, to the production of this third edition of *Canadian Corrections*. I would like to thank the external reviewers, whose comments and suggestions on the second edition of the text provided guidance in preparing the current edition.

There are a number of correctional professionals who have influenced my thinking on corrections and contributed ideas and materials for the text. I would like to thank Morgan Andreassen, Deputy Warden–Intervention, Matsqui Institution, and Kelly Chahal, probation officer with the Ministry of Correctional Services in British Columbia, for sharing their insights and experiences. I would also like to thank Tom Jackson of the Prisoners' HIV/AIDS Support Action Network in Toronto for his valuable assistance in facilitating the inclusion of the inmate poems that appear in Chapter 6. Special thanks to John A. McCullough, Chair, Ontario Parole and Earned Release Board for providing the materials included in Appendices 8.1 and 8.2. Invaluable assistance in preparing the text was provided by Danielle Murdoch, doctoral student in the School of Criminology at Simon Fraser University.

I would also like to acknowledge the students in my corrections courses in the School of Criminology who, over the past three decades, have made the teaching and study of Canadian corrections an exciting endeavour and whose curiosity and criticisms have been a continual source of inspiration. A further debt of gratitude is owed to the offenders and correctional officers and administrators who have shared their experiences and observations of corrections over the years.

As always, it has been a pleasure to work with the outstanding publishing team at Nelson Education Ltd.: Lenore Taylor-Atkins, Mark Grzeskowiak, Susan Ure, and David Tonen all brought a high level of enthusiasm, energy, and professionalism to the project. And, special thanks to the world's best copy editor, Matthew Kudelka.

Canadian Corrections

THIRD EDITION

CHAPTER 1

CANADIAN CORRECTIONS: AN OVERVIEW

CHAPTER OBJECTIVES

After reading this chapter you should be able to:

- *Describe the "who" and the "what" of corrections.*
- *Provide a definition of corrections.*
- *Outline the structure of contemporary Canadian corrections.*
- *Describe the purpose, principles, and goals of sentencing and the various sentencing options.*
- *Describe the special sentencing provisions for dangerous and long-term offenders as well as the sanction of judicial determination.*
- *Discuss the effectiveness of sentencing.*
- *Identify and discuss the challenges that confront correctional systems in the early 21st century.*
- *Identify and discuss the trends in contemporary corrections.*
- *Discuss the arguments that surround the use of the death penalty.*
- *Discuss the arguments that surround Section 718.2(e) of the Criminal Code.*
- *Speak to the arguments surrounding the potential expansion of the number of mandatory minimum sentences in the Criminal Code.*

KEY TERMS

Noncarceral corrections
Carceral corrections
Corrections
Canadian Charter of Rights and Freedoms
Constitution Act (1867)
Criminal Code
Corrections and Conditional Release Act
Two-year rule
General deterrence
Specific deterrence
Dangerous offenders
Long-term offenders
Judicial determination
NIMBY (Not in My Back Yard)/ NOTE (Not Over There Either)

PERSPECTIVE

Reflections of an Ex-dangerous Offender

"It started out when I was at a group home which consisted of 30 other children. I was sent there because I was labeled as being "incorrigible" under the Juvenile Delinquent's Act. This was in the late 1960s. My dad was physically abusive and so they took me away from my family. But the group home was full and I was called into the office and told that I was going to a bigger school, a school which I would learn quite a bit and would become a responsible boy. Initially I would start at a place called Bowmanville which was kind of a reception centre for boys coming into the training school system. I would be there for approximately ten days, and I would be classified as being too young to be there and so I was sent to a place called Coburn. Coburn Training School: what would go on in that training school for me, I felt, was probably the hardest part in my whole life, because there was a lot of discipline and discipline was really forced on you.

"I mean physically forced. We were made to sit in lockers in houses of 30 boys; each house consisted of 30 boys, and there were seven houses at the school. Everything was done military style, and we would have to sit in our lockers and if anybody, you know, acted up or something like that the house would be put onto routines. Routines sometimes consisted of running up and down fire escapes with big parkas on during the summer. This was referred to as being the sweat box, because it was summer and we would be up and down the fire escape. Some of the routines would last three or four hours. If one of the boys, or any of the boys didn't make it or fell down or gave up or whatever, the house was put on more routines. As a consequence, whoever causes the house to be put on longer routines would get beat. Sometimes the staff would suddenly get up and say he heard the telephone ring. That was the key to go and he was leaving and that some guy was going to get beat up. So at an early age we learned that fighting was part of the way of life, and that if you wanted to survive that you had to be physical, and also the fact that you weren't going to inform on anybody there, because if you did, you were a rat. So at an early age we were learning not to be a rat and also to fight. And, if somebody escaped, the whole house would be put on routines until the boy came back, providing that it was not a long period. So anyway, when this boy came back he would sometimes be put into a potato sack and tied into it. Then everybody would scramble him.

"Sometimes when visitors came they would give candy and chocolate bars and stuff like that. Well we were only allowed to have it on Friday night. So all of this candy was put away in a closet and on Friday night if the house had been good then we were able to get whatever candy we had. People like myself were unfortunate not to have visitors; so, they would have a box of candy and what they used to do is put like jelly beans or Smarties or something like that; they would give you a cup, then throw the candy in the middle of the floor. Everybody would scramble for it. So everybody was beating each other up to get a couple of candies.

"For me training school was probably, as I said earlier, the worst part of my experience with the criminal justice system. My mother and father never came to visit me, ever. Not when I was a juvenile or adult. I never saw my mother again. Due to the fact that I was very young and had just been taken away from my family and having no loved ones, I started to build this out of control kind of person, you know, in the sense that I would fight at the drop of a hat. The thing is I realized by doing that then I was protecting myself, so for my own protection I was developing these skills that as I got older would become very harmful to me, and to most other people I would come into contact with."

Source: Author's interview with ex-offender.

These are the reflections of an ex–dangerous offender who entered the youth justice system as an "incorrigible" at age seven in the 1960s under the Juvenile Delinquents Act. He would go on to serve 23 years inside youth and adult correctional institutions; for his last series of offences, he would be designated a dangerous offender. His story, while perhaps extreme, is similar to those of many others who find themselves involved in the correctional system. It also highlights the difficulty of escaping what, for many, becomes a perpetual "revolving door": from the community to the justice system and (sometimes) incarceration and back into the community. The challenge for community-based and institutional correctional systems is to intervene in a positive way so as to reduce the likelihood of reoffending. When this challenge is met, the offender is helped and the community is protected.

Corrections is perhaps the most fascinating and controversial component of the criminal justice system. Nearly everyone is interested in crime and criminal offenders and has an opinion to contribute to any discussion that arises. To illustrate this, raise the subject of capital punishment with your friends or family members over dinner. This interest in crime has not been lost on the media, which present an endless supply of police dramas and crime news. In the study of corrections, sorting fact from fiction and sifting through the sensational to discover the reality are not always easy tasks. One result is that most Canadians know little about this country's correctional system, except what they hear on the evening news.

Whatever your particular philosophy of corrections, whether you support strict enforcement of criminal laws or lean more toward treatment, you should be concerned about how our correctional systems operate. This is true not only because of the enormous outlay of tax dollars but also for reasons closer to home. Most people convicted of criminal offences will never serve a day in prison. Instead they will be fined, discharged, or subjected to some degree of supervision by correctional authorities while they continue to live at home. Those who do go to prison may well be "out of sight, out of mind," but almost all of them—including virtually everyone sentenced to life imprisonment—will eventually be released back into the community. They will live in our cities and towns, be our coworkers, stand in line behind us at the grocery store, and attend college or university with us or with our children.

These facts alone require us to examine how correctional systems, from the sentencing stage onward, respond to people convicted of violating the law. Just as important is the need to reflect on a question asked of C.T. Griffiths by a 19-year-old serving a lengthy sentence: "When I get out of here in 25 years, do you want to be my neighbour?" Remember also that each of us has a stake in our correctional systems. If only out of self-interest, it is crucial that we understand not only how these systems operate but also how they can be made more effective.

This chapter provides an overview of the systems of corrections in Canada and identifies a number of challenges that confront corrections, as well as several trends in corrections that are evident in the early 21st century. The discussion is designed to get you thinking about the different dimensions of corrections and to provide a backdrop for the more detailed discussions throughout the text.

THE "WHO" AND THE "WHAT" OF CORRECTIONS

"Corrections" describes such a wide range of structures and activities that it is often difficult to determine what is being discussed. Many people make the mistake of equating corrections with prisons (and many college and university texts have pictures of prisons or inmates in cells on their covers).

The "Who" of Corrections

All correctional systems have both **noncarceral** and **carceral** components. Noncarceral systems include offenders, corrections personnel, and programs that are outside an institution. People involved in noncarceral corrections include sentencing judges; probation officers; probationers; staff of nonprofit organizations such as the John Howard Society, the Salvation Army, and the Elizabeth Fry Society; staff of treatment and counselling programs; community service coordinators; Aboriginal organizations, such as friendship centres; community volunteers; religious organizations; the offender's family; parole board members; parole officers; parolees; and staff in community halfway houses.

Carceral corrections includes sentencing judges; inmates; superintendents and wardens; correctional officers; program staff; volunteers; the offender's family; treatment professionals; health-care providers; spiritual advisers such as chaplains and Aboriginal elders; Aboriginal organizations, including Native prison liaison workers; the inmates; and oversight agencies, which receive complaints from inmates. Note that both of the above lists include criminal court judges, because the correctional process really begins when the sentence is passed. More on this later in the chapter. Figure 1.1 presents a breakdown of the adult correctional population.

The "What" of Corrections

The "what" of corrections is somewhat more complicated. Correctional systems can be described in a number of ways:

Figure 1.1

Composition of the Adult Correctional Population, 2005–2006

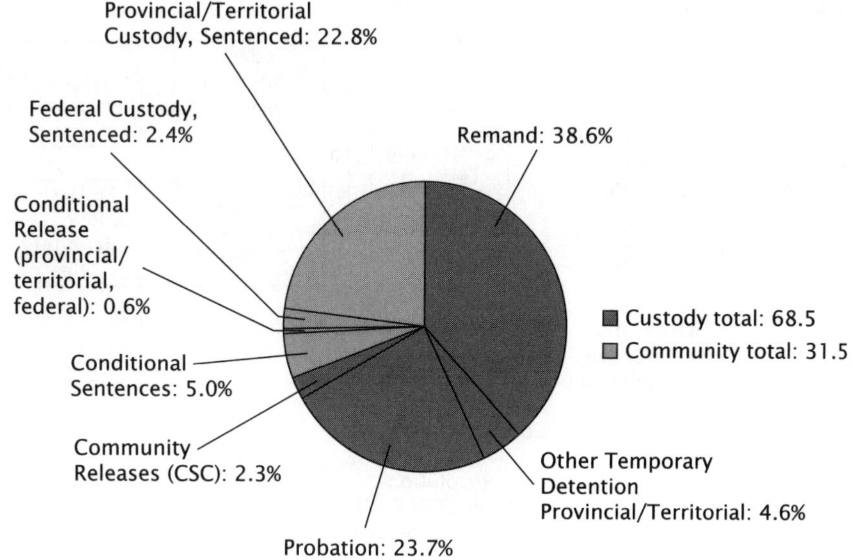

Source: Landry and Sinha 2008, 12.

Corrections as a Subsystem of the Criminal Justice System

Systems of corrections, together with the public, the police, and the criminal courts, provide the foundation of the criminal justice system. These components of the criminal justice system are interconnected—in other words, the activities of each affect the activities of the others. For example, the patterns of police enforcement and arrest affect the number of cases Crown counsel must handle, and the case-screening decisions of Crown counsel determine the caseloads of the criminal courts. For another example, the sentencing decisions of judges in criminal courts can influence the caseloads of probation officers and determine the number of admissions to correctional institutions, while the decisions of parole boards both contribute to the number of offenders who are incarcerated and the caseloads of parole officers. Throughout the criminal justice process, various key decisions affect the likelihood that an offender will end up under the supervision of a correctional authority. These key points are illustrated in Figure 1.2. Note as well that nearly all offenders will eventually return to the community.

The flow of cases through the criminal justice system has been characterized as a sieve or a funnel; in other words, the further into the process, the

Figure 1.2

The Criminal Justice System

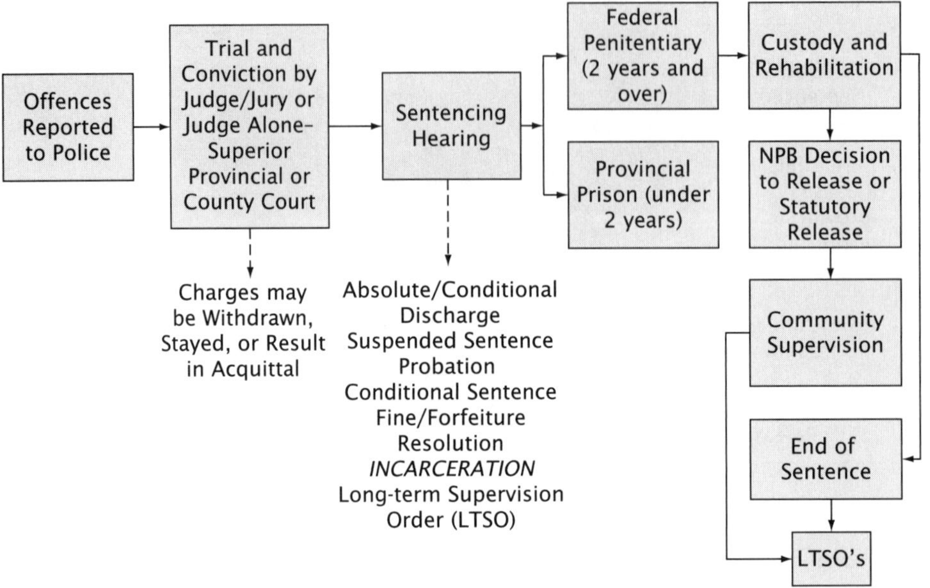

Source: Sampson 2007, 9.

smaller the number of cases (fewer than 5 percent) of the incidents reported to the police ultimately result in a prison sentence (see Figure 1.2).

Corrections as a Philosophy for Responding to Criminal Offenders

The term corrections, as the name implies, can refer to the approach taken in responding to convicted persons. Several philosophies have, at different times, provided the basis for the response to persons designated as criminal. These responses have ranged from the death penalty and corporal (physical) punishments, to treatment and rehabilitation (see Chapter 2).

Corrections as a Range of Programs and Services Delivered in Community and Institutional Settings

The majority of convicted offenders are not incarcerated; rather, they complete their sentences under some form of supervision in the community. This includes

Figure 1.3

The Criminal Justice Funnel

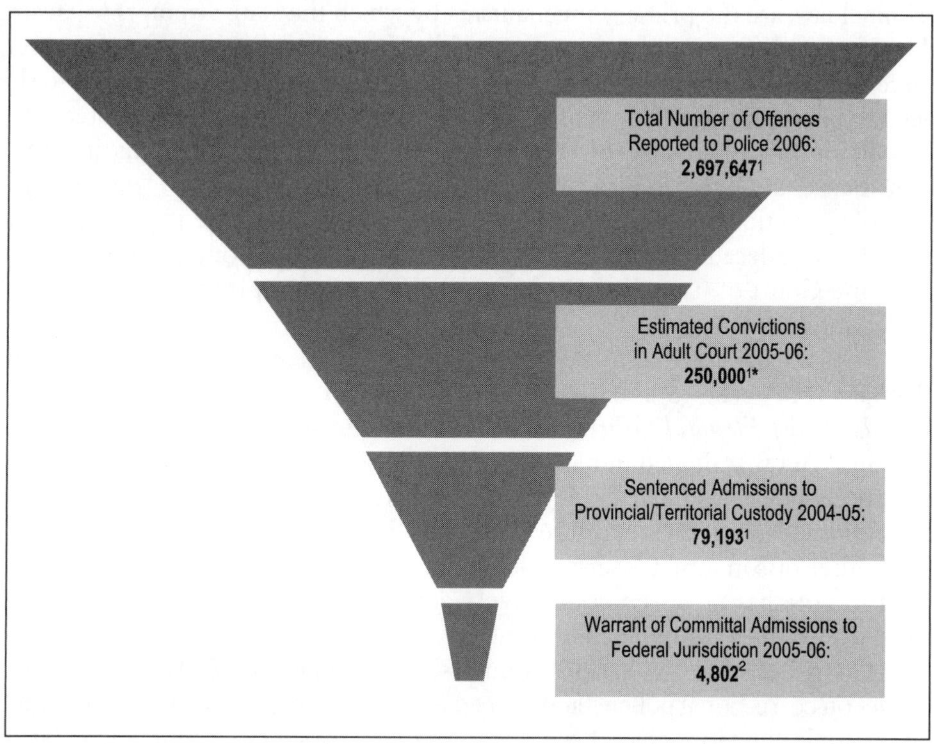

Source: Public Safety Canada Portfolio Corrections Statistics Committee 2007, 17.

offenders who are being supervised on probation, who are serving conditional sentences (often referred to as "house arrest"), or who have been released from incarceration on parole or statutory release. Probation and conditional sentences are discussed in Chapter 3; parole and statutory release are examined in Chapter 8. Correctional systems also offer programs and services to the relatively small number of offenders who are sentenced to a period of custody (see Chapter 7).

Defining Corrections

Combining all of the above dimensions, **corrections** can be defined as the structures, policies, and programs that are delivered by government, nonprofit agencies and organizations, and members of the general public to sanction, punish, treat, and supervise, in the community and in correctional institutions, persons convicted of criminal offences.

CORRECTIONS IN A DEMOCRATIC SOCIETY

Systems of corrections, along with the police and the criminal courts and the criminal law, are the primary mechanisms by which the state attempts to ensure the safety and security of the general public. In democratic societies, however, there are tensions among these systems of power and authority. There is also the need to ensure that the rights of accused and convicted persons are protected.

Prior to the passage of the Charter of Rights and Freedoms in 1982, Canadian courts were reluctant to involve themselves in lawsuits against systems of corrections, particularly those brought by convicted offenders. However, over the past decade a number of decisions by Canadian courts, including the Supreme Court of Canada, have had a significant impact on the operations of correctional systems.

Historically, for example, prison inmates were denied the right to vote in elections. However, in 2002, the Supreme Court of Canada held in *Suave v. Canada (Chief Electoral Officer)* (SCC 68) that the provision of the Canadian Elections Act that denied inmates serving two years or more in prison the right to vote violated the Charter. In the 2004 federal election, inmates in federal correctional facilities were for the first time allowed to vote. However, the issue of whether prison inmates serving less than two years in prison should have the right to vote has not been conclusively determined; at this writing, this right has been extended to inmates in some but not all provinces.

Court decisions and various commissions of inquiry have also had a strong impact on correctional policies and procedures and on how offenders are managed. For example, limitations have been placed on the use of solitary confinement, "strip searches," and the deployment of male correctional officers in women's prisons.

The Mission Statement of the Correctional Service of Canada reflects an attempt to balance protection of society with the rights of offenders: "The Correctional Service of Canada, as part of the criminal justice system and respecting the rule of law, contributes to the protection of society by actively encouraging and assisting offenders to become law-abiding citizens, while exercising reasonable, safe, secure, and humane control" (Note: The "rule of law" generally refers to a "system that attempts to protect the rights of citizens from the arbitrary and abusive use of government power"; http://www.uiowa.edu/ifdebook/faq/Rule_of_Law.shtml).

THE LEGISLATIVE FRAMEWORK OF CORRECTIONS

Correctional systems operate under a variety of federal and provincial/territorial statutes that establish the authority of correctional officials, set out jurisdiction, and provide the framework within which decisions are made and programs are administered. Among the more significant pieces of legislation are the following:

- **The Canadian Charter of Rights and Freedoms** is the primary law of the land and guarantees fundamental freedoms, legal rights, and equality rights for all citizens of Canada, including those accused of crimes.
- **The Constitution Act (1867)** sets out the respective responsibilities of the federal and provincial governments in many areas, including criminal justice. The federal government is assigned responsibility for enacting criminal laws and for establishing the procedures to be followed in criminal cases, and the provincial governments are given the authority to establish the necessary structures for the administration of justice. However, this is only a general division of responsibilities, and some boundaries remain ambiguous. For example, the federal government operates correctional facilities for offenders who receive a sentence (or sentences) totalling two years or more.
- The **Criminal Code** is a federal statute that defines most criminal offences, the procedures for their prosecution, and the penalties that sentencing judges can hand down.
- The **Corrections and Conditional Release Act (CCRA)** is the primary legislation under which the federal system of corrections operates. Sections in this act cover institutional and community corrections, conditional release and detention, and the office of the correctional investigator.
- Provincial legislation includes corrections statutes that set out the framework within which provincial correctional systems operate.
- Finally, there are international agreements and conventions to which the Canadian government is a signator. These include the Transfer of Offenders Act, the United Nations Standard Minimum Rules for the Treatment of Prisoners, and the International Covenant on Civil and Political Rights.

THE STRUCTURE OF CONTEMPORARY CANADIAN CORRECTIONS

Correctional systems in Canada are operated by the federal and provincial/territorial governments, which together spend around $3 billion a year on personnel, programs, services, and infrastructure.

The Split in Correctional Jurisdiction

A unique feature of Canadian corrections is the **two-year rule,** under which offenders who receive sentences of two years or longer fall under the jurisdiction of the federal government, and offenders receiving sentences of two years less a day are the responsibility of provincial/territorial correctional authorities. The historical record provides no clear explanation for why the two-year rule was established at Confederation in 1867. Observers have offered a number of reasons, including these: (1) the federal government was interested in strengthening its powers; (2) only the federal government had the resources to establish and maintain long-term institutions; and (3) offenders receiving short sentences were seen as in need of guidance, whereas those receiving longer sentences were seen as more serious criminals who had to be separated from society for longer periods (Ouimet 1969).

The split in corrections jurisdiction has a number of implications for offenders and correctional authorities. On the negative side, the relatively short period of time that offenders are confined in provincial institutions means that there is a high turnover of the population, which makes it difficult to provide treatment programs. As well, there are considerable variations among the provinces and territories in the noncarceral and carceral programs and services offered. Many offenders spend their entire "careers" in provincial/territorial facilities, and others spend time in both systems. On a more positive note, the two-year rule helps separate more serious offenders who receive lengthier sentences from those offenders who have committed less serious crimes. As well, provincial offenders have access to a wide range of alternatives to incarceration, including probation, conditional sentences, and electronic monitoring.

THE FEDERAL SYSTEM OF CORRECTIONS

The Correctional Service of Canada

The federal system of corrections is operated by the Correctional Service of Canada (CSC), an agency of Public Safety and Emergency Preparedness Canada. The CSC has five regions (Atlantic, Quebec, Ontario, Prairie, Pacific) and is headquartered in Ottawa. It provides corrections services from sea to sea to sea and operates a variety of facilities, including federal penitentiaries, halfway houses, healing lodges and treatment centres for Aboriginal offenders, community parole offices, psychiatric hospitals, reception and assessment centres, health-care centres, palliative care units, and an addiction research centre. Also, the CSC has partnered with not-for-profit organizations to operate halfway houses across the country.

The National Parole Board

A second important federal agency is the National Parole Board (NPB), which operates independently of the CSC and makes conditional release decisions.

The NPB makes the final decisions with regard to when (most) federal offenders will be released from custody. The NPB's decision making is examined in Chapter 8.

The Office of the Correctional Investigator

This is an independent federal agency whose mandate is to investigate the problems experienced by federal offenders in institutions and under supervision in the community and to ensure that the CSC meets its obligations to manage offenders in a manner that conforms to the law and that respects the rights of offenders (http://www.oci-bec.gc.ca).

PROVINCIAL/TERRITORIAL CORRECTIONAL SYSTEMS

The large majority (96 percent) of convicted offenders receive sentences that place them under the jurisdiction of provincial/territorial correctional authorities. Just over half of the custodial sentences imposed by the courts are for less than one year (Public Safety Canada Portfolio Corrections Statistics Committee 2007).

The diversity of programs and services that provincial/territorial corrections offer, the relatively short periods of time that provincial offenders remain in confinement, and the widely held view that provincial/territorial offenders represent a less serious threat in terms of their criminal behaviour have all conspired to keep the provincial/territorial correctional systems in relative obscurity.

In recent years a number of incidents have highlighted the importance of examining the workings of provincial/territorial correctional systems. Many provincial jails are faced with overcrowding, gang activity, high rates of communicable diseases (including HIV, tuberculosis, and hepatitis C), a lack of inmate safety, and poor working conditions for staff. The devastating riot that occurred in the Headingley Correctional Institution in Manitoba in 1996 (see Chapter 4) reminds us that provincial facilities are no strangers to violence and danger.

Provincial/Territorial Noncarceral and Carceral Corrections

All of the provinces/territories operate a variety of noncarceral programs and services, including probation, bail supervision, fine options, community service, and diversion programs. Other programs and services include electronic monitoring (most often used as a condition of probation or with temporary absences), house arrest, intensive supervision probation, attendance centres, temporary absences, and parole. Most of the offenders involved in provincial/territorial correctional systems are on probation.

The provincial/territorial governments operate about 150 facilities across the country. Their correctional systems are also responsible for housing accused persons who are on remand. Remanded individuals (a) have been charged with an offence, and the court has ordered they be held in custody while awaiting trial, or (b) have been found guilty at trial and are awaiting sentencing.

Two provinces—Quebec and Ontario—operate their own provincial parole boards, with provincial probation officers supervising offenders released on parole. In the other eight provinces, the NPB handles the release of some offenders and parole officers of the CSC supervise offenders. There are also provincial ombudspersons who have the authority to investigate citizen complaints against the decisions and actions of provincial government agencies and employees. These complaints include those made by offenders under the supervision and control of provincial correctional systems. Provincial/territorial correctional systems may also enter into exchange-of-service agreements with federal corrections so that inmates can remain close to their home community or have access to specific types of correctional programming.

THE PRIVATE, NOT-FOR-PROFIT SECTOR

There is a long history of involvement of private, not-for-profit organizations in the delivery of correctional services and programs. The John Howard Society is active in all of Canada's provinces and territories except the Yukon. Through its branches it operates a variety of programs, including bail supervision; community assessment and parole supervision; residential halfway houses; victim assistance and victim–offender mediation; and public and legal education. In Calgary, for example, the society operates a substance abuse program; a community conferencing program based on the principles of restorative justice; a number of counselling, advocacy, referral, and prerelease planning programs for offenders in correctional institutions; and a halfway house for special needs offenders (http://www.johnhoward.ca).

The Elizabeth Fry Society lobbies for reform at all levels of the criminal justice system, with a particular focus on women in conflict with the law. The society advocates for reform in correctional policy and develops and operates its own programs. It has had a significant impact on correctional policy for federal female offenders including the closing of the prison for women in Kingston, Ontario and the construction of small, regional facilities. The branch in Hamilton, Ontario, operates a community service order program and provides a range of services for female offenders, including counselling, community service programs, and prerelease services (http://www.elizabethfry.ca).

The Salvation Army has been involved in Canadian corrections since the late 1880s. It provides a range of services and programs, including community service order supervision, family group conferencing, substance abuse counselling, and supervision of offenders in the community (http://www.salvationarmy.ca).

Across Canada, affiliates of the St. Leonard's Society sponsor a wide range of programs and facilities for offenders. St. Leonard's Community Services London and Region, for example, operates a number of community-based and residential programs. These include an attendance centre program for youth as an alternative to custody, an employment readiness program, and Maison Louise Arbour, a residential centre program for women in conflict with the law and for women who have a mental illness (http://www.stleonards.ca).

In recent years there has been exponential growth in the involvement of Aboriginal organizations helping Aboriginal persons in conflict with the law as well as in efforts to reduce the overrepresentation of Aboriginal people in the justice system. The Native Counselling Service of Alberta (NCSA) is the oldest of the organizations involved in providing justice-related programs and services for Aboriginal people. The NCSA delivers a wide variety of institutional and community-based correctional programs and services for Aboriginal offenders, many under contract with the CSC. These include an adult and youth criminal court workers' program; the Stan Daniels Healing Centre (a 75-bed community residential centre) and an open custody centre, both in Edmonton; prison liaison services; and parole supervision (http://www.ncsa.ca).

SENTENCING IN THE CRIMINAL COURTS: BEGINNING THE CORRECTIONAL PROCESS

The Canadian judiciary is an independent component of the criminal justice system. The criminal courts can be identified as the beginning of the correctional process. It is here that judgments are passed on offenders and that specific sanctions are imposed through sentencing. The decisions made by criminal court judges not only determine which system of corrections (federal or provincial/territorial) the offender will enter, but also whether the offender will be under supervision and control in the community or be incarcerated. It is noteworthy that public opinion surveys over the past three decades have consistently found that 75 percent of Canadians view sentencing as too lenient. In a 2005 survey, 50 percent of Canadians supported mandatory sentencing, albeit with judges retaining some discretion to impose a lesser sentence in exceptional cases (Roberts, Crutcher, and Verbrugge 2007). Consider the issues surrounding mandatory sentencing as set out in "At Issue 1.1: Should there be more mandatory minimum sentences in the Criminal Code?" presented at the end of the chapter.

The Purpose and Principles of Sentencing

Section 718 of the Criminal Code sets out the purpose and principles of sentencing:

> *The fundamental purpose of sentencing is to contribute, along with crime prevention initiatives, to respect for the law and the maintenance of a just, peaceful and safe society by imposing just sanctions that have one or more of the following objectives:*
>
> *(a) to denounce the unlawful conduct;*
>
> *(b) to deter the offender and other persons from committing offences;*
>
> *(c) to separate offenders from society, where necessary;*
>
> *(d) to assist in rehabilitating offenders;*
>
> *(e) to provide reparations for harm done to victims or to the community; and*
>
> *(f) to promote a sense of responsibility in offenders, and acknowledgment of the harm done to victims and to the community.*

The Goals of Sentencing: The Cases of Mr. Smith and Mr. Jones

There are three primary groups of sentencing goals in the criminal courts: utilitarian, retributive, and restorative (Griffiths 2007). The real-life cases of "Mr. Smith" and "Mr. Jones" (not their real names) will be used to illustrate the application of these sentencing goals. Mr. Smith was a Quebec-based police chief and swimming coach who was convicted of four counts of sexual assault for fondling two girls aged 12 and 13. Mr. Jones, a computer engineer based in British Columbia, was convicted of sexual assault for fondling his young step-daughter over a two-year period. The cases of Mr. Smith and Mr. Jones—neither of whom had a prior criminal record—were highly publicized in their respective communities, and both men eventually lost their jobs.

Utilitarian Goals

Utilitarian sentencing goals focus on the future conduct of Mr. Smith, Mr. Jones, and others who might commit similar offences. The sentence is designed to protect the public from future crimes in the following ways:

- *General deterrence:* discouraging potential Mr. Smiths and Mr. Joneses from crime;
- *Specific deterrence:* discouraging Mr. Smith and Mr. Jones from doing it again;

- *Rehabilitation:* addressing the reasons why Mr. Smith and Mr. Jones did it; and
- *Incapacitation:* keeping Mr. Smith and Mr. Jones in jail to protect society.

Retributive Goals

The past, rather than the future, is the focus of retributive sentencing goals, which include the following:

- *Denunciation:* to express society's disapproval of Mr. Smith's and Mr. Jones's behaviour and to validate existing laws; and
- *Retribution:* to make Mr. Smith and Mr. Jones "pay" for their offences, based on the philosophy "an eye for an eye."

Central to the retributive goals of sentencing is the notion of proportionality: the sentences received by Mr. Smith and Mr. Jones should be proportionate to the gravity of the offence and the degree of responsibility of Smith and Jones.

Restorative Goals

The most widely used restorative approaches are victim–offender reconciliation programs, circle sentencing, and family group conferencing. Restorative justice is based on the principle that criminal behaviour injures not only the victim but communities and offenders as well. Any attempt to resolve the problems that the criminal behaviour has created should, therefore, involve all three parties. Restorative justice approaches also have a utilitarian function in that they are designed to protect the public from future criminal behaviour. Restorative justice is examined in greater detail in Chapter 3.

Since the victims in both these cases were children, they would be excluded from any restorative justice forum. However, the victims' families would have the opportunity to discuss the impact of the crimes, and Mr. Smith and Mr. Jones would be held accountable for their criminal behaviour.

What Sentences Did Mr. Smith and Mr. Jones Receive?

The offence of sexual assault carries a maximum penalty of ten years' imprisonment. Although neither Mr. Smith nor Mr. Jones had a prior criminal record and both had a good job history, the offences they committed were serious and had a significant impact on the victims. One of Mr. Smith's victims suffered long-term emotional and academic problems, while Mr. Jones's former spouse and children experienced considerable emotional difficulties. The child victims in both cases had been young and vulnerable. Mr. Smith had been an authority figure in the community, and parents trusted him to supervise their children, a trust he violated. Similarly, Mr. Jones violated the trust of his stepdaughter and most likely would have continued sexually abusing her had she not informed her mother of his improper behaviour.

Mr. Smith was sentenced to three years' probation (the maximum) and 180 hours of community service work. The Crown appealed the sentence on the grounds that it was too lenient. But the Quebec Court of Appeal upheld the sentence, in part because Mr. Smith had been fired from his job as police chief and so had already experienced a severe sanction. The appeal court acknowledged that child abuse typically demands a denunciatory sentence for the protection of society, but noted that each case must be judged on its merits.

Mr. Jones was not so fortunate. He was sentenced to 18 months' confinement in a provincial correctional facility and three years' probation (the maximum). In explaining the sentence, the presiding judge cited the objectives of denunciation and general and specific deterrence.

"They say time is money. I had a very generous judge."

SENTENCING OPTIONS

Among the sentencing options from which judges can select are the following:

- *Absolute discharge:* The offender is found guilty but is technically not convicted and is set free with no criminal record.
- *Conditional discharge:* The offender is released upon the condition that he or she comply with certain conditions. If the offender fails to meet the conditions, he or she may be returned to court to be sentenced on the original charge.

- *Fine:* The offender must pay a specific amount of money within a specified time or face the prospect of imprisonment for fine default.
- *Suspended sentence:* The offender is convicted of the offence, but the imposition of the sentence is suspended pending successful completion of a period of probation.
- *Probation:* The offender is placed under supervision in the community for a specified period of time (maximum three years), must fulfill general conditions, and may, as well, be required to adhere to or complete specific conditions (e.g., a number of community service hours).
- *Conditional sentence:* The offender receives a term of confinement (less than two years) and is allowed to serve it in the community under the supervision of a probation officer, provided he or she meets certain specified conditions (although the offender is not on probation and may be imprisoned for violation of conditions).
- *Imprisonment:* The offender is sentenced to a period of confinement.

Note that some of these options may be mixed and matched; for example, the courts may grant probation in conjunction with a sentence of two years less a day for offenders in provincial/territorial systems, or they may impose fines along with probation or a period of confinement. Most of these sentencing options are discussed in greater detail in Chapter 3.

Sentences imposed in court can be concurrent, consecutive, or intermittent.

- *Concurrent sentences:* The sentences received by the offender are merged into one sentence and served simultaneously. That is, an offender sentenced to two terms of 9 months each will serve a 9-month sentence (not an 18-month sentence).
- *Consecutive sentences:* These sentences are served separately: one begins after the other has expired. That is, an offender sentenced to two terms of 9 months each will serve 18 months.
- *Intermittent sentences:* These sentences are served on a "part time" basis (generally weekends, from Friday evening until Monday morning) and are generally no more than 90 days in length.

Provisions in the Criminal Code state that all sentences are to be concurrent unless the trial judge specifies that the sentences are to be consecutive. However, sentences under the Provincial Offences Act are to be consecutive unless the sentencing judge specifies that the sentences are to run concurrently.

Sentencing Aboriginal Offenders

There is a special provision in the Criminal Code for the sentencing of Aboriginal offenders. It is designed to reduce the overrepresentation of

Aboriginal people in correctional institutions. It was reaffirmed by the Supreme Court of Canada in *R. v. Gladue* ([1999] 1 S.C.R. 688). In that landmark case, the Court held that in cases where a term of incarceration would normally be imposed, judges must consider the unique circumstances of Aboriginal people. Specifically, judges must consider (1) the unique systemic or background factors that may have contributed to the criminal behaviour of the Aboriginal person before the court, and (2) specific sentencing procedures and sanctions (including restorative justice and traditional healing practices) that may be more appropriate for the individual Aboriginal offender. Contribute your thoughts to the At Issue 1.2: "Is Section 718.2(e) a valuable sentencing option or a misguided reform?" presented at the end of the chapter.

Dangerous Offender and Long-Term Offender Designations

Sections 752 and 753 of the Criminal Code set out the procedures and criteria for designating certain offenders as either **dangerous offenders** (DOs) or **long-term offenders.** On application by Crown counsel, judges may designate as dangerous offenders, those persons who have been convicted of committing a serious personal injury offence (except murder); or those persons who have a pattern of serious violent offences, are deemed to present a danger to society, and are highly likely to put the community at risk if not imprisoned. The application to designate an offender as dangerous must be made at the time of sentencing. A judge who makes a dangerous offender designation will order that the person serve an indeterminate period of time in prison. These offenders are eligible for a hearing before the NPB every two years after serving seven years from the day they were taken into custody.

The long-term offender designation, designed to deal with specific sexual offences, is another option for Crown counsel, particularly in cases in which the Crown falls short of the rigid requirements or level of evidence to file a dangerous offender application. As with dangerous offenders, there must be evidence that the offender presents a substantial risk of reoffending by committing a serious personal offence. However, there must also be risk assessment evidence demonstrating that the offender may be effectively managed in the community with appropriate supervision and treatment.

The designation is available only for those offenders who have received a sentence of more than two years. At sentencing, the judge sets the length of the long-term supervision order. This means that after the sentence ends (which includes confinement and postrelease supervision), the long-term supervision order comes into effect. This order requires that the offender be supervised by a parole officer for the remaining period of the order, which may be up to ten years. The NPB sets the conditions under which the offender will be supervised following the expiration of his or her sentence.

Judicial Determination

Section 743.6 of the Criminal Code gives sentencing judges the authority to impose, on some offenders receiving a sentence of imprisonment of two years or more, the requirement that the offender serve one-half of the sentence prior to being eligible for parole, instead of the typical one-third. The primary objectives of this provision are protection of the public and specific and general deterrence.

Offenders who are subject to **judicial determination** are those who have been convicted of one or more Schedule I and Schedule II offences (the former are specified crimes against the person, the latter are specified drug offences as listed in the Corrections and Conditional Release Act). Judges make limited use of judicial determination, imposing it on less than 5 percent of those offenders who qualify for it. Aboriginal offenders are overrepresented in the group of offenders receiving judicial determination. Offenders receiving judicial determination are more likely than other offenders to serve their entire sentence in confinement.

Life Imprisonment

Under the Criminal Code, persons convicted of murder are subject to life imprisonment. This means that the offender is under sentence for life, although he or she may serve this sentence both in prison and upon release on parole in the community. The Criminal Code sets out the minimum number of years that an offender must serve in prison before being eligible to apply for release on parole. The key word is *apply*—there is no guarantee that the parole board will grant a release.

There are several situations in which life sentences can be imposed:

- As a mandatory sentence for first degree murder with no eligibility for parole for 25 years (although Section 745 of the Criminal Code provides for judicial review for some offenders after 15 years).
- As a mandatory sentence for second degree murder with no eligibility for parole for 10 to 25 years, a period set by the sentencing judge.
- As an optional sentence for other offences, including manslaughter, with parole eligibility set at 7 years.
- As an indeterminate sentence imposed on those persons designated as dangerous offenders.

The death penalty was abolished by Parliament in 1976 and replaced with a mandatory life sentence without possibility of parole for 25 years in cases of first degree murder (although it was retained for a number of military offences, including treason and mutiny). The debate over the death penalty continues, however. Contribute your thoughts to the "At Issue 1.3: Should the death penalty be reinstated in Canada?" presented at the end of the chapter.

THE EFFECTIVENESS OF SENTENCING

Setting aside the controversies over leniency in sentencing and those cases covered heavily by the media, it is difficult to determine the effectiveness of sentencing and the extent to which a sentence imposed on a convicted offender ultimately fulfills the various objectives discussed earlier. There is no conclusive evidence that increasing sentence lengths for offenders reduces rates of reoffending, although prison sentences may be an effective deterrent for some offenders (DeJong 1997; Jones and Sims 1997). There are a number of reasons for this murkiness. While judges may include recommendations for treatment in their sentencing orders, once the offender is convicted, he or she becomes the responsibility of the correctional system. Judicial recommendations for placement and treatment programming are not binding on correctional decision makers. Also, matching specific sentencing options with the needs and risks of offenders is, at best, an inexact science. It is by no means clear that the sentences imposed by the criminal courts achieve the goals of specific or general deterrence.

There may also be disparity (different sentences handed down in similar types of cases) in sentencing practices among judges across the country. Criminal court judges are granted, by statute and precedence, considerable latitude when selecting sanctions for convicted offenders; this may lead to individual judges handing down different sentences in similar cases. With a few exceptions involving mandatory sentences, most offences have only a maximum penalty; thus, judges have considerable discretion in deciding both the objective of the sentence and the specific penalty. This latitude allows judges to consider a broad range of factors specific to the case and the offender; in other words, they are not forced to take into account only information related to prior offences and the current crime. Calls for increasing the number of mandatory sentences are prompted by concerns that sentencing judges have too much discretion, resulting in disparity in sentencing and lenient sentences.

In recent years there has emerged in the United States a move toward "smart sentencing." This has included focusing on "what works" to reduce crime and on altering traditional sentencing practices, which, in the words of one judge, "make no responsible effort to select or encourage sentences that are most likely to reduce an offender's criminal behavior. We produce cruelly avoidable victimizations and impose cruelly misdirected punishments. Most offenders sentenced for most crimes offend again. Most offenders who commit heinous crimes have been sentenced before with no meaningful attempt to choose a sentence that is most likely to prevent future crime" (Marcus 2006).

CHALLENGES FOR CORRECTIONS

Correctional systems in the early 21st century face a number of unique challenges. These include the following:

Providing Programs and Services for Offenders, Often for Lengthy Periods of Time

The police and the criminal courts spend very little time with individual offenders during the criminal justice process. It falls to corrections to provide programs and services over the long term, be it in the community or in institutional settings. The costs of providing these services are high, and they are rising. Unique challenges are provided by the small but growing number of offenders serving life sentences.

Serving a Diverse, Marginal Population

Many men and women become involved in the criminal justice system and end up in systems of correction. These people include offenders of various ethnicities, as well as specific categories of offenders, such as white-collar, violent, mentally disordered, long-term, and sex offenders, and increasingly, elderly offenders.

For many offenders, criminal behaviour is only a symptom of other difficulties in their personal lives. They may have other functional problems in their families, peer groups, and workplaces. While this is not universally true, many offenders were raised in dysfunctional homes afflicted by alcoholism and violence and were victims of child abuse (physical, sexual, or psychological) or neglect. As adults, many offenders have severe alcohol and/or drug addictions, low levels of formal education, few marketable skills, and low self-esteem.

Statistics indicate that Aboriginal inmates have higher levels of alcohol abuse and lower levels of education and employment than non-Aboriginal offenders. A high percentage of female offenders have been the victims of physical and sexual abuse and exhibit high rates of eating disorders, depression, and sleep disorders (Brzozowski, Taylor-Butts, and Johnson 2006). There is a much higher prevalence of mental health disorders such as schizophrenia, major depression, and bipolar disorder among carceral and noncarceral populations than among the general population. Federal female offenders are twice as likely as male offenders to have been previously hospitalized for psychiatric reasons and to have a mental health diagnosis. There are also high rates of communicable diseases, including HIV/AIDS, tuberculosis, and hepatitis B and C in institutional populations (Public Safety Canada Portfolio Corrections Statistics Committee 2007, 55).

The Changing Offender Profile

Offenders entering systems of corrections in the early 21st century present a broader range of risks and needs than in earlier years. There has been a significant increase in the number of federal offenders who are classified as maximum security at admission, as well as an increase in the proportion of offenders serving a sentence for homicide (as of 2007, one in four inmates). More offenders have mental health issues (12 percent of men, 25 percent of women) and substance abuse issues (four of five offenders). Rates of infectious diseases are increasing among inmates. As well, elderly inmates are a growing segment of institution populations, with just over 15 percent of federal inmates being over 50. The "greying" of Canada's prisons is the result of a number of factors, including changes in the Criminal Code and increased rates of reporting by crime victims, particularly of sexual offences that may have occurred many years earlier. Older offenders are more likely to have been convicted of more serious violent offences or of sexual offences, although in most cases they pose a lower risk to the community than younger offenders do (CSC 2007; NPB 2007a, 2007b).

Pursuing Conflicting Goals

Correctional systems and the other components of the criminal justice system have as their primary mandate the protection of society. However, there is often disagreement over how this goal can best be accomplished. Many observers argue that the protection of society is best assured by more severe sanctions—more arrests, more convictions, and longer periods of incarceration. Others argue that this "get tough" approach has failed in the past and that the criminal justice system should focus on addressing the causes of crime instead of merely reacting to criminal behaviour. The latter approach would mean focusing on the specific treatment needs of offenders in an attempt to reduce or eliminate future criminal behaviour. The persistence of these two views of the goals of corrections—punishment versus treatment—has resulted in what is often referred to as the "split personality" of corrections.

The Absence of a Knowledge Base

Corrections lacks a well-developed body of empirical knowledge that can be used to formulate policies and operate programs. Though the amount of research on various types of criminality and on various interventions has increased, the findings of these studies are often contradictory. Furthermore, research often has too little influence on correctional policies, programs, and services, which are affected by a variety of factors, including political considerations and public opinion.

The Plague of Disinformation

For most Canadians, the media are the primary sources of information about crime and criminal justice. However, the media tend to be biased toward sensational crimes and to simplify crime and justice issues, and the public for its part tends to generalize from specific events. All of this contributes to an uninformed and misinformed public (Roberts 2001). News reporting that focuses on the sensational is not strictly speaking erroneous; it does, however, result in disinformation because it is not balanced. For example, news items are more likely to highlight the crimes of a handful of parolees rather than the fact that most offenders succeed in completing their period of parole supervision following release from an institution. Riots, drug overdoses, hostage takings, and lockdowns tend to receive more media attention than positive initiatives that prison inmates have taken, such as running sports day programs for developmentally challenged youth in the institution, raising money for the fight against AIDS through annual walks within the institution, fighting forest fires, building trails and campgrounds, and completing community service projects. Corrections systems have found it difficult to counter and correct the images the media present to the public.

The Tense Relationship with the Public

Poll findings suggest that, except when it comes to the police (who consistently record an 80 percent overall approval rating), the Canadian public lacks confidence in the criminal justice system (Roberts 2004). Correctional systems, in particular, receive very low levels of public support from the general public. Only 18 percent of the respondents to the federal government's General Social Survey (Statistics Canada 2005) felt that the prison system was doing a "good job" at helping prisoners become law-abiding citizens. Only 15 percent of those surveyed felt that the parole system was doing a "good job" at supervising parolees, and only 18 percent felt that it was doing a good job at helping offenders become law-abiding citizens (ibid.). Note, however, that these ratings reflect a general public that by its own admission knows very little about corrections except for what it learns from negatively cast media stories.

Chapter 2 of this text will reveal that not so many decades ago, most offenders were punished in public view. Back then, community residents not only could witness sanctions—including hangings—but also could often participate in sanctions by showering offenders with insults, as well as the occasional rotten vegetable. Today, with a few notable exceptions, such as the

Community residents protest against a sex offender released from prison taking up residence in their neighbourhood.

CP PHOTO/Red Deer Advocate/Randy Fiedler

involvement of community residents as volunteers in correctional institutions and in community programs, the role of the public is primarily reactive. Community sentiment is often expressed through interest groups that lobby for more severe sanctions for criminal offenders, longer periods of incarceration, and more stringent requirements for release.

Because of public opposition, correctional systems have often found it enormously difficult to secure community participation in programs and services. A major obstacle to correctional programming in the community is the **NIMBY** (Not In My Back Yard) syndrome. This term refers to the resistance that communities display in response to correctional systems' efforts to locate programs and residences for offenders in their neighbourhoods. The reasons for community resistance include fear of crime, attitudes toward crime and offenders that are based largely on media accounts, and concerns that property values will be depressed (Benzvy-Miller 1990). A more recent phenomenon is **NOTE** (Not Over There Either), which refers to community residents resisting the placement of correctional facilities anywhere in the region. To date, correctional systems have devised very few effective strategies for addressing and counteracting the NIMBY and NOTE syndromes. Far too often, corrections personnel find themselves in the position of reactive crisis management—responding to the accusations of citizen interest groups, attempting to reassure a nervous public following an escape or the commission of a serious crime by an offender on parole, or the release of a high-risk offender into the community.

The difficulties that correctional systems encounter in securing the interest and involvement of community residents in delivering programs and services for offenders should not obscure the fact that people of all ages across Canada volunteer to work with offenders in a variety of institutional and community settings. This volunteer work includes regular visits to institutions by religious groups, service clubs, and sports teams, as well as one-on-one mentoring in literacy programs and prerelease planning. Citizens also volunteer as community sponsors for offenders on parole. And citizens are becoming increasingly involved in various restorative justice initiatives (see Chapter 4). There are also Citizen's Advisory Committees (CACs), which operate in all federal prisons. CACs are composed of local citizens who volunteer their time. Attempts are made to ensure that these committees reflect the ethnic, gender, socioeconomic, and cultural diversity of the community at hand. The goals of CACs include these: promoting public knowledge and understanding of corrections; contributing to the development of correctional facilities and programs; and increasing public participation in the correctional process. They are also meant to serve as impartial observers of the CSC's day-to-day operations. In carrying out their mandate, CACs provide advice to CSC managers, meet regularly with correctional staff and management, and serve as liaisons between correctional institutions and the community.

Corrections in a Multicultural Society

Multiculturalism is a defining characteristic of Canada. The primary source of this diversity is immigration, which has had a significant impact on Canadian society since Europeans first colonized the country. Visible minorities, most of whom live in Canada's major urban areas, now make up just over 10 percent of the population. There is no evidence that immigrants have higher rates of criminality than people born in Canada; in fact, the rate of offending for immigrants is lower. However, cultural diversity poses challenges to the criminal justice system and, more specifically, to systems of corrections. Many new immigrants speak neither English nor French and come from countries where there are is widespread distrust of the criminal justice system.

TRENDS IN CORRECTIONS

This introductory chapter concludes with a discussion of several trends in correctional systems. While by no means exhaustive, the areas covered illustrate the dynamic nature of corrections.

The "Americanization" of Canadian Corrections

A major development in Canadian corrections has been the emergence in recent years of a more conservative, American-style approach to correctional policy and practice. This new approach represents a radical departure from the more liberal model of correctional practice that has prevailed in Canada for the past several decades. It places public safety and security as the foremost objectives of the correctional system. The increasing move toward mandatory sentences in the Criminal Code, the proposal by the CSC Review Panel (Sampson 2007) to create large, regional correctional facilities, and the requirement that provincial inmates in Ontario earn time off for good behaviour (known as "earned remission") are examples of the shift in correctional policy at the federal and provincial levels.

Increasing Accountability and a Concern with the Rule of Law and Justice

In recent years there has been an increase in the accountability of systems of corrections and conditional release. This has coincided with the increasing involvement of the courts, which are now imposing on correctional agencies and personnel a duty to act fairly in managing offenders and to ensure that the decision-making process is fair and equitable.

In recent years, correctional authorities have been the target of an increasing number of civil suits launched by crime victims. In 2001, a B.C. woman who was raped at knifepoint by a career criminal with 63 prior convictions on statutory release and on a day pass from a minimum-security institution settled out of court for $215,000 (Hall 2001, A1, A4).

Correctional authorities are also being taken to court by the inmates themselves. Between 2004 and 2006, $1.2 million was paid to settle lawsuits filed by inmates. This included $5,000 paid to an inmate for exposure to second-hand smoke (since 2008, smoking has been banned in federal prisons) and $13,500 paid to an inmate who was subjected to a body search after sniffer dogs detected drugs on her (Harris 2006).

Focusing on Offender Risk/Needs Assessment and Risk Management

Risk assessment and risk management are the mantras of contemporary corrections. Personnel at all stages of the correctional process, from institutional staff to parole board members to parole officers, have access to theoretically or empirically based assessment instruments and tools. These assessment and management instruments provide correctional workers with information from which to develop effective management and treatment plans; they also reduce the liability and culpability of personnel should the offender commit serious crimes in the community.

Creating Alternatives to Incarceration

Correctional systems are focusing more and more on intermediate sanctions and on programs based on the principles of restorative justice. A number of jurisdictions have in place policies that encourage the development of forums for conflict resolution and mediation. Communities, religious organizations, and not-for-profit agencies are playing a major role in the development of alternatives to incarceration.

A driving force in the search for alternatives to incarceration is, quite simply, costs. A large portion of the $3 billion expended on corrections is spent on incarcerating offenders. Average annual costs per inmate are as follows: maximum-security institution: $113,645; medium-security institution: $75,251; and minimum-security institution: $82,676. The annual cost per female inmate is $170,684, which is more than twice that for a male inmate in a medium-security institution. These costs are due, in part, to the small number of female offenders and the high cost of operating the regional correctional facilities for women. In contrast, the average annual cost per offender of community supervision is $23,105, about one-quarter that of an inmate in a minimum-security institution. For inmates at all security levels, the annual costs are much more than the cost of obtaining a university degree and more than if the person were housed in a first-class hotel (Public Safety Canada Portfolio Corrections Statistics Committee 2007, 30).

The federal government and most provincial/territorial governments spend over 80 percent of their correctional budgets on custodial expenses. This, even though less than 5 percent of sentenced offenders are sent to prison. Conversely, though most offenders are under some form of supervision in the community, less than 20 percent of federal and provincial corrections budgets are spent on noncustodial programs and services.

Developing Policies and Programs for Female Offenders

Although female offenders make up only a small percentage of correctional populations, there has been a concerted attempt to develop correctional policies and programs specific to their needs, through a woman-centred philosophy that empowers women to make changes in their lives. A major component of this approach has been the construction of a number of small regional facilities for federal female offenders, including one designed specifically for Aboriginal women.

Expanding Aboriginal Corrections

In recent years, Aboriginal communities and organizations have become increasingly involved in designing and delivering correctional services in community and institutional settings. Aboriginal communities are involved in institutional programs through Native liaison workers, activities sponsored by Aboriginal organizations, and the participation of elders in providing treatment. Communities and the justice system are collaborating in programs, many of which incorporate elements of traditional Aboriginal spirituality and principles of restorative justice. These programs include sentencing circles, community mediation, and various sentencing advisory committees. Some Aboriginal communities are creating and controlling their own programs, including programs geared toward Aboriginal women.

In Manitoba, for example, First Nations and Métis community correctional agencies are involved in probation supervision, fine option programs, the preparation of presentence reports for the courts, and a variety of community-based treatment programs.

The Increasing Role of Information Technology and the Rise of "Technocorrections"

In their drive to become more efficient, systems of corrections are making increasing use of information technology. Many provinces are working to integrate their information systems across components of the justice system and, potentially, with the federal government. Federal corrections and most provincial/territorial systems of corrections have created offender management systems that make offender case file information available to more than those who possess the actual case file. Electronic monitoring programs allow offenders to serve their sentence in the community. Videoconferencing technology is being used for remand, bail hearings, and adjournment hearings to reduce transportation costs and the risks of assault among inmates during trips to court.

As correctional systems come under pressure to manage their operations in a cost-effective manner without compromising public safety, they are turning their attention to a field known as "techno-corrections." Electronic tracking and location systems to supervise offenders in the community, the use of drugs to control behaviour in correctional and community settings, and genetic and neurobiological risk assessments that focus on genetic predispositions to violent or criminal behaviour are just three of the emerging areas in techno-corrections.

AT ISSUE

ISSUE 1.1: Should there be more mandatory minimum sentences in the Criminal Code?

Historically, the Criminal Code has contained very few mandatory minimum sentences. There is a trend, however, toward increasing the number of these types of sentences.

Proponents of mandatory minimum sentences argue that they:

- reduce the crime rate
- increase public safety
- increase public confidence in the justice system
- reflect denunciation of serious crimes
- target a small number of offenders who commit serious crimes
- are an appropriate check on unfettered judicial discretion.

Opponents counter than mandatory minimum sentences:

- do not deter criminal activity or reduce crime rates
- do not address the root causes of crime
- are a political intrusion on judicial discretion
- increase prison populations
- increase correctional expenditures for new prisons while reducing resources for prevention and treatment programs
- discriminate against Aboriginal offenders and African Canadians.

Sources: Basen 2006; Canadian Association of Elizabeth Fry Societies 2005; Fraser 2007.

What do you think?

1. What is your opinion about mandatory minimum sentences?
2. Which of the above arguments do you find most persuasive?

AT ISSUE

ISSUE 1.2: Is Section 718.2(e) a valuable sentencing option or a misguided reform?

Supporters of Section 718.2(e) argue that:

- Section 718.2(e) requires only that judges consider sanctions other than confinement when sentencing.
- Non-Aboriginal offenders are not precluded from being considered for nonincarcerative sentences.

- Section 718.2(e) represents enlightened sentencing policy and is only one component of a wider effort to address the overrepresentation of Aboriginal people in correctional institutions.
- Aboriginal communities become more involved in assisting offenders.
- The development and use of restorative justice and traditional healing programs and practices is encouraged.
- Aboriginal offenders have the opportunity to participate in culturally based programs that may be more effective than institutional programs.

Critics of Section 718.2(e) counter that:

- Special sentencing provisions for Aboriginal people discriminate against non-Aboriginal offenders and are based on faulty assumptions.
- Complex historical and contemporary factors, rather than sentencing practices, are the primary reason for the high rates of Aboriginal incarceration.
- Research evidence shows that Aboriginal persons generally receive shorter sentences than non-Aboriginal offenders who have been convicted for comparable offences.
- Section 718.2(e) does not protect Aboriginal victims of crime.
- There is no evidence that judges systematically discriminate against Aboriginal offenders during sentencing.
- Section 718.2(e) is more a product of political correctness than of research findings.
- Defence lawyers will attempt to use the provisions in Section 718(2)(e) to mitigate the severity of sentencing for non-Aboriginal offenders, including visible and cultural minority offenders.

Sources: Haslip 2000; Stenning, LaPrairie, and Roberts 2001; Turpel-Lafond 2000.

What do you think?

1. What is your opinion of Section 718.2(e)?
2. Review the above points and counterpoints. What are the strongest arguments made by each side in the debate?

AT ISSUE

ISSUE 1.3: Should the death penalty be reinstated in Canada?

Proponents for the death penalty argue:

- *There is support for the death penalty.* While public opinion polls have revealed a drop in the levels of support for the death penalty since the mid-1990s, support continues to hover around the 50 percent mark.
- *The death penalty permanently removes dangerous offenders from society.* The offender will never again commit crimes.
- *The death penalty reaffirms society's right to respond severely to severe violence.* Whether capital punishment serves as a general deterrent is not the primary issue; rather, it is that society and communities have the right to respond severely to

violent criminal behaviour that transcends, morally and legally, the boundaries of acceptable behaviour.

- *The absence of the death penalty hinders general deterrence.* The failure to impose severe sanctions on violent criminal behaviour lessens the potential deterrent value of the criminal law.
- *The death penalty provides closure for the families of victims.* In the absence of the death penalty, the families of crime victims are revictimized by publicity surrounding the offender and by the offender's subsequent efforts to seek release. Further revictimization occurs when offenders who receive a life sentence can apply under Section 745 of the Criminal Code (the "faint hope" clause) to have their period of parole ineligibility reduced.

Opponents of the death penalty counter that:

- *Innocent people are put to death.* In the United States, people have been executed who were subsequently found to have been innocent. In Canada there have been several high-profile cases of individuals who were convicted of first degree murder and sentenced to life imprisonment but subsequently proven innocent; these people would have been executed had the death penalty still been in force in Canada. (Visit the website for the Association in Defence of the Wrongfully Convicted, http://www.aidwyc.org).
- *The death penalty is used disproportionately for minority offenders.* Figures from the United States indicate that a disproportionate number of offenders put to death are black. Indeed, in 80 percent of the cases reviewed, the victim's race was found to affect the likelihood of an offender being charged with capital murder and receiving the death penalty.
- *There is no empirical evidence that the death penalty serves as a general deterrent to crime.* There is no consistent research evidence from the United States that the death penalty has any impact on the rates of serious crime. The average time from conviction to imposition of the death penalty on offenders in the United States is more than 10 years.
- *Premeditated killing is immoral.* A question often heard from opponents of the death penalty is this: Why do we kill people to show that killing people is wrong? These people view the deliberate taking of another's life as immoral; they also raise concerns about the methods used (Hanks 1997; Reitan 1993). Many state courts have declared the electric chair cruel and unusual punishment. Lethal injection has been criticized as sanitizing death.
- *Use of the death penalty in the United States has failed to reduce the public's fear of crime.*
- *The death penalty does not save taxpayers' money.* The long legal process associated with death penalty appeals may result in higher costs than if the offender had been incarcerated for life in a correctional institution.

Sources: Decker and Kohfeld 1990; Kaufman-Osborn 2006; Klein, Berk, and Hickman 2006; Peterson and Bailey 1991; U.S. General Accounting Office 1990.

What do you think?

1. What is your opinion about the death penalty?
2. Which of the above arguments do you find most persuasive?

KEY POINTS REVIEW

1. Corrections is a philosophy for responding to criminal offenders; it is also a range of programs and services delivered in community and institutional settings.
2. In democratic societies, there are tensions between systems of correction and the need to ensure that the rights of accused and convicted persons are protected.
3. Correctional systems operate under a variety of federal and provincial/territorial statutes that establish the authority of correctional officials, set out jurisdiction, and provide the framework within which decisions are made and programs are administered.
4. The large majority of convicted offenders receive sentences that place them under the jurisdiction of provincial/territorial correctional authorities.
5. The criminal courts can be identified as the beginning of the correctional process.
6. The three primary groups of sentencing goals in the criminal courts are utilitarian, retributive, and restorative.
7. It is difficult to determine the effectiveness of sentencing in reducing rates of reoffending.
8. Prisons should not be used with the expectation of reducing reoffending.
9. Offenders entering systems of correction in the early 21st century present a broader range of risks and needs than in earlier years.
10. Corrections lacks a well-developed body of empirical knowledge upon which to base the formulation of policies and the operation of programs.
11. Correctional systems have very low levels of public support from the general public.
12. Systems of corrections face a number of challenges that distinguish them from their counterparts in the criminal justice system.
13. Among the trends in Canadian corrections are the "Americanization" of corrections, increasing accountability, a concern with the rule of law, a focus on offender risks and needs, Aboriginal corrections, and the development of alternatives to incarceration.

KEY TERM QUESTIONS

1. Describe the components of **noncarceral** and **carceral** corrections.
2. Define **corrections.**
3. Describe the role of each of the following in providing the framework for corrections: the **Canadian Charter of Rights and Freedoms,** the **Constitution Act,** the **Criminal Code**, and the **Corrections and Conditional Release Act.**
4. What is the **two-year rule,** and what role does it play in corrections?
5. Define and contrast **general deterrence** and **specific deterrence.**
6. Describe the process for designating offenders as **dangerous offenders** and **long-term offenders.**
7. What is **judicial determination,** and what are the objectives?
8. What is meant by the terms **NIMBY** and **NOTE,** and what is the importance of these terms for any study of corrections?

REFERENCES

Basen, I. 2006. "Doing the Crime and Doing the Time." *Reality Check*, January 5. http:www.cbc.ca/canadavotes2006/realitycheck

Benzvy-Miller, S. 1990. "Community Corrections and the NIMBY Syndrome." *Forum on Corrections Research* 2(2): 18–22.

Brzozowski, J.-A., A. Taylor-Butts, and S. Johnson. 2006. "Victimization and Offending Among the Aboriginal Population in Canada." Juristat 26(3). Cat. no. 85-002-XIE. Ottawa: Minister of Industry. http://www.statcan.ca/English/freepub/85-002-XIE/85-002-XIE2006003.pdf

Canadian Association of Elizabeth Fry Societies. 2005. "Opposition to Mandatory Minimum Sentences. Open Letter to the Minister of Justice." http://www.prisonjustice.ca/starkravenarticles/mandatorymin_1105.html

CSC (Correctional Service of Canada). 2007. *Departmental Performance Report* Ottawa: Treasury Board of Canada Secretariat. http://www.tbs-sct.gc.ca/dpr-rmr/2006-2007/inst/pen/pen01-eng.asp

Decker, S.H., and C.W. Kohfeld. 1990. "The Deterrent Effect of Capital Punishment in the Five Most Active Execution States: A Time Series Analysis." *Criminal Justice Review* 15(2): 173–91.

DeJong, C. 1997. "Survival Analysis and Specific Deterrence: Integrating Theoretical and Empirical Models of Recidivism." *Criminology* 35(4): 561–75.

Fraser, R. 2007. "Mandatory Prison Terms Do More Harm Than Good." *Huntingdon Herald Dispatch* (January 11). http://www.famm.org/PressRoom/FAMMintheNews/WVMandatoryprisontermsdomoreharmthangood.aspx

Griffiths, C.T. 2007. *Canadian Criminal Justice: A Primer.* 3rd ed. Toronto: Nelson Thomson.

Hall, N. 2001. "Woman Raped by Parolee Gets $215,000 from Government." *Vancouver Sun*, January 9, A1, A4.

Hanks, G.C. 1997. *Against the Death Penalty: Christian and Secular Arguments Against Capital Punishment.* Scottsdale: Herald.

Harris, K. 2006. "Feds Award Cons $1.2M to Settle Lawsuits." Canoe Network News, August 9. http://www.cnews.canoe.ca/CNEWS/Canada/2006/08/09/pf-1726284.html

Haslip, S. 2000. "Aboriginal Sentencing Reform in Canada: Prospects for Success—Standing Tall with Both Feet Planted Firmly in the Air." *Murdoch University Electronic Journal of Law* 7(1) http://www.murdoch.edu.au/elaw/isssues/v7n1/haslip71.html

Jones, M., and B. Sims. 1997. "Recidivism of Offenders Released from Prison in North Carolina: A Gender Comparison." *Prison Journal* 77(3): 335–48.

Kaufman-Osborn, T.V. 2006. "Critique of Contemporary Death Penalty Abolitionism." *Punishment and Society* 8(3): 365–83.

Klein, S.P., R.A. Berk, and L.J. Hickman. 2006. *Race and the Decision to Seek the Death Penalty in Federal Cases: Executive Summary.* Washington: U.S. Department of Justice. http://www.ncjrs.gov/pdffiles1/nij/grants/214729.pdf

Landry, L., and M. Sinha. 2008. "Adult Correctional Services in Canada, 2005/2006." *Juristat* 28(6). Cat. no. 85-002-XIE. Ottawa: Minister of Industry. http://www.statcan.gc.ca/english/freepub/85-002-XIE/85-002-XIE2008006.htm

Marcus, M. (Justice). 2006. "Justitia's Bandage: Blind Sentencing." http://www.sandstonepress.net/ijps/IJPS_sample.pdf

NPB (National Parole Board). 2007a. *Performance Monitoring Report 2006–2007.* Ottawa. http://www.npb-cnlc.gc.ca/reports/pdf/pmr_2006_2007/index-eng.htm

———. 2007b. Highlights—Profile of Federal Offenders 2006–2007. Ottawa. http://www.npb-cnlc.gc.ca/reports/pdf/pfo_2006-2007/profil-2006_2007-eng.htm

Ouimet, R. (Chairman). 1969. *Toward Unity: Criminal Justice and Corrections. Report of the Canadian Committee on Corrections.* Ottawa: Information Canada.

Peterson, R.D., and W.C. Bailey. 1991. "Felony Murder and Capital Punishment: An Examination of the Deterrence Question." *Criminology* 29(3): 367–98.

Public Safety Canada Portfolio Corrections Statistics Committee. 2007. *Corrections and Conditional Release Statistical Overview.* Ottawa. http://www.publicsafety.gc.ca/res/cor/rep/ccrso2007-eng.aspx

Reitan, E. 1993. "Why the Deterrence Argument for Capital Punishment Fails." *Criminal Justice Ethics* 12(1): 26–33.

Roberts, J.V. 2004. *Public Confidence in Criminal Justice: A Review of Recent Trends.* Ottawa: Public Safety and Emergency Preparedness Canada. http://ww2.ps-sp.gc.ca/publications/corrections/200405-2_e.asp

———. 2001. *Fear of Crime and Attitudes to Criminal Justice in Canada: A Review of Recent Trends.* Ottawa: Solicitor General Canada. http://ww2.ps-sp.gc.ca/publications/corrections/pdf/fearofcrime_e.pdf

Roberts, J.V., N. Crutcher, and P. Verbrugge. 2007. "Public Attitudes to Sentencing in Canada: Exploring Recent Findings." *Canadian Journal of Criminology and Criminal Justice* 49(1): 153–84.

Sampson, R. (Chair). 2007. *A Roadmap to Strengthening Public Safety. Report of the Correctional Service of Canada Review Panel.* Ottawa: Minister of Public Works and Government Services Canada.

Statistics Canada. 2005. *General Social Survey, Cycle 18.* "Overview: Personal Safety and Perceptions of the Criminal Justice System." *2004.* http://dsp-psd.tpsgc.gc.ca/Collection/Statcan/85-566-X/85-566-XIE2005001.pdf

Stenning, P., C. LaPrairie, and J.V. Roberts. 2001. "Empty Promises: Parliament, the Supreme Court, and the Sentencing of Aboriginal Offenders." *Saskatchewan Law Review* 64(1): 137–68.

Turpel-Lafond, M.E. 2000. "Sentencing Within a Restorative Justice Paradigm: Procedural Implications of *R. v. Gladue*." *Criminal Law Quarterly* 43(1): 34–50.

U.S. General Accounting Office. 1990. *Death Penalty Sentencing.* Washington: Government Printing Office. http://archive.gao.gov/t2pbat11/140845.pdf

WEBLINKS

Access to Justice Network

http://www.acjnet.org
A comprehensive website containing extensive materials on law and justice. Information is organized by jurisdiction, subject, and format. This website includes numerous links to other Canadian and U.S. criminal justice sites.

Public Safety and Emergency Preparedness

http://www.psepc-sppcc.gc.ca
This federal government "superagency" houses the core criminal justice agencies, including the RCMP, the Correctional Service of Canada, the National Parole Board, and the Canadian Border Services Agency. Its website contains links to these and other justice agencies and review boards.

Canadian Resource Centre for Victims of Crime

http://www.crcvc.ca
The website of this victim advocacy group contains access to a monthly newsletter and links to victim resources.

National Office for Victims

http://www.publicsafety.gc.ca/prg/cor/nov/nov-bnv-en.asp
A central resource for victims of crimes committed by offenders who fall under federal jurisdiction. The NOV ensures that the perspective of victims is considered in national policy development.

Federal Ombudsman for Victims of Crime

http://www.victimsfirst.gc.ca/serv/ov-ap.html
This office facilitates victim access to programs and services, serves as a referral centre, and works with federal justice personnel to ensure that victims' rights are respected. The website also contains links to victim services in the provinces and territories.

Canadian Criminal Justice Resource Page

http://db.c2admin.org/doc-pdf/Campbell-report-30.09.06.pdf
Links to sites dealing with criminal justice, policing, crime prevention, restorative justice, corrections, and crime victims, among others.

University of Toronto Criminology Information Service & Library

http://www.criminology.utoronto.ca/library
An excellent site for bibliographies on criminal justice and corrections issues.

Correctional Service of Canada

http://www.csc-scc.gc.ca
A comprehensive site that provides information on CSC services, programs, and organization, as well as links to relevant federal, provincial, and nongovernmental sites.

Elizabeth Fry Society

http://www.elizabethfry.ca
This site contains information on the organization and activities of Elizabeth Fry Societies across the country, annual reports, news items and press releases, conferences and presentations, position papers on women and corrections, and submissions to human rights commissions.

National Institute of Corrections

http://www.nicic.org/library
This website contains an extensive online library and access to a wide variety of research reports and articles.

National Criminal Justice Reference Service

http://www.ncjrs.gov
http://www.ncjrs.gov/abstractsdb/Search.asp
An excellent U.S.-based website that provides online abstracts on the full range of criminal justice and corrections literature.

CHAPTER 2

THE EVOLUTION OF PUNISHMENT AND CORRECTIONS

CHAPTER OBJECTIVES

After reading this chapter you should be able to:

- *Discuss the indicators of correctional change and the various perspectives on correctional history.*
- *Compare and contrast the conservative, liberal, and radical perspectives on crime, criminal offenders, and the criminal justice system.*
- *Discuss the features of crime and punishment in early Canada.*
- *Describe the influences and events that resulted in the building of the first penitentiary in Canada in 1835.*
- *Discuss the emergence of federal and provincial prisons and local jails across the country.*
- *Highlight the key developments in efforts to reform the penitentiaries and the move toward a treatment model of corrections following the Second World War.*
- *Describe the models of corrections that have been developing for the past two decades.*
- *Discuss the historical legacy of community corrections.*

KEY TERMS

Conservative ideology of corrections
Liberal ideology of corrections
Radical ideology of corrections
Classical school
Positivist school
Pennsylvania model (for prisons)
Auburn model (for prisons)
Moral architecture
Brown Commission
Medical model of corrections

PERSPECTIVE

Inmate G852, *Kingston Penitentiary*, 1920

The prisoner stood up. He steadied himself, then walked into the office ahead of the guard. Beside the man acting as Warden sat the Acting Deputy, Corby, the officer who used to run the blacksmith shop where he'd earned a small fortune turning a blind eye to the manufacture of wheels and boxes for the works sold up and down the range. At one end of the desk stood Beaupre looking out of place without his horse and the backdrop of pale layered stone. Beside the prisoner stood his escort guard. He was outnumbered four to one.

G852 you've been reported for possession of contraband, namely tobacco, and for insulting an officer. How do you plead?

The tobacco charge he'd expected, but the other surprised him, though his face registered nothing. For a first contraband report, a convicted could expect to lose remission and suffer bread and water for a couple of weeks. An insult charge was a ticket to the Hole.

Warden's Court was a misnomer: there would be no trial. No one defended the prisoner, and he was not allowed to speak, except to enter a plea. Only the officer's evidence was heard. And he was not presumed innocent: he was guilty the moment the report was filed. Passing sentence was the only business of the Warden's Court.

The prisoner considered pleading guilty to the contraband and not guilty to the insult charge. That was the truth. He had admitted right away that the tobacco was his. But truth counted for nothing here. If he dared tell his side of the story, it would only go harder for him. The less said, the better.

Stand up and answer the charge! How do you plead?

The guard at his side jabbed him in the ribs with his stick.

Guilty, Sir!

The man acting as Warden turned towards Corby and Beaupre. They spoke together in low voices as if they had a secret to share.

Now, then, you plead guilty to possession of tobacco, a substance banned inside the penitentiary. Tell me, where did you get this tobacco?

I found it.

Someone planted it in the quarry for you, is that not true? Who is your connection? Who gave you the contraband?

I told you. I found it.

G852, you understand that you are under suspicion of dealing in contraband. That is a very serious charge. We have been watching you. We know what you are up to. Until now you have had a fairly good record at the penitentiary. We want to help you. Tell us who your connection is and it will go easier for you.

I told you already. I found it. The prisoner looked the man straight in the eye. I don't know where it came from. Maybe somebody dropped it. I don't know. I found it, that's all.

Perhaps a few days in isolation will restore your memory. Take him away.

The guard marched the prisoner out of the office, past the other waiting convicts, through a narrow wooden door, all but unnoticeable, the entrance to a storeroom or a closet perhaps, down a flight of cement stairs, through an iron barrier, then left, into a narrow hall.

The stone cellar under the Keeper's Hall held nine cells flanked by a corridor on either side. The cells were larger than the ones on the range, as wide as they were long. There was a small sliding window at eye level to the left of the door and another on the opposite wall, both screened with wire mesh, the glass painted over. A wooden door was padlocked over the bars of every cell. Here was total privacy, the antithesis of the range, where a man was exposed at all times. Visibility made a man vulnerable; invisibility invoked the terror of what could be done to a man alone.

The walls, ceiling and floor of the cell were painted a slick, uniform green. The room was a concrete box, absolutely bare. No toilet, no sink, no bed. If he needed to go to the bathroom, the guard informed him, he was to yell. An officer would take him to the toilet at the end of the hall. Twice a day, he added, someone would bring him bread and a mug of water.

Put your hands through the bars.

The prisoner did as he was told. He refrained from pointing out that the Acting Warden had said nothing about shackling, or a starvation diet. He would do as he was told and hope for the best.

Higher.

The prisoner withdrew his hands and put them through the grate above his head. The guard snapped cuffs on his wrists, then secured the bolt on the iron gate.

The wooden door closed inches from the prisoner's face. He heard the padlock snap to, heard the guard's footsteps fade on the cement, heard the barrier at the bottom of the stairs shut, a muffled clang, listened for footsteps, almost indiscernible now, the door at the top of the stairs slammed, he imagined, though he never heard it close. Whatever sounds he heard from that moment on would be his own.

Almost no light made it through the painted windows of his cell. A ten-watt bulb screwed in the ceiling raised the illumination to a more uncomfortable pitch: too dark to discern anything without squinting hard, too light to be free of the desire to look. He stared into the fibres of the wooden door for a while, then twisted his upper body to survey the limits of his concrete cage. Graffiti covered every surface. Scratched into the paint, with what, he wondered. A man's bare fingernails? He strained to read the messages, the ones closest to him at first, then the marks further along the wall, spending long minutes, maybe hours determining if F14 might really be F19 and whether a sentence was 130 or 150 days . . .

Hours passed, perhaps days. No, probably hours. His arms went numb. He called out for the guard, called out again, and when no one came, he relieved himself, wetting his trousers. He let his thoughts roam free . . . He thought with longing of his cell. His book, his blankets, his plant of tobacco (they'd probably found that, too), his fold-out chair. Until now, he'd counted his loss of liberty from the moment he'd walked through the North Gate. But he'd adjusted to the constraints of penitentiary life, become accustomed to the bars, to the surveillance, to the line-ups and searches, to the toilet exposed to passersby, to the never-ending light, the silence and the cold. He had not realized that freedom was such a layered thing, that there were still so many freedoms to lose . . .

Source: Excerpted from Merilyn Simonds, *The Convict Lover* (Toronto: Macfarlane Walter & Ross, 1996), 164–67.

For many decades, Canadians have studied the evolution of punishment and corrections by examining materials from other countries. It is often assumed that the emergence of systems of corrections in this country closely mirrored events in the United States and Britain. In fact, although there have been influences from these countries, Canada has a unique history in corrections.

This chapter traces the emergence of punishment and corrections from the early days of settlement to the present, highlighting the legislation, events, and personalities that determined the response to criminal offenders and that provided the foundation for contemporary corrections. The discussion will highlight this critical point: systems of corrections exist within, not apart from, the broader societal context. Put another way, society's political, economic, and religious beliefs strongly influence who is identified as criminal and/or deviant, what sanctions are imposed on those convicted of criminal or deviant acts, and what the objectives of those sanctions are.

This historical review will show that the difficulties associated with incarcerating offenders have been extensively documented. Many reforms have been recommended, but the federal and provincial/territorial governments have found it difficult to act on those recommendations. Indeed, many of the issues that confront corrections today first arose almost two hundred years ago—which underscores the challenges that confront those who seek to implement reforms in corrections.

THE PROCESS OF CORRECTIONAL CHANGE

We can say that correctional change has taken place when one or more of the following occurs: (1) the severity of punishment of convicted offenders is modified; (2) explanations of criminal behaviour change; (3) new structural arrangements, such as the penitentiary, are created for sanctioning offenders; and (4) the number or proportion of offenders involved in the correctional process changes (Shover 1979).

Why do such changes occur? And why were prisons invented in the 18th century? Scholars of penal history study correctional change from a number of perspectives. Some have focused on early reformers' humanitarian ideals; others have argued that prisons were designed primarily to control people who were perceived as threats to the emerging capitalist system of industrialized Europe. Prisons were not a humane alternative to the death penalty and corporal punishment; rather, they were for isolation and punishment.

The different perspectives on correctional history are best illustrated by the various explanations that scholars have offered for why, during the 18th century, there was a gradual shift away from extensive use of the death penalty and corporal punishment—which were most often inflicted in public view—toward confinement for the purposes of punishment and reformation. Was this change a result of the philanthropy of well-intentioned people, or was it an attempt to exert even greater control over what was perceived to be a rising criminal class that threatened the social order? Following are the views of several notable scholars.

David Rothman, author of *The Discovery of the Asylum* (1990), argues that the building of the first penitentiary in America in the late 1700s was the result of changes in how crime was viewed. Originally, crime and other social problems were felt to be a natural part of society and not a threat to the social order, which was maintained by strong communities, religious faith, and the family. For a variety of reasons, crime and other forms of deviance came to be viewed as threats to social order. In response, Americans built prisons, houses for the poor, and asylums for the mentally disordered, in that hope that these institutions would cure social ills.

Michel Foucault, author *of Discipline and Punish: The Birth of the Prison* (1979), examined the use of imprisonment by the French monarchy. The prison, he argued, was designed to improve punishment rather than reduce it, by removing it from public view and shifting the punishment's focus from the body of the offender to his mind. Prisons as instruments of punishment were intended not only to maintain order but also to strengthen the power of the monarchy.

Michael Ignatieff, author of *A Just Measure of Pain: The Penitentiary in the Industrial Revolution—1750–1850* (1978), focused on the transformations caused by the Industrial Revolution in Europe and argued that prisons were built in an attempt to combat growing social disorder. Through isolation, punishment, and penitence, members of the lower classes would be reformed and become productive members of the new industrial society.

Notably, all of these observers ascribe the transformation in punishment at least in part to a desire to maintain social order, often at the expense of the lower classes of society. This explains why the use of imprisonment continued to expand even though there was evidence, very early on, that it was ineffective in reducing criminal behaviour. There is also evidence that during the 1700s the public became disenchanted with the spectacle of gruesome public punishments and supported the rise of what were purported to be humane alternatives, such as prisons.

No single explanation fully accounts for the transformation that resulted in imprisonment becoming an integral part of the sanctioning process. That said, the various perspectives do highlight the importance of considering the broader context within which systems of corrections develop and operate.

Cohen (1985) has identified four historical developments in the response to crime and deviance:

1. The increasing centralization of the response to crime and criminals, and the concurrent development of bureaucratic institutions to carry out this task.
2. The classification of criminals and deviants through the use of experts' "scientific knowledge."

3. The construction of prisons and asylums as places in which to reform criminals and deviants.
4. The lessening of the severity of physical punishment and an increased focus on the mind of the criminal/deviant.

When we review the history of systems of punishment and correction, several trends become evident:

- An increasing centralization and professionalization of punishment and correction, with formal agents of control assuming responsibility for the identification of, response to, and sanctioning of offenders.
- The diminishing role of the community in the punishment and correction of offenders.
- A concern with the effectiveness of the punishment response in protecting society and in reducing the likelihood that offenders will commit further offences.

PERSPECTIVES ON PUNISHMENT AND CORRECTIONS

This chapter's discussion of the history of punishment and systems of correction will reveal that explanations of crime and responses to criminal offenders have always been strongly influenced by social, political, religious, economic, and demographic factors. Which acts are defined as criminal, the explanations for criminal behaviour, the types of sanctions imposed on offenders, and the objectives of those sanctions are always changing. There are many competing perspectives on crime and criminal offenders and on what the objectives of corrections should be. Generally, these approaches can be categorized as **conservative, liberal,** and **radical** (see Box 2.1).

The conservative and liberal perspectives are, respectively, grounded in the **classical school** and the **positivist school** of criminological thought; the radical perspective is influenced by the writings of Karl Marx.

Following are the basic tenets of the classical school, as set out in the writings of Cesare Beccaria and Jeremy Bentham in the 1700s:

- The offender exercises free will and engages in criminal behaviour as a result of a rational choice; offenders are responsible for their crimes.
- Criminal behaviour is not influenced by external societal factors or by deterministic forces internal to the offender.
- The primary goal of the criminal justice system should be deterrence, not revenge.
- Offenders, like all people, engage in a hedonistic calculus in which they attempt to maximize pleasure and minimize pain; therefore, the costs of crime must outweigh any benefits (i.e., crime must not pay).
- Punishment, to be effective, must be certain and must fit the crime.

BOX 2.1

Perspectives on Crime, Criminal Offenders, and the Criminal Justice System

Issues	Conservative	Liberal	Radical
1. View of capitalism and the Canadian political system	• Principles fundamentally sound	• Principles need improvement; need greater economic and social equality	• Principles fundamentally unsound and exploitive; need to change to socialism
2. Reason for crime	• Social disorder—lack of discipline in society • Traditional institutions and values have broken down • Lenient criminal justice system—"crime pays"	• Poverty, racism, and other social injustices • Society is not meeting the human needs of people, and crime is a manifestation of this inadequacy in our system	• Capitalist exploitation: the rich exploit the poor and the poor prey on one another
3. Ways to stop crime	• Reestablish social order and discipline • Reassert traditional values that made Canada great • Increase the costs of crime by stiffer punishments	• Make a better social order through reform • Establish social programs to meet the needs of the disadvantaged • Establish a more humane and just criminal justice system • Focus on rehabilitation of the offender	• Eliminate the capitalist system and establish a new social order

(continued)

Issues	Conservative	Liberal	Radical
4. Focus of corrections	• On the victim of crime and on innocent citizens • Offender commits crime through free will	• On the criminal—help the disadvantaged criminal and prevent future victimization of society • Crime is a result of adverse social conditions, though increasingly, the attention is on the individual offender, who is easier to change than underlying social conditions	• On the inherent inhumanity of the system • Crime is a result of the way society is structured; any attempt to reduce crime must focus on the system rather than on individual offenders • Criminal justice system is used to repress lower classes
5. Source of crime problem	• Street crime	• Street and white-collar crime	• The crime of capitalism and the rich
6. Prime values	• Social order—"law and order"	• Protection of individual rights and humane treatment of the less advantaged—"doing justice" and "doing good"	• Total economic and social equality— "no classes and no exploitation"
7. Historical influences	• The classical and neoclassical schools of criminology • The notion of deterrence	• The positivist school of criminology	• The writings of Karl Marx
8. Strengths of the perspective	• Focuses on efforts to maintain social order as a determinant of correctional strategies	• Considers the role of environmental factors in crime	• Highlights the roles of economics and politics in the development and operation of justice systems

	• Emphasizes the role of free will in criminal behaviour	• Attempts to treat and rehabilitate offenders by giving them skills to manage their lives	• Considers the role of race and class in crime and administration of justice
9. Weaknesses of the perspective	• Fails to consider any external causes of crime • Ignores role of such societal conditions as poverty, race, and discrimination as contributors to criminal behaviour • Relies on reason alone to explain and respond to crime	• Fails to consider role of free will in crime • Ignores potential role of psychological and biological factors in crime	• Few empirical studies • Socialist agenda ignores broad public support for most laws • Gives little attention to victims

These three perspectives often overlap. People with a conservative view may support treatment programs for offenders, and adherents to all three perspectives generally support efforts to reduce unemployment as a way to prevent and reduce crime (Welch 1996).

WHAT DO YOU THINK?

Which of these three correctional ideologies is closest to your views of crime and justice? What evidence would you present in support of your position?

Source: Adapted from Cullen and Gilbert 1981, 41; Welch 1996, 82–118.

The basic principles of the positivist school, as set out in the writings of Cesare Lombroso, Enrico Ferri, and Raffaelo Garafalo in the 1800s, include the following:

- Criminal behaviour is determined by biological, psychological, physiological, and/or sociological factors.
- The scientific method should be used to study criminal behaviour and identify criminal types.
- Criminal offenders are fundamentally different from others in society.
- Explanations for crime centre on the individual, rather than on society.
- Sanctions should focus on treatment and be individualized to the specific needs of the offender.

The particular perspective that is taken as to why individuals engage in criminal behaviour will influence the sanctions imposed and the objective of those sanctions.

THE EVOLUTION OF PUNISHMENT: THE BRITISH LEGACY

How societies and groups have chosen to respond to those who violate norms, mores, and laws has varied over the centuries. Prior to the creation of the state and the development of formal written laws, personal retaliation was the primary response. This practice was later augmented by the "blood feud," in which the victim's family or tribe avenged themselves on the family or tribe of the offender. Before the Middle Ages (i.e., before AD 500), the predominant philosophy underlying the response to criminal offenders was punishment. The death penalty was carried out by hanging, burying alive, stoning, boiling alive, crucifying, or drowning.

Corporal punishment was also used, as were exile and fines. Imprisonment as punishment for convicted persons was rare, confinement being employed mainly for those awaiting trial, execution, or corporal punishment or as a means to force payment of fines. In fact, correctional historians have noted that although severe punishments were used up until the beginning of the 18th century, it was economic sanctions—including fines, confiscation, and restitution—that were most often imposed. With all of these sanctions, the goal was retribution; there was no attempt to rehabilitate the offender (Newman, 1978).

It is generally agreed that, with a few exceptions, imprisonment as a form of punishment was not used to any great extent until the 1500s in England and the early 1600s in Continental Europe. One exception was during the Inquisition, in the 1200s, when accused persons were often held for months or years. The first house of correction in England opened in a former royal palace in Bridewell,

London, in 1557. This facility operated on the principle that subjecting offenders to hard labour was the best solution to the increasing population of criminals. Private businesspeople under contract with the local government operated Bridewell, and within a few years, other "Bridewells" (as they became known) had been opened throughout England. Conditions in the houses of correction soon deteriorated until they mirrored those of the local jails.

The 1700s marked the beginning of industrialization in England and the breakdown of the feudal, rural-centred society. Courts increasingly resorted to the death penalty in an attempt to stem the rise of what the emerging middle class saw as the "dangerous classes." By 1780, under what had become known as the Bloody Code, legislation had rendered more than 350 offences punishable by death.

England disposed of a large number of offenders through transportation, a form of banishment that for centuries had been used as a sanction (often resulting in death). Between 1579 and 1776, England sent as many as two thousand offenders every year to her American colonies. These convicts were often

The hulk "Warrior," shown anchored off Woolwich, London in 1848, was one example of the floating prison.

used to clear and settle the land as indentured slaves. After the American War of Independence in 1776, more than 135,000 felons were sent to Australia, until the practice was discontinued in 1875. Convicts were also confined in hulks—that is, in decommissioned sailing vessels that had been converted into floating prisons, anchored in rivers and harbours. At its peak, the hulk prison system comprised eleven ships holding more than three thousand prisoners.

The Age of Enlightenment

During the 18th century, later known as the Age of Enlightenment, a number of ideas emerged that would strongly influence Western society's perception of and response to criminal offenders. During this time, a transition occurred from corporal punishment to imprisonment as a frequently used form of punishment. This change was in large measure the result of the writings of philosophers such as Montesquieu, Voltaire, Cesare Beccaria, and Jeremy Bentham. Their writings were a reaction to the arbitrary and corrupt systems of criminal justice in England and Europe at the time; they embodied a spirit of humanitarianism and a radically different view of human behaviour. Writers of this era saw crime as a choice, as an exercise of free will by a rational human being. The person could be dissuaded from choosing to commit a crime by the spectre of a certain, swift, and measured consequence (Radzinowicz, 1966).

In his major work, *Essay on Crime and Punishments*, published in 1764, Beccaria argued that the gravity of the offence should be measured by the injury done to society and that certainty of punishment was the most effective deterrent against criminal behaviour. Punishments that were too severe served only to embitter offenders and perpetuate criminal conduct.

Jeremy Bentham, who is considered the leading reformer of English criminal law during the 18th century, also had a significant influence on the response to offenders. Bentham posited a *hedonistic calculus*, which held that the main objective of intelligent human beings was to achieve the most pleasure while receiving the least amount of pain. According to Bentham, sanctions should be applied to ensure that the pain resulting from the punishment would outweigh any pleasure derived from the commission of the offence, but that punishment should be no greater than necessary to deter the potential offender. For Bentham, imprisonment was a more precise measure of punishment than corporal punishments: the more heinous the crime, the longer the period of confinement.

In retrospect, Beccaria and Bentham and their contemporaries were somewhat successful in mitigating the severity of punishments imposed on offenders. The increasing use of imprisonment as punishment, however, created an entirely new set of difficulties and controversies, many of which continue to this day.

John Howard and Elizabeth Fry: Pioneers in Prison Reform

John Howard was a pioneer in efforts to reform the conditions of English prisons during the late 1700s. In his classic work, *The State of Prisons in England and Wales*, published in 1777, Howard proposed a number of reforms relating to the use of confinement, including providing single sleeping rooms for convicts, segregating women and young offenders from men, building facilities for bathing, and employing honest and well-trained prison administrators. Although well intentioned, some of Howard's proposals—such as placing offenders in solitary confinement to protect them from the corrupting influences of other convicts and to provide the proper solitude for moral reflection—contributed to the deprivations that convicts experienced. Even so, John Howard's humanitarian ideals live on in Canada through the work of the John Howard Society.

Elizabeth Fry was one of the first volunteers to work with female convicts in early 19th-century England. She paid particular attention to convict mothers. For nearly two decades she read scriptures and conducted prison ministries. The work of the Elizabeth Fry Society in Canada reflects her legacy.

CRIME AND PUNISHMENT IN EARLY CANADA (1600s TO 1800s)

The historical record provides key insights into how offenders were sanctioned in early Canada. The punishment of criminal behaviour in early Canada was patterned on the systems of England and France. The sanctions imposed on convicted offenders were harsh, particularly when compared with today's standards. The death penalty was applied to offenders convicted of murder, grand larceny, sodomy, and rape, and a variety of sanctions were available for less serious offences, including branding, transportation, banishment, fines, and whipping.

Reflecting the English system, punishment was progressive: "Murderers were hung while thieves were branded with the letter 'T' on first conviction and hung for a second offence. The lash and stocks served as punishment for less serious crimes" (Coles 1979, 1). In general, sanctions were designed to deter both the individual offender and the public at large.

Public Punishments

Public shaming and humiliation were the cornerstones of many of the corporal punishments that were employed. The pillory was used in Lower Canada until 1842. This was a solid wood frame punctured with holes through which the head and hands of the offender were placed. When it was closed, the openings fit around the neck and wrists, holding the offender secure. The pillory was mounted on a pivot so that the person being punished could be made to face in any direction. In Upper Canada, offenders were often put into stocks, which were wooden structures with holes for arms and legs in which offenders were seated. This practice continued until 1872. Both of these structures allowed for public punishments, and members of the community often showered the offender with eggs and other refuse.

Illustrative of the types of sanctions imposed on offenders during the early 1700s is the sentence that was imposed on Robert Nichols in the community of Annapolis, in what is now the province of Nova Scotia. Nichols had been convicted of assaulting his master. In the words of the presiding judge,

> *The punishment therefore inflicted on thee is to sit upon a gallows three days, half an hour each day, with a rope about thy neck and a paper upon your breast whereon shall be writ in capital letters AUDACIOUS VILLAIN and afterwards thou art to be whipped at a carts tail from the prison house up to the uppermost house of the cape and from thence back again to the prison receiving each hundred paces five stripes upon your bare back with a cat of nine tails. (in Coles 1979, 1)*

In Halifax in the mid-1750s, men were hanged for petty crimes. A woman who had stolen two saucepans, a copper pot, a quart and a pint pewter pot, and two brass candlesticks, with a total value of five shillings, was spared hanging only by intervention of local clergy. As punishment, she was branded in the hand with the letter "T" and sent to jail for two months. Also in Nova Scotia, an offender convicted of counterfeiting was placed in the pillory for one hour, with one of his ears nailed to the pillory, and then whipped in public. Both men and women were branded, a sanction carried out in open court by the jailer. As late as the 1830s in Nova Scotia, nearly one hundred offences were punishable by death (Baehre 1990; Raddall 1988).

In New France, before the adoption of the English system, punishment was often inflicted on the offender at the location where he or she had committed the offence. In 1692, for example, a Montreal judge condemned an offender to have his right hand cut off and his limbs broken before being placed on the rack to die, all of this to be carried out in front of the house of the merchant he had killed (Morel 1963).

The historical record from Lower Canada reveals that men and women seem to have been treated equally in being sentenced to capital punishment and to less severe sanctions such as public humiliation. However, in cases between the two extremes, there was differential treatment. For example, whereas men were banished or sent to the galleys, women received terms of confinement in the Hôpital Général (Morel 1975).

Banishment

In the early 1800s, justice officials began to banish convicted persons, the offender being ordered "to depart the province at his or her own expense and peril." In Newfoundland, offenders were placed on boats and set adrift, ultimately landing (much to the consternation of those living downwind) in New York State or Prince Edward Island. This practice continued until the early 1900s.

Dissatisfaction with banishment as a sanction was one of the factors that precipitated the building of the first penitentiary in the 1830s. In 1831 the Select Committee on the Expediency of Erecting a Penitentiary wrote: "It is no punishment to a rogue to order him to live on the right bank of the Niagara River instead of the left and it is cruelly unjust to our neighbours to send among them thieves, robbers, and burglars" (Beattie 1977, 82). Banishment appears to have fallen out of favour largely owing to the diminishing number of places to send offenders as settlements spread and the population grew.

Transportation

Laws in both Upper and Lower Canada contained provisions for transporting convicts. In Upper Canada, the legal basis for sentences of transportation was provided for in the Act of Legislation of Upper Canada, passed in 1838. This act authorized judges to grant conditional pardons, even to persons who had been sentenced to death, "upon condition that they be respectively transported as convicts to her Majesty's Colony of Van Diemen's Land" (present-day Tasmania, an island 240 kilometres south of Australia). The length of the banishment could range from seven years to life. Some convicts from Canada were transported to England and confined in hulks, but most were sent to the Australian mainland and Tasmania, with a smaller number being sent to Bermuda (Boissey 1996).

Transportation as a sanction officially ended in 1853, but it was seriously reconsidered in 1871 when the colonial government attempted (unsuccessfully) to persuade England to establish a penal colony in Hudson Bay Territory to which convicts could be transported (Edmison 1976).

Workhouses

Although the use of incarceration for punishment was not widespread, there were several attempts during the 1700s to confine persons convicted of certain illegal activities. In 1754 the first workhouse was constructed in Nova Scotia. This facility held a wide variety of individuals in addition to criminal offenders, including vagrants, beggars, prostitutes, fortune tellers, runaways, gamblers, drunks, and orphans. This workhouse was patterned on the Bridewells that had been founded in England in the late 1500s to provide employment and shelter for London's riffraff while instilling in them the ethic of hard work (Coles 1979, 1).

By 1818 imprisonment in a workhouse had become the primary mode of punishment in Nova Scotia. Its use, however, was not without controversy. In 1818 a new workhouse was completed in Halifax, and the prisoners were employed cutting granite and laying roadbed. This employment in prisons precipitated a debate (which continues today) over whether convict labour unfairly competed with outside, or "free," labour. Workhouse authorities had no desire to have convict labour compete with free labour, but neither did they want the convicts to remain idle. The solution? A proposal to build a human treadmill, or "stepping mill," an "unproductive dispiriting device upon which prisoners would walk thereby moving sand back and forth or 'grinding the wind'" (Coles 1979, 2). A bill to create stepping mills was introduced in the legislature but it was defeated by one vote. The conflict between prison labour and free labour would resurface several years later when the first penitentiary was constructed at Kingston.

The Local Jails

During the 1700s, with the exception of the workhouses that were built in some areas, there was no use of confinement for the purposes of punishment. Rather, jails (local lock-ups, at the time spelled "gaols") held people who were either awaiting trial or who had been found guilty at trial and were yet to be punished. Toward the end of the 1700s, however, jails were constructed in Upper and Lower Canada. In 1792 the first Parliament of Upper Canada passed an act providing for the construction of a courthouse and a jail in each district in the province. It passed further legislation in 1810 that established jails as houses of correction, in which were to be confined "all and every idle and disorderly person, and rogues and vagabonds, and incorrigible rogues" (Strong 1969, 24). Similar legislation was passed in Lower Canada in 1799.

Records from Upper Canada reveal that in 1828, most admissions to provincial jails were for debt, although in the following years the percentage of debtors in jail populations declined, their numbers being replaced by persons convicted of more serious crimes (Talbot 1983, 153). Interestingly, there was little use of imprisonment for debt in Lower Canada (Kolish 1987).

In 1838 the Gaol Construction Act passed in Upper Canada. This legislation created a Board of Gaol Commissioners, whose primary function was to oversee the construction of new jails and to improve conditions for prisoners. Talbot has noted however, that "complaints about the conditions of district jails began almost as soon as a new jail opened" (1983, 283). Upper Canadians, however, seem to have been largely unconcerned about the poor conditions in which many convicts were confined.

CORRECTIONS ON THE FRONTIER

Communities in settled regions were slow to develop local jails and other alternatives for punishing convicted people; this was even more the case in the vast western portion of the country once known as Rupert's Land. Authorities and settlers on the Prairies attempted to replicate the systems of punishment found in Upper and Lower Canada and in England. Until the early 1800s, people charged with more serious offences were sent to England for trial. When this system became too costly, the government in England passed legislation providing that cases arising from Rupert's Land were to be heard in the courts of Upper or Lower Canada. Moreover, any sentences imposed were to be served there. This applied as well to Aboriginal persons who had been convicted of crimes. In the Far North, Aboriginal persons were often sentenced to periods in RCMP or military garrisons, or brought to urban areas such as Edmonton for trial and incarceration or for imposition of the death penalty.

One of the more unique aspects of the administration of justice on the early frontier was the role played by the Hudson's Bay Company (HBC). In 1670 the English monarchy gave the HBC exclusive control over a tract of land that covered most of the western region of the country, along with the authority to enact laws and other regulations to control its thousands of employees. The company operated courts until the federal government purchased Rupert's Land in 1869. As late as 1861, the presiding judicial officer of the HBC served as sheriff, jailer, chief medical officer, and coroner (Smandych and Linden 1996).

THE CREATION OF THE CANADIAN PENITENTIARY

The years between 1830 and Confederation in 1867 were among the most important in Canadian corrections. The most noteworthy development during this time was the building of the first Canadian penitentiary, in 1835 in Kingston, Ontario. Equally important was the reformatory movement and the spread of middle-range reformatories. A hierarchy of institutions developed, with the penitentiary at the top. During this relatively short period of time, several key events and personalities were to shape the course of correctional history. For a variety of reasons, these decades saw changes in the laissez-faire attitude toward building jails and in how the sordid conditions of the existing local jails were addressed. There were also changes in the attitudes of communities, particularly in terms of how they viewed crime and criminals.

An examination of the circumstances that led to the building of the penitentiary at Kingston provides insight into the factors that influence systems of punishment and corrections. Note as well at the outset that scholars disagree over the specific influences that resulted in the decision to build the penitentiary. Among the more likely reasons for the decision were influences from the United States and changes in the economic structure of Upper Canada, as well as in how communities viewed crime and criminality. Keep in mind that in the past (as in contemporary times), the majority of people who were convicted of crimes were not sent to local jails or prisons.

The Penitentiary in America

One development that influenced the building of the first Canadian penitentiary was the decision by authorities in several American states during the late 1700s to make more use of imprisonment as punishment. Although England and a number of other European countries had already developed workhouses and houses of correction by the late 1700s, it was in the United States that the widespread use of imprisonment as a form of punishment emerged in its modern form.

Between 1790 and 1830, profound shifts occurred in perceptions of crime and explanations of criminal behaviour. In part, this was a consequence of the philosophical thought of the time; another factor was demographic, social, and economic changes in colonial society. Crime came to be viewed as a consequence of community disorder and family instability rather than as a manifestation of individual afflictions.

Americans sought to create a setting in which the criminal could be transformed into a useful citizen. The setting was to be the penitentiary, so named because inmates could reflect on the error of their ways through religious contemplation and hard work. In 1790, amidst unbridled optimism, the Walnut Street Jail opened in Philadelphia, Pennsylvania. It was followed by the spread of penitentiaries across the eastern United States, which operated on either the Pennsylvania model or the Auburn model. The **Pennsylvania system** was a "separate and silent" system, in which prisoners were completely isolated from one another and even kept out of eyesight of one another. Inmates ate, worked, and slept in separate cells. The **Auburn system,** first applied in a penitentiary in Auburn, New York, allowed prisoners to work and eat together during the day and provided housing in individual cells at night. A system of strict silence, which forbade prisoners from communicating or even gesturing to one another, was enforced at all times. The Pennsylvania system became the model for prisons in Europe, South America, and Asia, whereas the Auburn system was the model on which most prisons in the United States and Canada were patterned.

Changes in Upper Canadian Society

Some historians contend that an increase in crime rates in the 1830s, coupled with overcrowding in the local jails, precipitated the construction of the penitentiary in Kingston. Others have argued that serious crime was not an issue, and that the primary influence was a change in Canadians' attitudes toward criminal behaviour. According to this latter view, criminality came to be seen as symptomatic of much deeper social evils that threatened the moral and social fabric of Upper Canadian society. Recently arrived immigrants, in particular, were perceived as a threat—as having suspect values and a poorer work ethic (Beattie 1977; Bellomo 1972).

Canadian criminologist Russell Smandych has made an important contribution to the discussion of the events that surrounded the building of the Kingston facility. He focuses on the Upper Canadian Tory government of the time and its "paternalistic sensibilities"—a key factor in the movement for penal reform. From this perspective, the Tory governing elite was the driving force behind reforms to the penal system. The initiative to build the penitentiary was part of the government's much broader effort to bring about a "'moral uplifting' of the population through education and religious instruction." The prison, then, was "another control mechanism that could be employed to maintain a 'well-ordered' society" (Smandych 1991, 137).

KINGSTON PENITENTIARY

J.C. Thomson, editor of the *Upper Canadian Herald* in Kingston, Ontario, presented a proposal to construct a penitentiary to the 1826–27 House of Assembly of Upper Canada. In 1831 he was named chair of a select committee to consider the proposal for a prison. In February of the same year, he visited the Bridewell prison in Glasgow, Scotland. He later travelled to Auburn, New York, to view the state prison that had been constructed there, using the most recent ideas about penitentiary punishment. Thomson then prepared a report in which he severely criticized Canada's existing penal system and offered a number of arguments for constructing a penitentiary, including these: (1) the levying of fines was unjust owing to the differential ability of convicted offenders to pay; (2) capital punishment was rarely being used to punish offenders; (3) confinement in the local jails was no longer a practical alternative because of overcrowding and the lack of proper classification of offenders; (4) corporal punishment was improper and degrading; and (5) banishment as a sanction was no longer practical or effective (Baehre 1977).

Goals of the Penitentiary

Thomson's recommendations were accepted by the House of Assembly and did much to shape the Penitentiary Act of 1834. The House of Assembly emphasized the use of the penitentiary both as a general deterrent and as a mechanism for reforming criminals through hard labour. The penitentiary would provide a setting for the moral reeducation of convicts. It would make religion a focal point of the punishment/reformation process. In this, chaplains would play an important role; indeed, they would be the first noncustodial personnel to work inside on a regular basis (James 1990).

When it was completed in 1835, Kingston Penitentiary was the largest public building in Upper Canada. It symbolized a **moral architecture,** one that reflected the themes of order and morality: "The penitentiary was an ideal society . . . Much more than a system of dealing with transgression of the law, it became a projection of the world as it should be" (Taylor 1979, 407). Kingston Penitentiary was to be a model for those confined in it, as well as for society. Among its goals was to eradicate what were widely perceived to be the underlying causes of crime: intemperance, laziness, and a lack of moral values.

The Early Years of Kingston

In its design, the new penitentiary differed considerably from the district jails. The prison separated offenders by gender and type of offence, and it allowed the prisoners to have their own bedding, clothing, and food. Design, however, did not translate into practice, and the conditions in which prisoners were kept soon deteriorated:

> *Inmates were kept in absolute seclusion from society and were detained in a state of complete inactivity during the non-working hours. The resultant effect was physical atrophy and mental stagnation. Rules of strict silence prevailed. Prisoners were mixed together young with old, sane with insane. As cells were too small to allow for free movement, inmates were forced to lie down for twelve to sixteen hours a day. (in MacGuigan 1977, 11)*

A central feature of life inside Kingston Penitentiary was the silent system. This system presented challenges to the inmates, the guards, and the administration. Prison regulations required convicts to:

- yield perfect obedience and submission to the keepers
- labour diligently and preserve unbroken silence
- not exchange a word or otherwise communicate with one another
- not exchange looks, winks, laugh, nod, gesticulate to each other

- not sing, dance, whistle, run, jump
- not carelessly or willfully injure their work tools, wearing apparel, bedding or any other thing belonging to or about the prison (in Talbot, 1983, 295).

Male inmates who violated prison regulations were generally whipped, while female convicts were placed in solitary confinement. The same punishments were applied to children, some as young as eight. Strict silence was maintained at all times; the inmates walked in lock step; and the constant ringing of bells controlled the convict's day. Convict life was centred on hard work, much of it performed in a stone quarry outside the institution. Breaches of prison regulations brought swift and harsh punishment, including flogging, leg irons, solitary confinement, and rations of bread and water (see Box 2.2).

Labour groups in the Kingston area raised concerns that teaching trades to inmates in the penitentiary would threaten tradespeople's economic well-being. Having failed to halt construction of the prison, in 1936 the tradespeople filed a petition with the Parliament of Upper Canada that called for convict labour to be restricted to "breaking stones, pumping water,

BOX 2.2

Entries from *The Punishment Book of the Prison* (1843)

Offence	Punishment
Laughing and talking	6 lashes; cat-o'-nine-tails
Talking in wash-house	6 lashes; rawhide
Threatening to knock convicts' brains out	24 lashes; cat-o'-nine-tails
Talking to Keepers on matters not relating to their work	6 lashes; cat-o'-nine-tails
Finding fault with rations when desired by guard to sit down	6 lashes; rawhide, and bread and water
Staring about and inattentive at breakfast table	bread and water
Leaving work and going to privy when other convict there	36 hours in dark cell, and bread and water

Source: Shoom 1966, 216.

and working at efforts that would not injure the interests of tradesmen" (Palmer 1980, 16).

As early as 1840, concerns were growing: Was the prison doing enough to punish and reform offenders? Was it resorting too often to corporal punishment? Critics pointed to the high rate of recidivism among offenders released from the prison.

Oblivious to these difficulties, the English novelist Charles Dickens wrote of his visit to Kingston in 1842: "There is an admirable jail here, well and wisely governed, and excellently regulated, in every respect" (in Edmison 1965, 255). Dickens's visit occurred just one month after a 12-year old girl named Eliza Breen had received six lashes (according to records, the sixth occasion on which she had been whipped).

The Brown Commission: 1848–49

Public concern over the treatment of prisoners in Kingston Penitentiary led to an 1848 Royal Commission, chaired by George Brown, editor of the *Toronto Globe*. The commission's mandate was to investigate charges of corruption in the institution—specifically, charges of mismanagement, theft, and mistreatment of convicts. The commission found that the warden, Henry Smith, had indeed mismanaged the institution and that there was excessive use of corporal punishment, including the flogging of men, women, and children, some as young as 11.

The first of the Brown Commission's two reports, released in 1848, condemned the extensive use of corporal punishment and recommended the removal of Warden Smith for failing to fulfill the institution's objectives (i.e., to impose order and discipline and to reform the inmates). The second report, released in 1849, stated that the primary purpose of the penitentiary was the prevention of crime and the rehabilitation of offenders, using the least possible force (Beattie 1977, 31–32).

The **Brown Commission** was the first systematic inquiry into the operations of Kingston Penitentiary. However, the impact of its reports on prison reform is unclear. Many of its recommendations were embodied in the Penitentiary Act of 1851, which established specific guidelines for the use of corporal punishment in the institution and restricted the practice of allowing citizens to buy admittance to the facility to view the prisoners. The same legislation called for mentally ill offenders to be removed to the Lunatic Asylum of Upper Canada and for the appointment of two inspectors who would oversee the operations of the asylum. In 1857 the Prison Inspection Act was passed, which provided for the construction of a separate facility for insane convicts and the building of a reformatory for young offenders, as

Kingston Penitentiary

National Archives of Canada/PA-046255

well as for a system of inspection for the penitentiary, the asylums, and the district jails.

Despite these changes, corporal punishment, the silent system, and hard labour remained prominent features of prison life. In retrospect, the Brown Commission can perhaps best be viewed as a missed opportunity for Canadians to reconsider the use of imprisonment and to explore potentially more effective ways to prevent crime and reform offenders.

DEVELOPING SYSTEMS OF CORRECTIONS: 1850 TO THE EARLY 1900s

By 1867 there were prisons in Kingston, Ontario, Saint John, New Brunswick, and Halifax, Nova Scotia. The prisons were at the top of the hierarchy of penal facilities, which included lockups and jails. At Confederation, in 1867, all three institutions came under the authority of the new Parliament of Canada. At that point the two-year rule came into effect.

In 1868, under the first Penitentiary Act, the structure of the federal penitentiary system was established. The Department of Justice was to oversee the administration of all justice matters not within the purview of the provinces. The 1870s saw a major expansion of the federal penitentiary system, with prisons being constructed in Montreal, Quebec (1873), Stony Mountain, Manitoba (1876), and New Westminster, B.C. (1878) (Zubrycki 1980). In 1880, a new penitentiary was opened in Dorchester, New Brunswick, and the prisons in Saint John and Halifax were closed. (For a history of Stony Mountain Penitentiary, see Edwards 2004.)

All of the new penitentiaries were constructed on the Auburn model: "Rows of lightless, airless cubicles were arranged back-to-back in tiers connected by steel walkways overlooking a central rotunda . . . The workshop, the chapel and the prison yard were the only common areas. Inmates ate their meals from trays in their cells" (Blanchfield 1985a, 7). Life inside these prisons centred on discipline and hard labour. The bell was the symbol of discipline and controlled the convict's day. The daily schedule of the Manitoba Penitentiary in 1879 is presented in Box 2.3. The food in the penitentiaries left much to be desired. The "coarse diet" was considered part of the punishment for convicts. Kitchen keepers often bought the cheapest foods available. The typical coarse diet for convicts confined during the 1880s is presented in Box 2.4.

BOX 2.3

Symbol of Discipline: The Bell

5:50 a.m.	Bell. Prisoners rise, wash, dress, make beds.
6:00 a.m.	Officers parade. Keys issued, slops collected. Cells, walls, halls and passages swept. Lamps collected and cleaned. Prisoners unlocked and escorted to work. Names of the sick taken. Night tubs [chamber pots] cleaned and placed outside the prison. Fuel distributed and ashes emptied. Random search of cells. Water pumped into tank.
7:30 a.m.	Bell. Prisoners marched to dining halls in groups of three.
7:40 a.m.	Bell. Breakfast over. Prisoners marched back to their cells and locked in. Guards have breakfast.
8:30 a.m.	Bell. Officers parade. Outside gangs unlocked and escorted outside. Inside workers escorted to their jobs. Surgeon attends the sick.
10:00 a.m.	Office hours. Convicts on report are taken to the warden.
12:15 p.m.	Bell. Prisoners marched back to their cells and locked up.
12:20 p.m.	Bell. Prisoners unlocked and marched to the dining room for lunch.
12:45 p.m.	Bell. Prisoners marched back to cells and locked up. Officers have lunch.
12:50 p.m.	Eligible prisoners unlocked for school.

1:30 p.m.	Bell. Officers parade. Prisoners unlocked and marched off to work. Random search of cells.
5:40 p.m.	Night tubs brought back into the prison.
5:50 p.m.	Bell. Prisoners marched to cells and locked up. Supper delivered to each cell. Convicts with special requests may use "signal sticks" to summon guards.
6:00 p.m.	Bell. Prisoners' clothing collected and placed outside cell door. All cells searched. Prisoners begin their meals. Guards on night shift take over. Keys collected. Chief keeper reads out daily orders.
7:00 p.m.	Patrol guards supply water to convicts who signal for it. Kitchen and dining hall locked up.
9:00 p.m.	Lights in cells turned down.
10:00 p.m.	Lights in passages turned down. Dampers of heating stoves closed. Lights out in officers' room.

(The bell, which was centrally located in the prison, was so hated by the inmates that it was destroyed during the 1971 riot at Kingston.)

Source: Blanchfield 1985b, 5.

BOX 2.4

A Typical Daily Menu for Inmates in the Manitoba Penitentiary in the Late 1880s

Breakfast	1 pint	pease coffee (sweetened with 1/2 oz. brown sugar)
	1/2 lb.	brown bread
	1/2 lb.	white bread or 1/2 lb. potatoes
	1/4 lb.	beef or pork (with beets and vinegar twice a week)
Dinner	1-1/2 pint	soup
	1/2 lb.	white bread or 3/4 lb. potatoes
	1/2 lb.	brown bread
	1/2 lb.	beef, mutton, or pork
Supper	10 oz.	white or brown bread
	1 pint	coffee (with 1/2 oz. brown sugar)

The food allowance for women inmates was generally smaller due to their lighter workload.

Source: Blanchfield 1985c, 5.

The conditions for the guards in these early penitentiaries were often only marginally better than those for the convicts. The guards were required to follow a strict regimen and were not permitted to exercise personal judgment. Salaries were low ($500 per year for guards at Kingston Penitentiary in the 1890s), and job security and pensions were nonexistent. In an attempt to address the deficiencies of the guards, the 1888 Penitentiary Regulations included the provision that "no person shall be employed as an officer for the prison who is not able to read and write with facility, or who cannot readily apply the rules of arithmetic" (cited in Dixon 1947, 3).

Local Jails and Provincial Prisons

Meanwhile, conditions in the local jails and provincial institutions continued to deteriorate. An attempt by the province of Nova Scotia to create a system of workhouses at the local level had failed. In 1834 a grand jury report called the facilities unfit for human beings. To keep costs down, prisoners were required to pay for their meals, liquor, and rent—and, upon release, for the jailer's fee for his services. Those inmates unable to pay the fee were often confined for additional periods of time or allowed to panhandle on the streets to raise the necessary funds (Coles 1979, 8). A review of historical records indicates that many of the prisoners in Halifax's local jails during the late 1800s were recidivists; between 1864 and 1873, 5 percent of the offenders were responsible for 32 percent of the committals. Many of these persons were destitute, and when not in jail were in the poorhouse (Fingard 1984, 84).

Most of the female offenders confined in the jails had been sentenced for morals offences rather than for more serious crimes against person and property. These offences included prostitution, vagrancy, and larceny. On the whole, these women were young and from the powerless segment of society (Price 1990). For a detailed examination of Canadian women and punishment between 1754 and 1953, see Greenwood and Boissery (2000).

In 1844 a new provincial penitentiary was opened in Nova Scotia, to which the majority of convicted offenders were sent. As the following description reveals, conditions in this institution soon deteriorated as well:

> *Within five years, prison life had tumbled to the lowest common denominator. Singing, whistling, smoking, cursing, drunkenness, and sloth became the order of the day. Gaol keepers fraternized with the prisoners and often came to work drunk and disorderly. The Prison's Governor, Thomas Carpenter, spent weeks at a time drunk in his quarters, and in 1849, in a rum-soaked stupor, Carpenter actually aided prisoners in an escape. (Coles 1979, 3–4)*

Female Inmates Standing in Front of Their Cells, Carleton County Gaol, 1895; Ottawa
CP PHOTO/National Archives of Canada/William James Topley

Similar problems existed at the local level in Ontario. In 1890 that province established a commission of inquiry under the direction of J.W. Langmuir to examine the operations of asylums and houses of correction. Langmuir found that municipalities were failing to provide sufficient funds to operate the facilities; that proper classification of inmates was either nonexistent or inadequate; and that half the admissions were for vagrancy and drunkenness. The majority of offenders were poor and destitute. In Toronto, for example, nearly 60 percent of the inmates of the Central Prison between 1874 and 1900 were either "unskilled" or "semi-skilled" (Oliver 1998). In the West, conditions in the jails were much the same.

The 1886 Penitentiary Act provided for the appointment of federal prison inspectors and outlined their powers and duties; addressed the need for the separate confinement of female offenders, mentally disordered inmates, and young offenders; and provided for the use of solitary confinement in federal penitentiaries. The Act Respecting Public and Reformatory Prisons (1886) included the following provisions for the operation of provincial correctional facilities:

- The mandatory separation of youthful and older offenders.
- Procedures for agreements to transfer offenders from federal to provincial institutions.
- Powers for provincial legislatures to establish regulations for the custody, treatment, discipline, training, and employment of prisoners.
- Authority for the provinces to establish prisons and to identify to which facilities offenders were sent.
- The earning of remission, or "good time," by offenders confined in provincial institutions.
- The creation of temporary leaves of absence from provincial institutions for medical, humanitarian, or rehabilitative purposes.

This legislation established much of the framework within which contemporary Canadian corrections operates and was the forerunner of the Prisons and Reformatories Act.

The Huron Jail in Goderich, Ontario, served as the county jail from its opening in 1842 until 1972.

From the Collection of the Huron County Museum & Historic Gaol

THE EARLY 1900s

In 1906 a new Penitentiary Act was passed. This legislation repealed all previous federal legislation relating to penitentiaries and included provisions relating to the administration of the federal penitentiary system, the conditions under which prison inmates could earn remission ("good time"), the powers and duties of the federal penitentiary inspectors, and the removal of youthful inmates and the mentally disordered from general penitentiary populations.

Despite this legislation, there was little change in the philosophy of corrections or in how prisons were operated. In many institutions, the quality of administration and staff was poor. Punitive practices documented by the Brown Commission nearly half a century earlier continued. Inmates were subjected to a variety of disciplinary sanctions, many of which continued in use until the 1930s. These punishments included being hosed by a powerful stream of cold water, wearing a ball and chain during work, being handcuffed to bars for hours at a time, and, as a "cure" for offenders with mental disorders, being immersed in a trough of ice and slush (MacGuigan 1977, 12).

The structure and operations of institutions at the provincial and local levels changed little during the first decades of the 20th century. The provinces passed legislation providing for the administration of the jails under their jurisdiction, but they made no major reforms, and the primary objectives of imprisonment remained deterrence and retribution.

THE BEGINNINGS OF MODERN REFORM: 1930–1970

During the 1930s there were some signs, particularly at the federal level, that the harsh regimen of penitentiaries was slowly changing. Prisoners displaying good conduct were given lighting in their cells in order to read, were permitted to write one letter every three months to their families, and were allowed half-hour visits by relatives once a month (ibid., 12). A major change was the modification of the strict rule of silence. Under the new regulations, prisoners were permitted to converse prior to work in the morning, during lunch breaks, and until seven p.m. Inmates also began to be paid for work performed in the institution, at a rate of five cents per day. Federal penitentiaries also attempted to improve their medical facilities.

Contributing to the shift in penal philosophy was the report of the Royal Commission on the Penal System of Canada, which concluded that the goal of prisons should be not only to protect society by incarcerating offenders, but also to reform and rehabilitate offenders (Archambault 1938). More specifically, the report recommended that improvements be made in

Paddling Table

© Canada's Penitentiary Museum, Kingston, Ontario

vocational training and education programs, as well as in the classification of offenders. The Archambault Report also found the quality of medical services for inmates lacking, particularly in many of the penitentiaries in the eastern regions of the country.

This strengthening focus on how offenders were treated was to provide the basis for the postwar era in Canadian corrections, which saw the development and expansion of vocational and education training programs, the introduction of various treatment modalities, and the creation of community corrections programs.

Yet corporal punishment continued to be used as a tool to manage offenders in federal and provincial institutions until the late 1960s. The "strap" was widely used to punish inmates who breached prison discipline and inmates who had received corporal punishment as part of their sentence at the time of conviction. In Kingston Penitentiary, the punishment was administered to inmates lying on a "strapping" table (see photo). The "strap" or "paddle" was applied to the bare buttocks of the inmate. Records indicate that between 1957 and 1967, the strap was used 332 times in Canadian federal prisons (Farrell 2002).

POSTWAR CORRECTIONS: THE MOVE TOWARD TREATMENT

After the Second World War there was a shift toward a treatment model of corrections. The federal prison system introduced vocational training and education as well as therapeutic intervention techniques such as group counselling and individual therapy. Concurrent with these developments was an increase in the numbers of psychologists and psychiatrists on prison staffs. In 1948 the Kingston prison opened the first prison psychiatric hospital. The philosophy of corrections at this time is best illustrated by the comments of the Commissioner of Penitentiaries in an 1957 annual report:

> *The asocial and antisocial type of individuals who are sentenced by the courts to the penal system have failed through unfortunate circumstances and the vicissitudes of their past life to develop mentally as the average person does . . . Reformation, which is the ultimate aim of incarceration, stands to succeed best when the deficiencies and needs of the inmate are known.* (1958, 47)

The rehabilitation model of corrections received additional support from the findings of a Committee of Inquiry, which argued that the basic principles of Canadian corrections should include a system of adult probation, a focus on treatment, the creation of minimum-security institutions, and the recruitment of professional staff (Fauteux 1956).

This and other reports highlighted the shift toward rehabilitation under what became known as the **medical model of corrections.** In brief, the medical model held that the offender was ill, physically, mentally, and/or socially. Criminal behaviour was a symptom of illness. As in medicine, diagnosis and treatment would ensure the effective rehabilitation of the offender. Concurrent with this development were the increasing involvement of psychologists and psychiatrists in institutional programs and the development of specialized institutions to meet the needs of offenders.

The 1960s constituted the height of the treatment model in Canadian corrections. A number of new medium- and minimum-security facilities were constructed across the country, all of them designed to hold small populations of offenders. Prisons expanded visiting privileges as well as education and training opportunities. Prison physicians were added to treatment teams in an attempt to address the offender's criminal behaviour. This involvement extended to conducting medical experiments on offenders. Throughout the 1960s and 1970s, prison inmates were used as subjects in a variety of experiments conducted by drug companies, federal government agencies, and universities. Psychiatrists played an increasing role in institutional treatment programs; their techniques included electroconvulsive shocks and drug therapy, which for many years could be administered without an inmate's consent.

The medical studies included trials of new pharmaceuticals, research on sensory deprivation, and pain studies that used electric shocks. In one set of experiments, doctors gave female inmates at the Kingston Prison for Women the hallucinogenic drug LSD as part of a psychology experiment. Included in the subject sample was a 17-year-old woman who was in solitary confinement at the time. The sponsors of the research experiments insisted that the inmates had volunteered to participate in the experiments; however, critics argued that the practice raised serious ethical questions. For example, were captive persons capable of giving informed consent?

Provincial correctional systems also moved to adopt the medical model, and terms such as *scientific treatment* began to appear in provincial correctional acts. A wide range of interventions, including plastic surgery (designed to correct disabilities that had possibly contributed to criminality), aversion therapy, group therapy, behaviour modification, electroshock therapy, and various other psychological treatments were being utilized by the early 1950s. Behavioural science professionals became increasingly involved in correctional programming. By the late 1960s, critics were raising concerns about the effectiveness of rehabilitation programs in reducing or eliminating criminal behaviour and were calling for a return to a punishment model.

The Shift in Correctional Policy

In 1969 the Canadian Committee on Corrections addressed the problems that were being encountered in efforts to rehabilitate offenders within correctional institutions. It suggested that treatment might more effectively be pursued in a community setting (Ouimet 1969). This report provided the basis for the expansion of community-based correctional facilities and programs operated by federal and provincial agencies, as well as by private, not-for-profit organizations such as the John Howard Society, the Elizabeth Fry Society, and the St. Leonard's Society. In 1975 a report by the Law Reform Commission argued that prisons should not be used for rehabilitation; a number of other federal reports and task forces made the same recommendation during the late 1970s. Interestingly, many of these reports documented the difficulties of implementing treatment in institutional settings yet gave little or no consideration to modifying the environments of correctional institutions to create environments more amenable to rehabilitation.

The 1970s were a decade of unrest and violence in federal penitentiaries. In 1975–76 alone, there were 65 major incidents, including strikes, riots, murders, and hostage takings. This unrest led to the appointment of the Sub-Committee on the Penitentiary System in Canada, chaired by Mark MacGuigan. The final report of the sub-committee contained 65 recommendations for improving life inside correctional institutions for both inmates and correctional officers.

There were further developments in the late 1970s: The Canadian Penitentiary Service changed its name to the Correctional Service of Canada (CSC). It was increasingly recognized that correctional institutions must consider the rights of inmates in their charge. Community correctional facilities were expanded. Special Handling Units were created for violent, dangerous offenders. Finally, the medical model, which presupposed that correctional officials could diagnose and treat criminal behaviour, was discarded. In addition, the CSC opened several regional psychiatric centres (now called regional health centres) across the country for inmates with specialized treatment needs. For an in-depth examination of correctional practices in Canada and in the province of Quebec during the years 1969 to 1999, see Lalande (2000).

1990 to the Present: Emerging Models of Correctional Practice

In the 1990s a clear split in correctional practice emerged between the federal government and several provincial jurisdictions. At the federal level, correctional policy and practice was firmly entrenched in the liberal European model of corrections, which placed a high value on proactive intervention in the lives of offenders and on the involvement of social and justice agencies in responding to crime. This was reflected in the closing of the Kingston Prison for Women, the construction of a number of small, regional facilities for federally sentenced women, the development of Aboriginal healing lodges in partnership with First Nations, and an emphasis on increasing the number of federal offenders under supervision in the community.

At the provincial level, the election of conservative governments in several provinces, including Ontario, led to correctional policies that mirrored the punishment-oriented American approach to corrections. In Quebec, however, the emphasis continued to be on prevention, alternatives to incarceration, and interagency cooperation (Quebec Ministry of Public Security 2000).

In the early 21st century there has been a discernible shift in the approach of federal corrections, in part a result of the election of a conservative government. Legislation passed or pending (as of late 2008) would significantly alter correctional practice. Some of it includes proposals to increase the number of mandatory minimum sentences in the Criminal Code and to eliminate statutory release for federal offenders (Sampson 2007).

These developments, however, should not obscure the emergence of innovative alternatives to incarceration that have emerged over the past decade. A number of these are discussed in Chapter 3.

THE LEGACY OF COMMUNITY CORRECTIONS: PROBATION AND PAROLE

The federal and provincial governments failed to pursue with any vigour the reform of correctional institutions in the late 1890s. Even so, by then the foundations were being laid for the increased use of noncarceral sanctions. In the 20th century, probation and parole became the cornerstones of what became known as community corrections, an ill-defined term that describes any program or initiative for offenders that is not delivered in an institution.

The State of Massachusetts shares with England the distinction of having pioneered the use of probation. Probation evolved in that state from the activities of one John Augustus, a Boston shoe cobbler who in 1841 appeared in court and requested that he be permitted to stand as bail for a man charged with being a common drunkard. When the man returned to court three weeks later showing obvious signs of reformation, he was given a nominal fine of one cent for an offence that normally resulted in imprisonment. Spurred by this success, Augustus "bailed on probation" nearly 2,000 people in the 18 years preceding his death in 1859.

In Canada, the practice of releasing offenders on their own recognizance rather than imposing a sentence was given legal authority in 1889 by the Act to Permit the Conditional Release of First Offenders in Certain Cases. This legislation permitted judges to suspend the imposition of a sentence in the criminal court and, instead, place the offender on "probation of good conduct." By 1892 probation was mentioned in the Criminal Code. In 1921 the Criminal Code was changed so as to require the offender to report to an officer of the court. The growth of probation, however, was slow and uneven; it remained relatively undeveloped until after the Second World War. This pattern of development was a consequence of probation being under the jurisdiction of provincial/territorial governments. Another factor was geography, in that rural and remote areas of the country had no facilities for supervising offenders (Hamai et al. 1995).

The practice of releasing offenders before the end of sentence—today called *conditional release*—originated in the days when English convicts were transported to penal colonies in Australia. For centuries, the only avenue for early release had been to petition the king or queen for a Royal Prerogative of Mercy, which included pardons and remission of prison sentences granted for humanitarian reasons or because the severity of the sentence far exceeded the severity of the crime. The work of 19th-century penal reformers such as Alexander Maconochie was rooted in the observation that the harsh and brutalizing conditions in prisons did little to encourage convicts to be good citizens and, in fact, did much to ensure that they would become hardened criminals.

Maconochie was the superintendent of Norfolk Island (off the coast of Australia), a penal colony where those offenders thought to be incorrigible and irredeemable were sent. He developed a "mark system" whereby a day's labour earned the offender 10 marks, and 10 marks shortened the sentence by one day. A day's rations and supplies cost between three and five marks, so inmates could earn one day toward early release for every two days of work (Barry 1973).

In the 1890s, some jurisdictions in Canada began adopting the indeterminate sentence and the mark system for use with juvenile offenders. For adults, the reformatory movement found expression in the concept of "ticket of leave." The Act to Provide for the Conditional Liberation of Penitentiary Convicts, known as the Ticket of Leave Act, was passed in 1899. This legislation allowed federal convicts to be at large from prison under specified conditions.

The Prison Gate Section of the Salvation Army undertook to assist those on tickets of leave, there being no equivalents to the modern-day parole officers to supervise and assist reintegrating offenders. The first Dominion parole officer, a brigadier in the Salvation Army, was appointed in 1905. His appointment established early on the role of private agencies during this stage of the correctional process. The parole officer made recommendations to the Chief of the Remission Service in Ottawa, as it came to be called. Acting on behalf of the Minister of Justice, the Remission Service made the final decision. But the parole officer was one man in a big country; thus, tickets of leave were limited in number, and the practice spread slowly.

An enormous change to the parole system occurred after a commission of inquiry in the mid-1950s (Fauteux 1956). The commission wanted an independent body affiliated with neither the penal system nor the government to make release decisions. The committee recommended the creation of the National Parole Board (NPB), to be made up of five full-time members and located in Ottawa. The NPB came into being with the passage of the Parole Act in 1959; the Ontario Parole Commission was established in 1910. For an in-depth description of the origins and evolution of parole in Canada, see the National Parole Board (2005).

PARTING THOUGHTS: REFORM EFFORTS

Although there have been innumerable attempts to reform systems of corrections—in particular, the handling and confinement of offenders—many of the challenges that confront systems of corrections at the beginning of the 21st century were first identified early in the 18th century. These challenges include developing structures to ensure that systems of corrections are accountable, finding ways to increase the involvement of communities in the prevention of and response to crime and offenders, the need for adequate classification of offenders, humane and safe conditions within institutions, and the founding of effective treatment and training programs.

The major commissions and inquiries that have examined corrections and their focus and impact on correctional policy and practice are set out in Box 2.5.

BOX 2.5

Commissions and Inquiries into Systems of Corrections

Year	Commission/Inquiry	Focus/Impact
1848	Royal Commission of Inquiry (Brown)	Investigated charges of corruption and mismanagement at Kingston Penitentiary; first report (1848) condemned use of corporal punishment and recommended that the warden be fired; second report (1849) identified crime prevention and the rehabilitation of offenders as primary purpose of penitentiaries; impact of prison reform uncertain; most accurately viewed as a missed opportunity to rethink the concept of the penitentiary.
1891	Report of the Commission Appointed to Enquire into the Prison and Reformatory System of the Province of Ontario	Documented problems with classification, poor physical facilities, and inadequate management of provincial and local institutions; contributed to early reforms in the Ontario correctional system.
1936	Royal Commission on the Penal System of Canada (Archambault)	Appointed to investigate federal prisons; report (1938) concluded that the goal of prisons should be not only to protect society by incarcerating offenders, but also to reform and rehabilitate offenders; gave impetus to an increasing focus on the development and expansion of vocational and educational training programs.

Year	Commission/Inquiry	Focus/Impact
1956	Report of a Committee Appointed to Inquire into the Principles and Practices Followed in the Remission Service of the Department of Justice of Canada (Fauteux)	Recommended adoption of a correctional philosophy centred on treatment, the expansion of probation, and recruitment and training of professional staff.
1969	Canadian Committee on Corrections (Ouimet)	Examined problems of attempting to rehabilitate offenders in correctional institutions and suggested most effective in community settings; recommendations provided the basis for expansion of community-based facilities and programs.
1973	Task Force on the Release of Inmates (Hugessen)	Examined the procedures for the release of offenders from institutions prior to the completion of their sentence; recommended the creation of five regional parole boards at the federal level and the appointment of part-time board members.
1977	Report of the Parliamentary Sub-Committee on the Penitentiary System in Canada (MacGuigan)	Prompted by riots and disturbances in federal prisons, the final report contained 65 recommendations for improving life inside correctional institutions for inmates and staff; the majority of the recommendations are accepted by the federal government.
1987	Canadian Sentencing Commission	Examined sentencing and identified the purposes and principles of sentencing; proposed sentencing guidelines and revisions to the maximum and minimum sentence structure.

(continued)

Year	Commission/Inquiry	Focus/Impact
1990	Task Force on Federally Sentenced Women (Creating Choices)	Examined issues surrounding correctional policy and programs for federal female offenders; recommended that the Kingston Prison for Women be closed and that small regional facilities for female offenders be created, along with a healing lodge for Aboriginal female offenders; recommendations were accepted by the federal government.
1996	Commission of Inquiry into Certain Events at the Prison for Women in Kingston (Arbour)	In-depth examination of a critical incident at the Prison for Women, during which female offenders were stripped of clothing by male members of the Institutional Emergency Response Team; contained 14 primary recommendations, addressing, among other issues, women's corrections, cross-gender staffing in correctional institutions for women, the use of force and Institutional Emergency Response Teams, the needs of Aboriginal women, the operation of segregation units, ways of ensuring the accountability of correctional personnel and adherence to the rule of law, and procedures for handling inmate complaints and grievances.
2007	Correctional Service of Canada Review Panel	A thorough review of all facets of the CSC's operations, including the availability and effectiveness of rehabilitation and mental health programs; programs for Aboriginal offenders; services and support for crime victims; safety and security issues; the transition of offenders into the community; and physical infrastructure; results in over 100 recommendations to CSC.

KEY POINTS REVIEW

1. There are a variety of explanations for correctional change.
2. There are many competing perspectives on crime and criminal offenders and on what the objectives of corrections should be.
3. How societies and groups have chosen to respond to those who violate norms, mores, and laws has varied over the centuries.
4. With few exceptions, imprisonment as a form of punishment was not used to any great extent until the 1500s in England and the early 1600s in Continental Europe.
5. The Age of Enlightenment had a significant impact on Western society's perception of and response to criminal offenders.
6. The punishment of criminal behaviour in early Canada was patterned on the systems of England and France.
7. The first Canadian penitentiary was constructed in Kingston, Ontario, in 1835. Within seven years, concerns were being raised regarding its effectiveness in punishing and reforming offenders.
8. The conditions in early jails and provincial institutions were generally quite bad.
9. Reforms in Canadian corrections began in the 1930s; following the Second World War, there was an increased emphasis on treatment.
10. In the early 21st century, there are signs that correctional systems are becoming more "Americanized."
11. There have been a number of commissions and inquiries into corrections that have had a major impact on correctional policy and practice.

KEY TERM QUESTIONS

1. Compare and contrast the **conservative, liberal,** and **radical** ideologies of corrections.
2. Compare and contrast the basic tenets of the **classical** and **positivist** schools of criminological thought.
3. Compare and contrast **the Pennsylvania model** and **the Auburn model** of prisons.
4. What is **moral architecture,** and how does it help us understand the goals of the first penitentiaries that were built in Canada?

5. What was the **Brown Commission** and why is it important in the study of Canadian corrections?
6. Describe the **medical model of corrections** and its perspective of offenders.
7. What were the basic tenets of the **medical model of corrections**, and how did this model represent a change from previous views of criminal offenders?

REFERENCES

Annual Report of the Commissioner of Penitentiaries, 1957. 1958. Ottawa: Queen's Printer.

Archambault, J. (Chairman). 1938. *Report of the Royal Commission to Investigate the Penal System of Canada.* Ottawa: King's Printer.

Baehre, R. 1977. "Origins of the Penitentiary System in Upper Canada." *Ontario History.* 69(3): 185–207.

Barry, J.V. 1973. "Alexander Maconochie." In *Pioneers in Criminology,* ed. H. Mannheim. Montclair: Patterson Smith. 84–106.

———. 1990. "From Bridewell to Federal Penitentiary: Prisons and Punishment in Nova Scotia Before 1880." In *Essays in the History of Canadian Law, Vol. III: Nova Scotia,* ed. P. Girard and J. Phillips. Toronto: University of Toronto Press. 163–99.

Beattie, J.M. 1977. *Attitudes Towards Crime and Punishment in Upper Canada, 1830–1850: A Documentary Study.* Toronto: Centre of Criminology, University of Toronto.

Bellomo, J.J. 1972. "Upper Canadian Attitudes Towards Crime and Punishment (1832–1851)." *Ontario History* 64(1): 11–26.

Blanchfield, C. 1985a. "A New Kind of Punishment: Imprisonment." In *Crime and Punishment: A Pictorial History, Part II: Let's Talk.* Special Report. Ottawa: Correctional Service of Canada.

———. 1985b. "Symbol of Discipline: The Bell." In *Crime and Punishment: A Pictorial History, Part III: Let's Talk.* Special Report. Ottawa: Correctional Service of Canada.

———. 1985c. "The Monotonous Round: Coarse Diet." In *Crime and Punishment. A Pictorial History, Part III: Let's Talk.* Special Report. Ottawa: Correctional Service of Canada.

Boissey, B. 1996. *A Deep Sense of Wrong: The Treason, Trials, and Transportation to New South Wales of Lower Canadian Rebels After the 1838 Rebellion.* Toronto: Dundurn.

Cohen, S. 1985. *Visions of Social Control.* Cambridge: Polity.

Coles, D. 1979. *Nova Scotia Corrections: An Historical Perspective.* Halifax: Corrections Services Division, Province of Nova Scotia.

Cullen, F.T., and K. Gilbert. 1981. *Reaffirming Rehabilitation.* Cincinnati: Anderson.

Dixon, W.G. 1947. *A Bibliography Relating to the History of the Canadian Penitentiary System and the United States Bureau of Prisons.* Chicago: School of Social Service Administration, University of Chicago.

Edmison, J.A. 1965. "Kingston Penitentiary and Charles Dickens." *Chitty's Law Journal* 13(9): 255–57.

———. 1976. "Some Aspects of Nineteenth-Century Canadian Prisons." In *Crime and Its Treatment in Canada*, 2nd ed., ed. W.T. McGrath. Toronto: Gage. 347–69.

Edwards, W.G. 2004. *Stony: A History of Manitoba Penitentiary (Stony Mountain Institution).* Stonewall: Interlake.

Farrell, C. 2002. "The Canadian Prison Strap." http://www.corpun.com/canada.htm

Fauteux, G. (Chairman). 1956. *Report of the Committee Appointed to Inquire into the Principles and Procedures Followed in the Remission Service of the Department of Justice of Canada.* Ottawa: Queen's Printer.

Fingard, J. 1984. "Jailbirds in Mid-Victorian Halifax." *Dalhousie Law Journal* 8(3): 81–102.

Foucault, M. 1979. *Discipline and Punish: The Birth of the Prison.* New York: Vintage.

Greenwood, F.M., and B. Boissery. 2000. *Uncertain Justice: Canadian Women and Punishment, 1754–1953.* Toronto: Dundurn.

Hamai, K., R. Ville, R. Harris, M. Hough, and U. Zvekic. 1995. *Probation Round the World: A Comparative Study.* London and New York: Routledge.

Ignatieff, M. 1978. *A Just Measure of Pain: The Penitentiary in the Industrial Revolution—1750–1850.* New York: Columbia University Press.

James, J.T.L. 1990. *A Living Tradition: Penitentiary Chaplaincy.* Ottawa: Chaplaincy Division, Correctional Service of Canada.

Kolish, E. 1987. "Imprisonment for Debt in Lower Canada, 1791–1840." *McGill Law Journal* 32(3): 603–35.

Lalande, P. 1999. *Evolution of Penal Policies and the Debate on Imprisonment in Canada and Quebec: 1969–1999.* Quebec: Ministère de la Sécurité publique du Québec http://msp.gouv.qc.ca/reinsertion/publicat/politiques_penales/politiques_penales_en.pdf

MacGuigan. M. 1977. *Report to Parliament by the Sub-Committee on the Penitentiary System in Canada.* Ottawa: Supply and Services Canada.

Morel, A. 1963. "La Justice criminelle en Nouvelle-France." Cité Libre XIV: 26–30.

———. 1975. "Reflexions sur la Justice criminelle Canadienne au 18e Siècle." *Revue d' Historie de L'Amerique Française* 29(2): 241–53.

National Parole Board. 2005. *History of Parole in Canada.* Ottawa. http://www.npb-cnlc.gc.ca/about/parolehistory_e.htm

Newman, G. 1978. *The Punishment Response.* New York: Lippincott.

Oliver, P.N. 1998. *"Terror to Evil-Doers": Prisons and Punishments in Nineteenth-Century Ontario.* Toronto: University of Toronto Press.

Ouimet, R. (Chairman). 1969. *Toward Unity: Criminal Justice and Corrections.* Report of the Canadian Committee on Corrections. Ottawa: Queen's Printer.

Palmer, B.D. 1980. "Kingston Mechanics and the Rise of the Penitentiary, 1833–1836." *Social History* 13(25): 7–32.

Price, B.J. 1990. "'Raised in Rockhead. Died in the Poor House': Female Petty Criminals in Halifax, 1864–1890." In *Essays in the History of Canadian Law, Vol. III: Nova Scotia*, ed. P. Girard and J. Phillips. Toronto: University of Toronto Press. 200–31.

Quebec Ministry of Public Security. 2000. "Correctional Reform: Towards the Moderate Use of Penal and Correctional Measures." http://www.msp.gouv.qc.ca

Raddall, T.H. 1988. *Halifax—Warden of the North*. Toronto: McClelland and Stewart.

Radzinowicz, L. 1966. *Ideology and Crime: A Study of Crime in Its Social and Historical Context.* London: Heinemann.

Rothman, D.J. 1990. *The Discovery of the Asylum: Social Order and Disorder in the New Republic*, 2nd ed. Boston: Little, Brown.

Sampson, R. (Chair). 2007. *Report of the Correctional Service of Canada Review Panel.* Ottawa: Minister of Public Works and Government Services Canada. http://www.publicsafety.gc.ca/csc-scc/cscrpreport-eng.pdf

Shoom, S. 1966. "Kingston Penitentiary: The Early Decades." *Canadian Journal of Corrections* 8(3): 215–20.

Shover, N. 1979. *A Sociology of American Corrections.* Homewood: Dorsey.

Simonds, M. 1996. *The Convict Lover.* Toronto: Macfarlane Walter & Ross.

Smandych, R.C. 1991. "Beware of the 'Evil American Monster': Upper Canadian Views on the Need for a Penitentiary, 1830–1834." *Canadian Journal of Criminology* 33(2): 125–47.

Smandych, R., and R. Linden. 1996. "Administering Justice Without the State: A Study of the Private Justice System of the Hudson's Bay Company to 1800." *Canadian Journal of Law and Society* 11(1): 21–61.

Strong, M.K. 1969. *Social Welfare Administration in Canada.* Montclair: Patterson-Smith.

Talbot, C.K. 1983. *Justice in Early Ontario, 1791–1840.* Ottawa: Crimcare.

Taylor, C.J. 1979. "The Kingston, Ontario, Penitentiary and Moral Architecture." *Social History* 12(24): 385–408.

Welch, M. 1996. *Corrections: A Critical Approach.* New York: McGraw-Hill.

Zubrycki, R.M. 1980. *The Establishment of Canada's Penitentiary System: Federal Correctional Policy, 1867–1900.* Toronto: Faculty of Social Work, University of Toronto.

WEBLINKS

Prisons: History—Early Jails and Workhouses, The Rise of the Prisoner Trade, A Land of Prisoners, Enlightenment Reforms

http://law.jrank.org/pages/1786/Prsons-History.html
This website contains extensive historical materials on the evolution of the prison system in the United States and includes sections on early jails and

workhouses, the Auburn plan, the Pennsylvania system, prisons as social laboratories, modern prisons, and prisoners' rights.

World Corporal Punishment Research

http://www.corpun.com/expl.htm
A comprehensive 2,500-page website devoted to the study of corporal punishment throughout the world, both historically and in present day. The site contains 4,000 media items from the 17th century to the present, video clips, and links to countries throughout the world.

Correctional Service of Canada

Corrections in Canada—An Interactive Timeline

http://www.csc-scc.gc.ca/hist/1900/index-eng.html
This site contains an overview of the evolution of corrections in Canada from pre-1920 to the early 21st century.

CHAPTER 3

ALTERNATIVES TO CONFINEMENT

CHAPTER OBJECTIVES

After reading this chapter you should be able to:

- *Comment on the concept of "community corrections."*
- *Describe the traditional alternatives to incarceration: diversion and probation.*
- *Discuss the recruitment, training, roles, and responsibilities of probation officers, including the dual role of probation officers in supervising offenders.*
- *Discuss the obstacles to effective probation practice.*
- *Describe the objectives of intermediate sanctions and the types of programs that have been developed as intermediate sanctions.*
- *Discuss conditional sentences as an alternative to incarceration, their use, and the issues that surround conditional sentences in Canada.*
- *Describe how electronic monitoring works.*
- *Describe the fundamental principles of restorative justice and how these principles differ from retributive justice.*
- *Identify and discuss the various restorative justice approaches that have been developed and how these approaches differ from those of the traditional criminal justice system.*
- *Identify and discuss the critical issues that surround restorative justice approaches.*

KEY TERMS

Community corrections
Diversion
Net widening
Probation
Presentence report (PSR)
Intermediate sanctions
Intensive supervision probation
Conditional sentence
Electronic monitoring (EM)
Restorative justice
Circle sentencing

PERSPECTIVE

Ex-offender

We should be providing offenders with more alternatives than incarceration. I think that what has to be done is that we have to work with our young offenders or our youths a lot earlier, with a lot more emphasis and a lot more money spent in the young offender area. Once a youth has entered an institution, it's going to be very, very difficult to get that person to change their ways, because once he gets in there he is going to be conditioned to the situation that is happening. It's a very negative environment. I know in my situation, I had been a youth in a training school. I was being conditioned to the adult person I would be for the longest time, and I would spend 23 years of my life in institutions. If you put that into dollars and cents, I think it could have been spent a lot better than it was on me.

PERSPECTIVE

Probation Officer

We're not going to have someone who stole a chocolate bar and received a sentence for theft under $5,000 and bombard them with services. You may just be doing them more damage. But if somebody is struggling over and over again and they keep getting in trouble when they are intoxicated or on drugs and you've tried to address their issues and you find that there is a whole history of abuse behind that. I think it is our responsibility to try to help individuals and to identify the issues that they have so they can begin working on themselves. For the offenders on my caseload, I try to help them with basic needs, such as food, shelter, employment training, and core programming that will help them develop their self-confidence and address their issues. It is important to have empathy and to understand the client's needs while also having realistic expectations of them. I try to see that the conditions of the probation order are followed while at the same time respecting the person. Very rarely will we get someone on probation who doesn't have a youth record. When you look back through an offender's file, you can often clearly identify that there were times in their life that they were at a crossroads when there was a need for immediate intervention, but, for whatever reason, it wasn't done.

Source: Personal communication with author.

This chapter examines a broad range of programs and strategies that are used by the criminal justice and correctional systems as alternatives to confinement. These strategies include the more traditional practices of diversion and probation, as well as a variety of intermediate sanctions and restorative justice initiatives. Recall from the discussion in Chapter 1 that most offenders who receive a sentence of supervision remain in the community and that only a very small number of convicted persons are sent to custody (see Figure 1.1). Indeed, alternative sanctions are being used more and more often for offenders charged with or convicted of serious offences, including sex offences and spousal assault.

The search for alternative measures has been driven by the escalating costs of confining offenders in correctional institutions and by research evidence that calls into question the effectiveness of incarceration as a general and specific deterrent (see Chapter 4). In addition, the use of alternatives to confinement for less serious offenders allows more resources to be directed toward those offenders who constitute a greater risk to society and who require specialized intervention in the controlled setting of the prison.

A WORD ABOUT COMMUNITY CORRECTIONS

At the outset, it is important to consider the term **community corrections**. Most texts on corrections have at least one chapter on community corrections, which generally appears in the latter part of the book. Into this chapter are grouped such disparate correctional strategies as bail supervision, fine option programs, probation, intermediate sanctions, and electronic monitoring, as well as parole and various programs for offenders who have served a period of confinement. Needless to say, the differences among these very different correctional strategies are often obscured, resulting in considerable confusion.

In this text there is a deliberate separation of probation, intermediate sanctions, and restorative justice (to be discussed in this chapter) from conditional release and reentry, which are discussed in Chapters 8 and 9 respectively. This separation is designed to highlight the substantial differences between true alternatives to confinement and those strategies that are applied to offenders who have served a period of time in confinement and are then released by a parole board or after having served their sentence, less time earned for good behaviour and/or positive performance in the institution.

The decision not to use "community corrections" as a chapter title was also intentional. This term is surrounded by many misconceptions and has been overused to the point that it is of limited use in the study of systems of corrections. For example, any program with the term *community* in it implies that community residents provide significant support and participate in the particular strategy. Yet community residents are noteworthy for their general lack of involvement in community-based correctional programs, and may even be hostile toward systems of corrections. In this text, *community corrections* refers to correctional programs—including the supervision of offenders—that take place in the community rather than in institutional settings.

DIVERSION

Diversion programs have been a feature of Canadian criminal justice for decades. Offenders can be diverted from the formal criminal justice process at several points—there are precharge police diversion programs and postcharge diversion programs, and there is also postsentencing diversion. All of these allow offenders to avoid incarceration. The objective of all diversion programs is to keep offenders from being processed further into the formal criminal justice system. More specific objectives of diversion programs include the following:

- avoidance of negative labelling and stigmatization
- reduction of unnecessary social control and coercion
- reduction of recidivism
- provision of services (assistance)
- reduction of justice system costs

These competing objectives often end up limiting the potential effectiveness of diversion programs.

Diversion programs tend to target first-time, low-risk offenders, which raises concerns about **net-widening**—that is, involving offenders who would otherwise have been released outright by the police or not charged by Crown counsel. Some diversion programs are directed toward specific offender groups and more serious offences. The drug courts that have been developed in several Canadian cities are one example. Offenders avoid incarceration by agreeing to abide by specified conditions—for example, by agreeing to participate in a drug-abuse treatment program and regular drug testing (Weekes et al. 2007). Examples of diversion programs include the following:

The Mid-Island Diversion Program operated by the John Howard Society in Nanaimo, British Columbia, is designed for minor, first-time adult offenders who have acknowledged responsibility for their actions. The objectives of the program include holding offenders accountable for their behaviour, reducing the costs of criminal justice, and ensuring victim involvement. Available programs include anger management, employment and education programs, and victim–offender mediation.

The Community Council Program in Toronto is directed toward urban Aboriginal offenders and is designed to return a greater degree of responsibility to the Aboriginal community, to reduce recidivism, and to instill in offenders responsibility and accountability for their behaviour. The offender is an active participant in discussions about the offence and lifestyle issues. The council, composed of Aboriginal people from the community, has at its disposal a number of sanctions it can impose to reintegrate the offender with the community and to begin the healing process. Available options include fines, the payment of restitution to the victim, completion of a number of community service hours, and referral to treatment resources.

The Calgary Diversion Program is a community-based program that provides an alternative to incarceration for persons with a mental disorder who commit minor offences. The program provides the offenders with access to social service and health services.

Most diversion programs require that offenders acknowledge responsibility for their behaviour and agree to fulfill certain conditions within a specified time. These conditions might include paying restitution to the victim or completing a number of community service hours. Box 3.1 presents a case study that illustrates how diversion works.

BOX 3.1

A Case from the Nova Scotia Adult Diversion Project

The offender was a 38-year-old divorced mother of two children who was receiving social assistance. She was accused of defrauding social assistance of $14,000. The victim and the offender agreed that restitution would be an acceptable resolution. The charge was laid (sworn) by the police but not placed on the court docket. The police made the referral directly to the program staff, established contact with the victim to determine their wishes and concerns, and interviewed the offender to determine her interest in participating in the diversion option. Following an assessment interview with the diversion (probation) officer regarding the offence and the proposed resolution, the client signed a written agreement outlining her obligation to make monthly payments of $100 directly to the social assistance office.

The offender had a part-time job but was highly motivated to acquire a better job and hoped to repay the restitution more quickly. If she failed to abide by the conditions of the diversion agreement, the matter would be referred to the crown for processing through court.

Source: Church Council on Justice and Corrections 1996, 89.

Besides the possibility of net widening, concerns have been raised that diversion can be coercive and punitive. Also, there is some ambiguity surrounding the notion of "choice" in the operations of diversion programs. A study of the "John School" diversion program in Toronto (a program for men apprehended for soliciting street prostitution) found that the program focused disproportionately on offenders of lower socioeconomic status and that criminal charges were withdrawn if offenders waived basic procedural rights in order to gain admission to the program (Fischer et al. 2002).

PROBATION

Probation was first used as a correctional strategy more than two hundred years ago, and remains to this day the most widely used alternative to confinement. Section 731 of the Criminal Code provides that, in cases in which no minimum penalty is prescribed, the sentencing judge may place the offender on probation. Probation is generally used as an alternative to confinement; however, it can also be used in conjunction with a period of incarceration—including an intermittent sentence, which is generally served in a provincial/territorial facility on weekends. The maximum time that a probation order can be in effect is three years.

Once ordered, probation falls under the authority of the provincial/territorial correctional system. It may be used alone or following a period of confinement. Probation is not available for federal offenders, except when the offender has been sentenced to exactly two years in confinement; in this instance, the judge may attach a probation order for up to three years. Probation is ordered in about 45 percent of cases. The proportion of cases receiving a sentence of probation has remained stable over the years (45 percent), as has the average length of probation orders (15 months) (Marth 2008).

Probation is popular largely because it is so versatile. The length and conditions of a probation order can be tailored to the individual needs and circumstances of the offender. There are five ways that adult offenders can be on probation:

- as part of a conditional discharge
- as a condition of a suspended sentence
- as part of an intermittent sentence
- as a sentence on its own (the most common)
- following a prison term of two years or less

Also, probation can be included with any of the following dispositions:

- fine
- imprisonment for a term of up to two years

- intermittent sentence
- conditional sentence

Offenders who receive a conditional discharge, a suspended sentence, or an intermittent sentence *must* be placed on probation. Those receiving a fine, incarceration, or a conditional sentence *may* be placed on probation. When probation follows a term of confinement, probation supervision begins either at the time of release or on the expiration of parole.

The Conditions of Probation

Each adult probationer *must* comply with all of these three mandatory conditions:

- Keep the peace and be of good behaviour.
- Appear before the court when required to do so by the court and,
- Notify the court or the probation officer of any change of name, address, or occupation.

The sentencing judge may also impose extra conditions, which are tailored to the offender's specific needs. The more common optional conditions of probation include the following:

- Report as required to a probation officer.
- Abstain from drugs and/or alcohol.
- Abstain from owning, possessing, or carrying a weapon.
- Provide for the support and care of dependents.
- Perform community service work.

Probation conditions must be reasonable and, ideally, designed with an eye to preventing the offender from committing additional crimes. During the period of supervision, the probation officer may request that the sentencing judge increase, decrease, or eliminate additional conditions, or reduce (but not lengthen) the total period of the probation order.

The Supreme Court has ruled that probation orders cannot contain a condition that the probationer must provide blood or urine samples to show that he or she is complying with the condition to abstain from alcohol or drugs. These provisions, the court held, violated the Charter of Rights and Freedoms (*R. v. Shoker*, 2006, SCC 44). This ruling has limited the ability of probation officers to monitor drug and alcohol use among probationers.

An adult probationer who, without reasonable excuse, fails or refuses to comply with a condition, or who commits a new offence, may be charged with breach of probation. A breach of probation is an elective (or hybrid) offence and can carry a maximum penalty of two years imprisonment if proceeded with by indictment.

Recruitment and Training of Probation Officers

As noted earlier in this chapter, probation falls under the authority of the provinces/territories. Each jurisdiction has developed its own procedures and standards for recruiting and training probation officers. Commonly there is a preemployment training model, wherein potential applicants must complete a number of courses (many of which are offered online), often at their own expense, prior to being eligible to apply for a position as a probation officer.

In Ontario, the training for probation officer recruits (and provincial parole officer recruits) takes 18 months. It includes an orientation to the local area, the learning of specific skills, two five-day residential courses, a self-study program, and two oral examinations. The training focuses on developing skills in report writing, supervision, and enforcement, as well as integrating the theory with the practice of probation.

Most jurisdictions also offer ongoing in-service training courses for probation officers. These focus on supervision of special populations (such as sex offenders and the mentally disordered) and the use of assessment instruments.

Role and Responsibilities of Probation Officers

The activities of probation officers centre around the following: assessing clients with respect to their needs and the risks they pose; providing individualized case management with the objective of reducing criminal behaviour; and supervising offenders on probation as well as persons who have been released on bail while awaiting trial. In Quebec and Ontario, probation officers supervise offenders released on provincial parole. Probation officers are also responsible for supervising offenders on bail.

Probation offices are involved in preparing **presentence reports** (PSRs) on adult offenders who have been convicted. The PSR contains a wealth of information on the offender's sociobiographical background and offence history, as well as victim impact information and assessments completed by treatment professionals. While probation officers in many provinces are prevented by policy from making recommendations on sentencing, the PSR will generally set out available community and institutional programs for the judge to consider in determining the sentence. Where probation officers do make sentencing recommendations, they are generally accepted. A study in Manitoba found that when the probation officer recommended a community disposition, this was followed 71 percent of the time by the sentencing judge. The study also found that judges were willing to follow the probation officer's recommendation for a community sentence 50 percent of the time in cases involving high-risk offenders. This suggests that judges place considerable stock in the treatment and risk management information presented in the PSRs (Bonta et al. 2005).

A major finding from this study was that PSRs have evolved over the past three decades into reports that are oriented toward treatment and case management.

Assessment of Offender Risk and Needs

A core component of the probation officer's role is completing assessments, which are designed to identify the offender's needs, evaluate risk, and assist in formulating a plan of supervision. These assessments are used not only in the case management process, but also by provincial parole boards in determining whether to grant conditional release to offenders in custody (more on this in Chapter 9). Probation officers in Ontario use the Level of Supervision Inventory, Ontario Revision (LSI-OR), which examines offender characteristics to determine the likelihood of reoffending. In Manitoba, probation officers use the Primary Risk Assessment (PRA)—a general risk/needs classification instrument—and the Secondary Risk Assessment (SRA), which is specific to the offence for which the offender has been convicted (e.g., sexual assault, domestic assault).

Effective case management requires the identification of the risks and needs of offenders so that the appropriate level of supervision can be determined (i.e., more intensive supervision for higher risk/needs offenders and less supervision for lower risk/needs offenders), and so that the services that will address the needs of offenders can be identified (Bonta et al. 2004).

Supervising Offenders on Provincial Parole

Probation officers also serve as parole officers in Ontario and Quebec, the two provinces that have provincial parole boards. In this capacity, probation officers prepare community assessments, which the parole board then uses to assess the viability of the inmate-applicant's release plan (more on this in Chapter 8).

Case Management and Supervision

Supervision is a critical part of probation. It follows that the relationship established between the probation officer and the probationer is very important. The attributes of a positive relationship include the following:

- establishing and maintaining good rapport
- considering the offender's individual needs
- empowering the probationer to take responsibility and initiative
- maintaining a proper balance between control and assistance
- engaging in differential supervision, based on the risk the offender presents

Effective probation practice requires probation officers to foster relationships in which the offenders can speak openly about their concerns and problems, feel that they are being treated as individuals, and view the probation officer as a person who genuinely cares about them. It is also important that probationers understand what is expected of them and that there be consistency in supervision. Probation officers have identified interpersonal communication and interviewing skills, knowledge of community resources, and the ability to cope with the offender's emotions as required core competencies for effective supervision (Bracken 2003a, 2003b).

A study of probation practice in Manitoba, however, found that the intervention plans developed by probation officers were not being informed by the findings from the risk assessment. As well, there was considerable room for improvement with respect to the efforts of probation officers to alter the attitudes and behaviours of the offenders they were dealing with (Bonta et al. 2004, 27–28).

It is important that the supervision strategies the officer employs match the needs and risks of the individual offender. For offenders who are less cooperative, an approach based on control may be effective; whereas for offenders who are motivated to change, the probation officer can provide encouragement, support, and assistance. Probation officers have the discretion to tailor their style of supervision to the needs and risks of the individual probationer.

Over the past decade there has been a strong shift in the role and orientation of probation officers toward control and surveillance in probation supervision (Burnett and McNeill 2005). This shift has been due in large measure to increasing caseloads, the focus on risk assessment in order to ensure accountability and reduce liability, and the increasing number of special higher risk categories of offenders—such as sex offenders and assaultive male offenders—who are receiving sentences of probation.

The Dual Role of Probation Officers in Supervising Offenders

Probation officers play a dual role: they provide assistance and support for offenders, and at the same time they enforce the conditions of the probation order. In carrying out the assistance and support role, the probation officer may help the offender address issues that have contributed to the offence and identify resources in the community such as alcohol and drug treatment programs, education upgrading courses, and mental health services. However, the probation officer must at the same time ensure compliance with the general and specific conditions of the probation order.

It is often difficult for probation officers to focus equally on both roles, and this may be a barrier to effective case management. For example, a probationer with a history of drug addiction who has relapsed and started "using" again (or who never ceased using drugs) may want to ask his or her probation officer for help finding a treatment program. However, that person could trigger a charge of breach of probation by disclosing the illegal drug use to the probation officer. On the other hand, failing to disclose the drug relapse could result in the commission of further criminal acts to support the addiction. A probation officer who becomes aware that the probationer is not adhering to the conditions of the probation order often has considerable discretion in deciding whether to revoke probation. The decision often depends on the severity of the breach.

Programs for Probationers

Provincial/territorial systems of corrections and not-for-profit organizations offer probationers a wide variety of programs and services. In B.C., for example, these programs include the Violence Prevention Program, Substance Abuse Management, Respectful Relationships, Living Skills, Cognitive Skills, and Educational Upgrading, as well as a Sex Offender program. These programs are offered by community corrections offices throughout the province and are available for both probationers and parolees. Participation is generally stipulated on the offender's probation order, although the programs also accept persons other than probationers. The John Howard Society operates a number of programs for probationers. These include the Family Violence Intervention Program, a 20-week nonresidential program in Kamloops, B.C., that is designed to teach men convicted of spousal assault to take responsibility for and effectively manage their anger, abuse, and violence; and the Learning Resource Program in St. John's, Newfoundland, which offers courses and counselling in a number of areas, including substance abuse, anger management, and cognitive skills. In Edmonton, Native Counselling Services of Alberta operates the Family Life Improvement Program, which comprises a number of services, including counselling, family life-skills training, anger management, education, and community service.

Obstacles to Effective Probation

The efforts of probation officers have been hindered by a variety of factors, including the following:

Increasing workloads. The duties of probation officers have continued to expand and now include providing bail supervision to adult criminal courts; preparing PSRs for the sentencing court; supervising offenders on conditional release orders; and liaising with social services, the police, and the courts. Probation officers must also conduct pretransfer inquiries when a probationer's file is being transferred from one region to another.

Increasing caseloads. Probation officers in many jurisdictions have experienced increases in their caseloads, some of which are in the 100+ range per officer. In B.C., for example, the number of sentenced offenders on probation has remained relatively stable but there has been a steady increase in the number of individuals on bail who are being supervised by probation officers (British Columbia Ministry of Public Safety and Solicitor General 2006, 13). One consequence is that probation officers may be limited in their ability to develop comprehensive intervention plans that address the issues identified in the needs assessment. Also, probation officers may only have time to "meet" with probationers via telephone, which imposes certain limitations in terms of case management.

A lack of probation officer–offender contact and intervention. A study of probation practices in Manitoba found that probation officers had, on average, 1.6 contacts per month with the offenders on their caseload. This was the average for low-, medium-, and high-risk offenders. While high-risk offenders were seen more often, there was no difference in the number of contacts involving low- and medium-risk offenders. The average length of probation officer–offender meetings was 22 minutes, which leads one to ask how much direction and assistance can be provided in such a short time frame. Interestingly, the study also found that caseload size was not associated with either number of contacts with the probationer or the length of the sessions. This suggests that the other roles and responsibilities of probation officers "eat into" face-to-face interaction. Note that caseload size was found not to be associated with the frequency of contacts with the offender, nor was it associated with the length of the meetings that were held (Bonta et al. 2004).

Increasing needs and risks of probationers. In recent years, the profile of offenders receiving a period of supervision under probation has changed. There has been an increase in the needs and risk levels of offenders placed on probation and in the numbers of offenders who have been convicted of sex-related crimes and crimes of violence, and who are mentally disordered. In the past, the typical probationer had been convicted of a nonviolent property offence and did not have an extensive criminal history. Today, more probationers (40 percent in 2005–6) have been convicted of a violent crime (Landry and Sinha 2008).

Probation caseloads are now increasingly populated by special categories of offenders, many of whom have been assessed as high risk. Between 1997 and 2006, for example, the percentage of offenders assessed as low risk in B.C. dropped from 50 to just under 30 percent; at the same time, there was an increase in offenders assessed as high risk, from 15 to 25 percent (British Columbia Ministry of Public Safety and Solicitor General 2006, 14). Also in B.C., men who have been convicted of spousal assault account for 30 percent of today's probation caseloads.

The growth in special categories of offenders has placed additional demands on probation services to develop specialized services and to provide close supervision. To effectively supervise and assist special categories of offenders, probation officers require specialized training courses. Provincial/territorial systems of corrections are increasingly shifting resources to high-risk offender groups. Many probation offices now have specialized supervision units composed of specially trained officers for offenders convicted of spousal assault, sex offences, and other specific types of crime. The caseloads are smaller, and the probation officer can see clients more often and do more external supervision, including home visits.

Providing probation services in remote and northern regions. There are unique challenges in providing effective probation services in remote and northern areas of the country. For example, community resources are absent, and it is difficult to recruit and retain probation officers. These difficulties are particularly acute given the high rates of crime and violence that afflict many northern and remote communities (see Box 3.2).

As a consequence of these and other challenges, the occupation of probation officer has become more and more stressful. This increases the likelihood that probation officers will suffer emotional exhaustion or become cynical toward their clients and the justice system, significantly affecting the effectiveness of probation as a correctional strategy.

Improving Probation

In a number of jurisdictions, efforts are being made to reinvent probation so as to make it more effective. The suggestions for improving probation include these:

- *Supervising probationers in the community rather than in the office.* It is important that probation officers have firsthand knowledge of the offender's residence and family situation, as well as other aspects of the offender's life.
- *24/7/365 supervision.* Community supervision must be carried out at night, on weekends, and on holidays, not just during "regular" business hours.
- *Focusing supervision on offenders who are higher risk and whose offences pose a public safety risk.* An example is sex offenders.
- *Ensuring strict enforcement of probation conditions.* Breaches of probation have often not been taken seriously by either the probationer or the supervising probation officer. It is rare for offenders to be convicted for breaching the conditions of their probation order. Pilot projects in the United States that involve strict enforcement of probation conditions

BOX 3.2

Probation in the Remote North

A study of crime and justice in the Baffin region, in what is now the territory of Nunavut, found that Inuit residents and justice and social service personnel had numerous concerns about the effectiveness of probation. Among the more serious problems with probation in Baffin communities were (1) the overuse and inappropriate use of probation; (2) the ineffectiveness of probation in controlling the offender and protecting the community; (3) the inability of supervisory personnel to enforce the conditions of probation; (4) the absence of community-based programs and services for probationers; (5) the ineffectiveness of existing counselling programs in addressing the needs of offenders; and (6) the questionable effectiveness of program personnel (Griffiths et al. 1995). Concern about the effectiveness of probation was reflected in the comments of an Inuit woman who had been the victim of violence in one of the communities:

> *He was charged with assault. Then, a few weeks later, he was in JP court and he got six months probation. I thought it was going to be ok because after the JP court he said he would quit beating me up. But after one month he started again. That was against his probation. He'd go see his probation officer every month and when he still had six or eight months to go, he quit going. Nobody said anything and nothing happened. He was still drinking when he was on probation. It's just a lot of words, no action. (ibid., 159)*

Contributing to the overuse and inappropriate use of probation in remote areas such as Nunavut is the reluctance of circuit court judges to sentence offenders to periods of confinement in correctional institutions, which may be hundreds of kilometres from the offender's home community.

with high-risk probationers (e.g., drug users) have achieved high rates of compliance with probation conditions.

- *Developing partnerships between probation and the community.* This provides offenders with prosocial support networks and increased access to treatment resources. It also increases citizen awareness.
- *Creating performance-based initiatives to assess the effectiveness of probation practice and programs.*
- *Injecting restorative justice approaches into probation supervision* (Corbett 1999; Bonta et al. 2004; National Institute of Justice 2008; Robinson and Raynor 2006).

In an effort to increase the effectiveness of probation, Ontario has implemented a service delivery model that focuses resources and supervision on offenders with the highest levels of criminal behaviour and/or the highest risk of reoffending.

INTERMEDIATE SANCTIONS

The term **intermediate sanctions,** also often referred to as *alternative sanctions* or *community sanctions,* describes a wide variety of correctional programs that generally fall between traditional probation and incarceration, although specific initiatives may include either of these penalties. Intermediate sanctions include fines, community service, day centres, home detention with or without electronic monitoring, intensive probation supervision, strict discipline camps (boot camps), conditional sentence orders, and halfway houses (Caputo 2004).

Intermediate sanctions may be directed toward specific offender groups. An example of a gender-specific alternative sanction is Summit House, in North Carolina. This is a residential alternative to an incarceration facility. There, female offenders live with their children and are involved in parenting groups and a variety of other programs designed to strengthen the mother–child relationship (Brennan 2007).

Intermediate sanctions have two sets of objectives:

- *Offender*-oriented objectives, which include the assurance of real punishment, retribution, and some degree of incapacitation and control of offenders.
- *System*-oriented objectives, which include reducing institutional populations and the costs of corrections, as well as rates of recidivism (Junger-Tas 1994, 11, 13).

The primary objective of intermediate sanctions is to hold offenders responsible for their behaviour through restrictive and intensive intervention; treatment and rehabilitation are generally secondary, although usually a component of these sanctions. Studies that have queried offenders about their perceptions of the severity of intermediate sanctions as opposed to incarceration confirm that alternatives to incarceration can be effective at punishing and controlling (Petersilia and Deschenes, 1994).

Intensive Supervision Probation

Intensive supervision probation (ISP) was originally designed as an intermediate sanction between traditional probation practice—which generally involves minimal supervision—and incarceration. ISP programs entail increased surveillance of probationers, various treatment interventions, efforts to ensure that offenders are employed, and reduced caseloads for probation officers.

With ISP programs, offenders are monitored closely and rigorous conditions are imposed on them, such as multiple weekly reporting requirements, strict enforcement of the mandatory and optional conditions on the probation order, and the requirement that offenders secure and maintain employment. ISP is more suited for offenders who are classified as posing a greater risk to reoffend in the community. Over the past two decades, ISP programs have been developed in every state in the United States, and a number of programs have been developed by provincial systems of corrections in Canada. An underlying premise of such programs is that they can help reduce the number of prison admissions, cut operational costs, and protect the public, while providing increased supervision of more serious offenders.

Conditional Sentences

Section 742 of the Criminal Code states that a convicted person who would otherwise be incarcerated for a period of less than two years can be sentenced to a conditional term of imprisonment, to be served in the community rather than in custody. This is a **conditional sentence,** and the offender is required to fulfill certain conditions attached to the conditional release. A failure to comply with the conditions of the conditional release results in the offender being returned to court, where the sentencing judge has a variety of options, including sending the offender to prison. The use of conditional sentences has increased steadily since their inception in 1996; this practice, however, has levelled off in recent years at around 12,000 offenders (Public Safety Canada Portfolio Corrections Statistics Committee 2007, 71).

All conditional sentence orders contain standard, compulsory conditions that are similar to those contained in probation orders. Optional conditions may also be prescribed and may be added to or reduced by the court over time. These include the following:

- abstaining from alcohol or other intoxicants
- abstaining from owning, possessing, or carrying a weapon
- providing for the support or care of dependents
- performing up to 240 hours of community service work
- attending a treatment program

Noncompliance with the conditions of a conditional sentence order can result in the offender being incarcerated. If an allegation is made that a condition has been breached, the offender may have to appear in court to prove that the allegation is not true. This is a reverse onus situation; in other words, it is up to the offender to prove that the breach did *not* occur. There is some evidence that conditional sentence orders are frequently violated. One investigation found that 40 percent of offenders in three jurisdictions across Canada breached the conditions of their conditional sentence (North 2001).

A judge who is satisfied, on a balance of probabilities, that a condition has been breached, has four options:

- Take no action.
- Add or eliminate optional conditions.
- Suspend the conditional sentence order and commit the offender to custody to serve a portion of the unexpired sentence (in which case the conditional sentence resumes when the offender is released from confinement).
- Terminate the conditional sentence order and commit the offender to custody to serve until the release on parole or the discharge possible date.

Offenders on conditional sentences are supervised in the community by probation officers; however, *these offenders are not on probation.* The Supreme Court of Canada has clearly defined the differences between conditional sentences and probation (*R v. Proulx*, [2000] S.C.R. 61). The major difference is that probation focuses on rehabilitation, while conditional sentences embrace the principles of rehabilitation *and* punitive justice. This means that the conditions attached to a conditional sentence will generally be more onerous and more restrictive than the conditions attached to a probation order. The Court directed that two key factors be taken into account in determining whether a conditional sentence is appropriate: (1) the risk that the offender will reoffend, and (2) the amount of harm the offender would cause in the event of reoffence.

The Use of Conditional Sentence Orders

Research on the use of conditional sentence orders has found the following:

- There is considerable regional variation in the use of conditional sentences, with judges in Quebec, Ontario, and B.C. using this sanction more than those in other jurisdictions.
- Reducing the use of imprisonment is the most frequently cited objective.
- Property crimes account for the highest percentage of conditional sentence orders, although CSOs are also used in cases involving crimes against persons.

- The average length of conditional sentence orders is eight months, and nearly half the orders are under six months.
- Judges desire more guidance from Courts of Appeal in the use of conditional sentences.
- Judges would impose conditional sentences more frequently if there were sufficient community resources.
- Most judges believe that the use of conditional sentences has reduced the number of admissions to correctional institutions.
- Judges believe that the general public does not understand conditional sentences but that those members of the public who *are* informed support their use (Roberts, Doob, and Marinos 2000; Roberts and LaPrairie 2000).

In Quebec, the management framework for conditional sentences includes both control and rehabilitation activities. Control activities involve extensive telephone checks and random home checks each month, while rehabilitative activities include frequent in-person meetings with the offender, which are often held at the offender's home.

The Controversy Surrounding the Use of Conditional Sentences

Conditional sentences are a popular sentencing option for judges. At the same time, they have been surrounded by controversy, particularly when conditional sentences are imposed on offenders convicted of violent crimes or for crimes causing death. Critics have cited numerous cases in which offenders were granted a conditional sentence when a period of incarceration should have been imposed. Illustrative of the types of cases that received extensive coverage in the press and that resulted in denouncements by community groups such as Mothers Against Drunk Driving is the case of Peter Leon Howe, who drove impaired after consuming 24 beers and half a bottle of whiskey and struck and killed a person. Howe was sentenced to house arrest for two years less a day (Mothers Against Drunk Driving 2007).

Newspaper headlines such as "No Jail Time for Molesting 10-year old Girl" and "No Jail Time for Sexually Assaulting 12-year Old Girl" contributed to the controversy (http://www.justicemonitor.ca/jurgensheitz.htm; http://www.justicemonitor.ca/deanedmondson.htm). It is likely that conditional sentences will continue to be controversial, particularly if judges continue to expand the use of this sentencing option. Share your thoughts on "At Issue 3.1: Should there be more strict limits on the use of conditional sentences? A case study" presented at the end of the chapter.

Electronic Monitoring

Electronic monitoring (EM) programs were originally developed in the United States and are now used by several provincial systems of corrections (a) for offenders serving sentences in the community or (b) to provide surveillance for offenders on parole. There are both "passive" and "active" EM programs. Active EM systems involve the offender wearing a transmitter to provide a "continuous signal" as to the offender's location. Passive systems utilize a computer to call the offender at either random or specified times in order to verify that the offender is where he or she is supposed to be.

EM equipment generally includes a bracelet strapped to the offender's ankle. This bracelet emits radio signals within a range of 45 metres (150 feet). A receiver attached to the offender's telephone receives the signals and relays them to a central monitoring system. Offenders are generally permitted to be absent from home for specific periods of time to attend work or school programs. The supervising officer may make random visits to the home or workplace.

The primary objectives of EM programs include these: to provide an alternative to incarceration; to reduce the operating costs for correctional systems; and to allow offenders under supervision and control in the community to remain employed and with their families. Only those offenders who have been convicted of less serious, nonviolent offences and who have a stable residence and a telephone are eligible to participate in EM programs. The current generation of EM systems is only able to verify an offender's location and is not able to prevent an offender from committing crimes (Bottos 2008).

First-generation EM technology only allows corrections personnel to verify the location of an offender. By contrast, GPS technology has the capacity to track an offender's movements on a continuous basis. This has the potential to provide greater protection for crime victims, who can then be notified if the offender travels outside preset boundaries (ibid.). Similar to EM systems, GPS systems can be active, passive, or hybrid. Active monitoring provides near–"real time" information on the offender's location. Passive systems gather GPS data during the day, which is then transmitted to the monitoring authority when the offender returns home and connects the GPS receiver to a charging unit. In hybrid systems the offender is passively monitored until there is an alert, at which point the system switches into active mode (Brown, McCabe, and Wellford 2007; and see Figure 3.1).

GPS monitoring makes it possible to determine where an offender is at any given moment. In addition, it is possible to "customize" tracking and to specify the boundaries of an offender's movements and to set out locations where the offender is not permitted (e.g., a sex offender may be prohibited

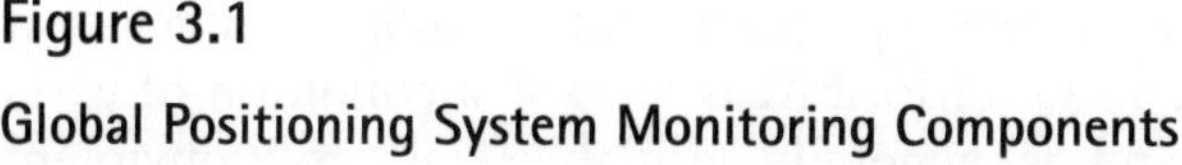

Figure 3.1

Global Positioning System Monitoring Components

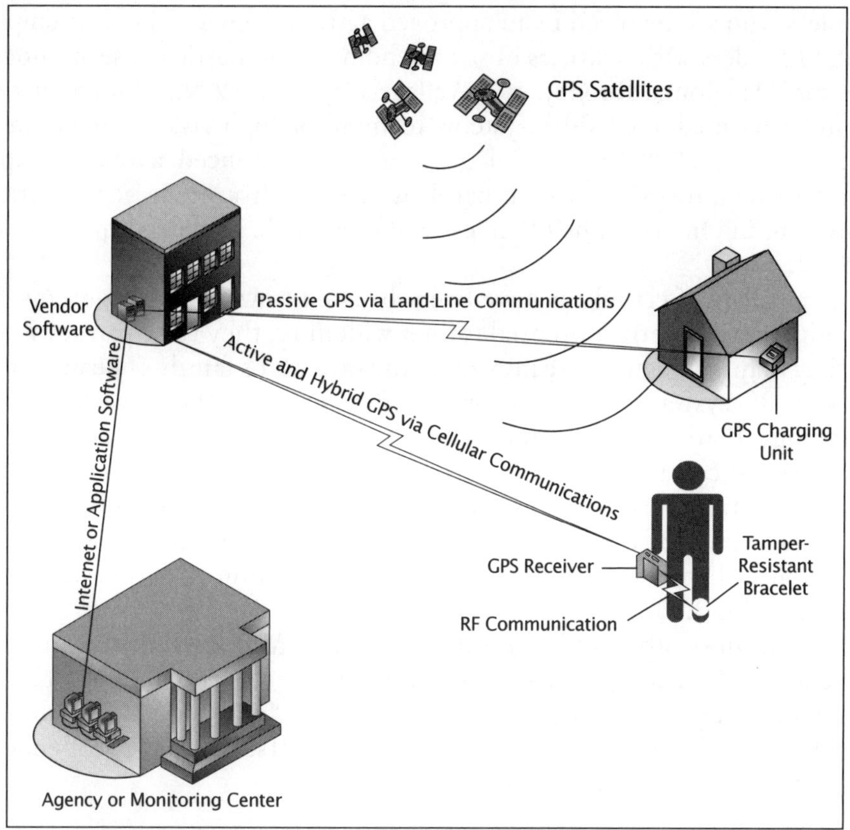

Source: Brown, McCabe, and Wellford, 2007. *Global Positioning System (GPS) Technology for Community Supervision: Lessons Learned.* Washington, D.C.: U.S. Department of Justice. p. 1.3. http://www.ncjrs.gov/pdffiles1/nij/grauts/219376.pdf; © 2007 Noblis

from going near schools or playgrounds). A monitoring program can be designed that will alert both the offender and the agency if the offender violates certain area restrictions.

EM Programs in Canada

There are both "front end" and "back end" EM programs, referring to the stage of the correctional process at which the strategy is used. In Saskatchewan, for example, EM is a front-end sentencing option that the judge may select at the time of sentencing, while in Ontario, EM is used as a condition of early release from incarceration and is generally available only to nonviolent offenders who are involved in an approved activity such as school or employment. Offenders with histories of sex offending or domestic abuse are not eligible for EM (Bonta, Rooney, and Wallace-Capretta, 1999). Nova Scotia and Manitoba have adopted GPS systems to monitor high-risk offenders in the community. In 2008 the federal government announced a one-year pilot project to monitor 30 high-risk parolees released from federal correctional institutions in Ontario. The offenders will wear ankle bracelets equipped with GPS receivers.

A number of criticisms have been directed toward EM programs. For example, they carry the potential for net widening, they raise privacy issues, and they may have a negative impact on the offender's family. The increasing use of GPS systems for monitoring offenders and the development of technology that will allow authorities to control the actual *behaviour* of offenders are certain to raise legal and ethical issues in the coming years. At the same time, research has found that offenders on EM hold generally favourable views of the program, citing the fact that EM allows them to stay employed and to remain with their families while attending treatment programs (ibid.).

For an in-depth examination of the use of EM and GPS in community corrections in Canada and the United States, see the report of the John Howard Society of Alberta (2006). Share your thoughts on "At Issue 3.2: Should electronic monitoring be expanded to include behavioural surveillance of offenders?" presented at the end of the chapter.

RESTORATIVE JUSTICE

Among the nations of the world, Canada has a long lead in the development of alternative justice policies and programs. **Restorative justice** is based on the fundamental principle that criminal behaviour injures not only victims but also communities and offenders and that any efforts to address and resolve the problems created by the criminal behaviour should involve all of these parties. The concept of restorative justice is best illustrated by comparing it with the principles of retributive justice, on which the adversarial system of criminal justice is based. The key differences are listed in Table 3.1.

It is important to note that restorative justice is not a specific practice; rather, it is a set of principles that together provide the basis for a community

Table 3.1 Comparison of Retributive and Restorative Justice Principles

Retributive Justice	Restorative/Community Justice
Crime violates the state and its laws.	Crime violates people and relationships.
Justice focuses on establishing guilt so that doses of pain can be meted out.	Justice aims to identify needs/obligations so that things can be made right.
Justice is sought through conflict between adversaries in which the offender is pitted against state rules, and intentions outweigh outcomes—one side wins and the other loses.	Justice encourages dialogue and mutual agreement, gives victims and offenders central roles, and is judged by the extent to which responsibilities are assumed, needs are met, and healing (of individuals and relationships) is encouraged.

Source: Zehr 1990.

and the justice system to respond to crime and social disorder. These general principles include the following:

- providing for the involvement of offenders, victims, their families, the community, and justice personnel
- viewing crimes in a broad social context
- embracing a preventative and problem-solving orientation
- ensuring flexibility and adaptability (Marshall 1999, 5)

Figure 3.2 depicts the interrelationships among the various parties that may be involved in a restorative justice approach.

The primary objectives of restorative justice are these:

- to fully address the needs of victims of crime
- to prevent reoffending by reintegrating offenders back into the community
- to enable offenders to acknowledge and assume responsibility for their behaviour
- to create a "community" of support and assistance for the victim and the offender, as well as for the long-term interests of the community
- to provide an alternative to the adversarial system of justice (ibid., 6).

Figure 3.2

The Relationships of Restorative Justice

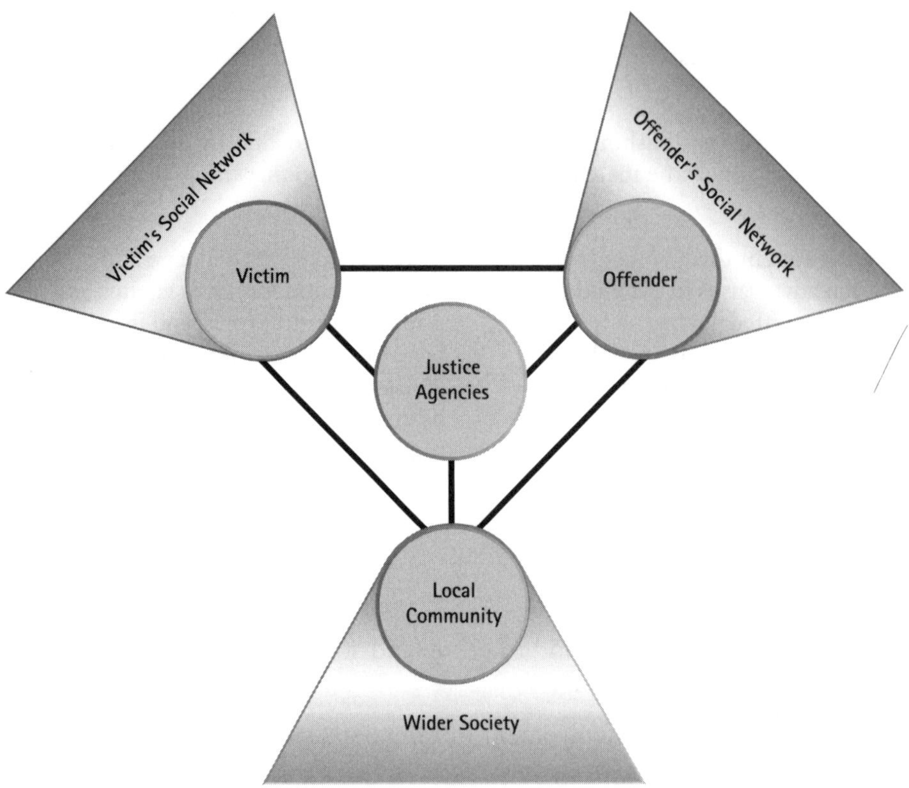

Source: Marshall 1999, 5.

Restorative community justice can be utilized at all stages of the justice process:

- Police: precharge
- Crown: postcharge, preconviction
- Court: postconviction, presentence
- Corrections: postsentence, prereintegration

Examples can be found of successful restorative justice programs operating in rural, suburban, and urban communities.

The Dimensions of Restorative Justice

Among the more common restorative justice initiatives are victim–offender mediation, circle sentencing, community holistic healing programs, and family group conferences. There are critical differences among the various models of restorative/community justice; these relate to their mandate and relationship to the formal adversarial system, the role of the crime victim and other participants, and the procedures for preparing for the event and for monitoring and enforcing the agreement (Bazemore and Schiff 2001; Johnstone and Van Ness 2006). The models also differ in terms of their objectives, the degree to which the model requires that the justice system share power with community residents, and the extent to which the model is designed to empower the community as well as address the specific incident and behaviour (Bazemore and Griffiths 1997; Dandurand and Griffiths 2006).

Victim–Offender Mediation

Victim–offender mediation (VOM) programs (also often referred to as victim–offender reconciliation [VOR] programs) take a restorative approach in which the victim and the offender are provided with the opportunity to express their feelings and concerns. With the assistance of a mediator, who is a neutral third party, the offender and the victim are able to resolve the conflict and address the consequences of the offence and, ultimately, to understand each other (see Box 3.3 for an example of a VOM program).

There are generally four phases of a mediation: (1) intake of the case from a referral source, (2) preparation for the mediation, which involves the mediator meeting separately with the victim and the offender, (3) the mediation session, and (4) postsession activities, including ensuring that any agreement reached during the mediation session is fulfilled.

In recent years, VOM and VOR programs have been extended to cases involving crimes of violence and have included incarcerated offenders.

Circle Sentencing

Circle sentencing was first developed in several Yukon communities as a collaboration between community residents and territorial justice personnel, primarily RCMP officers and judges from the Territorial Court of Yukon. In circle sentencing, all of the participants, including the judge, defence lawyer, prosecutor, police officer, victim and family, offender and family, and community residents, sit facing one another in a circle. Through discussions, those in the circle reach a consensus about the best way to dispose of the case, taking into account both the need to protect the community and the rehabilitation and punishment of the offender. Circle sentencing is premised on traditional Aboriginal healing practices and has multifaceted objectives, which include addressing the needs of communities, victims, the families of victims, and offenders through a process of reconciliation, restitution, and reparation. A

BOX 3.3

The Restorative Resolutions Program, Winnipeg

Restorative Resolutions is an intensive supervision program using victim–offender mediation to achieve restorative justice. The program is an alternative to incarceration for offenders who are willing to take responsibility for their behaviour and to compensate their victims. Among the services provided are counselling, anger management, and intensive supervision. The program is operated by the John Howard Society of Manitoba and staffed by workers trained in probation practices and restorative justice.

A Case Study

A 32-year-old man with a lengthy youth and adult record of assault and break and enter was charged with four new counts of break and enter and theft. The Crown attorney wanted a period of incarceration. Restorative Resolutions staff prepared an alternative plan, recommending that the judge issue a suspended sentence, with supervision of the offender to be carried out by Restorative Resolutions; and that the offender complete the Interpersonal Communication Skills Course; complete the Addictions Foundation of Manitoba assessment; attend AA regularly; complete the conditions outlined in the mediation agreement; and receive literacy training. The judge accepted the plan.

Source: Church Council on Justice and Corrections 1996, 5.

fundamental principle of circle sentencing is that the sentence is less important than the process used to select it. A circle sentencing case from Yukon is presented in Box 3.4.

There are a number of important stages in circle sentencing, each of which is vital to its success. Circle sentencing is generally only available to offenders who plead guilty. The operations of circle sentencing are specific to communities; in other words, the process may (and should) vary between communities and relies heavily on community volunteers (Stuart 1996). Both Aboriginal and non-Aboriginal victims, offenders, and community residents participate in sentencing circles. To date, the majority of offenders who have had their cases disposed of through sentencing circles have been adults, although the number of youth cases has been increasing. Circle sentencing has spawned a number of variations, including community sentence advisory committees, sentencing panels, and community mediation panels. There is some evidence that circle

BOX 3.4

Circle Sentencing: A Case Study

The victim—the wife of the offender, who had admitted to physically abusing her during two recent drunken episodes—spoke about the pain and embarrassment her husband had caused her and her family. After she had finished, she passed the ceremonial feather (used to signify who would be allowed to speak next) to the next person in the circle, a young man who spoke about the contributions the offender had made to the community, the kindness he had shown toward the elders by sharing fish and game with them, and his willingness to help others with home repairs. An elder then took the feather and spoke about the shame the offender's behaviour had caused to his clan, noting that in the old days, the offender would have been required to pay the woman's family substantial compensation.

After hearing this discussion, the judge confirmed that the victim still wanted to try to work things out with her estranged husband and that she was receiving help from her own support group (including a victim's advocate). Summarizing the case by again stressing the seriousness of the offence and repeating the Crown counsel's opening remarks that a jail sentence was required, the judge then proposed that sentencing be delayed for six weeks until the time of the next circuit court hearing. The judge would not impose the jail sentence if, during that time, the offender (1) met the requirements presented earlier by a friend of the offender who had agreed to lead a support group, (2) met with the community justice committee to work out an alcohol and anger-management treatment plan, (3) fulfilled the expectations of the victim and her support group, and (4) completed 40 hours of service under the group's supervision. After a prayer, in which the entire group held hands, the circle disbanded and everyone retreated to the kitchen area of the community centre for refreshments.

Source: Bazemore and Griffiths 1997. Reprinted by permission of the Administrative Office of the U.S. Courts.

sentencing may be highly effective at reducing and eliminating criminal and disruptive behaviour, particularly that of offenders who have lengthy records in the formal criminal justice system.

Table 3.2 compares the attributes of the formal, adversarial criminal court with the community-based, restorative approach as exemplified by circle sentencing.

Healing circle, Aboriginal Ganootamaage Justice Services (Winnipeg)

The Winnipeg Free Press, Joe Bryska, March 27, 1999. Reprinted with permission.

Table 3.2 Comparison of the Criminal Court Process and Restorative Justice

	Formal Court Process	Restorative/ Community Justice
People	Experts, nonresidents	Local people
Process	Adversarial State vs. offender	Consensus Community vs. problem
Issues	Laws broken	Relationship broken
Focus	Guilt	Identify needs of victim, offender, and community
Tools	Punishment/ Control	Healing/support
Procedure	Fixed rules	Flexible

There are some significant differences between the processes and principles of circle sentencing and those of the formal, adversarial system of criminal justice. These differences are outlined in Table 3.3.

It is important to note that offenders who have their cases heard in a sentencing circle may still be sent for a period of incarceration. However, a wide range of other sanctions are available, including banishment (generally to a wilderness location), house arrest, and community service.

Circle sentencing is an example of how the principles of restorative justice can be applied within a holistic framework in which justice system personnel share power and authority with community residents. In contrast to the adversarial approach to justice, circle sentencing:

- reacquaints individuals, families, and communities with problem-solving skills
- rebuilds relationships within communities
- promotes awareness and respect for the values and the lives of others
- addresses the needs and interests of all parties, including the victim
- focuses on the causes, not just the symptoms, of problems
- recognizes existing healing resources and creates new ones
- coordinates the use of local and government resources
- generates preventive measures

Table 3.3 Differences between Criminal Court and Circle Sentencing Principles

Criminal Courts	Community Circles
View the conflict as the crime	View the crime as a small part of a larger conflict
Hand down sentence to resolve the solution	View the sentence as a small part of the conflict
Focus on past conduct	Focus on present and future conduct
Take a narrow view of behaviour	Take a broader, holistic view
Avoid concern with social conflict	Focus on social conflict
Result (i.e., the sentence) is most important	Result is least important; the process is most important, as the process shapes the relationship among all parties

Source: Griffiths 2007. Reprinted by permission of Justice Barry D. Stuart.

Restorative Justice Initiatives in Aboriginal Communities

Aboriginal communities have become increasingly involved in developing restorative justice services and programs that are designed to address the specific needs of community residents, victims, and offenders. These initiatives have been developed as part of a process of cultural and community revitalization and in conjunction with the increasing movement to reassert Aboriginal people's authority over all facets of community life (Griffiths and Hamilton 1996). Communities have also begun to explore alternatives to confinement in order to reduce the disproportionate numbers of Aboriginal people incarcerated in correctional institutions.

These initiatives vary widely with regard to the types of offences and offenders processed; the procedures for hearing cases, reaching dispositions, and imposing sanctions; and the extent to which they involve justice system professionals. Restorative/community justice initiatives in Aboriginal communities *may* be premised (i.e., not necessarily) on customary law and traditional practices. Many involve elders and emphasize healing the victim(s), offenders, and, as required, the community. Instead of focusing solely on the offender and the offence, the response to criminal behaviour occurs within a broader, holistic framework. This holistic approach facilitates the inclusion of crime victims and their families, the offender's family, and community residents in responding to the behaviour and formulating a sanction that will address the needs of all parties (Green 1997, 1998).

Another attribute of these initiatives is that the Aboriginal band and/or community maintains a high degree of control over the disposition. In addition, sanctioning processes are either controlled by the community or shared on a partnership basis with justice system personnel (as in the case of circle sentencing). Other programs are more autonomous and are controlled by the community. The Community Holistic Circle Healing Program on Hollow Water First Nation in Manitoba is an example of a community-controlled program (see Box 3.5).

Restorative/Community Justice in Urban Centres: The Collaborative Justice Project, Ottawa–Carleton Judicial District

In discussions of the potential for developing restorative justice initiatives, it is often assumed that programs such as circle sentencing, which involve substantial community participation, are suited only to rural and remote communities with a strong cultural identity and foundation. This assertion is often used to deflect suggestions that justice personnel in suburban and urban areas should explore the potential for restorative justice approaches that would better serve

BOX 3.5

Community Holistic Circle Healing Program, Hollow Water, Manitoba

The Community Holistic Circle Healing Program was designed as a community-based response to the high rates of sexual and family abuse that afflicted the community. It includes a 13-phase process, illustrated in Figure 3.3.

The Special Gathering in the Hollow Water program is a public event that shares many similarities with the traditional justice ceremony described below. Traditional healing practices are used in an attempt to restore the community, the family, and individual peace and harmony. The offender signs a healing contract and apologizes publicly to the victims and to the community for the harm done. The circle healing process is designed to consider the needs of all of the parties to the abuse—the victim, the offender, and the community—and is directed beyond merely punishing the offender for a specific behaviour.

Figure 3.3

The 13 Phases of the Hollow Water Community Holistic Circle Healing Process

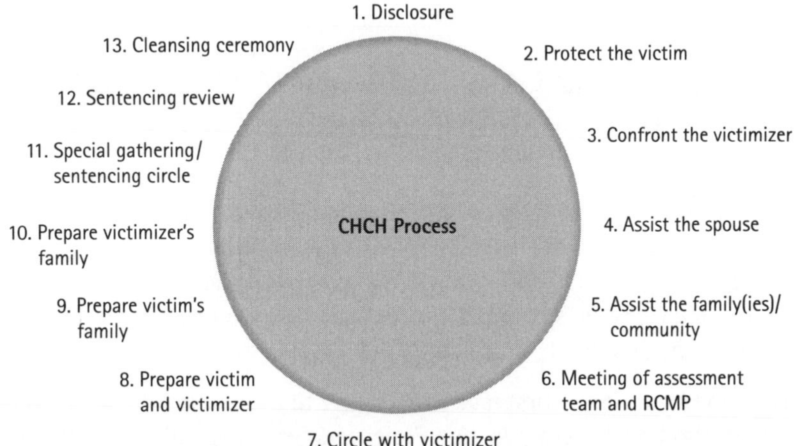

Source: Lajeunesse and Associates, Ltd. 1996, 33. Reprinted by permission of Manitoba Justice.

the needs of offenders, their victims, and the community. The Collaborative Justice Project (see Box 3.6) illustrates that restorative justice programs can succeed in urban centres. It also indicates that the use of restorative justice approaches is not restricted to minor offences but can be applied successfully to serious crimes, including crimes of violence, and may be used in conjunction with a period of incarceration.

The Collaborative Justice Project operates in the Ottawa–Carleton judicial district. Its aim is to demonstrate how a restorative approach can be used in cases of serious crime to deliver more satisfying justice to victims, the accused, and the community. The project considers cases of serious offending, including robbery, break and enter, assault causing bodily harm, weapons offences, and driving offences that involve death or bodily harm and for which a conviction would normally result in a period of incarceration. Cases are referred to the project by a variety of sources, including the judiciary, judicial pretrials, the Crown or defence counsel, the police, the probation office, and victim services. The accused person must be willing to take responsibility for the crime and to work to repair the harm done by it. The project is a postplea, presentence restorative justice program.

Three criteria must be met before a case is accepted by the project:

- The crime is serious and the Crown is seeking a period of custody.
- The accused person displays remorse and is willing to take responsibility for the crime and to work to repair the harm done.
- There is an identifiable victim who is interested in participating.

A summary of one case is presented in Box 3.6.

BOX 3.6

Impaired Driving Causing Death: A Case Study from the Collaborative Justice Project

The facts: The accused, Robert, was driving the wrong way on a multilane divided highway, entering by the off-ramp. After traveling 2 km in the wrong direction, narrowly missing several vehicles, he collided with the victim's car, killing a 60-year-old man and slightly injuring his wife. Robert had close to three times the legal limit of alcohol in his blood and was charged with impaired driving causing death and criminal negligence causing death.

Work done: The case worker first met with Robert to assess his interest in and appropriateness for the Collaborative Justice Project. Robert was willing to take responsibility for his offence and to work toward some form of reparation, without knowing in advance what that might look like. Robert was prepared to meet with the victim's family if it would help them. He was extremely emotional.

Satisfied that Robert met the criteria, the caseworker then met with Phillip, the adult son of the victim, and his mother, Claire. Phillip wanted something good to come out of the tragedy. He felt that Robert might speak to people about drinking and driving, or even go with Robert to speak to groups. However, Phillip believed that Robert would not be willing or able to speak publicly, so he didn't expect his hope could be realized. Phillip wanted to meet with Robert to learn who Robert was and whether he would drink and drive in the future. His mother didn't wish to meet Robert, but needed more information about the accident from the police so that she could move on with her own grieving process.

The caseworker obtained and forwarded the information to Claire. The caseworker met with Robert regularly over the next six months to discuss his alcohol problem, how he had ended up in this situation, the family he had harmed, and what he might do to assist the healing process. Robert was receiving ongoing psychological and addiction counselling. Similarly, the caseworker was meeting with Phillip to support him and his family, to explore what he needed from the process, and to prepare for a possible meeting with Robert. The caseworker conveyed information between Robert and Phillip so that each had a better understanding of the other's situation and needs.

Six months later, Robert and Phillip met in a mediation. They talked to each other in a supportive manner about the impact of the incident on them and their families, and about what they would like to see happen. While Robert had previously indicated that he felt unable to speak publicly about what had occurred, after meeting with Phillip he agreed to do so with him. Robert and Phillip met on four further occasions and together addressed a high school class where students were deeply moved by the presentation.

Sentence and follow-up: Robert received a sentence of two years less a day in provincial jail. The Crown attorney's original position of three to five years was mitigated in light of the work done by the accused and the victim's son and their interest in continuing such work. During the following year, there was continuing periodic contact with Robert and Phillip. Arrangements were made for Robert to be released on temporary absence passes from time to time to speak publicly with Phillip about impaired driving and their personal experiences.

Note: The names of the participants have been changed.

Source: http://cfsc.quaker.ca/pages/documents/RestorativeJusticeinPrisons.pdf

Critical Issues in Restorative Justice

The emergence of restorative justice in Canada has been uneven. In recent years it has been spurred by governments' attempts to reduce the costs associated with incarcerating offenders, by the increasing involvement of communities as partners in the criminal justice system, and by the efforts of Aboriginal communities to reassert control over responses to crime and social disorder (Clairmont 2000).

One obstacle has been that many of the key principles of restorative justice are unfamiliar to politicians, policymakers, and criminal justice personnel, including judges. Terms such as *forgiveness*, *community*, *empowerment*, *healing*, and *spirituality* are not found in the Criminal Code of Canada and are foreign to many criminal justice practitioners. This has slowed the development of restorative justice programs.

A number of critical issues will have to be addressed before restorative justice programs become established as alternatives to the adversarial system of criminal justice (Dandurand and Griffiths 2006). These include, but certainly are not limited to, the following:

Crime Victims and Restorative Justice

Crime victims are often marginalized by and excluded from the formal adversarial system of criminal justice. Concerns have been expressed that, as well, restorative/community justice initiatives may give inadequate attention to the rights and needs of vulnerable groups, specifically women, adolescents, and children. As a consequence, crime victims may find themselves revictimized by restorative/community justice. Aboriginal women, for example, have voiced concerns about the high rates of sexual and physical abuse in communities and have questioned whether restorative/community justice provides adequate protection for victims of violence and abuse and whether the sanctions imposed are appropriate (Presser and Van Voorhis 2002).

The Effectiveness of Restorative/Community Justice

Few evaluations have been conducted regarding the extent to which restorative/community justice strategies achieve their stated objectives. Despite the widespread publicity accorded circle sentencing, for example, no controlled evaluations of this strategy have been completed (Roberts and LaPrairie 1997).

Attempts to assess the effectiveness of restorative/community justice programs face a number of challenges. One is that the holistic approach and multifaceted objectives of many restorative justice programs require a broader evaluative framework than has been used for traditional crime-control initiatives.

Program objectives may encompass macrolevel dimensions such as cultural and community revitalization and empowerment, as well as community, family, and individual healing.

The Dynamics of Justice in the Community

The significant role that communities in restorative justice initiatives assume requires a close consideration of the strengths—as well as the potential pitfalls—of community justice. Canadian observers have raised a number of concerns and have identified several factors, which, if left unaddressed, may undermine the efficacy of restorative justice initiatives. These concerns relate, for example, to (1) ensuring that the general "health" of the community, including community leaders and those who would assume key roles in any restorative justice initiatives, is adequate; (2) acknowledging that there are, within all communities, power and status hierarchies that may undermine consensus building and place certain residents, be they victims or offenders, in positions of vulnerability; and (3) ensuring that the legal rights of offenders are protected (Griffiths and Hamilton 1996). For a review of the more common critiques of restorative justice and a "critique of the critics," see Morris (2002).

BOX 3.7

Research Summary: The Effectiveness of Alternative Sanctions

Diversion: Few formal evaluations have been conducted. Traditional diversion programs tend to target low-risk, first-time offenders convicted of minor offences. Programs may "widen the net," resulting in offenders being placed under supervision who otherwise would not have been subjected to any sanction. There is no evidence that diversion has any impact on correctional populations, but diversion may increase the justice system's workload and costs (Bonta 1998; Nuffield 1997). Preliminary results from the Drug Treatment Court in Toronto have been positive and suggest that this approach may reduce reoffending among repeat offenders with significant criminal records (Public Safety Canada 2007). An evaluation of the Calgary Diversion Program for mentally disordered offenders found high rates of client satisfaction and participation, a significant reduction in charges and court appearances and in the need for acute services (Mitton et al. 2007).

(continued)

Probation: Despite its long history and extensive use in correctional systems, the effectiveness of probation as a corrections strategy continues to be questioned. Few specific programs for probationers have been evaluated. Research studies suggest that probation is most effective with those offenders who are in a stable personal relationship, are employed, have higher levels of education, and do not have an extensive criminal record. Also, it appears that specialized supervision units can be effective in increasing offender accountability and reducing rates of reoffending, and have a positive impact on victim satisfaction (Klein et al. 2008).

How supervision is carried out is an important factor in the success of probationers. Formal evaluation of the Restorative Resolutions program in Winnipeg (see Box 3.3) indicates that this program has been successful in reducing recidivism (Bonta, Wallace-Capretta and Rooney, 1998).

Intensive Supervision Probation (ISP): There is no evidence that ISP programs reduce prison overcrowding. Close monitoring of offenders may result in more offenders being violated and sent to prison. There is some evidence that IPSs that include treatment services can produce small reductions in recidivism and that offenders under ISP remain longer in the community with no increase in revocations for violent offences. Studies of whether ISP programs result in cost savings are inconclusive. ISPs are effective in providing close supervision of high-risk offenders (Serin and Vuong 2003; Smith, Goggin and Gendreau, 2002).

Home Confinement/Electronic Monitoring Programs: Mixed results have been produced by studies that have examined whether the use of EM reduces rates of revocation and reoffending. A study of 75,000 offenders on home confinement in the United States found that EM significantly reduced the likelihood of reoffending and absconding, even when controlling for sociobiographical attributes of the offender as well as for current offence, prior record, and term of supervision (Padgett, Bales, and Blomberg 2006). There is no evidence that EM programs reduce prison admissions; however, in some jurisdictions it has been found that EM is a cost-beneficial resource that can be used to offset the costs associated with more expensive options, such as incarceration (Aos, Miller, and Drake 2006; Bonta, Wallace-Capretta, and Rooney 1999; Padgett, Bales, and Blomberg 2006). The limitations of EM include problems with the technology, the need to supplement the technology with treatment programs, and the stigma that offenders wearing bracelets may encounter (Bottos 2008).

An evaluation of EM programs in British Columbia, Saskatchewan, and Newfoundland that compared a sample of offenders under EM with inmates and 30 probationers, matched on key risk factors, found that EM resulted in net widening: many of the offenders under EM were low-risk and could have been effectively managed in the community without EM supervision. This indicates that EM was not generally being used as a true alternative to confinement (Bonta, Wallace-Capretta, and Rooney 2000).

Conditional Sentence: Studies of the effectiveness of conditional sentences, as compared to probation or incarceration, have not been conducted. It is uncertain whether conditional sentences have reduced rates of incarceration.

Restorative Justice: Research findings indicate that restorative justice approaches can be more effective in reducing reoffending than traditional correctional strategies such as probation. Restorative approaches generally receive high marks from crime victims, and there is some evidence that these approaches reduce the levels of trauma among victims. In some jurisdictions, restorative justice programs have reduced court costs and case-processing times (Dandurand and Griffiths 2006; Latimer, Dowden, and Muise 2001). An evaluation of the Hollow Water program found that the program has increased community awareness of sexual abuse and family violence and the rates of disclosure by offenders. It has also significantly reduced the rates of alcoholism in the community, improved educational standards, and increased services for at-risk children and youth (Couture, et al., 2001).

Note: It is important to be mindful that the findings presented in the research summary are not conclusive, but rather suggestive. This is because of the absence of well-designed evaluative studies and the fact that the studies cited are from a number of jurisdictions in Canada and the United States. It is likely that key factors surrounding the implementation and operations of individual programs, the specific program criteria (e.g., the qualifications for offenders to participate), and the methods and data used by the researchers will affect the research findings.

AT ISSUE

ISSUE 3.1: Should there be more strict limits on the use of conditional sentences? A Case Study

While the Criminal Code limits the use of conditional sentences in cases involving serious injury, this alternative to confinement is available to sentencing judges in nonviolent offences such as fraud. Consider the following summary of a case in Victoria, B.C. Graeme Bryson, a former vice president of a shipyard company who defrauded the company of more than $600,000, was given a conditional sentence of two years less a day, including one year of house arrest. He had pled guilty to fraud over $5,000 for nine illegal wire transfers. The stolen money was used to support a lavish lifestyle that included buying artwork and other luxuries. Bryson subsequently paid back all of the money, plus an additional $100,000 to help cover legal expenses and other costs.

In passing sentence, the judge stated: "The likelihood of the accused reoffending is minimal at most. The breach of trust is also obvious." The defence lawyer stated: "These sentences are often more severe than jail." Bryson had no prior record.

What do you think?

1. Do you think that a conditional sentence was appropriate in this case? Why? Why not?

Source: McMillan 2008. Used with permission by the Victoria Times Colonist.

AT ISSUE

ISSUE 3.2: Should electronic monitoring be expanded to include behavioural surveillance of offenders?

Current EM technology allows correctional authorities to verify the location of offenders, and the addition of Global Positioning Satellite (GPS) provides the capacity to track offender movements. It is likely that in the coming years, extensive use will be made of GPS technology, particularly once technology is developed to extend the monitoring of an offender's location to provide control over his or her behaviour. Possible scenarios would include developing the capacity to monitor brain activity, heartbeat, and other vital signs. When paired with chemical implants, it might be possible to monitor and, where required, control an offender's behaviour.

What do you think?

1. Would you support the development and application of technology that could both monitor an offender's location and provide behavioural control?
2. If yes, what limits, if any, would you place on the application of such technology? For example, securing offender consent, limiting it to high-risk offenders, and so on.

3. If no, what major arguments would you present against the deployment of this type of technology?

KEY POINTS REVIEW

1. Alternatives to confinement include diversion, probation, intermediate sanctions, and restorative justice initiatives.
2. There are concerns that diversion programs may widen the net and may be coercive and punitive.
3. Probation is the most widely used alternative to confinement.
4. Probation officers have a variety of roles and responsibilities, including preparing presentence reports, assessing offender risk and needs, and providing supervision and assistance.
5. Among the obstacles to effective probation are increasing workloads and caseloads, limited contact time with clients, increasing risk and needs of probationers, and providing probation services in rural and remote regions.
6. The primary objective of intermediate sanctions is to hold offenders responsible for their behaviour through restrictive and intensive intervention; treatment and rehabilitation are generally secondary, although usually a component of these sanctions.
7. There are significant differences between probation and conditional sentences.
8. There are both "front end" and "back end" electronic monitoring programs.
9. Restorative justice is not a specific practice, but rather a set of principles that provides the basis for a community and the justice system to respond to crime and social disorder.
10. There are significant differences between the criminal court process and restorative justice.
11. Aboriginal communities have become increasingly involved in developing restorative justice initiatives.

KEY TERM QUESTIONS

1. Discuss the issues surrounding the term **community corrections.**
2. Identify and discuss the objectives of **diversion** programs.
3. What is **net widening** and why is it a concern associated with diversion programs?

4. Describe the correctional strategy of **probation** and discuss the issues surrounding this strategy.
5. What is a **presentence report (PSR)** and what role does it play in sentencing?
6. Identify and discuss the objectives of **intermediate sanctions** and provide examples of these types of sanctions.
7. Describe the attributes of **intensive supervision probation.**
8. Define **conditional sentence order,** discuss what research findings have revealed about the use of conditional sentences in Canada, and describe the controversy that has surrounded their use.
9. Describe the use of **electronic monitoring,** including the potential role of GPS technology, as a corrections strategy.
10. What are the underlying principles of **restorative justice,** and how do these compare with the principles of retributive justice?
11. Describe the process of **circle sentencing.**

REFERENCES

Aos, S., M. Miller, and E. Drake. 2006. *Evidence-Based Public Policy Options to Reduce Future Prison Construction, Criminal Justice Costs, and Crime Rates.* Olympia: State Institute for Public Policy. http://www.wsipp.wa.gov/rptfiles/06-10-1201.pdf

Bazemore, G., and C.T. Griffiths. 1997. "Conferences, Circles, Boards, and Mediations: The 'New Wave' of Community Justice Decisionmaking." *Federal Probation* 61(2): 25–37.

Bazemore, G., and M. Schiff. 2001. *Restorative and Community Justice.* Cincinnati: Anderson.

Bonta, J. 1998. "Adult Offender Diversion Programs" Research Summary. *Corrections Research and Development* 3(1). Ottawa: Solicitor General Canada. http://ww2.ps-sp.gc.ca/publications/corrections/199801a_e.asp

Bonta, J., G. Bourgon, R. Jesseman, and A.K. Yessine. 2005. *Presentence Reports in Canada.* Ottawa: Public Safety Canada. http://ww2.ps-sp.gc.ca/publications/corrections/200401_e.asp

Bonta, J., T. Rugge, B. Sedo, and R. Coles. 2004. *Case Management in Manitoba Probation.* Ottawa: Public Safety Canada. http://ww2.ps-sp.gc.ca/publications/corrections/200401_e.asp

Bonta, J., J. Rooney, and S. Wallace-Capretta. 1999. *Electronic Monitoring in Canada.* Ottawa: Solicitor General Canada. http://ww2.ps-sp.gc.ca/publications/corrections/pdf/em_e.pdf

Bonta, J., S. Wallace-Capretta, and J. Rooney. 1998. *Restorative Justice: An Evaluation of the Restorative Resolutions Project.* Ottawa: Solicitor General Canada. http://ww2.ps-sp.gc.ca/publications/corrections/199810b_e.asp

———. 2000. "Can Electronic Monitoring Make a Difference? An Evaluation of Three Canadian Programs." *Crime and Delinquency* 46(1): 61–75.

Bottos, S. 2008. *An Overview of Electronic Monitoring in Corrections: The Issues and the Implications.* Ottawa: Research Branch, Correctional Service of Canada. http://www.csc-scc.gc.ca/text/rsrch-eng.shtml

Bracken, D. 2003a. "Skills and Knowledge for Contemporary Probation Practice." *Probation Journal* 50(2): 101–14.

———. 2003b. *Operation, Organization, and Style of Probation Service.* http://www.kih.gov.hu/data/cms7676/Kerezsi_Klara_Workshop_bevezetoje.pps

Brennan, P.K. 2007. "Intermediate Sanction That Fosters the Mother–Child Bond: A Process Evaluation of Summit House." *Women and Criminal Justice* 18(3): 47–80.

British Columbia Ministry of Public Safety and Solicitor General. 2006. *The Strategic Plan of B.C. Corrections. A Commitment to Public Safety 2006–2009.* Victoria.

http://www.pssg.gov.bc.ca/corrections/pdf/StrategicPlan2006-2009.pdf

Brown, T.M.L., S.A. McCabe, and C. Wellford. 2007. *Global Positioning System (GPS) Technology for Community Supervision: Lessons Learned.* Washington: U.S. Department of Justice. http://www.ncjrs.gov/pdffiles1/nij/grants/219376.pdf

Burnett, R., and F. McNeill. 2005. "The Place of the Officer–Offender Relationship in Assisting Offenders to Desist from Crime." *Probation Journal* 52(3): 221–42.

Caputo, G.A. 2004. *Intermediate Sanctions in Corrections.* Denton: University of North Texas Press.

Church Council on Justice and Corrections. 1996. *Satisfying Justice: Safe Community Options That Attempt to Repair Harm from Crime and Reduce the Use or Length of Imprisonment.* Ottawa: Correctional Service of Canada. http://www.csc-scc.gc.ca/text/pblct/stisfy/juste.pdf

Clairmont, D. 2000. "Restorative Justice in Nova Scotia." *Canadian Journal of Policy Research* 1: 145–49.

Corbett, R.P. 1999. *Transforming Probation Through Leadership: The 'Broken Windows' Model.* New York: Center for Civic Innovation, Manhattan Institute. http://www.manhattan-institute.org.

Couture, J., T. Parker, R. Couture, and P. Laboucane. 2001. *A Cost–Benefit Analysis of Hollow Water's Community Holistic Healing Process.* Ottawa: Solicitor General of Canada and Aboriginal Healing Foundation. http://eric.ed.gov/ERICDocs/data/ericdocs2sql/content_storage_01/0000019b/80/10/77/08.pdf

Dandurand, Y., and C.T. Griffiths. 2006. *Handbook on Restorative Justice Programmes.* Vienna: UN Office on Drugs and Crime. http://www.unodc.org/pdf/criminal_justice/06-56290_Ebook.pdf

Fischer, B., S. Wortley, C. Webster, and M. Kirst. 2002. "The Socio-Legal Dynamics and Implications of 'Diversion.'" *Criminology and Criminal Justice* 2(4): 385–410.

Green, R.G. 1997. "Aboriginal Community Sentencing and Mediation: Within and Without the Circle." *Manitoba Law Journal* 25(1): 77–125.

———. 1998. *Justice in Aboriginal Communities: Sentencing Alternatives.* Saskatoon: Purich.

Griffiths, C.T. 2007. *Canadian Criminal Justice: A Primer*, 3rd ed. Toronto: Thomson Nelson.

Griffiths, C.T., and R. Hamilton. 1996. "Sanctioning and Healing: Restorative Justice in Canadian Aboriginal Communities." In *Restorative Justice: Theory, Practice, and Research*, ed. J. Hudson and B. Galaway. Monsey: Criminal Justice Press. 175–91.

Griffiths, C.T., E. Zellerer, D.S. Wood, and G. Saville. 1995. *Crime, Law, and Justice Among Inuit in the Baffin Region, N.W.T., Canada.* Burnaby: Criminology Research Centre, Simon Fraser University.

John Howard Society of Alberta. 2006. *Electronic (radio frequency) and GPS Monitored Community Based Supervision Programs.* http://www.johnhoward.ab.ca/PUB/PDF/monitorupdate.pdf

Johnstone, G., and D.W. Van Ness. 2006. *Handbook of Restorative Justice.* Portland: Willan.

Junger-Tas, J. 1994. *Alternatives to Prison Sentences: Experiences and Developments.* New York: Kugler.

Klein, A.R., D. Wilson, A.H. Crowe, and M. DeMichele. 2008. *Evaluation of the Rhode Island Probation Specialized Domestic Violence Supervision Unit.* Washington: U.S. Department of Justice. http://www.ncjrs.gov/pdffiles1/nij/grants/222912.pdf

Lajeunesse, T., and Associates, Ltd. 1996. *Evaluation of Community Holistic Circle Healing: Hollow Water First Nation, Vol. 1: Final Report.* Winnipeg: Manitoba Department of Justice.

Landry, L., and M. Sinha. 2008. "Adult Correctional Services in Canada, 2005/2006." *Juristat* 28(6). Cat. no. 85-002-XIE. Ottawa: Minister of Industry. http://www.statcan.gc.ca/english/freepub/85-002-XIE/85-002-XIE2008006.htm

Latimer, J., C. Dowden, and D. Muise. 2001. *The Effectiveness of Restorative Justice Practices: A Meta-Analysis.* Ottawa: Department of Justice Canada. http://www.justice.gc.ca/eng/pi/res/rep-rap/2001.rp01_1-dr01_1/index.html

Marshall, T.F. 1999. *Restorative Justice: An Overview.* London: Research Development and Statistics Directorate, Home Office. http://www.homeoffice.gov.uk/rds/pdfs/occ-resjus.pdf

Marth, M. 2008. "Adult Criminal Court Statistics, 2006–2007." *Juristat* 28(5). Cat. no. 85-002-XIE. Ottawa: Canadian Centre for Justice Statistics, Statistics Canada. http://www.statcan.ca/english/freepub/85-002-XIE/85-002-XIE2008005.pdf

McMillan, T. 2008. "Ex–Oak Bay Marine Group VP Sentenced in Fraud Case." *Victoria Times Colonist*, August 2.

Mitton, C., L. Simpson, L. Gardner, F. Barnes, and G. McDougall. 2007. "Calgary Diversion Program: A Community-based Alternative to Incarceration for Mentally Ill Offenders." *Journal of Mental Health Policy and Economics* 10(3): 145–51.

Morris, A. 2002. "Critiquing the Critics: A Brief Response to Critics of Restorative Justice." *British Journal of Criminology* 42(3): 596–615.

Mothers Against Drunk Driving. 2007. "No Justice Served with Conditional Sentences for Killing." http://www.madd.ca/english/news/pr/p20070330.htm

National Institute of Justice. 2008. "HOPE in Hawaii: Swift and Sure Changes in Probation." *IN SHORT: Towards Criminal Justice Solutions.* Washington, D.C.: Office of Justice Programs, U.S. Department of Justice. http://www.ncjrs.gov/pdffiles1/nij/222758.pdf

North, D. 2001. "The Catch-22 of Conditional Sentencing." *Criminal Law Quarterly* 44(3): 342–74.

Nuffield, J. 1997. *Diversion Programs for Adults.* Ottawa: Solicitor General Canada. http://ww2.ps-sp.gc.ca/publications/corrections/pdf/199705_e.pdf

Padgett, K.G., W.D. Bales, and T.G. Blomberg. 2006. "Under Surveillance: An Empirical Test of the Effectiveness and Consequences of Electronic Monitoring." *Criminology and Public Policy* 5: 61–92.

Petersilia, L., and E.P. Deschenes. 1994. "What Punishes? Inmates Rank the Severity of Prison vs. Intermediate Sanctions." *Federal Probation* 58(1): 308.

Presser, L. and P. Van Voorhis. 2002. "Values and Evaluation: Assessing Processes and Outcomes of Restorative Justice Programs." *Crime and Delinquency* 48(1): 162–88.

Public Safety Canada Portfolio Corrections Statistics Committee. 2007. *Corrections and Conditional Release Statistical Overview.* Ottawa: Public Safety Canada. http://www.publicsafety.gc.ca/res/cor/rep/ccrso2007-eng.aspx

Public Safety Canada. 2007. *Toronto Drug Treatment Court Project.* Ottawa: National Crime Prevention Centre. http://www.publicsafety.gc.ca/prg/cp/bldngevd/2007-es-og-eng.aspx

Roberts, J.V. and C. LaPrairie. 1997. "Sentencing Circles: Some Unanswered Questions." *Criminal Law Quarterly* 39(1): 69–83.

———. 2000. *Conditional Sentencing in Canada: An Overview of Research Findings.* Ottawa: Research and Statistics Division, Department of Justice. http://www.justice.gc.ca/eng/pi/rs/reprap/2000/rr00_6/p4.html

Roberts. J.V., A.N. Doob, and V. Marinos. 2000. *Judicial Attitudes to Conditional Terms of Imprisonment: Results of a National Survey.* Ottawa: Department of Justice. http://www.justice.gc.ca/eng/pi/rs/rep-rap/2000/rr00_10/rr00_10.pdf

Robinson, G., and P. Raynor. 2006. "The Future of Rehabilitation: What Role for the Probation Service?" *Probation Journal* 53(4): 334–46

Serin, R., and B. Vuong. 2003. *Intensive Supervision Practices: A Preliminary Examination.* Ottawa: Correctional Services of Canada. http://www.csc-scc.gc.ca/text/rsrch/briefs/b31/b31-e.pdf

Smith, P., C. Goggin, and P. Gendreau. 2002. *The Effects of Prison Sentences and Intermediate Sanctions on Recidivism: General Effects and Individual Differences.* Ottawa: Solicitor General Canada. http://ww2.ps-sp.gc.ca/publications/Corrections/200201_Gendreau_e.pdf

Stuart, B. 1996. "Circle Sentencing in Yukon Territory, Canada: A Partnership of the Community and the Criminal Justice System." *International Journal of Comparative and Applied Criminal Justice* 20(2): 291–309.

Weekes, J., R. Mugford, G. Bourgon, and S. Price. 2007. "Drug Treatment Courts: FAQs." Canadian Centre on Substance Abuse. http://www.ccsa.ca/2007%20CCSA%20Documents/ccsa-011348-2007.pdf

Zehr, H. 1990. *Changing Lenses: A New Focus for Crime and Justice.* Scottsdale: Herald.

WEBLINKS

Centre for Restorative Justice

http://www.sfu.ca/crj
The centre is a repository for restorative justice materials and contains an extensive online library.

Restorative Justice Online

http://www.restorativejustice.org
A clearing-house for restorative justice materials, including a library, resources, videos, and current practice.

Probation Officers Association of Ontario

http://www.poao.org
The website of the professional association of probation officers in Ontario. Includes position papers and links to federal, provincial, and justice-related organizations and initiatives.

CHAPTER 4

CORRECTIONAL INSTITUTIONS

CHAPTER OBJECTIVES

After reading this chapter you should be able to:

- *Identify the types of correctional institutions.*
- *Discuss the structure, operation, and management of institutions.*
- *Identify and discuss the eras of prison architecture and how these reflected changes in correctional philosophy.*
- *Identify and discuss the attributes of the modern prison.*
- *Discuss the incident at the Kingston Prison for Women as a breakdown in the rule of law and administrative leadership.*
- *Identify and discuss the challenges of operating and managing correctional institutions.*
- *Describe the various prevention and interdiction strategies used by correctional systems to prevent the spread of HIV/AIDS and infectious diseases, as well as the issues that surround harm-reduction efforts.*
- *Discuss the riot at the Headingley Correctional Institution, and examine that incident as a case study of the factors that can contribute to the breakdown of stability and control in a correctional institution.*
- *Discuss the issues surrounding the involvement of the private sector in operating correctional institutions, including the Ontario "experiment" with a privately operated correctional facility.*
- *Discuss the use and effectiveness of incarceration.*

KEY TERMS

Minimum/medium/maximum security institutions
Special Handling Unit (SHU)
Multilevel institutions
Static security
Dynamic security
Total institution
Continuum of correctional institutions
Prevention strategies (for HIV/AIDS and infectious diseases)
Interdiction strategies (for HIV/AIDS and infectious diseases)

PERSPECTIVE

Deputy Warden, federal correctional institution

When you step into the world of the prison for the first time, the thing that always stays with you is the sound of the door clanging behind you. When I first went to work as a correctional officer, everything inside seemed to be in chaos. You wonder what the heck is going on. It takes a few months to get in tune with the place. After you've been there awhile you get to know who the major players are, how different correctional officers approach situations. You develop a rapport with the inmates and begin developing relationships with them. I've always said that being a correctional officer is an art ... to know how to balance the authority you have with the realities of life inside.

In terms of inmates, the long-term inmates are more manageable than short-term inmates. They understand they are going to have to get along with other inmates and the staff. There is an adjustment period ... When they first come in, they get really depressed and we have them on suicide watch. They lose hope. After they've been in a few weeks, they come to terms with the fact that they are going to be in jail a long time. That's when you begin to see more prosocial behaviour out of these guys. The long-term guys are the ones that end up being on the inmate committees and taking a more balanced view of things. It's the short-term guys that are the most difficult to manage. They are part of the 20 percent of the inmates in the prison who are difficult to manage and it's this group that causes all of the problems. That's the 20 percent you always see coming back. They go out on statutory release and screw up or they serve to their warrant expiry date and they go out and commit another crime and end up coming back. And those are the guys that can make you cynical—that nothing is working. It's the quiet guys that are there, doing their own time, working their way through the programs, getting out on parole and not coming back—those are the guys you don't even remember and that's the vast majority of guys. The 20 percent are the guys who commit the serious offences in the community—like a guy goes out of prison and commits an armed robbery three days later. Then the public and the politicians get up in arms about the system not being tough enough. Meanwhile, the other 80 percent who are going out and not getting into trouble don't get any attention.

I don't think that punishment works with a lot of these guys. Most of them have grown up in terrible social environments and were abused mentally and physically. Pushing them around and mistreating them is what they expect. It's when you treat them differently, with respect, while making them responsible. That often impacts their behaviour because they are not expecting it. If you model prosocial behaviour with a lot of these guys, you can change the way they think and act.

Source: Personal communication with author.

Only 5 percent of those who come to the attention of the criminal justice system are ultimately incarcerated for their offences. Yet the prison is one of the most visible and controversial components of corrections and has been the subject of a great deal of study. Federal and provincial/territorial systems of corrections spend the largest proportion of their budgets on institutions. This chapter examines a variety of topics related to correctional institutions, ranging from their structure and operations to the key challenges that confront the senior correctional personnel who manage institutional populations. A case study of a prison riot is provided to illustrate what happens when management loses control of a correctional institution.

TYPES OF CORRECTIONAL INSTITUTIONS

The federal government and provincial/territorial governments operate a wide variety of correctional facilities. The designations given to these institutions can be quite confusing. Here are some of the more common terms:

- correctional centres, reformatories, établissements, penitentiaries: used to confine sentenced offenders
- jails, detention centres: used to house short-term inmates and offenders on remand
- remand centres: used to confine offenders awaiting trial on remand
- correctional camps, farms, detention centres, treatment centres, community residences: used to house lower-risk inmates in a minimum-security setting or those on conditional release

Federal Correctional Institutions

Federal correctional facilities are categorized in terms of these security levels:

- **minimum-security institutions:** These institutions allow unrestricted inmate movement, except during the night, and generally have no perimeter fencing.
- **medium-security institutions:** In this institutional environment, inmates are surrounded by high-security perimeter fencing but have more freedom of movement than in maximum security.
- **maximum-security institutions:** In these highly controlled institutions, surrounded by high-security perimeter fencing, inmates' movements are strictly controlled and constantly monitored by video surveillance cameras.
- **Special Handling Unit (SHU):** A high-security institution for inmates who present such a high level of risk to staff and other inmates that they

cannot be housed in maximum-security facilities. There is a Special Handling Unit at the Regional Reception Centre in Ste-Anne-des-Plaines, Quebec. The Correctional Service of Canada (CSC) also operates a number of regional health centres. These facilities house violent offenders and offer treatment programs that focus on violence and anger management.

- **Multilevel institutions:** These institutions contain one or more of the above security levels in the same facility or on the same grounds. In addition, there may be distinct inmate populations within the same institution that, for security and safety reasons, are not allowed to comingle. For example, Kent Institution, a federal maximum-security institution east of Vancouver, houses three separate populations: close custody, general population, and protective custody.

The CSC operates nearly 50 facilities across the country, ranging from minimum-security work camps to maximum-security prisons. These include a number of small, regional facilities for female offenders (see Box 4.1).

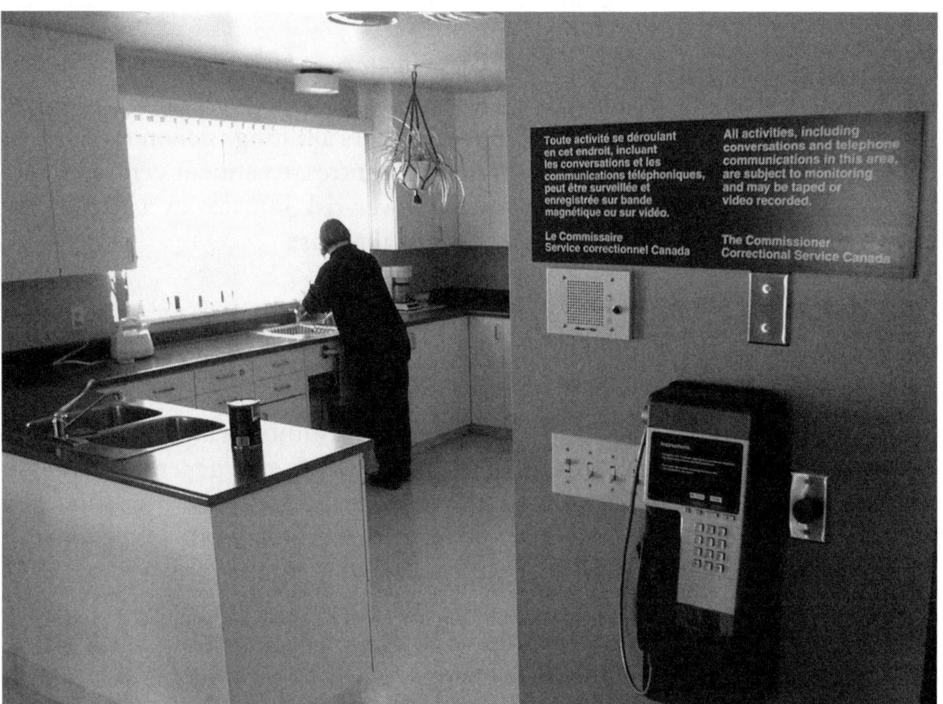

An inmate uses the kitchen area of the unit she shares with nine other women at the Joliette Institution in Joliette, Quebec.

CP PHOTO/Ryan Remiorz

BOX 4.1

Institutions for Federally Sentenced Women

Nova Institution for Women (Truro, NS)
Springhill Institution (Springhill, NS)*
Joliette Institution (Joliette, QC)
Grand Valley Institution (Kitchener, ON)
Saskatchewan Penitentiary (Prince Albert, SK)*
Regional Psychiatric Centre (Saskatoon, SK)
Okimaw Ohci Healing Lodge (Maple Creek, SK)
Edmonton Institution for Women (Edmonton, AB)
Fraser Valley Institution (Sumas, BC)

*Institutions for men with on-site facilities for maximum-security women.

Many Canadians do not realize that the federal government (not the CSC) also operates the Canadian Forces Service Prison and Detention Barracks (CFSPDB) in Edmonton, Alberta (see Box 4.2).

Provincial/Territorial Institutions

The provinces and territories operate about 160 facilities with different levels of security, though there are no uniform designations. It is interesting that the provinces/territories make more extensive use of maximum-security institutions than the federal CSC, primarily because they are responsible for housing persons who are on remand awaiting trial or sentencing. These individuals represent a broad range of security risks, and in the absence of time to assess individual offenders, all are detained in maximum security. Provincial correctional systems also operate treatment facilities for special populations, such as sex offenders.

In Ontario, the jails and detention centres house offenders who are awaiting trial (or other court proceedings) as well as offenders serving short sentences. Jails are often small, old buildings, whereas detention centres tend to be large, modern facilities built to meet the needs of several municipalities. The province also operates correctional centres for offenders, who typically are serving terms of up to two years less a day.

One of the more unique prisons in the world is the Baffin Correctional Centre, located in the Nunavut town of Iqaluit. This is the only correctional

BOX 4.2

Hard Time: The Canadian Military Prison

Members of the Canadian military can be convicted of offences under the Canadian Criminal Code *and* the Canadian Forces Code of Service Discipline Military Code of Conduct. The Canadian Armed Forces have their own justice system, including police, defence lawyers, prosecutors, courts, and prison. Established in 1949, the Canadian Forces Service Prison and Detention Barracks receives male and female members of the military who have been sentenced for periods from fifteen days to two years less a day. Offenders with longer sentences are then transferred to a federal correctional facility to serve the remaining portion of their sentence. These offenders are eligible for parole, as are any federal inmates.

The regimen inside the military prison is quite different from that of other correctional institutions. Inmates rise at 5:30 a.m. and follow a tightly controlled schedule until 9:00 p.m. The facility operates on strict discipline: both the guards and the inmates move through the day with military precision. Conjugal (overnight) family visits are not permitted. New inmates cannot speak to one another during the first two weeks of confinement. Activities such as watching television and reading are privileges that inmates must earn. Unlike civilian institutions, the military prison has a low incidence of violence, and contraband weapons and drugs are unknown. Less than 5 percent of the inmates are repeat offenders.

Source: Harris 2008.

facility in the world in which inmates are permitted to handle loaded firearms. The Land Program allows inmates to leave the centre under the supervision of an Inuit staff member and hunt for seal, walrus, caribou, whale, or Arctic hare, depending on the season. Most of the game harvest is donated to elders or to infirm residents in the community. A small portion is prepared by the kitchen staff at the institution.

FEDERAL/PROVINCIAL JOINT INITIATIVES

Efforts to increase the efficiency and effectiveness of correctional services have led to increased cooperation between federal and provincial correctional authorities in developing programs and services. On Prince Edward Island, the Offender Program Resource Centre provides services to both federal and provincial offenders. In Newfoundland, the West Coast Correctional Centre in

Stephenville operates primarily as a provincial institution for federally sentenced offenders. Staff have been certified to deliver federally developed programs in substance abuse and cognitive skills training. Federal and provincial corrections personnel make joint decisions about case management, and provincial probation officers may provide supervision for federal offenders on conditional release.

ABORIGINAL HEALING CENTRES AND LODGES

The federal government has entered into agreements with First Nations groups across the country to develop and operate healing lodges. These include Pê Sâkâstêw (Cree for "new beginning" and pronounced "Bay Sah-ga-stay-o"), a minimum-security facility near Hobbema, Alberta, on the Samson Cree Nation; the Prince Albert (Saskatchewan) Grand Council Spiritual Healing Lodge for male Aboriginal offenders in the Wahpeton Dakota First Nation Community; and the Waseskun Healing Centre, near Montreal, which offers residential

The Aboriginal Healing Range at the Stony Mountain Institution, Manitoba

CP PHOTO/Winnipeg Free Press/Ken Gigliotti

therapy for men and women referred from Aboriginal communities and from provincial and federal correctional institutions. Healing lodges operate under the auspices of the CSC, but they are also accountable to a governing council composed of elders and other First Nations representatives. Chapter 7 discusses specific treatment programs offered by these healing lodges.

SECURITY AND ESCAPES

All correctional facilities have two types of security:

- **Static security** includes perimeter fencing, video surveillance, and alarms, as well as fixed security posts, such as control rooms and position posts, where officers remain in a defined area.
- **Dynamic security** includes ongoing interaction, beyond observation, between correctional officers and inmates. It includes working with and speaking with inmates, making suggestions, providing information, and—in general—being proactive.

Though prison escapes are a Hollywood staple, they are in fact quite rare. Federally, most involve inmates walking away from minimum-security facilities. At the provincial/territorial level, most "escapees" are offenders who fail to show up to serve weekend, intermittent sentences.

PRISON ARCHITECTURE

One way to trace the changing philosophy of corrections and punishment is by examining the architecture of correctional institutions. As noted in Chapter 2, the first prisons constructed in Canada during the 1800s were designed to reflect the role of such institutions in Canadian society at that time as well as the objectives of incarceration. The term "moral architecture" was used to underscore that institutions were places where inmates would be taught proper attitudes and values through a strict regimen. Much has changed in the past half-century, and inmates and correctional personnel from earlier years would not recognize many of the correctional institutions that have been constructed in recent years.

The Eras of Prison Architecture

A review of the history of prison architecture in Canada reveals a number of distinct design phases that can be related to shifts in correctional philosophy. These eras are reflected in the federal correctional institutions that have been constructed, beginning with the Kingston Penitentiary in 1835 and continuing into the present. Note that the timeline dates presented in Box 4.3 are general rather than definite. Also, only some of the more distinctive attributes of each era have been identified.

BOX 4.3

The Eras of Prison Architecture

Pre-1835

Imprisonment was not used as a sanction, and little consideration was given to the structure in which offenders were housed while awaiting trial or punishment. Institutions had congregate housing with little or no separation of offenders by age, gender, or offence.

1800s–1940s

The first penitentiary at Kingston was built on the Auburn plan, with inmates working and eating together during the day and housed separately in cells at night. A rigid silent system (in effect in some institutions until the early 1950s) was used to prevent moral contamination among inmates. Living conditions improved in some institutions with the installation of plumbing and ventilation. The institutional design usually consisted of tiers (floors) of small, barred, windowless cells built in tiers like stacked cages overlooking a tall common space. Institutions built during this era include Dorchester Penitentiary (NB, 1880); Kingston Penitentiary (ON, 1835); Collins Bay Institution (ON, 1930); and the Prison for Women (ON, 1934).

1950s

During this decade there was an emphasis on privacy, with smaller tiers and larger cells with a solid door and a view window. Security was static. Institutions incorporating this design include LeClerc Institution (QC) and Joyceville Institution (ON).

1960s

During the 1960s, prison architecture reflected efforts to "dilute" the prison as a distinct building form. There was an attempt to normalize the institutional environment, and buildings were designed to reduce inmates' isolation and loss of personal dignity. A number of facilities were constructed that incorporated a campus-style layout and

(continued)

that included residential-scale buildings for living units. There was an increase in the use of dynamic security, which encouraged positive staff–inmate interaction. Among the institutions incorporating this design were Matsqui Institution (BC); Springhill Institution (NS), and Drumheller Institution (AB).

1970s

Institutional designs continued to reflect efforts to create physical spaces that would increase interaction between staff and inmates. Designs included living units, each of which housed a number of inmates supervised by a unit management team. There was an emphasis on providing space for rehabilitation programs, and efforts were made to create a more relaxed environment. Mission Medium Security Institution (BC) is an example of this design approach.

1980s

A mixed design approach was evident during this era, with some new institutions reflecting the trend toward creating physical facilities and institutional environments conducive to increased inmate responsibility and improved staff–inmate interaction. There was less use of traditional security barriers. At the same time, a number of existing institutions were upgraded to increase security and control over inmates. Bowden Medium Security Institution (AB) reflects the new designs during this era. It has cells that inmates can lock and unlock at will (except at night) as well as open, common areas for each cell cluster.

1990s

In this decade, several federal institutions were renovated to create "neighbourhood housing"—that is, small, autonomous housing units for five to eight inmates with reduced direct surveillance. Small regional facilities were constructed for female offenders, and several healing lodges for Aboriginal inmates were built that incorporated elements of Aboriginal culture and spirituality in the design. For example, Pe Sakastew Institution in Alberta was designed by an Aboriginal architect and uses a circular layout and building design.

Pê Sâkâstêw Institution, Hobbema, Alberta

Contemporary Prison Design

Prison design in the early 21st century continues to reflect different approaches by federal and provincial correctional systems. In many facilities, inmates live in "clusters"—that is, in inmate bedrooms surrounding a common living area. The objectives of the new "moral architecture" in federal corrections are to promote positive group interaction among small groups of inmates, to encourage inmates to become more responsible, and to prepare inmates for life outside the institution.

At the Grand Valley Institution for Women in Kitchener, Ontario, there are no cells and no uniforms, and the frontline staff are called "primary workers" rather than guards or correctional officers. There are a number of cottages, and each female inmate has her own bedroom, which can be locked from the inside. Some bedrooms have space for baby cribs. In contrast, several provincial jurisdictions, including Ontario and British Columbia, continue to focus on the development of "big box" correctional facilities that house large numbers of inmates.

One issue is how the changing composition of inmate populations in federal prisons may affect prison architecture in the future. A high proportion of federal offenders (nearly 70 percent in 2007) are serving sentences for violent offences, and there has been a decrease in the federal parole grant rate (Public Safety Canada Portfolio Corrections Statistics Committee 2007, 63). This means that offenders are serving longer periods of time in confinement. Also, at the provincial level, the expansion of alternatives to incarceration such as probation and conditional sentences has resulted in provincial inmate populations with more serious criminal profiles that require more secure facilities. All of these factors have limited the ability of correctional systems to design facilities that provide more freedom of movement and increased responsibility for inmates.

The Union of Canadian Correctional Officers has expressed concerns about the design of regional facilities for federal female offenders, particularly with respect to managing high-risk, maximum-security inmates. Citing threats and assaults on correctional officers and inmates, the Union of Canadian Correctional Officers has argued that "the frequency with which these events recur has long since invalidated the notion that new models of incarceration and new institutions would by themselves resolve most of the problems that were common in previous penitentiary approaches" (2007, 39).

Another issue is this: the extent to which prison architecture contributes to postrelease success among inmates has not been determined. There have been no evaluative studies to determine whether federal female offenders residing in the smaller regional facilities have lower rates of postrelease recidivism than women who served time and were released from the now-closed Kingston Prison for Women. Similarly, though extensive criticism has been levelled against the "big box" prisons constructed by provincial systems of correction, there is no evidence that these facilities contribute to higher rates of reoffending upon release.

It is also not certain that the new prison designs have significantly altered the dynamics of life inside correctional institutions; nor is it clear that those designs have mitigated the long-standing challenges of drug use, violence among inmates, and other features of life inside. The highly publicized death of a mentally ill female offender at Grand Valley in 2007 (see Chapter 6) suggests that, while prison design may reflect changes in correctional philosophy, it may do little to address the challenges and needs of those who live and work inside correctional institutions.

There are significant changes underway in federal correctional policy that may affect prison design. The final report of the CSC Review Panel (Sampson 2007) recommended that the CSC move away from the philosophy of constructing small, stand-alone correctional facilities and toward a regional-complex approach. Regional complexes would contain accommodations for minimum-, medium-, and maximum-security inmates in separate but adjoining facilities. These facilities would share (albeit segregated by security level) food services, prison industries, and core programs, among other things. In the view of the committee, "a regional complex approach would provide an opportunity to more effectively and efficiently manage larger groups of inmates and use a larger pool of resources to address the needs of inmates in a more targeted manner" (ibid., 157). If the federal government acts on this recommendation, it will represent a profound shift in correctional philosophy and reflect an "Americanization" of corrections at the federal level, similar to the trends that are apparent in several provincial jurisdictions. This bears watching.

THE ATTRIBUTES OF THE MODERN PRISON

Correctional institutions have a number of unique features that distinguish them from other public- and private-sector agencies and organizations. These features determine the daily challenges that confront correctional managers as well as the patterns of interaction that occur among the various groups who live and work inside correctional facilities. Three of the more significant features are discussed below.

Prisons Are Asked to Pursue Conflicting Goals

The primary goal of correctional institutions is to protect society by housing offenders who pose a serious risk to the community. However, correctional institutions are also charged with preparing offenders for eventual release into the community as law-abiding and contributing members of society. These two goals underscore the split personality of corrections. The resulting conflicts are reflected in many of the interactions that occur within the prison, including interactions between correctional officers and treatment staff (see Chapter 5). They are also evident in how treatment programs are delivered (see Chapter 7).

Prisons Are Political and Public Institutions

The role played by social, political, and economic forces in the creation and operation of Canadian prisons was illustrated in Chapter 2. These forces continue to determine the goals of incarceration and the extent to which they are achieved. Politicians, provincial legislatures, and the federal government exercise considerable control over how correctional institutions are operated, the goals they are asked to pursue, and the resources that are made available to corrections personnel. These aspects are part of the external environment. (The external and internal environments of a correctional institution are depicted in Figure 4.1.)

Figure 4.1

The External and Internal Environments of a Correctional Institution

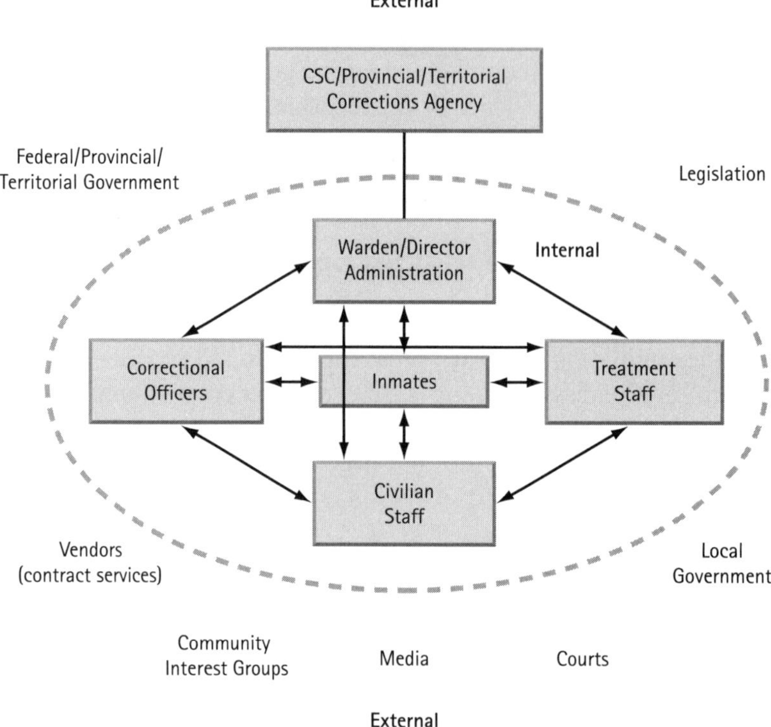

Prisons Are Total Institutions

One of the more significant contributions to the study of corrections was made more than 40 years ago by the sociologist Erving Goffman, who introduced the concept of the prison as a **total institution.** According to Goffman, a total institution is "a place of residence and work where a large number of like-situated individuals, cut off from the wider society for an appreciable period of time, together lead an enclosed, formally administered round of life" (1961, xii).

In his treatise, Goffman outlined the major attributes of life inside total institutions, among which he included mental hospitals, military installations, and prisons:

- All aspects of life are conducted in the same place under the same single authority.

- Each phase of the patient's daily activity is carried on in the immediate company of a group of others, all of whom are treated alike and required to follow the same regimen.
- All phases of the day's activities are tightly scheduled and controlled by an administrative hierarchy (ibid., 6).

The daily inmate routine in an Ontario provincial prison is set out in Box 4.4.

BOX 4.4

A Day in the Life of an Adult Offender, Province of Ontario

Morning

1. Wake-up call at approximately 06:30 hours
2. Inmate stand to count
3. Breakfast
4. Health-care rounds
5. Inmate: releases, transfers, and courts
6. Unit cleanup
7. Work gangs out to their assigned areas (community work, laundry, etc.)
8. Education and recreation periods

Afternoon

1. Lunch
2. Recreation period for inmates on work details
3. Health-care round
4. Rehabilitative programming or quiet time
5. Visits
6. Inmate stand to count

Evening

1. Supper
2. Unit cleanup

(continued)

3. Inmate stand to count
4. Visits
5. Evening recreation and/or other programs (e.g., Alcoholics Anonymous)
6. Health-care rounds
7. Showers
8. Televisions off
9. Bedtime/lights out at approximately 2300 hours

Source: Ministry of Public Safety and Security, Correctional Services, from a page on the website http://www.mpss.jus.on.ca (since deleted).

Though the living conditions inside Canadian correctional facilities have improved significantly over the years, the movements and activities of inmates are still subject to control and surveillance, and the common theme remains: denial of freedom.

While all correctional institutions share a common identity as total institutions, some are more "total" than others. Correctional facilities vary in terms of their affiliation (federal/provincial/territorial), security classification, size, management style, inmate characteristics, and other key factors that affect the patterns of activity and interaction within them. To reflect this variability, a rough **continuum of correctional institutions** can be constructed, based on the extent to which individual prisons reflect Goffman's description. At one end of such a continuum would be minimum-security and community correctional facilities; at the other would be maximum-security institutions. As one might expect, the dynamics of everyday life inside institutions at either end of the continuum would be considerably different. Even institutions at the same security level have their own "personalities"—a function of history, the attitudes of administrators, specific attributes of the inmate population, and other less tangible factors.

An important feature of the prison as a total institution is a split between the inmates and the institutional staff. Interactions between the inmates, who are essentially powerless within the hierarchy, and the correctional officers, who enforce the rules and regulations at the line level, are a prominent feature of prison life. These patterns of interaction are explored in greater detail in Chapter 5.

THE ORGANIZATION OF THE PRISON

Perhaps the best way to understand the dynamics of life inside a prison is to view it as a formal organization with its own goals, rules, and regulations and with its own hierarchical structure of authority. Like all organizations, correctional institutions are also affected by forces in the external environment (see Figure 4.1).

Institutional Management Models

Federal correctional facilities are structured around an institutional management model. In maximum- and medium-security male institutions, key roles in the management model are played by the Assistant Warden, Operations, and the Assistant Warden, Interventions, each of whom oversees a variety of personnel. The Assistant Warden, Operations, oversees the activities of several correctional managers (Scheduling and Deployment, Operations, and Desk/Sector); the latter two correctional managers are responsible for supervising the CO1s and CO2s. The Assistant Warden, Interventions, oversees assessment and intervention, the chaplaincy, programs, and the psychologists. The same person is also responsible for the interventions sentence management officers and the Aboriginal liaison officer.

Many provincial/territorial institutions are structured around the **unit management system.** Each unit in the institution has a unit manager, who reports to a deputy warden. The unit manager's responsibilities include security, case management, programming, health and safety issues, and administrative duties.

The Legislative and Policy Framework

All correctional institutions operate within a legislative and policy framework. Federal institutions, for example, are subject to the following:

- The Corrections and Conditional Release Act (CCRA) and other legislation.
- Guidelines, which are the principal way that CSC Headquarters communicates and codifies policy for all of Canada's regions.
- Regional instructions, which are issued by the CSC Regional Headquarters and which elaborate on Commissioner's Directives or address specific regional issues.
- Standing orders, which repeat or elaborate on provisions in the CCRA commissioner's guidelines as well as regional instructions. They also provide procedural instructions for specific activities within the institution.

- Post orders, which provide more in-depth guidelines and outline the responsibilities for staff members who occupy specific positions, or posts, within the facility.
- Policy manuals on such topics such as security, case management, and the conducting of investigations.

Despite this myriad of directives, rules, and regulations, the federal system of corrections has, at times, found it difficult to ensure that the principles of the rule of law are applied in policy and practice. This difficulty was evident in an incident that occurred in the Kingston Prison for Women in 1996.

The Incident at the Kingston Prison for Women (P4W): A Breakdown in the Rule of Law and Administrative Leadership

On April 22, 1994, a brief but violent physical confrontation took place between six inmates and several correctional officers at the Kingston Prison for Women (which has since been closed). As a result of the incident, the women were placed in segregation and criminally charged (five of the six inmates later pleaded guilty). Immediately after the incident, a high level of tension developed in the institution, compounded by the presence of a large number of overworked, overstressed, and relatively inexperienced correctional staff and correctional officers. A lack of leadership from the prison's warden contributed to the events that unfolded over the next several days.

Two days later, on April 24, three other inmates who were housed in the segregation unit caused further disruption by slashing, taking a hostage, and attempting suicide. On April 26, correctional officers from the institution demonstrated outside its walls, demanding that the inmates involved in the clash on April 22 be transferred to a higher security institution.

On the evening of that same day, the warden sent an all-male Institutional Emergency Response Team (IERT) to extract eight inmates in the segregation unit from their cells and strip-search them. Six of the eight had been involved in the initial confrontation on April 22. The IERT did not complete the cell extractions until early the following morning, at which time the eight women were left in empty cells in the segregation unit. The women had been stripped (in the presence of male members of the IERT), dressed in paper gowns, and placed in restraints and leg irons. All of the cell extractions and strip searches were recorded on videotape as per routine procedure. The following evening, seven of the eight inmates were subjected to body cavity searches. Six of the women involved in the original April 22 incident then were placed in segregation for many months.

The CSC investigated the incidents, but the report it issued left out many details. In February 1995 the report of the correctional investigator was tabled in the House of Commons. This report criticized the CSC's actions, the correctional staff, and the IERT. Pressure on the federal government to take action increased when portions of the videotape, showing the cell extractions and strip searches by the IERT, were shown on national television. An independent judicial inquiry was demanded, and one was appointed in April 1995. It was headed by the Honourable Louise Arbour, a highly respected member of the Quebec judiciary.

The inquiry's final report (Arbour 1996) was extremely critical of the actions taken by correctional staff, the IERT personnel, and the warden. The same report sharply criticized the response of senior CSC officials. In the end, the commissioner of corrections resigned.

The inquiry's report documented numerous violations of policy, the rule of law, and institutional regulations. For example, it criticized the use of segregation, the use of force by the IERT, and the manner in which the women had been strip-searched and subjected to body-cavity searches. The same report raised serious concerns regarding whether, without intervention and monitoring, the CSC was capable of implementing the necessary reforms to ensure adherence to justice and the rule of law. The Arbour Report made 14 key recommendations relating to the following: cross-gender staffing in correctional institutions for women; the use of force and of IERTs; the operations of segregation units; the needs of Aboriginal women in correctional institutions; ways of ensuring accountability and adherence to the rule of law by correctional personnel; and procedures for handling inmate complaints and grievances.

The Arbour Report has had a strong impact on the CSC's operations and on the development of women's corrections (Glube 2006). For example, a Deputy Commissioner for Women has been appointed, a use-of-force policy has been developed that stipulates that all-male institutional emergency response teams are never to be used as a first response in women's correctional institutions, and it is now forbidden for male staff to be present when female inmates are being strip-searched. The report also accelerated the closing of the Prison for Women and the opening of smaller, regional facilities for federal female offenders (see Hayman 2006).

THE CHALLENGES OF OPERATING AND MANAGING CORRECTIONAL INSTITUTIONS

Meeting the Requirements of Legislation and Policy

The legal framework within which correctional systems operate has become increasingly complex. Senior correctional personnel must not only remain informed about changes in law and policy but also ensure that the operations of the institution and the activities of the institutional staff comply with those laws and policies. Regarding the incident at the Kingston Prison for Women, the warden had failed to ensure that staff followed the rule of law and administrative policies.

Wardens and other correctional officials are sometimes the targets of legal actions initiated by inmates, by the families of inmates who have been victimized in prison or who have died there, and by crime victims and their families. In addition, institutions are subject to periodic external audits to ensure that they are following proper administrative and fiscal procedures.

Wardens of correctional institutions are also required to comply with CSC policies that are developed on an ongoing basis. Such policies may pose challenges to the institution's everyday operations. In 2008, for example, the CSC implemented a total ban on tobacco in federal facilities that also applies to all correctional personnel and staff. Tobacco is now contraband in prisons.

Managing Staff

Wardens and other senior administrative personnel in correctional institutions often spend as much time on staff-related issues and concerns as they do on the inmates. The smooth functioning of the institution on a day-to-day basis requires good morale and a shared sense of purpose among staff, including correctional officers and program staff. A failure of leadership can result in a poor working environment that, if left unaddressed, may culminate in incidents and disruptions. The Headingley riot in Manitoba, described later in this chapter, was in part a result of low staff morale and weak institutional leadership.

Overcrowding

Until the 1990s, correctional systems in Canada had largely avoided overcrowding and the double-bunking of inmates (note that double-bunking is, in itself, not an indicator of overcrowding). Changes in judicial sentencing patterns, the increase in the number of long-term inmates, the growing reluctance of parole boards to release offenders into the community, and the absence of new facilities have all resulted in some institutions operating at overcapacity. The remand population in B.C., for example, showed a steady increase during 2002–6 (British Columbia Ministry of Public Safety and Solicitor General 2006). In 2008 the same province announced that, owing to a prison population that was growing at a rate of 4 percent a year, at least 260 new cells would be constructed in existing provincial correctional facilities (Gilbert 2008). Similarly, in Quebec, a recent report of the provincial ombudsman expressed concern that programs for drug rehabilitation and conjugal visits had been cancelled in several provincial institutions as a result of overcrowding (Authier 2007).

Overcrowding can strongly affect daily prison life by heightening tensions among inmates and between inmates and correctional officers, by compromising security, by taxing program resources, and by compromising security and treatment programs.

Outbreaks of gang violence in the Saskatchewan Penitentiary in 2008, for example, were attributed in part to overcrowding in the institution. A situation had been created there in which known gang members were sleeping in classrooms and the gymnasium because there was no space for them in the gang unit. A prisoner counsellor commented on the impact of overcrowding on rehabilitation programs: "There is no classroom. There is no library. All the books have been put into boxes. It's unreal what's happening out there in terms of programming for the guys who want it" (Canadian Press 2008).

As of late 2008 the federal government was proposing to eliminate Statutory Release; if it does, the large majority of federal inmates who have not been granted (or not applied for) parole will not be released into the community under supervision after completing two-thirds of their sentence. It is estimated that eliminating Statutory Release will result in a 20 percent increase in the number of inmates in federal facilities. Similarly, an increase in the number of mandatory minimum penalties for certain offences and more severe sanctions for gun-related offences could increase inmate counts in federal and provincial correctional facilities, which would exacerbate overcrowding. These are obvious examples of how prisons are affected by factors in their "external" environment.

Facilitating Rehabilitation

In any prison population there is considerable variability in how inmates adapt to confinement and in the extent to which they adhere to institutional rules and display an interest in participating in prosocial activities and programs. One challenge confronting correctional administrators is how to accommodate those inmates who are interested in making positive changes, while at the same time controlling the more negative influences and behaviours of those inmates who are engaged in illicit and disruptive behaviours.

Corrections personnel in provincial/territorial institutions find themselves challenged to implement effective treatment interventions when offenders in these facilities serve, on average, less than one month in confinement.

Inmate Gangs

A growing challenge for prison administrators are inmate gangs that have their origins in the community and that import their affiliations and tactics into correctional institutions. It is estimated that one in six federal inmates is affiliated with a known gang or with organized crime (Sampson 2007). There seems to have been an increase in levels of gang activity in many provincial and federal institutions, especially in the Prairie provinces. This is partly a result of increasing legislative and enforcement efforts that have targeted gangs in the community. In addition, there has been exponential growth in Aboriginal gangs in urban and rural areas of the Prairie provinces. Aboriginal youth are particularly susceptible to the recruiting efforts of gangs—a consequence of poverty as well as disenfranchisement from family, school, and community.

Aboriginal gangs are prominent in the Prairie region. The most notable of these groups are the Alberta Warriors, Indian Posse, Redd Alert, Native Syndicate, and Manitoba Warriors. Other gangs include the Asian Crazy Dragons in Alberta, the U.N. gang in B.C., and the multinational Hells Angels. Inside correctional institutions, gangs are involved in a variety of activities, including smuggling and dealing drugs and extortion. This may be contributing to critical incidents and, in extreme cases, to riots (see discussion of the Headingley riot below).

Gang members often resort to assault and intimidation in order to secure and maintain power and influence within the prison. On April 28, 2006, at Bowden Institution, a federal prison near Calgary, an inmate was left with a splintered arm and a mangled face that would require reconstructive surgery. Authorities believe that the assault was part of a dispute between the Alberta Warriors and the Asian Crazy Dragons (insideprison.com 2006).

Ensuring Inmate Safety

The accountability of corrections officials extends to ensuring the safety of inmates in their charge—an onerous task, particularly in federal maximum-security institutions. Wardens have little say in how many inmates are sent to their facility, or in what types of inmates they take in (the latter is initially a classification decision; see Chapter 7), but they *are* held responsible for the safety and security of the inmates once they have arrived.

In recent years there have been a number of high-profile incidents within prisons, some of them involving inmates murdered by fellow inmates. This has increased the pressure on the CSC to ensure that operational policies and procedures provide protection for inmates. One such incident happened in 1996 at the then recently opened Edmonton Institution for Women (one of the small regional facilities built for federal female offenders). At the time, minimum-, medium-, and maximum-security inmates were mixed into one population. For one inmate, this had fatal consequences (see Box 4.5).

BOX 4.5

The Murder of Denise Fayant

Thirty hours after arriving at the Edmonton Institution for Women, 21-year-old Denise Fayant was strangled by her former lover with a bathrobe sash. She died two days later in hospital. An investigation into the death, which was originally ruled a suicide, found that she had been slain by two inmates, one of whom had been her former lover and against whom she was scheduled to testify. A subsequent inquiry conducted by an Alberta provincial court judge found that Fayant had repeatedly told corrections officials that she would fear for her safety if they transferred her to the newly opened institution. Thirty hours after arrival, she was dead. Two inmates were later convicted and sentenced to additional federal time for the death. The investigating judge concluded that Fayant's death was a result of "callous and cavalier" actions on the part of Corrections Canada and that she was a "victim of a process intent upon implementing an untested concept to manage federally sentenced women inmates. She was the test. The process failed tragically and inhumanely. Her death was avoidable" (in Cowan and Sheremata 2000). Prison officials insisted that they had been assured by inmates in the prison that no harm would come to Fayant.

It was noted in Chapter 1 that Canadian courts have become more active in addressing the rights of inmates. This includes the right to serve time in a safe and secure environment. In 2006 the federal government was required to pay $700,000 to an ex-inmate who had been beaten to near-blindness while serving a sentence in a federal penitentiary. And in 2008 three correctional officers were charged with criminal negligence in the death of a female inmate (see Chapter 6).

HIV/AIDS and Infectious Diseases

Perhaps the most critical challenge to correctional authorities is the spread of communicable diseases in inmate populations, including HIV/AIDS, tuberculosis, and hepatitis B and C. In many American prisons, AIDS is the leading cause of inmate death, and there are alarmingly high rates of infection in federal and provincial/territorial institutions in Canada.

Though the HIV virus can be transmitted via anal intercourse between inmates, the largest increase in the infection rate is a result of intravenous drug use and the sharing of HIV-contaminated needles and syringes. HIV and other blood-borne diseases such as hepatitis B and C are also transmitted by pens, pencils, and wire instruments that inmates use for body piercing and tattooing. In addition, many offenders are already infected by the time they enter systems of corrections.

Estimates are that the rate of HIV/AIDS infection in federal prisons is ten times that of the general population. It is a serious concern that the rates are continuing to rise. The HIV infection rate for Aboriginal offenders is even higher. Moreover, these figures are based on cases *known* to correctional authorities; many offenders may not have disclosed their medical condition or may not be aware that they are infected. There are also high rates of infection among provincial inmates, with the rates particularly high among Aboriginal offenders incarcerated in provincial facilities in the three Prairie provinces.

Statistics also indicate that the rates of hepatitis C (HCV) are higher than the HIV/AIDS prevalence rates. For example, as many as 75 percent of the women in the Edmonton Prison for Women are known to be HCV-positive, compared to less than 1 percent of the Canadian population (Lines 2002). Note that these figures are based on *reported* cases. Many inmates choose not to disclose their medical condition, do not know they are infected, or refuse to be tested.

Provincial/territorial and federal systems of corrections face immense challenges in responding to the increasing numbers of inmates with infectious diseases. These challenges include providing short- and long-term health care, providing medication, and developing policies to combat high-risk behaviour in inmate populations. The triple-drug therapy, or "cocktail," for AIDS patients costs over $1,000.00 per patient each month. The treatment for hepatitis C is also very expensive.

Prevention Strategies

Systems of correction have developed a number of **prevention strategies** in their efforts to prevent and reduce high-risk behaviours among inmates and to reduce the levels of infection. The CSC, for example, provides inmates with condoms, lubricants, dental dams, and bleach kits for needles (though not needles). In several federal institutions, inmates are trained as peer health counsellors to educate others on the various types of prevention as well as on how to reduce the risks of infection. The federal government has also expanded its methadone maintenance program for heroin-addicted offenders. The Canadian Aboriginal AIDS Network has developed a peer education model for Aboriginal offenders in federal correctional facilities. An in-depth study of actions taken on HIV/AIDS found considerable variability in the prevention and intervention initiatives undertaken by federal and provincial/territorial systems of corrections.

It "graded" each jurisdiction on a number of criteria, including the availability and accessibility of bleach; condoms, dental dams, and lubricants; methadone treatment; and needle exchange. It awarded B.C. with a "B," identifying that province as a leader in the field. The federal CSC was graded "B-" and Newfoundland and Labrador "D." All other jurisdictions were given an "F" (ibid.).

Federal institutions have developed Intensive Support Units (ISUs). These units are available to inmates who have substance-abuse issues as well as to inmates who wish to reside in a "drug-free" environment. Preliminary evaluations indicate that the units have strong support from both inmates who utilize the units and from correctional staff (Varis 2001). As of late 2008, however, there were no findings regarding the impact of ISUs on rates of reoffending or on subsequent drug use among inmates who utilize them.

Provincial/territorial systems of correction have undertaken similar efforts, though there is considerable variation in the harm-reduction resources provided to inmates. The challenges are considerable, given the higher turnover of inmates and the short periods of confinement. The dilemma for correctional administrators is this: To what extent should government be involved in harm-reduction initiatives, such as providing condoms and bleach kits, and how can such initiatives be reconciled with the requirement to enforce institutional regulations against drug use and sexual relationships between inmates? After reading this chapter, share your thoughts by utilizing "At Issue 4.1: Should the Federal and Provincial/Territorial Governments Initiate/Expand Harm-Reduction Programs in Prisons?"

Federal and provincial/territorial systems of correction also offer a variety of substance-abuse programs (see Chapter 7). For an in-depth examination of promising approaches to preventing the spread of HIV and hepatitis in correctional institutions, see Dias and Betteridge (2007).

Interdiction Strategies

The general public would be surprised to learn how prevalent illegal drugs are in correctional institutions. The CSC uses a number of proactive **interdiction strategies** in its efforts to reduce the use of illegal drugs and other high-risk behaviours, such as tattooing. These strategies include frequent searches, a urinalysis program, drug dogs, video surveillance, and ion scanners that can detect drug residue on clothing and other objects on visitors as well as on inmates returning from absences in the community. For a time, in an effort to reduce rates of infection, tattoo parlours were established in several federal institutions; that experiment was terminated in 2006. After reading this chapter, share your thoughts by utilizing "At Issue 4.2: Should the Federal and Provincial/

Territorial Governments Allow Supervised Tattoo Parlours to Operate in Prisons?"

The effectiveness of these strategies is uncertain. One concern is that the various drug-detection strategies may lead to an *increase* in hard-drug use in institutions, because drugs such as marijuana and hashish remain in the bloodstream for many days, whereas heroin stays in the body's system for approximately 48 hours. This makes the chances of being caught by a random urinalysis test higher for those inmates who use "soft" drugs.

The Union of Canadian Correctional Officers (2007) has criticized the CSC's antidrug policy—specifically, searches of correctional officers entering the institution—and has argued that what is required are proper cell searches and more severe sanctions for inmates and visitors involved in importing drugs.

PRISON RIOTS: THE BREAKDOWN OF ORGANIZATIONAL STABILITY AND CONTROL

Riots and disturbances continue to be a feature of life in correctional institutions. Every prison riot is the culmination of a unique set of circumstances and events; that said, riots are also symptomatic of a breakdown of policy and practice from the most senior administrative levels to the line-level correctional staff.

More minor disturbances are often the result of cutbacks in programs or changes in institutional policy. An in-depth examination of the circumstances surrounding the 1996 riot at the Headingley Correctional Institution, a provincial facility in Manitoba, provides an opportunity to explore the circumstances that create the conditions for a major disturbance.

A Case Study: The Riot at Headingley Correctional Institution

Any assumptions that only federal correctional institutions are susceptible to major prison disturbances were erased by the brutal and devastating riot that occurred at the Headingley Correctional Institution, a provincial facility in Manitoba, on April 25–26, 1996. The riot was started by an inmate who was attempting to prevent correctional officers from discovering drugs during a cell search and investigating his involvement in beating another inmate. The attempted search took place in a section of the jail housing members of two rival Aboriginal street gangs—the Manitoba Warriors and the Indian Posse.

The failure of correctional officers to follow proper procedures in the cell search led to the officers being beaten by the inmates, who seized the officers'

Aftermath of the Headingley riot, April 25–26, 1996

The aftermath of the Headingley riot. Courtesy of the Winnipeg Sun.

keys and went on a drug-fuelled rampage in the institution. The inmates set fires and severely beat inmates in protective custody, mutilating several by cutting off their fingers. One protective custody inmate was the victim of an attempted castration. The riot lasted 24 hours and caused $3.5 million in damage to the institution. Eight correctional officers and 31 inmates were beaten during the melee. Twelve inmates were subsequently sentenced to between two and eight years for their role in the uprising. Two years after the riot, one-quarter of the corrections staff remained off the job because of stress or physical injuries.

An independent review of the role and activities of senior provincial corrections officials, the director of the facility, correctional officers, and inmates documented the conditions that existed in the institution at the time of the riot and identified a number of factors that sparked the outbreak (Hughes 1996). Interviews with correctional staff and inmates revealed that, at the time of the riot, the atmosphere in the institution was extremely negative and that "the staff was a dysfunctional conglomerate torn apart by strife, hatred, bitterness, unpleasantness, and nastiness" (ibid., 7). There was distrust and ill will between the correctional officers and the administration. There were also conflicts among the correctional officers. Many of the institutional staff interviewed by the independent investigator mentioned the "Headingley mentality," a negative, militant approach to work in the institution.

The report of the independent investigator identified several key factors that had contributed to the unstable institutional environment at the time of the riot. Several of these factors (discussed below) seriously affected the ability of correctional officers and the administration to respond to the disturbance in an effective manner.

The Adoption, Several Years Earlier, of the Unit Management System

This resulted in a significant change to the management structure of the institution. The position of unit manager was created, and these personnel were responsible for all activities in the living units. Many of these duties had till then been the responsibility of shift managers (or duty officers), who continued to work in the units. There was often conflict between these two groups.

Introduction of the unit management system also altered the role of the correctional officers, who had previously been responsible only for security and for "turning keys." Under the unit management system, correctional officers were required to become actively involved in case management and in programs and to have more extensive knowledge of the inmates under their care and control. This was a role that many of the older officers, in particular, were either unable or unwilling to accept.

The Appointment, Several Years Earlier, of an Inexperienced Person as Superintendent of the Institution

The superintendent of the institution at the time of the riot had entered the field of corrections via the private sector, where he had been involved primarily in personnel administration. Before coming to Headingley, the superintendent had never worked in a correctional institution that included dangerous inmates in its population, nor did he have the skills and experience to manage the conflicts that existed between the administration and correctional officers.

A Poor Working Relationship Among Senior Administrative Personnel in the Institution

Also owing to a lack of experience, the superintendent was unable to facilitate a collaborative and cooperative working relationship among senior staff in the institution. The institutional management team was beset with interpersonal conflicts and competition and was, in effect, nonfunctioning. The ineffectuality of the management team is illustrated by the finding that "during the night of terror, the Deputy Superintendent, the number two person responsible for the entire facility, was at home. He first heard of the riot when his wife brought him the daily newspaper the following morning, which reported the rampage of the night before" (ibid., 23).

The Lack of Awareness of the Conditions at Headingley Among Senior Provincial Corrections Officials

For a variety of reasons, senior corrections personnel in Manitoba seem to have had little knowledge of the conditions at Headingley. Neither the provincial Minister of Justice nor the Deputy Minister of Justice received any information about the serious conflicts that existed between correctional officers and the administration at the prison or about the tense conditions these conflicts had created in the facility.

The Prevalence of Illegal Drugs in the Institution

A key feature of institutional life in Headingley was the presence of large quantities of illegal drugs. The intimidation and extortion among inmates caused by the flow of drugs into the institution as well as by drug use contributed to the unstable environment within the facility. The independent investigator documented the various ways in which illegal drugs entered the institution; for example, weaker inmates were coerced into having drugs brought in from the outside.

The Composition of the Inmate Population

There is general agreement that inmate populations in provincial institutions are becoming more violent and defiant. This is due to a variety of factors, including the development of a wide variety of alternatives to confinement (see Chapter 3) and liberal temporary-absence programs (see Chapter 8), which result in only the most dangerous and high-risk offenders being incarcerated and remaining inside. The independent investigator found that correctional institutions such as Headingley had not been built to accommodate this type of inmate population, which increasingly includes members of rival street gangs. Another feature of the inmate population is the high percentage (approximately 70 percent at Headingley) of Aboriginal inmates, many of whom have extremely dysfunctional backgrounds and special needs. These inmates are especially susceptible to being recruited by street gangs while in the community and are highly likely to continue their activities while incarcerated.

The Lessons from Headingley

Senior provincial corrections officials, the prison administration, correctional officers, and inmates all played a significant role in creating the conditions for the Headingley riot. Though the inmates in the institution initiated the riot and caused harm to staff, other inmates, and the facility itself, the independent review found that correctional personnel within and outside the institution were also responsible for the riot and its consequences.

The final report of the independent investigator documented the breakdown of the institution's social organization and of the collaborative and cooperative relationships that must exist among the administration, correctional officers, and inmates if institutions are to operate smoothly and safely. The next two chapters will provide a more in-depth examination of correctional officers' role and activities and of the dynamics that surround "doing time" in prison.

In the aftermath of the Headingley riot, correctional authorities in Manitoba took steps to more effectively manage the provincial correctional population. A new medium-security unit was constructed at Headingley to house offenders convicted of violent and gang-related offences. A maximum-security unit—the first in the province—was also constructed. The Headingley riot highlights an area of Canadian corrections—provincial correctional institutions—that has remained largely unstudied.

PRIVATE PRISONS: COMING SOON TO A COMMUNITY NEAR YOU?

As noted in Chapter 1, a major trend in corrections is the increasing involvement of the private sector in the delivery of correctional services. Not-for-profit groups such as the Salvation Army have a long tradition of involvement in community-based and residential programs for offenders; today, these groups are encountering stiff competition from for-profit organizations. This development is due in part to the search by governments for more cost-effective ways to operate institutions and to lower rates of reoffending.

The private sector is most extensively involved in the United States, Puerto Rico, Britain, and Australia, where it designs, constructs, and manages prisons. The first experiment with privatization in Canada was in 2001, when Ontario contracted Management and Training Corporation Canada (MTCC, a U.S.-based company) to operate the 1,184-bed Central North Correctional Centre (CNCC), a new maximum-security megajail in Penetanguishene. CNCC is the "identical twin" of another newly constructed megajail in Ontario, the Central East Correctional Centre (CECC) in Lindsay.

The provincial government intended to commence operations in the two facilities at the same time and then to compare their performance outcomes and costs. The contract with MTCC was terminated five years later, in 2007, at which time the facility's operations reverted to the province. An evaluation of the experiment found the following:

- MTCC operated in compliance with its contractual obligations to the province, including standards for safety, security, and health care.
- MTCC saved the province $23 million in operating expenses, with a projected additional $11 million had the contract been extended another five years.
- CNCC scored higher on training compliance, as well as on variety and volume of programming (particularly in the education area, where it secured accreditation from the American Correctional Association), while CECC scored higher on risk/need classification, the quality and effectiveness of programming, and health services.
- Inmates released from CNCC had higher rates of reoffending than those who had been confined in CECC.

It was acknowledged, however, that there were a number of "complicating" factors that prevented the intended "apples to apples" comparison of the two facilities and that may have compromised the evaluation. These factors included construction delays at the private jail that limited the performance data to a one-year period; the fact that CECC did not have an infirmary and transferred its sick inmates to CNCC, creating the potential for more critical incidents; the use of a longer period of monitoring of inmates released from CNCC; and the fact that CECC received all of the immigration "holds," who were deported upon release and who, therefore, were not included in the analysis of reoffending (Ontario Ministry of Community Safety and Correctional Services 2006). The difficulties in comparing the performance of privately operated prisons with that of government-operated facilities have been extensively documented in American studies. The former director of research for the U.S. Bureau of Prisons, for example, has cautioned that "cost comparisons are deceivingly complex, and great care should be taken when comparing the costs of privately and publicly operated prisons" (Gaes 2008).

The debate over the involvement of the private sector in operating Canadian prisons is likely to continue. After you have finished reading the chapter, share your thoughts by considering "At Issue 4.3: Should There be Private Prisons in Canada?"

THE 21ST-CENTURY HIGH-TECH PRISON

The exponential growth in high technology, combined with the needs of governments to operate prisons cost-effectively, has led to the emergence of the high-tech prison in Canada. These institutions incorporate the latest in electronic security and video-surveillance technology, allowing larger numbers of inmates to be housed, monitored, and controlled with fewer staff. The potential applications of technology in correctional institutions seem limitless.

Though institutions utilizing high technology may be less expensive to operate, high costs may occur as a result of disturbances and riots by inmates and increased rates of recidivism when inmates are released from these facilities. Technology may improve security, but it also reduces contact between the correctional staff and inmates. This lack of contact may have significant implications for the development of effective treatment interventions (see Chapter 7) and for the involvement of correctional officers in positive interactions with inmates (see Chapter 5). As one former correctional officer observed: "Warehousing people in high-tech structures with vapid environments not only hardens the core of the still-changeable criminal, but burdens the taxpayer with long-term social costs. Both law-breaker and law-abider lose" (Yates 1993:312).

THE USE AND EFFECTIVENESS OF INCARCERATION

There appears to be considerable variation across the country in the use of incarceration for convicted offenders. This suggests but does not prove that sentencing disparity exists. For example, in 2003–4 a high percentage of cases (58 percent) in Prince Edward Island resulted in a term of confinement; compare that percentage to the ones in Saskatchewan, Quebec, and Nova Scotia, where about 25 percent of cases during the same time period resulted in imprisonment. Even considering the impact of different patterns of crime in these jurisdictions, this is a significant difference in the use of incarceration. Statistics indicate that 91 percent of offenders convicted of impaired driving for the first time in PEI are sentenced to confinement, compared to 29 percent in Newfoundland and Labrador. For all jurisdictions, terms of incarceration are short: 60 percent are for one month or less (NPB 2007).

Serious concerns have been raised regarding the effectiveness of incarceration, although the research evidence is far from conclusive owing to the absence of evaluation studies and various issues relating to how studies are conducted (Villettaz, Killias, and Zoder 2006). The research evidence suggests that prisons should not be used with the expectation of reducing reoffending and that the excessive use of incarceration as a sanction can have substantial cost implications. Nor does there appear to be an optimal sentence length that serves to reduce recidivism rates (Smith, Goggin, and Gendreau 2002). Also, there is some evidence that offenders who spend their time under supervision in the community have lower rates of reoffending within twelve months of the termination of supervision than offenders released from correctional institutions (Statistics Canada 2006). An additional consideration is that community-based sentences are less costly than incarceration. In Ontario, for example, the cost of supervising a provincial offender on house arrest is about $1,600 per year, compared to just over $50,000 if the offender is confined in a provincial facility (Basen 2006).

These findings are likely due to a number of factors, including the dynamics of life inside correctional institutions (see Chapter 6), the fact that higher risk offenders are likely to be incarcerated, the difficulties of delivering treatment programs inside prisons (see Chapter 7), and the fact that, for some offenders, correctional institutions may be viewed as "home."

In their study of crime and justice in the Baffin region (now part of Nunavut), Griffiths and his colleagues (1995) found that sending Inuit offenders from the villages in the region to the Baffin Correctional Centre in Iqaluit had little impact on their criminal behaviour. Many of these offenders viewed confinement as a welcome break from the monotony of life in an isolated village. In the words of one social worker: "The bulk of offenders are under the age of 25 and their trip to jail is their only chance to get out of here" (in Griffiths et al. 1995, 164).

The correctional institution may also mark a significant improvement over the quality of life in the offender's community and home environment.

Offenders who are unemployed, have no permanent living address, are drug addicted, and/or are living with a medical conditions such as HIV/AIDS or hepatitis C may view confinement as a way to get three meals a day and a bed (often referred to as "three hots and a cot"), a paid job, and plenty of rest. In the words of one inmate incarcerated in a provincial correctional facility: "A lot of the guys who come in here are drug sick. They had served their sentence, or been granted parole, went back out on the street, and got right back into the drug life. They come back, get well, put on a few pounds, and they are ready to go out and start it all over again" (personal communication with C.T. Griffiths).

For some offenders, residing in a controlled environment has been a key feature of their youth and adult life. Many adult offenders have served lengthy periods of confinement beginning in their teenage years and continuing into adulthood. These "state-raised" offenders have few if any noncriminal associates and are not involved in any prosocial activities or networks that would help them live a law-abiding life. For many of these state-raised offenders, surviving in the outside, free community often poses a far greater challenge than doing time in prison (more on state-raised offenders in Chapter 6).

AT ISSUE

ISSUE 4.1: Should the federal and provincial/territorial governments initiate/expand harm-reduction programs in prisons?

In an attempt to prevent and reduce infection in prison populations, the Correctional Service of Canada and many provincial/territorial correctional systems provide inmates with methadone, condoms, lubricants, dental dams, and bleach kits for use in cleaning needles.

Proponents of harm-reduction programs in provincial and federal corrections make these points:

- Condoms, bleach kits, and methadone maintenance reflect the reality that drugs will always be available to inmates.
- Condoms and bleach kits help reduce the risk of HIV and other infectious diseases.
- Methadone maintenance reduces the use of hard drugs inside and helps inmates overcome their addiction.
- There is no evidence that these programs jeopardize the security of the institution.

Opponents of harm-reduction programs inside correctional institutions counter with these points:

- Providing condoms will encourage inmates to violate institutional regulations prohibiting sexual relations.
- Condoms do not prevent nonconsensual sex.
- Providing bleach kits and clean needles will encourage rather than discourage drug use in prison, which not only violates institutional regulations but also is against the law.
- Inmates could use needles as weapons against correctional staff.
- Inmates can overcome their addiction to hard drugs by abstaining from drug use inside and by adhering to institutional regulations prohibiting drug use.
- Methadone is an addictive drug that does little to eliminate drug dependency and that may prolong the inmate's involvement in the drug culture.

The Research Evidence

Canada is one of the few countries in the world where condoms and bleach kits are made available to inmates (although not to inmates in all provincial/territorial facilities). There are no published research studies on whether providing condoms and bleach kits reduces the risk and levels of infection among inmate populations. Needle exchange programs operate in Swiss, German, Spanish, and Australian prisons and appear to help reduce rates of infection. It is uncertain whether these programs have reduced the levels of hard drug use among inmate populations. Research on methadone maintenance programs in the community has produced mixed results. It is uncertain, for example, whether these programs have reduced the levels of heroin addiction, and there is the added problem that methadone itself is an addictive drug.

What do you think?

1. Do you agree with the CSC's harm-reduction programs?
2. Should the CSC consider providing clean needles to inmates? Would you support the implementation of this policy? Why or why not?
3. What do you see as the most beneficial aspects of these policies for reducing risk in prison populations? What are the most negative aspects?

AT ISSUE

ISSUE 4.2: Should the federal and provincial/territorial governments allow supervised tattoo parlours to operate in prisons?

In 2005, in an attempt to reduce infection rates in federal prisons, tattoo parlours were established in six federal prisons for a one-year trial. The cost of the program was $100,000 per year per site (total: $600,000). The tattoo shops were run by prisoners and supervised by correctional staff. Inmate tattoo artists were provided with training in preventing infections and also served as peer health educators. The program was terminated by the federal Conservative government in 2006.

The perspectives of proponents and opponents of tattoo parlours in federal correctional institutions are reflected in the comments of a spokesperson for the Canadian HIV/AIDS Legal Network and the federal Minister of Public Safety. Both were commenting on the federal government's decision to cancel the program.

> *Canadian taxpayers are either going to pay now or they are going to pay later . . . When prisoners return to the community, the diseases they've acquired in prison come with them and are spread through sex, drug use, and other behaviours.*
>
> *– spokesperson for the Canadian HIV/AIDS Legal Network*
>
> *Canada's new government will not spend taxpayers' money on providing tattoos for convicted criminals."*
>
> *– federal Minister of Public Safety*

What do you think?

1. Do you support or oppose the reinstatement of the tattoo-parlour program in federal correctional facilities? In provincial/territorial facilities?

AT ISSUE

ISSUE 4.3: Should there be private prisons in Canada?

Even though Ontario has terminated the contract of a private company that was operating one of its correctional institutions, the debate over privatization continues. The discussion centres on whether this approach (1) is a faster and cheaper way for correctional systems to add capacity; (2) reduces operating costs; (3) improves the quality of service provided to inmates; (4) reduces rates of reoffending; and (5) relieves government of the responsibility to sanction offenders. The debate over privately operated correctional facilities in Canada, however, has not diminished.

Proponents of privately operated prisons assert the following:

- They are more cost-effective than "public" prisons.
- They are more flexible and are able to expand physical capacity and programs more quickly than government-operated facilities.
- They are more accountable to monitoring and review than public prisons.
- They are an important yardstick against which to measure the performance of public prisons.

Opponents of the privatization of correctional facilities counter as follows:

- Private-sector companies that construct and manage prisons and those that manufacture prison "hardware" are components of the prison-industrial complex, "a set of bureaucratic, political, and economic interests that encourage increased spending on imprisonment, regardless of the actual need" (Schlosser 1998, 54).
- Politicians have used the public's (largely unjustified) fear of crime to promote private-sector involvement in building more prisons, as have communities that benefit economically from institutions built in their locales.
- "Punishment for profit" is unethical.
- The involvement of the private sector in operating prisons is a costly and ineffective response to crime, and any cost savings recorded by private prisons are a result of lower, nonunion wages paid to employees.

The Research Evidence

Developing measures of the effectiveness of prisons, be they operated by government or by private contractors, is a difficult task. Efforts to determine whether private prisons are more effective than public prisons are even more challenging, particularly when we factor in the ethical and moral dimensions of the debate. The absence of private prisons in Canada (except for the above-noted five-year experience in Ontario) precludes assessments of the effectiveness of privatization in this country.

Research studies conducted in other jurisdictions, including the United States and England, suggest that the performance of private prisons is much the same as that of public prisons. For example, there are more similarities than differences in vocational and educational programs for inmates, as well as in rates of prison disturbances.

Sources: Austin and Coventry 1999; Camp and Daggett 2005; Thomas 1998.

What do you think?

1. After considering the arguments for and against private-sector involvement in operating correctional institutions, what is your position on this issue? What would you consider the strongest arguments in favour of your position?
2. Would you support allowing private companies to build and manage correctional institutions on a trial basis in Canada? What is the basis for your position?

KEY POINTS REVIEW

1. Only a very small percentage of convicted offenders are incarcerated in correctional institutions.
2. A wide variety of correctional facilities are operated by the federal government and provincial/territorial governments.
3. One way to trace the changing philosophy of corrections and punishment is by examining the architecture of correctional institutions over the past 200 years.
4. A new moral architecture is being reflected in the design of federal correctional facilities, particularly those for female offenders and Aboriginal offenders.
5. Correctional institutions have a number of unique features that distinguish them from other public- and private-sector agencies and organizations.
6. The incident at the Kingston Prison for Women in 1994 involved a breakdown in the rule of law and of the administrative leadership of the prison.
7. Operating correctional institutions involves a number of inherent challenges, including these: meeting the requirements of legislation and policy, managing staff, addressing overcrowding, facilitating rehabilitation, combating inmate gangs, and ensuring inmate safety.
8. HIV/AIDS and infectious diseases present immense challenges to correctional authorities, who have developed a number of prevention and interdiction strategies.
9. The riot at the Headingley Correctional Institution in 1996 was the consequence of organizational, administrative, and staff deficiencies, as well as the actions of inmates.

10. Ontario's experiment with private-sector involvement in operating prisons was short-lived. A comparative evaluation of government-operated and privately operated correctional institutions produced mixed results.

KEY TERM QUESTIONS

1. Describe the attributes of the **minimum/medium/maximum security facilities** and the **multilevel institutions** and the **Special Handling Unit,** operated by the federal Correctional Service of Canada.
2. Compare and contrast **static security** and **dynamic security**.
3. Why are prisons viewed as **total institutions**?
4. What is the **continuum of correctional institutions**, and how does this concept assist our understanding of life inside prisons?
5. Discuss the **prevention strategies** and **interdiction strategies** that correctional systems have implemented in their efforts to reduce the rates of HIV/AIDS and other infectious diseases inside correctional institutions.

REFERENCES

Arbour, The Honourable L. (Commissioner). 1996. *Commission of Inquiry into Certain Events at the Prison for Women in Kingston.* Ottawa: Public Works and Government Services Canada. http://www.justicebehindthewalls.net/resources/arbour_report/arbour_rpt.htm

Austin, J., and G. Coventry. 1999. "Are We Better Off? Comparing Private and Public Prisons in the United States." *Journal of the Institute of Criminology* 11(2): 177–201.

Authier, P. 2007. "Prison Overcrowding Killing Rehab Programs: Ombudsman." *The Gazette*, June 7. http://www.pssg.gov.bc.ca/corrections/pdf/StrategicPlan2006-2009.pdf

Basen, I. 2006. "Doing the Crime and Doing the Time." *Reality Check*, January 5. http://www.cbc.ca/canadavotes2006/realitycheck

Benzvy-Miller, S. 1990. "Community Corrections and the NIMBY Syndrome." *Forum on Corrections Research* 2(2): 18–22.

British Columbia Ministry of Public Safety and Solicitor General. 2006. *The Strategic Plan of B.C. Corrections: A Commitment to Public Safety 2006–2009.* Victoria. http://www.pssg.gov.bc.ca/corrections/pdf/StrategicPlan2006-2009.pdf

Camp, S.D., and D.M. Daggett. 2005. *Evaluation of the Taft Demonstration Project: Performance of a Private-Sector Prison and the BOP.* Washington: Federal Bureau of Prisons. http://www.bop.gov/news/research_projects/published_reports/pub_vs_priv/orelappin2005.pdf

Canadian Press. 2008. "Prisoner Advocate Says Overcrowding to Blame for Gang Fight at Sask. Prison." April 26. http://www.pssg.gov.bc.ca/corrections/pdf/StrategicPlan2006-2009.pdf

Cowan, P., and D. Sheremata. 2000. "Death in Experimental Prison Unit—'She Was Helpless.'" *Edmonton Sun*, February 9.

Dias, G., and G. Betteridge. 2007. *Hard Time: HIV and Hepatitis C Prevention Programming for Prisoners in Canada*. Ottawa: Canadian HIV/AIDS Legal Network and Prisoners' HIV/AIDS Support Action Network (PASAN). http://www.pasan.org/Publications/Hard_Time.pdf

Gaes, G. 2008. "Cost, Performance Studies Look at Prison Privatization." *NIJ Journal* 259. http://www.ncjrs.gov/pdffiles1/nij/221507.pdf

Gilbert, R. 2008. "British Columbia Building More Prison Cells." *Journal of Commerce*, February 25. http://www.joconl.com/article/id26520

Glube, C. (Chair). 2006. *Moving Forward with Women's Corrections*. Ottawa: Correctional Service of Canada. http://www.csc-scc.gc.ca/text/prgrm/fsw/wos29/wos29-eng.shtml

Goffman, E. 1961. *Asylums: Essays on the Social Situation of Mental Patients and Other Inmates*. Garden City: Doubleday.

Griffiths, C.T., E. Zellerer, D.S. Wood, and G. Saville. 1995. *Crime, Law, and Justice Among Inuit in the Baffin Region, N.W.T.*, Canada. Burnaby: Criminology Research Centre, Simon Fraser University.

Harris, K. 2008. "Inside Canada's Military Prison." *Toronto Sun*, January 29. http://www.torontosun.com/News?Canada/2008/01/29/4799260-sun.html

Hayman, S. 2006. *Imprisoning Our Sisters*. Montreal and Kingston: McGill-Queen's University Press.

Hughes, the Hon. E.N. (Ted). (Chair). 1996. *Report of the Independent Review of the Circumstances Surrounding the April 25–26, 1996, Riot at the Headingley Correctional Institution*. Winnipeg: Ministry of Justice, Province of Manitoba.

insideprison.com. 2006. "A Snapshot of Prison Gangs and Youth Gangs in Canada: Well-Known Gangs, Membership, Offences, Risk, and Reconviction." http://www.insideprison.com/prison-gangs-canada.asp

Lines, R. 2002. *Action on HIV/AIDS in Prisons: Too Little, Too Late—A Report Card*. Montreal: Canadian HIV/AIDS Legal Network. http://www.aidslaw.ca/publications/interfaces/downloadFile.php?ref=179

NPB (National Parole Board). 2007a. *Performance Monitoring Report 2006–2007*. Ottawa. http://www.npb-cnlc.gc.ca/reports/pdf/pmr_2006_2007/index-eng.htm

Ontario Ministry of Community Safety and Correctional Services. 2006. *Central North Correctional Centre Review and Comparison to Central East Correctional Centre*. Toronto. http://privateci.org/private_pics/CNCC.pdf

Public Safety Canada Portfolio Corrections Statistics Committee. 2007. *Corrections and Conditional Release Statistical Overview*. Ottawa. http://www.publicsafety.gc.ca/res/cor/rep/ccrso2007-eng.aspx

Sampson, R. (Chair). 2007. *Report of the Correctional Service of Canada Review Panel: A Roadmap to Strengthening Public Safety.* Ottawa: Minister of Public Works and Government Services Canada. http://www.publicsafety.gc.ca/csc-scc/cscrpreport-eng.pdf

Schlosser, E. 1998. "The Prison-Industrial Complex." *Atlantic Monthly* 282(6): 51–77.

Smith, P., C. Goggin, and P. Gendreau. 2002. *The Effects of Prison Sentences and Intermediate Sanctions on Recidivism: General Effects and Individual Differences.* Ottawa: Solicitor General Canada. http://ww2.ps-sp.gc.ca/publications/corrections/200201_Gendreau_e.pdf

Statistics Canada. 2006. *The Daily* (December 15). Ottawa. http://www.statcan.gc.ca/Daily/English/061215/d061215b.htm

Thomas, C.W. 1998. "Issues and Evidence from the United States." In *Privatizing Correctional Services,* ed. S.T. Easton. Vancouver: Fraser Institute. 15–61.

Union of Canadian Correctional Officers. 2007. *Rewards and Consequences: A Correctional Service for the 21st Century. A Brief to the Independent Review Panel Studying the Future of Correctional Service Canada.* Montreal. http://www.ucco-sacc.csn.qc.ca

Varis, D.D. 2001. "Intensive Support Units for Federal Inmates: A Descriptive Review." *Forum on Corrections Research* 13(3). http://www.csc-scc.gc.ca/text/pblct/forum/e133/e133m-eng.shtml

Villettaz, P., M. Killias, and I. Zoder. 2006. *The Effects of Custodial vs. Noncustodial Sentences on Reoffending. A Systematic Review of the State of Knowledge.* Lausanne: Institute of Criminology and Criminal Law, University of Lausanne. http://db.c2admin.org/doc-pdf/Campbell-report-30.09.06.pdf

Yates, J.M. 1993. *Line Screw: My Twelve Riotous Years Working Behind Bars in Some of Canada's Toughest Jails.* Toronto: McClelland & Stewart.

WEBLINKS

The Prisoners' HIV/AIDS Action Network (PASAN)

http://www.pasan.org
PASAN is a community-based organization that is active in HIV/AIDS prevention and education and in providing support services to inmates, ex-offenders, and youth in custody as well as their families. It produces the newsletter *Cell Count*, which contains topical information on HIV/AIDS and which offers a forum for inmates to share their perspectives and experiences. The website contains information on the organization's activities, as well as extensive links to prisoner-advocacy organizations across Canada and to a number of PASAN-sponsored publications.

CHAPTER 5

THE CORRECTIONAL OFFICERS

CHAPTER OBJECTIVES

After reading this chapter you should be able to:

- *Discuss the roles and responsibilities of correctional officers.*
- *Discuss the arrangements for the recruitment and training of correctional officers.*
- *Describe the normative code that exists among correctional officers.*
- *Examine the relationships between correctional officers and inmates.*
- *Describe the attitudes and orientations that correctional officers have toward inmates and toward the organizations in which they work.*
- *Describe the accommodative relationships that develop between correctional officers and inmates and the roles that correctional officers can play in these relationships.*
- *Speak to the decision making of correctional officers and the exercise of discretion.*
- *Discuss the relationships between correctional officers and treatment staff and administration.*
- *Identify and discuss the sources of stress for correctional officers.*
- *Consider the issues surrounding cross-gender staffing in women's correctional facilities.*

KEY TERMS

Staff Application, Recruitment, and Training Program (START)
Normative code of behaviour (of correctional officers)
Custodial agenda (of correctional officers)
Correctional agenda (of correctional officers)
Post-Traumatic Stress Disorder (PTSD)
Critical Incident Stress Debriefing (CISD)
Cross-gender staffing

PERSPECTIVE

A Correctional Officer

I see many sorrows; few real honest smiles and less joy. The sorrows come by many things; one person may have missed an approved visit that he may have worked hard to get. The reason may have been that the inmate broke a rule and the visit was denied or postponed as punishment, or "his people" didn't come for some reason, or no reason at all.

Many sorrows come by a death in the family or perhaps an illness, and the inmate cannot get in touch with anyone to find out what has happened, or what is being done about the situation. I have heard an inmate not much older than myself, preparing funeral arrangements for one of his parents from prison. I caught myself trying to grasp how he must have felt, and I could not imagine the pain or sorrow. Many times the only thing they can do is to sit and wait, for hours—sometimes days. I have watched grown men break down and cry from frustration over things you and I don't ever stop to think about, such as a busy signal on a telephone.

Many of us consider no mail as a blessing, sometimes; however, many inmates consider "junk mail" as a blessing because it was sent to them alone. Many receive no mail at all, ever. Some inmates don't know where their family is, or how to contact them, sons, daughters, wives or grandchildren. No one. Many inmates have only a letter or a postcard to hold on to, to keep them going. I have sat for hours and talked with men about their problems. I have sat and looked at pictures of families, a wife, of children and pets and many other things. I have heard stories and the tales about the people in the pictures and felt compassion for both of them. (letter from a correctional officer to *Prison Talk*, January 19, 2003, http://www.prisontalk.com/forums/showthread.php?t=8744)

This chapter considers the activities of correctional officers (COs), including the patterns of interaction that develop among the officers themselves and the relationships with the prison administration, treatment staff, and inmates. Given the extensive interaction that officers have with inmates, particular attention is given to the orientations and attitudes of COs.

The examination of COs is hindered by a lack of Canadian research. Most of the published materials are from the United States, though some research has been conducted on federal COs in this country. Studies of COs in provincial/territorial institutions are virtually nonexistent, even though the majority of incarcerated offenders in Canada are under provincial jurisdiction.

ROLES AND RESPONSIBILITIES

Correctional officers play a pivotal role in correctional institutions. On a daily basis, it is COs who have the most contact with the inmates. Though systems of corrections make extensive use of high technology, such as video surveillance and various warning devices (static security), COs are the primary mechanism by which institutional policies and regulations are implemented and by which the inmates are controlled (dynamic security). COs are also a key part of efforts to rehabilitate offenders.

The authority of COs in prisons is both legal and moral. With respect to legal authority, though COs do not have the power to discipline inmates, in enforcing the policies and regulations of the institution, officers are able to initiate the punishment process. The decision making of COs is examined in greater detail later in the chapter. Note that the authority of COs is not established by policies and regulations. Equally important is their moral authority, which is based on establishing functional relationships with the inmates. The dynamics of officer–inmate relationships are discussed later in the chapter.

The responsibilities of COs have grown more complex and challenging in recent years. Their duties centre on providing static and dynamic security. These duties include carrying out motorized and foot patrols, staffing control posts, counting and escorting offenders, searching for contraband, enforcing institutional regulations, and providing emergency response. COs mediate conflicts, control inmate movement within the facility, admit and process new arrivals, and serve as an information and referral source for inmates. In many institutions, COs play an active role in case management. In some provincial institutions, they are involved in providing core programming to inmates. In short, the tasks of COs centre on four major tasks: (1) security, providing surveillance inside the prison; (2) service, looking after inmate needs; (3) helping inmates adjust to life inside; and (4) helping inmates prepare to reenter the community.

In federal institutions, CO1 officers are responsible for dynamic and static security, establishing working relationships with inmates and other staff members, and supporting the case management process. The priority of the CO1 is security. CO2 correctional officers focus on case management and on facilitating and encouraging inmate participation in programs. The activities of COs can be encapsulated as follows:

> *Correctional staff are engaged in guiding, mentoring, facilitating, developing and watching inmates. If an inmate needs assistance with a job, getting along with others, programming, interacting with staff, or obtaining privileges, then correctional officers are their more likely resource, given their proximity and frequency of contact. (Hemmens and Stohr 2000, 327)*

Despite the critical role played by COs and the increasing efforts to professionalize the occupation, many officers feel alienated from the organizations in which they work and hold negative or cynical attitudes toward inmates, treatment staff, and their coworkers. As well, officers may experience considerable stress associated with working inside institutions on a daily basis.

RECRUITMENT AND TRAINING

In referring to the criteria used to hire correctional officers until the 1960s, one correctional administrator told C.T. Griffiths: "About the only qualification was that the potential applicant had to be able to walk around the top of the wall (of the prison) without falling off." The low pay and lack of training reflected the low status of correctional officers. As late as the 1980s, one corrections observer noted that the only requirements for security personnel assigned to guard towers were "20/20 vision, the IQ of an imbecile, a high threshold for boredom, and a basement position in Maslow's hierarchy" (Toch 1978, 87). Today, working inside a correctional institution requires much more than the ability to turn a key. Officers must have good communication and interpersonal skills, exercise common sense and good judgment, be aware of legal and procedural issues, and be adaptable to changes in correctional philosophy and policy.

Recent years have seen changes in the demographic profile of CO recruits. More Aboriginal people and other visible minorities are being selected for training—a measure of the success of efforts to promote diversity in Canadian corrections.

Correctional Service of Canada Recruiting and Training Programs

At the federal level, each of the CSC's five regions (Atlantic, Quebec, Ontario, Prairies, Pacific) is responsible for recruiting, selecting, assessing, and hiring correctional officers using national standards. Applicants interested in applying for an entry-level CO position must apply to the region where they are interested in working (visit http://www.jobs.gc.ca). They must successfully pass a general aptitude test, the Bona Fide Occupational Requirements (BFOR) for COs, and a set of medical and physical standards, including the COPAT (Correctional Officer Physical Abilities Test). This is followed by an in-depth interview that focuses on the applicant's background and personal integrity. The CSC has dropped the requirement that applicants have a university degree; it now requires only a high-school diploma or high-school equivalency.

Successful applicants are required to complete the Correctional Training Program, an online learning module that includes law and policy. The recruits then attend a six-week program at the Staff College, which focuses on developing skill sets in interpersonal and communication skills, security procedures and strategies, self-defence, firearms, and interviewing techniques, among other things. The Union of Canadian Correctional Officers has expressed serious reservations about this new training regime. Previously, new recruits spent 12 weeks in residence at the Staff College. On completion of training, new officers are deployed to institutions in the region where there are vacancies. After building up seniority, officers may request a transfer to another institution.

The CSC has developed a special process for selecting and training staff to work in institutions for federally sentenced women. Specific criteria are used to identify personnel who are sensitive to women's issues, their life histories, and their unique needs. Besides the training provided to all new COs, staff selected to work in women's facilities must complete a "women-centred training" course. This course consists of a number of modules covering areas such as these: women's criminality and its links to personal history, self-injury, and suicide; same-sex relationships; cultural sensitivity; and dealing effectively with lifers (Lajeunesse et al. 2000).

One of the most ambitious studies of Canadian COs examined how the attitudes of officers change between the training phase and the field. A survey questionnaire was administered to 147 federal COs on the first day of the training program, then after two weeks, and again after three months. It was found that the new recruits held positive views about correctional work generally and toward the idea of rehabilitation, although female recruits scored higher on attitudes toward rehabilitation and on motivation than the male recruits (Bensimon 2005a).

The survey instrument was then administered to the same officers after they had been assigned to a correctional institution for three months, six months, and twelve months. It was found that after one year on the job, the officers continued to display positive attitudes towards correctional work and feelings of empathy, although the scores for the women officers on these items was higher than for the male officers. However, they also identified a number of disadvantages of the job after one year, including stress associated with shift work and concerns about personal security and negative features of the work environment (e.g., poor relations with colleagues). It was also found that over the twelve months, the officers' concerns had increased regarding lack of challenge in their work and their low degree of decision-making autonomy. They were also beginning to sense that they lacked the personal capacity to meet many of the challenges confronting them (Bensimon 2005b).

Provincial/Territorial Recruiting and Training Programs

There are no nationwide standards for recruiting and training COs for provincial/territorial systems of corrections. Each province/territory has established its own procedures, standards, and training courses. In most provinces, new recruits are trained using some combination of initial and on-the-job training programs. Increasingly, potential recruits are required to assume the costs of their own training. Some jurisdictions offer pre-employment courses through community colleges.

Box 5.1 outlines Ontario's CO **Staff Application, Recruitment, and Training Program (START).**

BOX 5.1

The Ontario START Program

Candidates for employment in Ontario provincial corrections must complete, at their own expense, the CO START program, which includes the following components:

The Admission Process

There are three stages in the admission process:

Stage 1: Qualifications

Applicants must:

- be eligible to work in Canada;
- have Ontario grade 12 graduation diploma or formal equivalency; and,
- have current Emergency First Aid and CPR Heartsaver certificates

(continued)

Stage 2: Testing and Evaluation

Several times a year, information, testing, and evaluation sessions are presented at various locations throughout the province. Candidates are provided with information on the activities and duties of correctional officers and also complete a testing and evaluation process, which includes:

- the Correctional Officer Counting Test;
- the Canadian Achievement Survey Test for language expression and comprehension;
- a video-based judgment test;
- a video and written observation skills test;
- a personality inventory

Stage 3: Personal Interview

A personal interview, centred on core competencies required of corrections officers, is conducted. Those candidates who successfully complete this stage are then required to undergo a medical exam, physical abilities test, and security, employment reference, and character reference checks.

Pre-employment Training

Candidates who successfully complete the admissions process are invited to enroll in the six-week Pre-Employment Training Program with a focus on either adult or youth offenders. Vacancies in correctional facilities are filled from a list of those persons who have successfully completed the Pre-employment Training Program and have met the medical and security requirements. Candidates are required to pay tuition fees as well as room and board costs while at the training centre.

Institutional Orientation

Provincial institutions offer a three-week orientation for new correctional officers—who generally start out as "unclassified employees" on a contract basis—when they are hired. This orientation provides the new officer with information on the rules and operating procedures of the institution, programs and services, case management, and other features of daily institutional life.

Source: Ministry of Community Safety and Correctional Services, 2006.

In British Columbia, the various stages of recruitment and training are similar to those in Ontario. One difference is that applicants in B.C. apply directly to one or more of the provincial facilities. Qualified applicants are first hired as "security officers." After working for 18 months with successful performance reviews and having completed all required training, they are eligible to become COs (http://www.jibc.bc.ca/ccjd/adultCorrections.htm). In most jurisdictions, someone who is interested in a career as a CO can enroll in a certificate course offered by a community college or justice training centre. These courses may enhance an applicant's chances of being hired, but they do not guarantee a successful application outcome.

GOING INSIDE: THE SOCIALIZATION OF NEW CORRECTIONAL OFFICERS

A number of challenges confront new COs, not the least of which is the lack of knowledge of what it will be like working inside a prison. A new CO probably has not visited a correctional institution in any capacity before being hired. Indeed, most new COs have been exposed to prison life solely through movies and sensational reports in the media.

In learning to exercise discretion and carry out their tasks effectively, new COs must learn the subtle nonverbal cues that will help them "read" individual inmates. They must also become familiar with the various intricacies of the inmate social system, the methods used to distribute and use contraband goods and drugs, and other activities such as gambling, strong-arming, and debt collection. Early on, the inmates will "test" new COs to determine how they will exercise their discretion and authority. These processes of adaptation and learning and of developing strategies to cope with the pressures and demands of everyday life in the prison are similar to those undergone by new inmates.

Another challenge confronting new COs involves gaining acceptance from coworkers. The new officers must demonstrate their solidarity through their actions. There is often a "probationary" period during which the neophyte must prove that he or she can be trusted and has the abilities to perform the job.

Patterns of Relationships Among Correctional Officers

It has long been assumed that COs, much like their police counterparts, constitute an occupational subculture with definable attributes. The tenets that are said to provide the foundation for a **normative code of behaviour** among COs include the following:

- Always assist another officer who is in real or potential danger.
- Do not become overly friendly with the inmates.
- Do not abuse your authority with inmates.
- Always back your colleagues in decisions and actions; don't backstab.

- Do your job and don't leave work for other officers to do.
- Defer to the experience of veteran officers (Farkas 1997; Kauffman 1988).

Among the factors that have been identified as contributing to the development of solidarity among COs are these: the ever-present potential for injury on the job; the hostility directed toward COs by inmates; the often conflicting demands made on COs, largely as a consequence of shifting correctional philosophies; a work environment where rewards and recognition are few and far between; and the reliance of officers on one another (Grossi and Berg 1991). The resulting normative code of behaviour provides a mechanism for COs to cope with the demands of both inmates and the prison administration.

On closer examination, however, the subculture of COs seems not to be monolithic. Indeed, COs as a work group may be as fragmented as the inmates are. Line-level security personnel group into friendship networks, which may be gender based or centred around a shared experience, such as having completed a university degree. The degree to which COs exhibit solidarity depends on a number of factors, including the security level of the institution; the age, gender, and experiential backgrounds of the officers; the relations between the officers and the administration; and other factors that are less tangible, including the extent to which the COs in any one institution perceive that they are threatened by the inmates or by administrative policies. For example, in high-security institutions, where the daily regimen is more controlled and the threat (real or perceived) of injury is greater, solidarity among officers is likely to be more evident. Similarly, there may be greater solidarity among officers working in institutions where the administration provides neither clear guidelines for officer activities nor support for the decision making of officers.

In fact, for many COs it is their *colleagues*, not the inmates, who are the main source of job-related stress. COs who gossip among themselves, who share information with inmates, and who are perceived as too authoritarian are potential sources of stress for line-level personnel. Conflict may also arise when certain officers are viewed as "slackers"—for example, because they sleep during graveyard shifts and fail to make their rounds at the appointed times.

ORIENTATIONS AND ATTITUDES

Because they staff the prison 24 hours a day, COs have the most extensive contact with inmates of anyone in the building. For this reason alone, it is important to examine and understand the orientations and attitudes of COs. Even when they are not directly involved in delivering treatment programs or managing cases, they are well positioned to act as change agents and to foster positive attitudes and behaviours among inmates. Or, on the negative side, to hinder the efforts of the program staff.

A Typology of Correctional Officers

Attempts have been made to categorize COs based on their orientation and attitudes toward the inmates, their coworkers, their occupation, and the institutional environment. Though such efforts are fraught with difficulty, as it is unlikely that any single officer will exhibit all of the attitudinal and behavioural features of one particular type, it does sensitize us to the fact that not all COs think and act the same way. Studies have found that some officers are more rule and enforcement oriented, while others rely on communication skills and common sense to solve problems (Farkas 2000). COs can be located on a continuum based on how they exercise their discretionary authority. At one end are those who are rigid and who attempt to enforce all the rules at all times; at the other are officers who do little or no rule enforcement. This latter group may include officers who are close to retirement. In the middle are officers who are consistent in their decision making and straightforward with inmates, who do not make arbitrary decisions, and who temper their exercise of authority with common sense and a respect for the rule of law. These officers have good judgment, have the ability to mediate potentially explosive behavioural situations, and are good judges of character.

One correctional officer in a federal institution described the different approaches that fellow officers took toward inmates: "Some officers are pretty stiff and enforce the rules and regulations. Some people are pretty lax, although some of the staff over the years have adopted the attitude, 'Well, if I don't bother the cons, they're not going to bother me.' Well, that's not a good idea, because you might have an easy shift once in a while, but they are going to take advantage of it eventually" (Harris 2002, 45-46).

Attitudes toward Inmates

A number of studies have reported that COs hold negative attitudes toward inmates, including the view that inmates are manipulative and that the likelihood of rehabilitation is slight (Whitehead and Lindquist 1989). In addition, COs may believe that inmates have too much power and control, which places officers at an increased risk of injury or even death. COs often attribute this risk to weak administrators who, often inadvertently, have imposed policies that undermine the authority of COs and that upset the routine and regimen of daily prison life. In comparison with administrators and treatment staff, COs may exhibit attitudes that are more punitive, less empathetic, and less supportive of rehabilitation (Larivière 2002; Larivière and Robinson 1996).

A number of factors appear to influence the attitudes that COs harbour toward inmates, including the following:

- *Institutional setting:* COs in minimum-security facilities tend to hold more favourable attitudes toward offenders than those in medium- and maximum-security institutions (Jurik 1985; Larivière and Robinson 1996).
- *Age and experience:* There is some evidence that more positive attitudes toward inmates are held by older COs with years of experience. This is most likely a consequence of officers adjusting to the realities of their workplace and developing strategies for coping with inmates and with the variety of stressors that they experience in carrying out their tasks (Larivière and Robinson 1996; Plecas and Maxim 1987).
- *Region of the country:* The research on federal COs suggests that there are regional variations in officers' attitudes. It has been found, for example, that federal COs in the Pacific region are more empathetic and less punitive toward offenders, whereas federal COs in Quebec are less empathetic as well as the most punitive of any region. More research is required to explore and identify the sources of these regional differences.

There do not appear to be any significant differences between male and female COs in their attitudes towards inmates.

Job Satisfaction and Commitment to the Organization

The factors that relate to job satisfaction among COs can be roughly divided into (1) personal characteristics of the CO, and (2) work environment factors (Lambert, Hogan, and Barton 2002). Studies have attempted to determine the impacts of race, gender, age, level of education, and length of service on the perceptions that officers have of their work environment and on levels of job satisfaction. Following are among the more significant findings with respect to the personal characteristics of COs:

- Female COs and those with more years of experience are more satisfied with their work.
- COs who were empathetic, nonpunitive, and supportive of rehabilitation programs are more committed to their work, are more satisfied with the work they perform, and experience less stress on the job.
- Contrary to expectations, there may be an inverse relationship between level of education and job satisfaction.

- COs' attitudes vary with length of time in service. There is evidence of a "mellowing effect"—that is, officers who are older and who have more years on the job tend to be more positive in their attitudes.

With respect to the role of environmental factors and organizational commitment, the following can be said:

- Compared to other institutional staff, COs often score lowest on perceptions of staff empowerment, staff recognition, fair treatment of employees, and overall job satisfaction.
- Perceived dangerousness does not seem to have an impact on the commitment of officers to the organization.
- Those officers who evidence higher levels of organizational commitment are more likely to exhibit positive "citizenship" and to work in a manner that benefits the prison (Hogan et al. 2006; Lambert, Hogan, and Griffin 2008; Morgan, Van Haveren, and Pearson 2002).

The extent to which level of job satisfaction among COs is affected by the personalities and background experiences of individual officers, as well as by the work itself, has yet to be researched.

A prerequisite for correctional staff to be effective is commitment to the organization in which they work. Findings from surveys of federal COs indicate the following:

- Correctional officers and case managers showed lower levels of commitment to the CSC than supervisory staff.
- New staff had higher levels of commitment than officers who had been in the service for a number of years.
- Female staff tended to be more committed than their male counterparts.
- Neither education nor age were related to level of commitment to the organization (Robinson, Porporino, and Simourd 1992).

COs have also been found to be more critical of their work environment than any other employee group in the system. That said, the lower the security level of the institution, the more favourable are staff's attitudes toward their work environment. (Price-Waterhouse 1994, 15–1, 15–2) This dissatisfaction is, perhaps, understandable, given the position of correctional officers in the prison staff hierarchy:

> *The correctional officer is a civil servant underling who occupies the lowest rung in the penitentiary hierarchy, just above the inmates. As an individual, he/she does not participate in the formulation of prison policy or in that of the tasks that he/she is required to perform. (Union of Canadian Correctional Officers 2002, 105)*

Correctional officers' unions in Canada are active in representing the interests and concerns of their members. The Union of Canadian Correctional Officer represents federal COs and is active in conducting research, submitting briefs to government and commissions of inquiry, and advocating for reform in prison policies and practices. The Union of Canadian Correctional Officer's position is that the authority of COs has diminished in recent years and that COs should be treated as justice system professionals. In a brief to the CSC Review Panel (Sampson 2007), the union set out a number of challenges facing correctional officers, including these: the changing offender profile, deficiencies in the disciplinary regime in correctional institutions, inadequate security equipment, the rising presence of drugs and weapons in prisons, and the increasing number of inmates with mental health problems.

Internal chat sites abound with concerns that the work of COs does not receive sufficient recognition and support. Box 5.1 presents the contributions of two participants to an on-line discussion of an incident at a Maryland prison. Several COs had been fired after severely beating an inmate. Though the expressed views are, perhaps, on the extreme end of the opinion continuum, the opinions do reflect a widely-held view that the work of COs is undervalued.

BOX 5.2

Response to the Firing of Two Correctional Officers

earnhardtlvr, May 22, 2007. I personally think firing these CO's is a bunch of crap. They go to work every day with people who committed crimes and been convicted!! I mean, how scary is that? I know quite a few COs and I have to say I feel for their family every day they have to go to work. People talk about excessive force, but I think that's a load of crap too. If you don't come down hard on them they will all be trying to pull this crap! I mean, they weren't smart enough not to commit the crime that got them there in the first place, but then not to follow the rules inside . . . well that's even dumber, and maybe they should be beat. Our jails are overpopulated and CO's are so understaffed it is ridiculous! Obviously going to jail is not a deterrant for committing a crime, so if punishment isn't swift in the jails what kind of order will u have on the inside?

missyhairlady, February 28, 2008. These officers put their lives on the line everyday "babysitting" these criminals. Criminals who are allowed to have more freedoms &

(continued)

perks than some people on the outside. They get 3 meals a day, a bed to sleep in, recreation, schooling, etc . . . and who's paying for it? YOU and ME!

These officers are already underpaid, unappreciated, and short staffed. Remember 2 years ago there was an Officer KILLED by an inmate, and now they are gonna fire officers for putting these criminals in their place? Is it fair that they have committed a crime, put in a prison and treated like they are living at the Hilton hotel, not in jail?? Hardly!! These officers are basically made to treat these criminals with love and respect . . . but do they get it in return, NOPE, they get urine and feces thrown at them, spit at, and many other gross and disgusting things. So is that fair, should officers be fired for putting up with scum??? NOPE!!

Source: http://your4state.com

In a brief to the CSC Review Panel, the Union of Canadian Correctional Officers identified a number of areas of concern regarding operational policies, including the following:

Prison discipline. According to the Union of Canadian Correctional Officers, the discipline regime in federal prisons was undermining the authority of COs by imposing light sanctions (mainly fines and suspended sentences) for inmate behaviour that jeopardized the institution's security as well as officers' safety. In support of this position, the union cited findings from an analysis of 3,600 major offence reports in Donnacona, a maximum-security prison, between January and December 2006. Nearly 1,500 of these offence reports had been postponed owing to time constraints.

The analysis also revealed that 41 percent of the reports resulted in a guilty finding and that in almost 60 percent of these cases, the sanction was either a suspended sentence or a fine. The incidents for which reports were filed most often involved the following: "Disobeys a justifiable order of a staff member" (30 percent); "Creates or participates in a disturbance or any other activity that is likely to jeopardize the security of the penitentiary" (22 percent); "Fights with, assaults, or threatens to assault another person" (9 percent); and "Without prior authorization, is in possession of, or deals in, an item that is not authorized by a Commissioner's Directive or by a written order of the Institution Head" (9 percent). The study found that only one inmate in ten received a sanction involving confinement.

Security equipment. In 2004, in a suit brought by the Union of Canadian Correctional Officers, a federal court ruled that federal COs could carry handcuffs on their uniforms. While acknowledging that this was a victory, the union argued to the review panel that COs should also wear OC (pepper) spray on their uniforms.

Attacks with bodily fluids. Under current CSC regulations, organic-liquid (urine, feces, spit) attacks on COs are not classified as "attacks." In the Union of Canadian Correctional Officer's view, such incidents are assaults with a weapon, given the level of infectious diseases among the inmate population. Yet because of privacy laws, correctional staff do not have the right to be told which inmates are infected.

The role of UCCO is to advocate for correctional officers, further research is required to explore these issues.

CO–INMATE RELATIONSHIPS AND PATTERNS OF ACCOMMODATION

Even though a core principle of correctional officers is "never trust an inmate," the unique features of daily life inside institutions create pressures for COs and inmates to develop accommodative relationships, which, for inmates, help reduce the pains of imprisonment, and, for COs, ensure daily stability and order. Relations with inmates are generally not a source of stress for COs, though the officers realize that they are outnumbered by the inmates and that peace and order in the institution require the cooperation of the inmates.

The specific patterns of interaction that develop between COs and inmates depend on a variety of factors, including the individual CO, the size of the inmate population, the security level of the facility, and the policies and management style of the senior administration. Generally, inmates serving life sentences (twenty-five-year minimum) are the easiest group to deal with. By contrast, younger offenders (often referred to as "new school inmates"), many of whom have a "get high today, the hell with tomorrow" attitude, are often a source of instability in the institution for both COs and other inmates. Ironically, then, even as the conditions within correctional institutions have improved, life has become more unpredictable for COs and staff.

Instability and lack of routine in correctional institutions may be in part a result of the erosion of the traditional "inmate code" (see Chapter 6). This erosion has brought about changes in how inmates relate to one another. Not so long ago, some inmates functioned as "elder statesmen," maintaining control in the units and helping maintain peace and stability in the institution as a whole. But today, in the words of one CO, "it's all intimidation, and brute force, and who has the most drugs to sell" (in Harris 2002, 48).

The Custodial Agenda of Correctional Officers

The public or **custodial agenda** of COs is constructed around the image of the officer as a "mindless and brutal custodian" (Johnson 1996, 197). The historical record of correctional institutions is heavy with documented cases of COs using arbitrary and excessive force. Today, however, COs are better trained; they are also supervised and held accountable for their actions. Though there are occasional well-publicized incidents involving the abuse of authority by COs (see the Ashley Smith case in Chapter 6), it would be inaccurate to portray officers as predisposed to violence or as systematically abusing their authority.

Here we must also consider the extent to which the prison environment itself, with its total institutional features, contributes to many of the problems that arise. As one researcher has observed:

> *Officers and inmates are the chief antagonists in prison conflict. As such, they are typically blamed for problems that plague prisons. Just as prisons are regarded as deviant environments, those who live and work in them are dismissed as possessing deviant characters and interests ... The intractable problems posed by prisons are not rooted in the identities and characters of officers or inmates. The problems are much more fundamental. They are rooted in the nature of the goals prisons are erected to serve. (Kauffman 1988, 264–65)*

The Correctional Agenda of Correctional Officers

Even if COs cannot build relationships with inmates that are based on trust, this does not preclude them from engaging in activities that are helpful to the inmates. This duty is part of the private **correctional agenda** and involves the CO functioning as a change agent and using his or her authority to help inmates cope with the problems of living in confinement.

COs must find ways to maintain an appropriate "distance" from the inmates; at the same time, they must develop relationships that allow them to provide assistance. "Keeping one's distance involves a subtle synthesis of proximity and remoteness, the former providing the means to earn the inmate's respect and cooperation, while the latter implies the physical separation that is essential to the exercise of authority" (Union of Canadian Correctional Officers 2002, 120–21).

Even while maintaining an appropriate social distance, COs can extend various human-services activities to inmates. For example, they can:

- ensure that the inmates receive basic goods and services, such as food, clothing, medication, and sundry items, in a timely manner, thereby reducing tensions;
- act as referral agents and advocates for inmates, often by serving as intermediaries between the inmate and the institutional bureaucracy; and,

- help inmates solve problems related to their incarceration, including the management of personal crises (Johnson 1996, 229–41).

COs have considerable discretion to help inmates and ease the difficulties that often surround daily life in incarceration. Following are two contributions by the partners of inmates to a web-based forum that illustrate this point:

> *Yesterday, Mr. D and I were working on an old issue that always ends up with me in tears. Yesterday's discussion was no different. Shortly after we finished talking about it, Mr. D. went to go use the washroom. The visiting room c/o, who is usually courteous but not friendly, started walking around the room. She stopped when she came to our table and said, "Are you OK?" I was startled at the concerned look on her face and her question and didn't answer right away, so she asked again. I assured her that YES, I was OK . . . its just a hormonal thing. When Mr. D. came back, I told him about it and he was surprised too . . . especially coming from this c/o. When our visit was over, I thanked her for her concern . . . I wanted to let her known that it was deeply appreciated – because it was. (http://www.prisontalk.com/forums/showthread.php?t=18347)*
>
> *Ya know, some people are pretty cool.*
>
> *I am moving to a new apartment in a different town and will have to get a new phone number. The facility that my guy is at only allows them to add phone numbers to their list once a quarter, and Oct. 1 was the last time until January. So I called and talked to the guy in charge of the phones to see if I could forward my calls from my old number to my new number, or if that was against the rules. He said, yes, it is against the rules, but as long as my guy keeps his mouth shut about it, that he would allow it until the next time they can add numbers! How cool is that? I have to admit, though, for the most part, the Cos and staff at this place have been quite helpful and generous with letting visits go longer than they're supposed to. (http://www.prisontalk.com/forums/showthread.php?t=2800)*

Those officers who develop a rapport with inmates beyond the basic "keeper and the kept" level are generally more effective in maintaining order in the units. A positive relationship with inmates may increase the amount of information that "snitches" or "information providers" pass along to officers and may also allow inmates to inform officers of problems that develop in the unit. It seems that generally speaking, the majority of inmates "get along" with COs.

COs often feel that little value is placed on the assistance they provide to inmates. This extends to a perception that the media is only interested in critical events in prisons. In the words of one former CO:

> *Countless times I and others had called journalists to persuade them to do stories on interesting programs we had cooked up. Nothing. Many of these people I knew in my writing capacity, others were people I had known or who had worked for me when I was a CBC executive. I couldn't budge them even by calling in favours they owed me. They showed up only to report escapes, riots, or allegations of "excessive force" by staff. (Yates 1993, 306)*

Exercising Authority: Correctional Officer's Discretion and Decision Making

> *The central dilemma faced by guards is that they can neither expect inmate cooperation nor govern without it ... To achieve a smoothly running tour, a guard has to gain inmate acquiescence with the carrot rather than the stick. The best reward a guard can offer is to ignore certain offenses when they are committed or to make sure that s/he is not around when a rule is being broken. (Hewitt, Poole, and Regoli 1984, 446)*

COs have a high degree of discretion in carrying out their daily activities and in determining when and how they will enforce the rules and regulations of the institution. Officers are well aware that full enforcement of all institutional regulations at all times would make life unbearable for both themselves and the inmates. A former CO recalled that a general principle was this: "Read the book, but don't throw the book. Do not go prescriptively into any situation" (Yates 1993, 115).

Much like police officers, COs cannot walk away from confrontations and crises that occur in the prison. That said, COs have considerable flexibility when applying many of the more minor institutional regulations. In the context of the accommodative relationships that develop between officers and inmates, minor and in some instances major transgressions may be ignored or not responded to in a formal manner, depending on the circumstances and the inmate(s) and CO(s) involved. Officers also know that there are limits to the use of incident reports as a way to secure inmate compliance. Thus, officers may resort to "informal punishments" such as refusing or "forgetting" to provide certain services for the inmate (e.g., "misplacing" an inmate's paperwork) (Union of Canadian Correctional Officers 2002, 123).

Styles of Correctional Officer Decision Making

It was noted earlier that COs exhibit different attitudinal and behavioural tendencies in carrying out their tasks. COs can be placed on a continuum, based on how they exercise their discretionary authority. At one end are those who are rigid and who attempt to enforce all of the rules at all times; at the other are those who do little or no rule enforcement. This latter group may include officers who are close to retirement. In the middle are officers who are consistent in their decision making and straightforward with inmates, who do not make arbitrary decisions, and who temper their exercise of authority with common sense and a respect for the rule of law. These officers have good judgment, have the ability to mediate potentially explosive behavioural situations, and are good judges of character.

Commenting on decision making and the role of experience, one former CO noted:

> *If you are not a shrewd assessor of human character, then you had better learn to be one fast. Some people are inside because they never had a break in their lives and some are in because they were "born to lose." You give the former the benefit of the doubt and you bend the rules for the latter only when it suits your purpose. In certain circumstances, you think of the inmate as an individual, a fellow human being. In others, you must first think of the good of the institution in general. It's a matter of making judgment calls, and it can't be taught except through experience. (Yates 1993, 115)*

Abuse of Authority and Misuse of Force by Correctional Officers

The low visibility of daily life inside correctional institutions, combined with the broad discretion exercised by COs, may create situations in which officers abuse their authority and sometimes even violate the law. Research conducted in Ontario provincial institutions raised the issue of whether COs were systematically abusing their discretionary powers when dealing with black inmates. The perception was widespread among black inmates that they were being punished more often and more severely, for less cause, than white inmates. Black inmates also felt more vulnerable to physical violence by COs. Support for these views was provided by some of the COs interviewed for the study (Gittens and Cole 1995).

An examination of COs' disciplinary practices revealed that black inmates were more likely to be charged with misconduct that involved interpreting behaviour (i.e., "attitude"), whereas white inmates were more likely to be disciplined for incidents where the COs' discretion was more limited, such as the discovery of an inmate with contraband. There was also evidence that black and white inmates were treated differently when penalties for misconduct were imposed, with black inmates being overrepresented in the punishment category of closed confinement (i.e., segregation).

Determining the extent to which COs abuse authority and discretion is made difficult by a number of factors, including the low visibility of the decisions that officers make every day inside institutions; the culture of silence among officers, which may result in officers protecting one another; and the relatively short periods of time for which provincial inmates are incarcerated. Increasingly, COs are being held civilly and criminally liable for their actions. In a number of incidents, COs have been fired following riots or inmate deaths. In 2007, three COs and their supervisor at the Grand Valley Institution for Women in Kitchener, Ontario, were charged with criminal negligence causing death in the suicide of a nineteen-year old inmate (see Chapter 6).

RELATIONSHIPS WITH THE PRISON ADMINISTRATION

> *In the view of the Union, the professional judgment and experience that correctional officers have developed as the frontline staff of our institutions is often given inadequate weight or consideration when decisions are made that radically affect their ability to do their jobs effectively. Invariably, this has been due to common misperceptions and stereotypes that cloud the reality of the work of this hidden profession. (Union of Canadian Correctional Officers 2007, 6)*

Research on the orientation and attitudes of COs (see above) has revealed that a key source of stress and alienation is the relationship between COs and the prison administration. COs may view administrators with a mixture of distrust and cynicism and may see them as being distant from the everyday realities of the prison. COs are especially critical of administrators who fail to provide clear and consistent operational policies. COs may view the administration as overly concerned with fiscal and administrative issues that have little relevance to line-level officers. In the words of one former CO: "There is a high wall between line screws and all corrections personnel . . . It becomes a situation of guards and cons against the system. The inmate code of silence and the guard culture are distorted mirror images of one another" (Yates 1993, 60). You will recall from Chapter 4 that the severely troubled relations between COs and senior administration were a major factor in the Headingley riot.

RELATIONSHIPS WITH TREATMENT STAFF

Many COs hold a rather dim view of treatment programs. Just over half of the federal COs surveyed in a Price-Waterhouse (1994) study felt that rehabilitation programs were a waste of money. The COs' view that few inmates have the ability, resources, and motivation to make significant changes in their attitudes and behaviours may limit the potential of COs to be effective change agents in the institution. In the present day, much of the impetus for a given inmate's participation in treatment programs comes from the plan prepared by the inmate's case management officer. Some support for this view is provided by a survey of federal inmates, which found that one in four inmates admitted they signed up for treatment programs only to please their case managers (Makin 1996, A5). There is also the perception that many inmates become involved in treatment programs primarily to improve their chances of release on parole, rather than for self-improvement. Officers may also be suspicious of positive statistics on recidivism generated by systems of correction, perceiving that such figures are used to justify expenditures on treatment programs.

Federal correctional officers at the CO2 level are involved in case management; however, the majority of provincial/territorial COs have little input into the case management process and indeed often find themselves at odds with case managers. This conflict is in part a consequence of the different roles that COs and case management officers play in the institution: the primary role of many COs is security, whereas case managers are charged with developing, implementing, and monitoring the offender's plan of treatment. For example, COs who charge offenders for violations of institutional rules may be asked or coerced by case managers to remove this information from the offender's file, if such information is seen as jeopardizing the plan for the inmate, such as transfer to a lower-security facility. Tension may result, as line-level security personnel may perceive that case managers are not fully aware of the inmate's conduct in the institution.

One CO remarked to C.T. Griffiths: "The inmates are on their best behaviour from nine to four during the week. It's after hours and on the weekends that we have to deal with disruptive behaviour. The treatment staff and case management officers don't see this." COs may assign more responsibility to inmates for their behaviour than do case management officers and other treatment staff. Case management officers may have few opportunities to interact with COs, who spend most of their time in the units or on the tiers.

SOURCES OF STRESS FOR CORRECTIONAL OFFICERS

As they carry out their tasks and responsibilities, COs can experience high levels of stress. Some common sources of this occupation stress are discussed below.

Threats to Personal Security

Concerns about personal security are a leading cause of stress among COs (Millson 2002). Many of them feel that institutional policies and procedures are not adequate to ensure their personal security. The threat of violence is a primary concern. There is some evidence that female correctional officers have higher levels of perception of danger in their work environment, though the perceptions of danger held by male and female COs vary across institutions. As one might expect, COs working in maximum-security institutions perceive higher levels of danger than officers working in minimum-security facilities (Garcia 2008). The slayings of two provincial COs in Quebec in 1997 highlighted the risks that COs face on the job (See Box 5.3). Statistics indicate, however, that there has been a steady decline in the rate of COs' injuries due to assaults by inmates in federal correctional facilities (the same for the rate of inmate injuries due to inmate assaults) (CSC 2007, 11).

Among the safety concerns of COs is the danger of exposure to inmates who are infected with HIV/AIDS, hepatitis, and tuberculosis. There is no mandatory testing of inmates for HIV/AIDS, and as a matter of policy, COs are not told which inmates are HIV-positive. This means that officers must be trained in universal precautions—in other words, they must be instructed to assume that every inmate with whom they have contact may be infected with a communicable disease.

Owing to safety concerns, COs in federal maximum-security institutions and multilevel institutions, as well as those assigned to segregation units in medium-security institutions, wear stab-resistant vests for protection. As well, all inmates on escorted temporary absences from maximum-security institutions or who have not had a risk assessment are accompanied by armed COs.

BOX 5.3

Death on the Job

In 1997 two Quebec correctional officers were killed by ambush while in the community. Diane Lavigne was killed in June while she was driving home from her job at Bordeaux jail, and Pierre Rondeau was ambushed in September while he was driving a bus to pick up prisoners from a provincial jail. The gangland-style attacks were carried out by a biker gang, the Nomads, who were affiliated with the Hell's Angels. Two members of the gang were subsequently charged and convicted of the slayings and sentenced to life imprisonment with no possibility of parole for twenty-five years.

The killings of the COs were part of an ongoing war between two Montreal biker gangs—Hells Angels and the Rock Machine—to control the illicit drug trade. The killings were likely intended to intimidate the authorities, who had mounted a crackdown on the gangs. Under pressure from the COs' union, the provincial government agreed to allow COs to carry arms and wear bulletproof vests while transporting prisoners.

Source: Fitterman and Gatehouse 1998. Reprinted by permission of the Montreal Gazette.

Lack of Support and Respect

There is a widespread feeling among COs that senior managers, the media, and the general public neither understand nor respect their profession. This view is reflected in the words of one officer: "We are asked to work in an environment that imposes a heavy personal toll on us, and we get no recognition for it. We do not feel valued by management, and we certainly are not valued by either the inmates or the general public. We're the only ones who understand the difficult environment" (Joint Committee on Federal Correctional Officers 2000, 54).

A related source of frustration for COs is the absence of communication with and support from management and the fact that policies are often developed without consultation from front-line workers. Research has found that uncertainty among officers as to their roles, lack of direction and guidance, and unreasonable expectations of senior management are significant stressors (Hogan et al. 2006). Note here that some studies have found the stress levels among correctional supervisors to be low (Owen 2006).

The Emphasis on Inmate Rights

Recall from Chapter 1 that a key trend in corrections has been an increasing focus on accountability, the rule of law, and the rights of inmates under the Canadian Charter of Rights and Freedoms. Many COs perceive that the new emphasis on inmate rights has come at the expense of their own rights. There is even the perception among some officers that it is the inmates who are running the institutions. In the words of one CO: "No two ways about it, we can do nothing to them now. Absolutely nothing. At one point, at least we had the threat of being able to lock them up and charge them, or some type of control. Now you tell them you are going to charge them—they laugh at you" (in Harris 2002, 49).

Multiple Tasks

The duties of federal COs may include not only patrolling, conducting searches, and intervening in inmate disturbances, but also issuing permits and passes, performing casework and reclassification, transferring and processing inmates, and answering the telephone. In short, in addition to the security requirements of the job, COs are called on to play the multiple roles of "nurse, psychologist, parole officer, administrator, police, criminologist, fireman, and teacher" (in Environics Research Group 2000, 7).

A source of considerable stress is the conflicting demands of casework and security. In the words of one CO at Kingston Penitentiary:

> *A difficulty is handling the two philosophies of corrections right now, which is security and rehabilitation. Having a caseload and security. The caseload . . . it's hard to be a guard and hug him in the morning and them mace him in the afternoon because he's been a bad person. Don't laugh, it happens. (ibid.)*

Inadequate Training

A common complaint among COs is that the duration and content of training is insufficient for the variety of tasks they are asked to perform. As a consequence, a considerable amount of learning occurs "on the job." A review of training for federal COs found that training needs and requirements have not kept pace with the increased knowledge and skills required of COs (Joint Committee on Federal Correctional Officers 2000, 84). Given the broad range of tasks that COs perform, however, it is likely that experience on the job will remain a key feature of the position.

The Impact on Personal Life

> *Early in our careers as line officers, we are admonished to "leave it at the gate." I've yet to meet a prison guard who can leave it at the gate successfully. We're told to find someone we can talk to, who will help us "offload" the stress. Then we're told that it's against the law to speak to a civilian (your spouse, your best friend) about an incident or a case. The guards we might like to speak to likely were there at our side during the very incident we need to offload. (Yates 1993, 313)*

Many COs find it difficult to separate their work life from their personal life. At the same time, many of them are unwilling or unable to talk about their work experiences with people outside the profession. In the words of one CO:

> *[The job] screws up your relationships. You limit the friends that you've got. How many people are you going to talk to about, other than a cop or an ambulance driver, what kind of mayhem you went through that day…it's indescribable. (in Environics Research Group 2000, 15)*

Shift Work

COs generally work rotating shifts. For federal officers, the most common schedule is twelve-hour shifts on a two-day, two-night, five-days-off rotation. Shift work often results in loss of sleep and a disruption of the circadian rhythm (or biological clock), which controls the body's sleep, wake, and arousal periods. Disruptions of the circadian rhythm result in a feeling similar to jet lag: fatigue, nausea, irritability, and loss of appetite. Shift workers may be more prone to poor performance, accidents, and health problems.

Shift work can also affect a CO's private life and make the management of family and other personal relationships more difficult. It may limit the opportunities for officers to interact with their children during nonschool hours and to participate in community activities. A survey of federal CO1s and CO2s found that over 70 percent of officers at each level felt that shift work had a negative or very negative impact on their family life. In addition, the level of job satisfaction was lower (and stress higher) among those who reported highly negative impacts of shift work on family relations (Grant 1995). A study of Ontario COs found that officers who switched from an eight-hour to a twelve-hour workday and compressed work week had higher levels of absenteeism than other officers (Venne 1997).

The Institutional Environment

There is some evidence that levels of stress among COs are related to the specific correctional environment in which the officer is working. Maximum-security institutions, as well as more "secure" medium-security facilities, may have more tension and a greater potential for violence both between inmates and directed toward officers. In one Canadian study, problems with coworkers were rated as a greater source of stress than inmate-related problems (Hughes and Zamble 1993). The potential for stress arising from interactions with coworkers may be heightened by generational differences among officers. A deputy warden in a federal prison complained that "there is no loyalty and commitment from many in the new generation of officers . . . . If they want Christmas off, they'll take it off, regardless of whether they are scheduled to work . . . It's a very me-focused bunch." This represents a significant change from past generations of officers. In Chapter 6 it will be seen that similar changes have occurred in the inmate population, with "new school" inmates heightening the pressure and unpredictability of prison life for inmates as well as COs.

Contributing to the stress experienced by COs are the conflicting expectations placed on them by the various groups in the institution:

> *Each of the officer's audiences within the prison demands something different: administrators look to officers to lead inmates rather than relate to them or otherwise deal with them in interpersonally skillful ways; inmates value interpersonal skills in officers, especially as these relate to problem-solving in everyday prison life, and are suspicious of efforts to lead them. (Johnson 1996, 206)*

The Impact of Critical Incidents

In the course of their careers, COs may be exposed to a wide variety of critical incidents, including disturbances and riots, hostage takings, inmate murder, inmate self-mutilation and suicide, threats to the officer's safety, and injury to the officer. These incidents may result in symptoms generally associated with **post-traumatic stress disorder (PTSD),** an extreme form of critical incident stress, the symptoms of which include nightmares, hypervigilance, intrusive thoughts, and other forms of psychological distress (Rosine 1995). In its most extreme forms, such as that found among veterans of combat, sufferers experience flashbacks during which they relive the trauma as if they were there.

A study of federal COs in Ontario found that during their career, the respondents had been exposed to an average of 27.9 critical incidents. Also, 60 percent of the officers had been injured at work, with a majority requiring leave time, and a number of the officers had experienced severe critical incident stress and had later been diagnosed as having PTSD. The most common symptoms experienced by officers were sleep disturbances, nightmares, and exaggerated startle response (i.e., hypervigilance). About 95 percent of the officers rated the impact of these symptoms on their personal life as severe. Significantly, only 40 percent of the officers sought professional assistance for their problems (Rosine 1992).

The results of this survey highlight the need for systems of correction to develop policies for critical incident stress management centred on **critical incident stress debriefing (CISD).** This technique involves on-scene debriefing of the CO by a trained intervenor after a critical incident has occurred; "defusing" by a mental health professional or trained peer, during which the symptoms of stress are identified and strategies for stress management are provided; a formal critical incident stress debriefing; and, if required, a follow-up critical incident stress debriefing. The main objective of CISD is to provide protection and support for the CO, while imparting information and strategies that will help the officer cope with any symptoms of critical incident stress that might later arise.

In addition, COs have access to federal or provincial/territorial employee assistance programs, which provide financial support and legal assistance as well as help with family- and work-related issues, substance abuse, and mental and physical health. The culture of COs may be a barrier to accessing these sources of assistance. Much like police officers, COs may view any disclosure of stress as "emotional weakness." This has led officers to deny that corrections work has any impact on their well-being (Fisher 2000).

Coping with Stress

Though COs experience a considerable amount of stress working in institutions, the evidence suggests that most officers have developed effective coping mechanisms and are generally satisfied with their occupation. In contrast to the stereotype of COs that has developed largely as a result of studies in the United States, a Canadian study found that officers did not drink to excess, spent a large portion of their off-duty time with their families, and did not limit their socializing to activities with other officers. A further reflection of the adequacy of the coping skills of most COs is that officers, as a group, report relatively the same alcohol consumption patterns as the general population (Holden et al. 1995; Hughes and Zamble 1993). For many officers, interpersonal relationships (having someone to speak to about problems on the job) are an important source of support in coping with the stresses of the job. For an in-depth discussion of programs and strategies for addressing CO stress, see Finn (2000).

FEMALE CORRECTIONAL OFFICERS

Historically, women were confined to clerical and noncustodial positions in correctional facilities. Considerable resistance was encountered as women were hired as COs. Women were (and often still are) perceived by male coworkers and supervisors as lacking the mental or physical toughness to survive the rigours of institutional life, to control inmates when required, and to back up male officers in crisis situations. In addition, male COs may believe that women are more prone to victimization and manipulation by the inmates (Lawrence and Mahan 1998). There is also the issue of the privacy of male inmates, particularly in relation to frisks and strip searches. In *Conway v. Canada* ([1993] 2 S.C.R. 872), however, the Supreme Court of Canada reaffirmed the right of women to be employed as COs in male institutions.

Research studies have found that the resistance and hostility of male officers tend to diminish as women demonstrate their abilities as COs. Furthermore, there is no evidence that female COs are assaulted more frequently or are more easily manipulated by inmates than their male counterparts. Research on the experiences of female COs in the United States has revealed that female officers have a positive impact on the management of inmates in maximum-security institutions, are less likely than their male counterparts to be assaulted by inmates, and are less confrontational and often more able to defuse potentially explosive situations (Rowan, 1996).

Sexual Harassment

Though systems of correction have made concerted efforts to recruit qualified female applicants, and though women are employed as COs in all types of institutions, problems remain. Several internal surveys conducted by the CSC have found a high incidence of sexual harassment, discrimination, and abuse of authority in many federal institutions. Over 50 percent of female employees in the Ontario and Prairie regions indicated that they had been subjected to harassment or abuse. In one federal institution, 62 percent of the female staff stated that they had been harassed by a coworker. At this particular institution, female COs were openly called "100-pound weaklings," along with more vulgar names. Female COs in Ontario cited instances in which threatening notes had been left on the windshields of their cars and in which they had been harassed and embarrassed by male coworkers in the presence of inmates. The report concluded that senior management was responsible for harassment being an integral part of the daily life in many institutions (in Canadian Press 1995; Price-Waterhouse, 1994). It is not clear how well the CSC has addressed the issues that were first documented more than a decade ago.

CROSS-GENDER STAFFING IN WOMEN'S INSTITUTIONS

The incidents at the Kingston Prison for Women in April 1994 (see Chapter 4), which involved an all-male Institutional Emergency Response Team extracting female inmates from their cells and stripping them of their clothing, rekindled the debate over male staff in women's correctional facilities. Men work at all levels in federal and provincial/territorial women's institutions, from senior management positions to the line level. In 1998 the CSC appointed a Cross-Gender Monitor to provide an independent review of the policy and operational impact of **cross-gender staffing** in federal women's correctional facilities. The final report of the project included the recommendation that male COs working in women's facilities not be permitted to carry out security functions in living and segregation units or serve as members of cell-extraction teams (Lajeunesse et al. 2000).

The issue of cross-gender staffing in women's correctional facilities is the focus of continuing debate. Share your thoughts on this topic in the "At Issue 5.1: Should Male Correctional Officers Work in Women's Institutions?"

AT ISSUE

ISSUE 5.1: Should male correctional officers work in women's prisons?

Proponents of cross-gender staffing offer a number of arguments in support of men working in women's institutions:

- The presence of male correctional officers help normalize daily institutional life.
- Male employees should be treated fairly and equally rather than excluded from job competitions, deployments, and other staffing procedures on the basis of gender.
- For female inmates who have never had a positive relationship with a respectful, nondiscriminatory male, there is rehabilitation and reintegration value in having men work in front-line positions.
- There is a divergence of opinion among female inmates as to whether men should be employed in women's facilities.

Opponents of cross-gender staffing make these points:

- The presence of male correctional officers and treatment staff has a negative impact on female inmates who have histories of abuse by men.
- The unique power imbalances in correctional officer-inmate relationships require measures that do not replicate standard employment practices.
- The presence of men as front-line correctional workers increases the risk for privacy violations and sexual misconduct.
- The high number of female inmates who have been abused by men in positions of authority requires that only women serve as front-line workers.

What do you think?

1. What is your position on cross-gender staffing in women's correctional facilities?
2. Which of the above arguments do you find most persuasive? Least persuasive?
3. If men are prohibited from being front-line workers in women's institutions, should the same restrictions apply to women working in male institutions? Why? Why not?

Source: Arbour 1996; Glube 2007; Lajeuesse et al. 2000.

KEY POINTS REVIEW

1. The authority of correctional officers is both legal and moral.
2. There have been changes in the demographic profile of correctional officer recruits in recent years, with more Aboriginal people and visible minorities being selected for training.
3. Among the challenges confronting new correctional officers is learning the subtle, nonverbal cues that will assist them in interacting with inmates and gaining the acceptance of their coworkers.

4. There is a normative code among correctional officers that guides their relationships with the inmates and with fellow officers.
5. Research studies have found that some correctional officers are more rule and enforcement oriented, while others rely on communication skills and common sense to solve problems.
6. Institutional setting, age and experience, and region of the country appear to influence the attitudes that correctional officers have toward inmates.
7. The features of daily life inside prisons create pressures for correctional officers and inmates to develop accommodative relationships.
8. Correctional officers have a high degree of discretion in carrying out their daily activities and in determining when and how they will enforce the rules and regulations of the institution, though officers exhibit different attitudinal and behavioural tendencies in carrying out their tasks.
9. A primary source of stress and alienation for correctional officers is the relationships between officers and the senior prison administration.
10. Correctional officers may hold a dim view of treatment programs, perceiving that many inmates lack the motivation and capacity to make significant changes in their lives.
11. Among the sources of stress for correctional officers are threats to their personal security, a perceived lack of support and respect from corrections officials and the general public, the impact of the job on their personal life, and critical incidents.
12. Female correctional officers often face unique challenges, including hostility from male officers and sexual harassment.

KEY TERM QUESTIONS

1. Describe the Correctional Service of Canada **Correctional Training Program.**
2. Describe the components of the Ontario provincial corrections **Staff Application, Recruitment, and Training (START)** program.
3. What is the **normative code of behaviour** of correctional officers, and what factors may mitigate against officer solidarity?
4. Compare and contrast the **custodial agenda** with the **correctional agenda** of correctional officers.
5. What is **post-traumatic stress disorder (PTSD)** and why is it a potential source of stress for correctional officers?

6. Describe **critical incident stress debriefing** (CISD) and its objectives.
7. Discuss the issues surrounding **cross-gender staffing** in women's institutions.

REFERENCES

Arbour, the Honourable L. (Commissioner). 1996. *Commission of Inquiry into Certain Events at the Prison for Women in Kingston.* Ottawa: Public Works and Government Services Canada. http://ww2.ps-sp.gc.ca/publications/corrections/pdf/199681_e.pdf

Bensimon, P. 2005a. *Correctional Officer Recruits During the Training Period: An Examination.* Ottawa: Correctional Service of Canada. http://www.cac.scc.gc.ca/text/rsrch/reports/r165/r165_e.pdf

———. 2005b. *Correctional Officers and Their First Year: An Empirical Investigation.* Ottawa: Correctional Service of Canada. http://www.csc-scc.gc.ca/text/rsrch/reports/r179/r179-eng.shtml

Canadian Press. 1995. "Female Guards Complain of Harassment." *Globe and Mail,* January 9, A4.

CSC (Correctional Service of Canada). 2007. *Departmental Performance Report.* Ottawa: Treasury Board of Canada Secretariat. http://www.tbs-sct.gc.ca/dpr-rmr/2006-2007/inst/pen/pen01-eng.asp

Environics Research Group. 2000. *Focus Group Report to the Joint Committee of the Public Service Alliance of Canada, Treasury Board, and Correctional Service of Canada on the Jobs and Working Environment of Federal Correctional Officers and RCMP Officers.* Ottawa: Public Service Alliance of Canada, Treasury Board, and the Correctional Service of Canada.

Farkas, M.A. 2000. "A Typology of Correctional Officers." *International Journal of Offender Therapy and Comparative Criminology* 44(4): 431–49.

———. 1997. "The Normative Code Among Correctional Officers: An Exploration of Components and Functions." *Journal of Crime and Justice* 20(1): 23–36.

Finn, P. 2000. *Addressing Correctional Officer Stress: Programs and Strategies.* Washington: Office of Justice Programs, U.S. Department of Justice. http://www.ncjrs.gov/pdffiles1/nij/183474.pdf

Fisher, P.M. 2000. *The Road Back to Wellness: Stress. Burnout & Trauma in Corrections.* Victoria: Spectrum.

Fitterman, L., and J. Gatehouse. 1998. "Biker Boss's Murder Trial Delayed: Another Hell's Angel-Turned-Witness Pleads Guilty in the Slaying of Prison Guard." *The Gazette* (Montreal), March 20, A5.

Garcia, R.M. 2008. *Individual and Institutional Demographic and Organizational Climate Correlates of Perceived Danger Among Federal Correctional Officers.* Washington: U.S. Department of Justice. http://www.ncjrs.gov/pdffiles1/nij/grants/222678.pdf

Gittens, M., and D. Cole (co-chairs). 1995. *Report of the Commission on Systemic Racism in the Ontario Criminal Justice System: A Community Summary.* Toronto: Queen's Printer for Ontario.

Glube, C. (chair). 2007. *Moving Forward with Women's Corrections.* Ottawa: Correctional Service of Canada. http://www.csc-scc.gc.ca/text/prgrm/fsw/wos29/wos29-eng.shtml

Grant, B. 1995. "The Impact of Working Rotating Shifts on the Family Life of Correctional Staff." *Forum on Corrections Research* 7(2): 40–42.

Grossi, E.L., and B.L. Berg. 1991. "Stress and Job Dissatisfaction Among Correctional Officers: An Unexpected Finding." *International Journal of Offender Therapy and Comparative Criminology* 35(1): 73–81.

Harris, M. 2002. *Con Game: The Truth About Canada's Prisons.* Toronto: McClelland & Stewart.

Hemmens, C., and M.K. Stohr. 2000. "The Two Faces of the Correctional Role: An Exploration of the Value of the Correctional Role Instrument." *International Journal of Offender Therapy and Comparative Criminology* 44(3): 326–49.

Hewitt, J.D., E.D. Poole, and R.M. Regoli. 1984. "Self-Reported and Observed Rule-Breaking in Prison: A Look at Disciplinary Response." *Justice Quarterly* 1(4): 437–47.

Hogan, N.L., E.G. Lambert, M. Jenkins, and S. Wambold. 2006. "Impact of Occupational Stressors on Correctional Staff Organizational Commitment: A Preliminary Study." *Journal of Contemporary Criminal Justice* 22(1): 44–62.

Holden, R.W., L.W. Swenson, G.K. Jarvis, R.L. Campbell, D.R. Lagace, and B.J. Backs. 1995. "A Survey of Drinking Behaviors of Canadian Correctional Officers." *Psychological Reports* 76: 651–55.

Hughes, G.V., and E. Zamble. 1993. "A Profile of Canadian Correctional Workers." *International Journal of Offender Therapy and Comparative Criminology* 37(2): 99–113.

Johnson, R. 1996. *Hard Time: Understanding and Reforming the Prison.* Belmont: Wadsworth.

Joint Committee on Federal Correctional Officers. 2000. *A Comparison of the Duties, Working Conditions, and Compensation Levels of Federal Correctional Officers, Uniformed RCMP Officers, and Selected Provincial Correctional Officers.* Ottawa: Public Service Alliance of Canada, Treasury Board Secretariat, and Correctional Service of Canada. http://dsp-psd.pwgsc.gc.ca/Collection/BT43-102-2000E.pdf

Jurik, N.C. 1985. "Individual and Organizational Determinants of Correctional Officer Attitudes Toward Inmates." *Criminology* 23(3): 523–39.

Kauffman, K. 1988. *Prison Officers and Their World.* Cambridge, MA: Harvard University Press.

Lajeunesse, T., C. Jefferson, J. Nuffield, and D. Majury. 2000. *The Cross Gender Monitoring Project: Third and Final Report.* Ottawa: Correctional Service of Canada. http://www.csc-scc.gc.ca/text/prgrm/fsw/gender3/cg-eng.shtml#P12_37

Lambert, E.G., N.L. Hogan, and S.M. Barton. 2002. "Satisfied Correctional Staff: A Review of the Literature on the Correlates of Correctional Staff Job Satisfaction." *Criminal Justice and Behavior* 29(2): 115–43.

Lambert, E.G., N.L. Hogan, and M.L. Griffin. 2008. "Being the Good Soldier: Organizational Citizenship Behavior and Commitment Among Correctional Staff." *Criminal Justice and Behavior* 35(1): 56–68.

Larivière, M. 2002. "Antecedents and Outcomes of Correctional Officers Attitudes Toward Federal Inmates: An Exploration of Person-Organization Fit." *Forum on Corrections Research* 14(1): 19–23.

Larivière, M., and D. Robinson. 1996. *Attitudes of Federal Correctional Officers Towards Offenders.* Ottawa: Research Division, Correctional Service of Canada.

Lawrence, R., and S. Mahan. 1998. "Women Corrections Officers in Men's Prisons: Acceptance and Perceived Job Performance." *Women & Criminal Justice* 9(3): 63–86.

Makin, K. 1996. "Inmates Fear Attacks. Drug Use Common." *Globe and Mail*, June 7, A1, A5.

Millson, W. 2002. "Predictors of Work Stress Among Correctional Officers." *Forum on Corrections Research* 14(1): 45–47.

Morgan, R.D., R.A. Van Haveren, and C.A. Pearson. 2002. "Correctional Officer Burnout: Further Analyses." *Criminal Justice and Behavior* 29(2): 144–60.

Owen, S.S. 2006. "Occupational Stress Among Correctional Supervisors." *Prison Journal* 86(2): 164–81.

Plecas, D.B., and P.S. Maxim. 1987. *CSC Correctional Officer Development Study: Recruit Survey.* Ottawa: Correctional Service of Canada. http://www.csc-scc.gc.ca/text/rsrch/reports/r102/r102-eng.shtml

Price-Waterhouse. 1994. *CSC All Staff Survey: Final Report.* Ottawa: Correctional Service of Canada.

Robinson, D., F.J. Porporino, and L. Simourd. 1992. *Staff Commitment in the Correctional Service of Canada.* Ottawa: Research and Statistics Branch, Correctional Service of Canada. http://www.csc-scc.gc.ca/text/rsrch/reports/r21/r21e-eng.shtml

Rosine, L. 1992. "Exposure to Critical Incidents: What Are the Effects on Canadian Correctional Officers?" *Forum on Corrections Research* 4(1): 31–37.

———. 1995. "Critical Incident Stress and Its Management in Corrections." In *Forensic Psychology—Policy and Practice in Corrections*, ed. T.A. Leis, L.L. Motiuk, and J.R.P. Ogloff. Ottawa: Correctional Service of Canada. 213–26.

Rowan, J.R. 1996. "Who Is Safer in Male Maximum Security Prisons?" *Corrections Today*, April 1. http://thefreelibrary.com/_/PrintArticle.aspx?id=18339824

Sampson, R. (chair). 2007. *Report of the Correctional Service of Canada Review Panel: A Roadmap to Strengthening Public Safety.* Ottawa: Minister of Public Works and Government Services Canada. http://www.publicsafety.gc.ca/csc-scc/cscrpreport-eng.pdf

Toch, H. 1978. "Is a 'Correctional Officer' by Any Other Name a 'Screw'?" *Criminal Justice Review* 3(2): 19–35.

Union of Canadian Correctional Officers. 2007. "*Rewards and Consequences: A Correctional Service for the 21st Century.*" *Brief to the Independent Review Panel studying the future of Correctional Service Canada.* Montreal. http://www.ucco-sacc.csn.qc.ca

———. 2002. *Towards a Policy for Canada's Penitentiaries: The Evolution of Canada's Prison System and the Transformation of the Correctional Officer's Role (1950–2002).* Montreal. http://www.ucco-sacc.csn.qc.ca

Venne, R.A. 1997. "The Impact of the Compressed Work Week on Absenteeism: The Case of Ontario Prison Guards on a Twelve Hour Shift." *Industrial Relations* 52(2): 382–400.

Whitehead, J.T., and C.A. Lindquist. 1989. "Determinants of Correctional Officers' Professional Orientation." *Justice Quarterly* 6(1): 69–87.

Yates, J.M. 1993. *Line Screw: My Twelve Riotous Years Working Behind Bars in Some of Canada's Toughest Jails.* Toronto: McClelland & Stewart.

WEBLINKS

Union of Canadian Correctional Officers–SACC

http://www.ucco-sacc.csn.qc.ca
Website of the Union of Canadian Correctional Officers, which represents federal correctional officers. The site offers position papers, research studies, and submissions of government inquiries.

CHAPTER 6

DOING TIME: THE INMATES

CHAPTER OBJECTIVES

After reading this chapter you should be able to:

- *Provide a general profile of inmate populations.*
- *Discuss the experience of inmates entering and living inside correctional institutions.*
- *Discuss the inmate social system, the key tenets of the inmate code, and the extent to which these are operative in correctional institutions.*
- *Describe how inmates attempt to cope with incarceration.*
- *Describe the challenges that confront offenders serving long-term sentences.*
- *Discuss the patterns of violence and exploitation among inmates and the strategies that inmates use to reduce their risk of being victimized.*
- *Describe the challenges that confront the inmate family and, in particular, inmate mothers and the issues surrounding inmate mother–child programs.*
- *Discuss the inmate grievance system and the work of provincial ombudspersons and the Office of the Correctional Investigator.*
- *Discuss the issues surrounding self-injurious behaviour and suicide among inmates in correctional institutions.*
- *Comment on the issues that arise relating to inmate rights in prison.*

KEY TERMS

Mortification
Status degradation ceremonies
Pains of imprisonment
Inmate subculture/inmate social system
Importation theory (of inmate social system)
Deprivation theory (of inmate social system)
Prisonization
Institutionalized
Inmate code
Niches (of inmates)
Social (or argot) roles
Mature coping
State-raised offenders
Expressive violence
Instrumental violence
Passive precautions (against violence)
Aggressive precautions (against violence)

PERSPECTIVE

Inmates

"A lot of people here blame the external world for their troubles: they're not big enough to accept the fact that they are responsible for their own situations. There's guys here that I can deal with on a one-to-one basis, guys that understand what I'm going through, guys that you can talk to, eh. And oh, there's people you can associate with and people you can't associate with, people you can trust, people you can't trust." (cited in Murphy and Johnsen, 1997:60)

"If I come out at fifty-six, as a thirty-one-year-old, after twenty-five years in prison, I'll be the same mental age as my children. How do you deal with that? Assuming that I make it through this sentence, if I'm fortunate enough to, and I pray that I am, I don't want to die any more than any other person, I like living just as much as anybody else and if I make it through, I still wouldn't see my children. I would make a point of not seeing them. It's far better for them to have me not interfere with their life in any way, shape, or form." (cited in Murphy and Johnsen 1997,79)

A GENERAL PROFILE OF INMATE POPULATIONS

Offenders confined in correctional institutions tend to be:

- *male:* Women comprise just under 10 percent of provincial/territorial inmate populations and about 4 percent of admissions to federal facilities.
- *young:* Most offenders fall into the 20–34 age range, though the average age of admission for Aboriginal offenders is lower than for non-Aboriginal offenders.
- *single parents:* About 60 percent of male offenders and nearly 70 percent of female offenders have children or stepchildren.
- *marginally skilled:* Inmates are more likely to have low levels of education and to be unemployed at the time of conviction.
- *disproportionately Aboriginal:* Aboriginal offenders comprise 18 percent of the federal inmate population and as high as 75 to 80 percent of provincial inmate populations, but only 3 percent of the general population.
- *disproportionately black:* Black men comprise 5 percent and black women 7 percent of federal institution populations. In Ontario the figures are 11 percent and 9 percent respectively.
- *convicted of a property offence:* That said, offenders convicted of violent crimes comprise a greater part of the populations in federal institutions. Also, Aboriginal offenders in federal prisons are more likely to be serving sentences for violent offences.
- *addicted.*
- *poor at solving problems.*
- *serving a short sentence:* More than half (55 percent) of all custodial sentences are for less than one month (Landry and Sinha 2008; Public Safety Canada Portfolio Corrections Statistics Committee 2007).

The treatment needs of inmates are significant: rates of alcohol and drug abuse are high, and at least 10 percent of inmates exhibit mental-health problems at the time of admission. Most inmates fall under the jurisdiction of provincial/territorial systems of correction, which tend to have fewer resources than the federal system. Also, the average time that provincial/territorial inmates spend in confinement (less than one month) makes it difficult to address their needs.

Some inmates require specialized facilities and interventions. Generally speaking, female offenders share with their male counterparts a marginalized background of poverty, alcohol and/or drug dependency, limited education, and minimal employment skills. In addition, female offenders may have suffered sexual and physical abuse and may be responsible for children or stepchildren.

Box 6.1 presents a composite profile of an Aboriginal woman serving time in a federal institution.

BOX 6.1

Profile of an Aboriginal Woman Serving Time in a Federal Correctional Institution

The Aboriginal female offender is generally twenty-seven years old with a grade nine education. She is also single, with two or three children. She has limited education and employment skills and is usually unemployed at the time of her crime. Contributing factors that may negatively affect the life of an Aboriginal woman include moving to an urban centre (isolation and loneliness); alcoholism and violence in the family home; lack of family support and supervision; lack of financial resources; and lack of opportunities to become involved in positive interactions with others.

Generally the Aboriginal offender experimented with drugs and alcohol at a young age. Often she came into conflict with the law as a youth; more recently, because of lack of intervention, she has continued into the adult system. She is likely to have left school at a young age to associate with friends who are streetwise. On the street, her abuse of drugs and alcohol continued to the point where she became a prostitute to continue her addiction. Under the influence of her associates and a negative lifestyle, she became more streetwise and committed more serious crimes such as robberies, assaults, or murder.

She may have left home because she experienced violence (whether she was abused or she witnessed abuse) and her home life became unbearable. Or she may have lived under very rigid conditions that she fled because she wanted to become independent. Or she may have been lured away by friends who were living a life of drugs, alcohol and partying. She may have worked the streets because she needed money to live on and did not have the education, skills, and training to get a job. She may have been subjected to racism, stereotyping, and discrimination because she was Aboriginal. Her experience on the streets became violent as she continued to experience sexual, emotional, and physical abuse. She probably became involved in an abusive relationship. There usually have been children born from this relationship, and the social, emotional, and economic struggle has continued. The cycle of an unhealthy family continues.

A high percentage of Aboriginal women who come into conflict with the law are convicted of crimes committed while under the influence of drugs and alcohol. These contributing factors are often related to their history of physical, psychological, and emotional abuse, and they have not dealt with the effects of this abuse. This harmful way of dealing with the past history of dysfunctional behaviour may continue unless these past abuses and effects are dealt with.

Source: Correctional Service Canada, 2000. "Profile of an Aboriginal Woman Serving Time in a Federal Correctional Institution. http://www.csc-scc.gc.ca/text/prgrm/abinit/know/5-eng.shtml

More and more inmates today are elderly, and this presents challenges for systems of correction. Chronic illnesses, disabilities, hearing and vision loss, incontinence, mental disorientation, and Alzheimer's disease require special attention and resources. In addition, older inmates (especially those serving their first prison term) may have difficulty adjusting to the prison regimen; it is they who account for the highest rates of suicide. As well, the treatment needs of this population may be different from those of younger inmates. Older inmates may require educational upgrading and vocational skills training if they are to succeed in the job market upon release. In response to these challenges, the Correctional Service of Canada (CSC) has created the Older Offenders Division, whose mandate is to develop policies and programs for this population of offenders.

Sex offenders are a high-profile offender group. They present unique challenges to corrections in terms of treatment programming and supervision in both institutional and community settings. Sex offenders are less likely to exhibit the marginal attributes of other inmates; at the same time, they have cognitive and behavioural difficulties that must be addressed. Also, correctional administrators may have to take steps to ensure that sex offenders are safe from other inmates.

Long-term offenders are defined as those inmates serving life terms, indeterminate sentences, or sentences of 10 years or more. These offenders have specific programming needs and place unique demands on correctional administrators.

GOING INSIDE

> *I remember the day that I came in; the first time I went to the cafeteria and I could feel a hundred sets of eyes on me. I could see everybody wondering who you are, what you're in for, how long you're doing. (lifer, in Murphy and Johnsen 1997, 41)*

On entering the prison, offenders undergo a process of **mortification,** during which they are transformed from free citizens into inmates (Goffman 1961, 18–20). This psychological and material stripping of the individual, which involves a series of **status degradation ceremonies,** includes the issuing of prison clothing, the assignment of an identification number, the loss of most personal possessions, and the end of unhindered communication with the outside community (Cloward 1969). These procedures are the mechanism by which the offender is moved from residency in the community, with its attendant freedoms, to the world of the prison, with its rules, regulations, informal economy, and social system.

Unfortunately, though systems of corrections have perfected the mechanisms for transforming citizens into inmates, there are no *status restoration ceremonies* at the end of the inmate's confinement that would function to convert the inmate back into a citizen. The consequences of this for the reentry and reintegration of offenders released from correctional institutions will be explored in Chapter 9.

The specific impact that entry into the prison has on the individual offender will vary, depending on a variety of factors, including his/her personality, offence history, and previous incarcerations. First-time offenders may experience severe cultural shock, whereas offenders with extensive criminal histories and previous confinements are likely to be relatively unaffected. For these inmates, the processes and procedures related to entry into the institution and confinement are well known, as are many of the correctional officers (COs) and inmates in the facility. Indeed, returning to the prison may be more of a homecoming than a banishment. For the uninitiated inmate, however, adjusting to the regimen of prison life can be stressful and frightening.

In Box 6.2 a former inmate, who served nearly 20 years inside youth and adult correctional institutions, describes entering Kingston Penitentiary for the first time at age 18.

BOX 6.2

A Young Inmate Enters the Prison

The judge said to me that I was a danger to the community and that I would be sentenced to three years in Kingston Penitentiary. I was transferred to the Don Jail (in Toronto) and placed on a range where people were going to the penitentiary. A lot of stories were told to me there about what happens to young kids going into the big house, because when I was a kid I was always told that, "Robert, some day you are going to the big house", and now it was becoming a reality. I was going to the big house, and I was very scared, especially after hearing all these stories, right? And the thing is, I was told that as long as you fight, you won't have a problem.

So I went to Kingston, and we got through the two clanging doors you have to go to to get into it off King Street. You go through the first door, and "Clang!" Then, you are waiting between the two doors to go into the prison. When I look back in retrospect, I feel that if I had been given a chance at that point to get out, to go back and maybe be in a home or something like that, then maybe I would not have to go through the rest of the life that I would go through. I was really scared at that time, but it seems like once you go through the second clanging door, you start to lose a lot of that fear and you turn that fear into hate and anger.

Source: Personal communication with author.

Though all incoming inmates are provided with copies of the institutional regulations and an orientation, each inmate is left to his or her own devices (and wits) to adjust to life inside and to develop strategies and techniques of coping and survival. Following is a portion of the advice given by one inmate to a second inmate who had just arrived at Millhaven, a federal correctional facility:

> *Drugs and alcohol are everywhere and I urge you to avoid that trip. Ninety percent of all killings revolve around the dope scene . . . Don't accept anything from anyone, because you don't want to put yourself in a position where you'll have to repay the favor. Nothing is free . . . It's in your best interest to avoid cliques. You'll be spending a lot of time on your own—it's much safer that way . . . Don't encourage conversation with anyone. Be brief and polite . . . Don't promise anyone anything . . . Stay quiet and mind your own business. (Dube 2002, 238–39)*

LIVING INSIDE

> *The cells are filthy. The walls are pocked with the carcasses of dead flies. During the day, the roaches visit, at night the mice. The door and door frames to the cells are solid steel, and every time they close, steel against steel, the sound is deafening. It seems as if there is a contest among the guards to determine who can make the doors bang loudest on closing. A constant reminder, if you need one, of where you are and the role you have to play. (inmate's description of life in the reception centre at Millhaven Institution, Ontario, in Ault 1997, A14)*

The Pains of Imprisonment

A key concept in understanding the carceral experience is the **pains of imprisonment.** In his classic study of a maximum-security prison, presented in the book *Society of Captives*, Gresham Sykes (1958) identified a number of deprivations experienced by inmates. These include the loss of liberty, of access to goods and services, and of access to heterosexual relationships, as well as the loss of personal autonomy and personal security.

Of all the pains of imprisonment, the loss of liberty is perhaps the most devastating for most offenders, especially in a society that places a high premium on the rights and freedoms of its citizens. In prison, inmates must find ways to cope with the loneliness, boredom, and hopelessness that are associated with the loss of freedom. Though federal and provincial/territorial systems of correction have family-visit programs, many inmates are not visited by anyone. An inmate may go for years without receiving a letter, much less a personal visit. The pains of imprisonment may be especially acute for Aboriginal and Inuit inmates, who are often incarcerated hundreds or even thousands of kilometres from their home communities.

It also appears that the pains of confinement may be much more severe for female offenders. This is for a number of reasons, including these: many federally sentenced women are housed in facilities that are far from home; many are mothers who have been separated from their children; and confinement can have a strong impact on women who have experienced physical and emotional abuse as children and/or adults. For insightful, first-person accounts of female offenders in prison, see Lamb (2004; 2007).

THE INMATE SOCIAL SYSTEM

A universal attribute of correctional institutions is the existence of an inmate social system, often referred to as the **inmate subculture.** For decades, criminologists have attempted to determine the origins, components, and functions of the inmate social system. These efforts have provided insights into prison life and the experience of incarceration.

From his study of life inside a maximum-security prison, Sykes (1958) concluded that the inmate social system developed as a result of inmates' attempts to mitigate the pains of imprisonment. Through participation in this social system, inmates could gain access to goods and services (albeit illicit), attain some measure of personal security and autonomy, and have access to consensual sexual relations. The social system also provided inmates with friendship networks, which helped reduce loneliness and boredom and created a sense of solidarity. By banding together, inmates could present a united front against COs and the administration. This view came to be known as the **deprivation theory** of inmate social systems.

Several years later, the criminologists John Irwin and Donald Cressey (1962) proposed an alternative explanation—the **importation theory**—for the origins of the inmate social system. They argued that rather than being a response to the pains of imprisonment, the attitudes and behaviours that characterized the inmate social system were imported into the institution by offenders who had criminal careers on the outside. Research studies have found that both theories are useful in understanding the origins of inmate social systems.

In the classic work *The Prison Community*, Donald Clemmer (1940) used the term **prisonization** to describe the process by which inmates become socialized into the norms, values, and culture of the prison. This process includes becoming immersed in the inmate social system and adopting the behavioural tenets of the inmate code. Prisonization is not a uniform process, however. Those inmates with extensive carceral experiences are likely to already have developed antisocial, criminally oriented attitudes and behaviours. These offenders have considerable difficulty adapting to a law-abiding life in the community once released from a correctional institution. Prisonization also appears to be a function of the degree to which the inmate feels powerless and the extent to which he or she relies on fellow inmates for information and support (Lawson, Segrin, and Ward 1996). Offenders are said to be **institutionalized** when they have become prisonized to such a degree that they are unable to function in the outside, free community.

Inmates without an extensive criminal history or record of confinement may be highly susceptible to becoming prisonized, depending on their personality, the level of support they receive from family and friends while confined, and the length of their incarceration. The longer an inmate is confined, the more difficult it may be to retain prosocial attitudes and behaviours, especially when the inmate is confined with offenders with more criminal orientations.

A major challenge confronting systems of correction is preventing offenders from becoming so immersed in the culture of the prison that staff's efforts to promote positive values and behaviours cannot succeed. There is also the challenge of how to "unprisonize" inmates as they move closer to their release date. This step would be part of a process of status restoration, which currently does not exist. Unfortunately, many of the attitudes and values that are embedded in the inmate social system are antithetical to those of the outside, law-abiding community.

The Inmate Code

A key component of the inmate social system is the **inmate code,** first identified by Sykes and Messinger (1960). The inmate code is a set of behavioural rules that govern interactions among the inmates and with institutional staff. Box 6.3 outlines the basic tenets of the code in its ideal form.

It appears that the inmate code as a behavioural guideline for inmates has changed significantly over the years. In a survey of inmates in several federal institutions, Cooley (1992) identified a set of informal rules of social control; these rules provided cohesion among inmates while also dividing them. The rule sets included the following:

- *Do your own time.* Don't rat on other inmates; stay out of other inmates' business.

BOX 6.3

The Inmate Code

1. Don't interfere with inmate interests:
   - never rat on a con
   - don't be nosy
   - be loyal to your class—the cons

2. Don't lose your head:
   - play it cool and do your own time

3. Don't exploit inmates:
   - don't break your word
   - don't steal from cons
   - don't sell favours
   - don't be a racketeer
   - don't welch on debts

4. Don't weaken:
   - don't whine
   - don't cop out (or cry guilty)
   - don't suck around
   - be tough; be a man

5. Don't be a sucker:
   - don't accept the guards' view of the world
   - be sharp

Source: Welch 1996, 150.

- *Avoid the prison economy.* Avoid debt, which can result in psychological intimidation and victimization.
- *Don't trust anyone.* Don't offer information—the less other inmates know about you, the less likely you are to be snitched on.
- *Show respect.* Don't be a "goof"—don't act out, interrupt, or cause disruptions.

However, unlike the traditional inmate code, which was purported to increase inmate solidarity and provide a united oppositional front against COs and the prison administration, each of these sets of informal rules can either increase cohesion among the inmates or separate and divide them. For example, the rule that inmates should do their own time and not interfere with other inmates encourages stability and cohesion among inmates; on the other hand, it can isolate inmates from one another, as individuals attempt to avoid becoming involved in activities that may place them at risk of being victimized.

From extensive correspondence with inmates in Canada and the United States, Thompson provides the following description of "do your own time":

> *It means keep yourself separate from everything and everybody. Don't comment, interfere, or accept favours. Understand that you are "fresh meat" and need to learn the way of the joint. You have to deal with the "Vikings" (slobs, applied to both guards and cons), "booty bandits" (someone looking for ass to fuck), and the "boss," "hook," "grey suit" or "cookie" (all terms for prisons officials of various ranks) without "jeffing" (sucking up) to the staff. You have to deal with other cons who want you as a "punk" or a "fuck boy." Anybody can be carrying a "shank" (home-made knife) made out of a toothbrush and a razor blade or a piece of sharpened steel. Probably the more innocent someone looks, the more you have to worry. (2002, 15–16)*

These informal rules of social control create institutional environments that are, in Cooley's words, "'partially unstable': the prison is neither in a constant state of turmoil nor in accord" (1992, 34). Contributing to the lack of loyalty and solidarity among inmates is the rat (or snitch) system, by which inmates may improve their own position and prospects with COs and the administration, often at the expense of fellow inmates.

The current state of the inmate code is that, while most inmates pay at least "lip service" to it, an inmate's greatest source of danger is other inmates. It can be anticipated that adherence to the inmate code may be more prevalent in high-security institutions, where inmates are likely to be prison veterans with more entrenched criminal attitudes and behaviours.

Note that the inmate writing in Box 6.4 makes a distinction between "convicts" and "inmates" (or "new school kids"), and perceives the latter as not respecting the traditional inmate social system. These observations were echoed by a deputy warden in a federal correctional facility: "These 'new school kids' think nothing of going into another inmate's cell in groups of four or five and punching out the inmate and taking his TV. That would never happen in the past, and it makes life in the institution much more unpredictable than in previous years."

Status and Power Among Inmates

The days when one inmate "boss" controlled an entire population in an institution are over. That said, there is still a hierarchy of status and power among

BOX 6.4

An Inmate's Lament

In *Cell Count*, a newsletter for Canadian inmates, one inmate lamented the demise of the "solid con":

> *I sit here in the shiftiest environment I've ever experienced in my life. I've seen friends stabbing friends, box thieves who claim they're "solid," rats, punks, and to top it all off, "new school" kids who have no respect for anyone or anything.*
>
> *From what I've seen thus far there's "cons" and then there's "inmates." Cons respect each other at every chance, cons don't "muscle" anyone, cons don't start problems, cons do their "own" time. New inmates on the other hand think respect is not earned but instead it's taken, cause problems for not only themselves but for everyone else around them, and give their "word" out like it's completely meaningless. WTF is up with this?*
>
> *I have to be one of the youngest cons in this pen and yet I know I have more respect in my little finger than most you'll see here. Even though I may be young I am still very "old school" and I'm also a "con."*
>
> *What I don't get is that we're all put here by the same people, we all have to live together, and we're all grown men. So what gives? What's with all the BS? What's with people thinking going to the pen is a status symbol?*
>
> *Why can't we all be cons fighting the system as one and not fighting each other? Cons are supposed to be united against "the man," cons respecting each other . . . at least that's how it's supposed to be. All I see now is "inmates," not "cons." Don't get me wrong, "cons" are still around, it's just that we've become an endangered species among the wave after wave of "new school" inmates that keep flooding into our home, onto our ranges and they're doing nothing but fucking-up our time!*
>
> *If I had one wish it would be for cons to reunite once again. Instead of fighting each other, let's fight for each other, let's fight united, let's fight the system!*
>
> *So pull up "inmates" because this isn't a joyride or another notch to add to your belt. It's time to start fighting as one, it's time for respect. Stop making*

(continued)

our time harder than it has to be because "the man" already does that for us. It's time to pull up and unite once again as "cons"!

A Fellow "Con"

Source: http://www.pasan.org/Cell-Count/Issue_48.pdf. © David Timothy Jackson

inmates. Some of them wield considerable influence in the prison. High status is generally accorded to inmates who are serving life sentences, who are intelligent and are able to articulate the concerns and issues of the inmate population, and whose pre-prison status and activities are well known and admired. Other inmates exercise power based on gang affiliation, their ability to control illicit goods and services within the institution (including drugs and gambling), and their sheer physical strength (Faulkner and Faulkner 1997).

Then there are other inmates who, because of their personality, offence, or physical weakness, have little or no power and influence. Inmates confined for sexual offences, especially against children, have low status in most institutional populations and may be subject to victimization.

A defining feature of life in contemporary correctional institutions is that inmates tend to group themselves into **niches,** or friendship networks. These networks may be based on associations formed during previous incarcerations or in the outside community; on shared ethnicity or culture; or on length of sentence (e.g., lifers may group together). It is this friendship group, rather than the inmate population as a whole, that provides the individual inmate with security and support and that is the recipient of the inmate's loyalty. These groups create an inmate population that is characterized by pluralism rather than by uniformity of thought and action.

Inmate Social Roles

A number of **social** (or **argot**) **roles** are associated with the inmate social system. These roles are based on the inmate's friendship networks, sentence length, current and previous offences, degree of at least verbal support for the inmate code, and participation in illegal activities such as gambling and drug distribution. Though the specific names may vary, several of the more common roles include the following:

- *Square-john.* Exhibits prosocial attitudes and behaviours; not involved in the inmate social system; positive toward staff and administration.
- *Right guy.* Antisocial; heavily involved in the inmate social system; opposed to staff and administration.

- *Rat* (also known as *squealer* or *snitch*). Provides information on inmates, illegal activities, and plans to COs; despised by inmates; at high risk of physical injury if detected; may be placed in protective custody for safety.
- *Tough* (also known as *outlaw*). Violent, aggressive, and often unpredictable; is willing to use violence to intimidate and secure goods and services; often feared by both inmates and COs; disruptive to the daily routine of the institution and to the accommodative relationships that exist between COs and inmates.
- *Wolf*, *fag*, and *punk*. Sexual roles in the prison. The wolf actively seeks out other inmates to have sexual relations with; the fag voluntarily assumes a passive role in sexual relations; and the punk is coerced or bribed into a passive role in sexual encounters.
- *Merchant* (also known as *peddler*). Extensively involved in importing and distributing contraband, including drugs and money; prospers at the expense of other inmates (Welch 1996, 150).

That these types of roles exist among inmate populations provides strong evidence that the inmate code is not the defining feature of inmate behaviour. In fact, inmate relations are characterized by considerable intimidation, fear, violence, and manipulation, depending on the particular correctional institution and the offenders housed in it.

A related feature of inmate society is a specialized vocabulary. Examples of prison slang—a constantly changing vocabulary—are provided in Box 6.5.

BOX 6.5

The Inmate Vocabulary

Term	Meaning
beef	type of crime (e.g., murder beef, sex beef)
bit	sentence (e.g., five-year bit)
book	life sentence (e.g., doing book)
bug juice	any drug used to calm an inmate
bugs	inmates others see as annoying or crazy
date	sentence warrant expiry date

(continued)

deuce less	sentence of less than two years
fish	new inmate
goof	inmate who acts inappropriately (i.e. whistles)
hole	segregation unit (generally 23-hour lockup)
house	prison cell
kite	illegal letter or note
piped	hit on the head with a metal pipe
rats	informers
shakedown	the searching of an area within the prison
shank	homemade knife
short	inmate who is close to release
skinner	sex offender
waterhead	see *goof*
yard	recreation area

Interestingly, this vocabulary may be shared by COs in the prison.

Source: Murphy and Johnsen 1997, xvii–xix; National Parole Board n.d.

Parting Thoughts on the Inmate Social System

The early research on inmate social systems provided invaluable insights into the dynamics of life inside correctional institutions. The question is to what extent the findings from these studies apply to the modern prison and, more specifically, to Canadian correctional institutions. Though the absence of Canadian research limits our ability to answer this question conclusively, it is possible to update the discussion on inmate social systems by piecing together the findings of Canadian and American studies. Unfortunately, the lack of research on life inside correctional institutions for women makes it difficult to include more than passing comment on this important area of Canadian corrections.

Though contemporary prisons share many features of their earlier counterparts and are total institutions, in many respects the contemporary prison is less "total" than its predecessors. Increasingly, prison administrators and correctional staff are being held accountable to the rule of law, and inmates have recourse through grievance procedures and the courts for perceived injustices. The living conditions of inmates have improved dramatically. New regional facilities have been constructed for federal female offenders; facilities incorporating elements of Aboriginal culture and spirituality have been established for Aboriginal offenders; and in several minimum- and medium-security facilities, new architectural designs allow inmates to live in apartment-like residences.

It is likely that inmate social systems are the most highly developed in federal correctional facilities, which house offenders with more extensive criminal records for longer periods of time. The relatively rapid turnover of inmates in provincial/territorial institutions would seem to mitigate against the development of an inmate social system. On the other hand, many provincial/territorial inmates have been incarcerated on previous occasions and may be well schooled in the various facets of doing time. To date, there have been no studies of inmate social systems in provincial/territorial facilities. While it can be assumed that some type of social system exists among the inmates, the specific forms these systems take, the extent to which there is an inmate code, and whether social roles exist have yet to be determined.

Despite the improvement in correctional institutions, incarceration is still a painful experience. The pains of imprisonment ensure that the inmate social system will remain a key feature of institutional life. That said, it is important not to mythologize "the good old days" in prisons. It is unlikely that inmates ever constituted a united front against the guards and administration. Certainly, institutional life during these times was not free from violence and exploitation among inmates, and not all inmates had equal power and status.

COPING WITH CONFINEMENT

While incarcerated, inmates spend considerable energy attempting to reduce the pains of imprisonment. Inmates often become involved in obtaining, distributing, and/or using illicit goods and services, including drugs and other contraband. Consensual sexual relationships may also be entered into. Participation in the underground economy, however, is not without risk. Inmates who incur gambling debts, for example, may risk being physically harmed or may be pressured to have family members smuggle drugs and contraband into the prison. To protect themselves, these inmates may have to request placement in a protective-custody unit, where their freedom of movement within the institution and access to programs are severely curtailed.

Drugs and Contraband

> *Illicit drugs and alcohol are the central driving force in the lives of inmates: they not only supply ways of escaping the deadening routine of doing time but also confer currency, collateral, and power on their dealers. Just as on the street, substance abuse in prison leads to violence and further crime. (Harris 2002, 185)*

In most federal and provincial/territorial correctional facilities, drugs are as freely available as they are on the street. Inmates use drugs or alcohol to cope with their environment, forget their problems, or just to relax. Many offenders become addicted to drugs while in confinement (Chubaty 2002; Plourde 2002).

The smuggling networks are extensive and sophisticated. Organized gangs play a major role in the importing and distributing of drugs, especially in federal institutions. Drug distribution and use are commonly associated with intimidation, extortion, and staff corruption. The warden of a federal correctional institution in Ontario observed that "80 percent of the drugs come in the front door and 20 percent through the back door" (Harris 2002, 67–68). Moreover, both violence and victimization among inmates are often the result of nonpayment for illicit drugs. This presents a risk to the safety and security of inmates and staff. Of particular concern is "homebrew," a concoction made by inmates with ingredients (bread, fruit, or vegetables) stolen from the kitchen or dining hall. Most illicit drugs in prison have the effect of "downing out" inmates; by contrast, homebrew consumption can precipitate violence.

The problem of illicit drugs and contraband inside prisons might be surprising at first glance, given the strict regimen of correctional institutions, the various static and dynamic security arrangements, and drug interdiction strategies. The latter include metal detectors, ion scanners, nonintrusive searches of all visitors, drug-sniffing dogs, cell searches and physical searches of inmates, and, at the federal level, a national random-urinalysis program that tests the urine samples of 5 percent of the inmate population each month. In reality, however, it is virtually impossible for correctional staff to adequately monitor or eliminate the flow of drugs and contraband. There is extensive contact between inmates and outside visitors; offenders leave institutions on temporary absences and day parole; and inmate labour is used in a variety of noninstitutional settings, including community service, forestry work, and firefighting.

Alcohol is generally brewed on the premises. Illicit drugs flow into prison through several channels, including these: (1) family members (including children and infants, who are not searched on entry into the prison) and friends on visiting days; (2) inmate work crews deployed outside the institution; and (3) drop-offs on prison property by family members or friends. The most common way that drugs are moved into institutions is through rectal or vaginal insertions.

In Box 6.6 a CO in a correctional facility in Manitoba describes how drugs were moved into the prison, transferred to an inmate, and taken into the living unit. In this particular case, a family member had placed the contraband in a condom and inserted it into a body cavity on visiting day and then removed it in the washroom in the visitors' area. The description picks up at that point.

BOX 6.6

Condoms, Coke Machines, and Contraband

One of the tricks they used—we have a Coke machine in there, did at that time, a pop machine. A girl would go up and buy a drink. She would put the money in and she would deposit the drugs in the little opening where the pop would come out. She'd put the condom of drugs in there. She'd buy a drink, take the drink, and leave. The person who was now going to get the drugs, it's usually a kid, first timer, we'd never suspect he was a drug carrier. He would go and buy a drink, along with the condom of drugs and he'd take them back to the location. He would do that for fear of being badly beaten if he didn't agree to it . . .

The only people really chosen at random for a strip search at the end of visiting are known drug users, guys who are really bad characters, guys who are giving staff a lot of problems. We would strip-search them. A young kid, that's the first time into the building, that's the guy the inmates would get to carry their drugs back, because we wouldn't suspect him . . . He would insert the drugs in his rectum. Quite often we'd search and we'd find the rear of their pants would be sliced and their underwear would be sliced and they would be sitting right at the table. As rude and crude as that sounds, that's the culture we're dealing with. And this may be a well-educated, blond-hair, blue-eyed kid. But he was going to do it or he was going to get a terrible licking when he got back to his range. So, he took the risk and did it.

Source: Hughes 1996, 49. Reprinted by permission of Manitoba Justice.

Sexual Gratification

Inmates also attempt to cope with the deprivation of heterosexual relationships and to secure sexual gratification. Masturbation and consensual sexual relations with another inmate are the two most common types of sexual activity in correctional institutions. Consensual sex, while technically homosexual, is an adaptation to a unique circumstance; inmates revert to heterosexual sexual activity when they return to the community. The extent to which prison authorities should tolerate sexual relations between inmates is a topic of ongoing discussion. Contribute your thoughts to the "At Issue 6.1: Should there be limits on sexual relationships in prison?" presented at the end of the chapter.

Little is known about how gay inmates adapt to confinement and how their attempts at sexual gratification are viewed and responded to by heterosexual inmates. A less common means of sexual release, which is also a manifestation of power and control in the inmate social system, is the rape of an inmate (see page 226).

Humour

Another way that inmates cope with the deprivations of confinement is through humour, an underresearched feature of doing time. Inmates often relate to fellow inmates sad tales about their experience with the justice system, especially the sentence they received, in a humorous way. Inmates also often mock the rules and regimen of the prison in subtle and not so subtle ways. Following is a researcher's description of "insubordinate farting" by inmates in a jail:

> *A standing rule exists stating all inmates must be silent until count is cleared. Violation of this requirement can result in a loss of privileges for all inmates, regardless of who breaks the rule. During count the men sit or lie on their three-tier high bunks in silence while a guard walks up and down the dorm counting the bodies on the beds. With an expression that can be seen as nothing less than defiance, inmates will, once the guard has passed their bed area and is a safe enough distance away to insure their anonymity, fart loudly. The resulting laughter obviously mocks the guard. It also, in a safe way, attacks the system, or, in this case, the people responsible for creating the rule that all must be silent during count. It also allows the inmates to break the rules and reaffirm, at least for themselves, their own power. (Terry 1997, 32)*

Mature Coping

Though there are many opportunities to participate in illegal activities during their confinement, inmates may choose to mitigate the pains of imprisonment through more constructive means. **Mature coping** is a positive approach to adapting to life inside. There are three components to mature coping that inmates must learn: (1) dealing with problems in a straightforward way rather than engaging in denial and manipulation; (2) avoiding the use of deception and violence in addressing problems; and, (3) making an effort to care for oneself and others—being altruistic (Johnson 1996). Inmates engage in mature coping when they take a proactive approach toward problems, plan specific courses of action, and abstain from reacting to events until carefully considering the nature of the problem. Through positive coping actions, inmates develop self-esteem and maturity, learn to manage failure, and use the incarceration experience for positive growth. Positive coping, in turn, increases the likelihood that the inmate will benefit from participation in rehabilitation programs and succeed on release from the institution.

There are obstacles to the practice of mature coping. First, the ability of individual inmates to fulfill the behavioural requirements of mature coping may be seriously affected by the regimen and dynamics of prison life. In many respects, the features of the prison as a total institution are antithetical to inmates taking responsibility for their actions and exercising independent judgment. Inmates who lack power and status in the inmate social system are hardly in a position to be altruistic, lest they become even more vulnerable to victimization.

Second, it is difficult to predict how individual offenders will respond to confinement and how the various dynamics of life inside correctional institutions will interact with personal attributes of the inmate to determine the strategies he or she adopts to survive the carceral experience. Needless to say, if inmates are required to expend considerable energy on developing strategies to ensure their safety and security in the prison and to cope with the pains of imprisonment, their receptiveness to programs designed to promote prosocial values and behaviours may be limited.

Finally, there are the abilities of individual inmates. As noted in Chapter 1, many people confined in correctional institutions are marginal in terms of background, skill level, and offence history. A history of substance abuse, exposure to physical and emotional abuse as children, mental illness, and a long history of confinement in youth and adult facilities may diminish the inmate's ability to adopt mature coping as a response to incarceration and to benefit from treatment intervention. For self-change to occur, an inmate must not only be committed to altering attitudes, values, and behaviours, but also have the capacity to pursue such a course of action (more on this in Chapter 7).

DOING LIFE

> *Picture yourself falling into a tunnel, totally dark, and it's going to take you twenty-five years to walk out . . . one step at a time. (lifer, in Murphy and Johnsen 1997, 43)*

As noted in Chapter 1, Canada abolished the death penalty in 1976 and replaced it with mandatory penalties of long-term confinement. Concerns have been raised about the morality and effectiveness of long-term sentences and how to prepare long-term offenders for their eventual reentry back into the community.

Coping with Long-Term Confinement

An offender serving life offered the following observation:

> *I've been in for two and a half years, just about going on three years. Seems like forever already. It's hard to remember what it's like out there. So many things can happen in three years. It's a terrible transition period; it's a*

> *terrible thing to go through. Especially when you don't see a light at the end of the tunnel anywhere. You're just stuck here and you're herded into your cell every few hours for a count. You feel like cattle. You get a feeling like you're helpless. Herd you in, lock the door. They count you like diamonds and treat you like shit. (Murphy and Johnsen 1997, 30)*

Long-term sentences present challenges not only for systems of correction in terms of housing and programming, but also for the individual inmate. How lifers cope with confinement and their views on doing long sentences are important, because one day nearly all will be released back into the community. The CSC operates a program called Life Line In-Reach, which is designed to help lifers (a) effectively manage their time and their program opportunities during confinement and (b) prepare for judicial review and/or release on parole.

Though they are all serving long sentences, there are considerable differences among long-term offenders in terms of their attitudes and how they adjust to confinement. These differences are reflected in a survey of long-term offenders, which found that first-term lifers are at greater risk of being victimized during the early years of their confinement, rather than later; and that life-sentence offenders are at a high risk of suicide and homicide (Porporino 1991).

After losing freedom, the loss of relationships and contact with family, friends, and children is perhaps the most serious pain of imprisonment for the long-term offender. Some inmates cope with this deprivation by severing all ties with family members, while others try to maintain contact, which may, inadvertently, add to their frustration and anxiety. Realistically, it is highly unlikely that most long-term offenders will be able to sustain their pre-prison relationships, especially if relations with a spouse and/or children were unstable.

The loss of family is a catalyst for the bonds that develop among inmates doing life. In the words of one lifer: "Once you get over the initial hurdle of being separated from your family . . . the lifers become your comrades. They become the guys you really become close to. I've got twenty years in, so I really don't feel that close to the short-timers that are coming in, because they're just like shadows" (Murphy and Johnsen 1997, 197).

The Impact of Long-Term Confinement

Despite these pains of imprisonment, there is no empirical evidence that long-term confinement leads to mental and physical deterioration in inmates or to impaired coping abilities. More specifically, the duration of confinement is unrelated to changes in attitude or personality among inmates, to feelings of bitterness and demoralization, or to a loss of perceptual-motor or cognitive functioning. It seems that over time, most inmates adapt to confinement by becoming involved in work, sports, and other activities. These findings, while not conclusive (many of the studies did not consider the age of the inmate or prior prison experiences), are nevertheless quite surprising, given the many negative features of life inside correctional institutions (Paulus and Dzindolet 1992; Zamble and Porporino 1988).

An offender who had served fifteen years in confinement at the time he was interviewed offered the following observations:

> *How has my thinking changed in prison? Well, I think it's more or less just aging. I've aged and that's made a lot of changes on how I see things. Because perception changes with age and in little stages it hits you that it's changed. I don't know that I'd do too many things differently. I don't think my lifestyle would change a whole lot, other than I wouldn't be trafficking in drugs, simply because I would get in a lot of trouble. And I'm going to have a lot of heat, so that's more or less deleted from my repertoire, right? Some of my tastes have changed. I'm now a writer. I don't think I'm going to go roofing again. But it's not the work part that bothers me. It's just the change of interest, basically . . . Not living in today, period, with no idea that there's a tomorrow at all. That's changed. (Murphy, Johnsen, and Murphy 2002, 41)*

Note well, however, that though long-term confinement may not produce the predicted negative impacts on inmates, neither does it promote positive changes. Though most inmates seem to ultimately adjust to life in prison, this may make it more difficult for them to survive in the outside, free community on release.

PRISON AS "HOME": THE STATE-RAISED OFFENDER

> *Those who happen not to be in prison at the moment tend to think of themselves as free. Those who were locked behind bars early in their lives and have become "institutionalized" feel free only when in jail. These people have no talent or disposition for filing tax returns, remembering Aunt Flossie's birthday, obeying the speed limit, or attending the P.T.A. Being told by people like me when to rise, when to eat, when to change their clothes, suits them just fine. Just as it's hard for people on the outside to understand how anyone can love being in prison, the "institutionalized" cannot understand how anyone can love mowing the lawn, joining the Rotary Club, or running for office. (former correctional officer, in Yates 1993, 313)*

There are offenders who have spent most of their youth and adult lives confined in correctional institutions. These **state-raised offenders** have experienced only limited periods of freedom in the community and may have neither the social skills nor the ability to function outside the total institutional world of the prison. Many have become institutionalized and are frightened at the prospect of having to cope with the fast pace of modern life. For the state-raised offender, the prison provides security, friends, room and board, and a predictable routine, none of which is guaranteed in the outside community. The prison, not the community, is their home. State-raised offenders present challenges to systems of corrections, especially when these offenders reenter the community.

VIOLENCE AND EXPLOITATION AMONG INMATES

Male inmates in Canadian federal institutions have a higher likelihood of being murdered than males in the outside, free community. This risk, along with violence in institutions generally, has increased in recent years. Toughness is a central feature of inmate identity, and inmates may use extreme violence for self-protection, to achieve and maintain power and status, and to retaliate against snitches. Though COs are sometimes the source of brutality inflicted on inmates, other inmates present the greatest danger to inmates' safety. Not all inmates, however, are at equal risk of being victimized. The degree to which an inmate is vulnerable to attack and exploitation by other inmates depends in large measure on his or her status, power, and friendship network. Weak and vulnerable inmates may be coerced to provide sexual services, to pay money or goods for protection, to repay loans or favours at high interest, or to persuade family members to bring drugs into the institution.

For inmates in many correctional institutions, the potential for violence and exploitation is a fact of daily life. In contrast to the physical aggression that characterizes life inside institutions for male offenders, in women's facilities such aggression appears to be more indirect and to take the form of verbal bullying, threats, ostracism, intimidation, and gossip (Ireland and Archer 1996).

Violence between inmates in institutions can be categorized as **expressive violence** or **instrumental violence.** Expressive violence is neither planned by the perpetrator nor deliberate. Rather, it is a result of specific problems that the inmate-initiator is experiencing (including stress), problems in adjusting to life in the institution, and difficulties in anger management. Instrumental violence, on the other hand, is used by the perpetrator as a means to an end. The motive of the aggressor is to gain or maintain status or to intimidate other inmates in order to secure illicit goods and services (Leschied, Cunningham, and Mazaheri 1997).

The level of violence in individual correctional institutions is a function of many factors, including conditions in the institution, the actions of COs and administrators, overcrowding, and competition among inmate gangs for turf. Violence can erupt over what, in the outside community, would be a nonissue. Situations that would be insignificant in the outside, free community often precipitate violence inside the prison. An inmate in the Don Jail recalled watching one inmate beat another inmate to within an inch of his life over who owned a slice of toast. Prescriptions for avoiding violence include never looking at—let alone touching—other people's possessions, never whistling, never reaching over anybody's food, and never talking too much. Even making eye contact with another inmate can be dangerous, as it may signal either a sexual advance or a challenge to the power and status of an inmate (Shephard 1997, F1).

Many inmates live in constant fear for their safety. Among the more fearful are young inmates and those who do not have strong friendship networks. Given the patterns of violence in prison, this fear is most likely justified. Issues related to inmate safety have come to the attention of the courts. In 2004 the Supreme Court of Canada acquitted a former inmate on a charge of possessing a dangerous weapon. Jason Kerr had stabbed another inmate to death with a homemade knife. The court ruled that Kerr had the knife for self-defence after having been threatened with harm by the victim and that possession of the weapon did not endanger the public (*R v. Kerr*, 2004 SCC 44). This decision was strongly criticized by the federal Union of Canadian Correctional Officers as one that would encourage the proliferation of weapons inside prisons (Union of Canadian Correctional Officers 2007).

It is difficult to determine the actual incidence and patterns of prison victimization. In comparing inmate-reported victimization with official data, researchers have found that the actual rates of assaults and of inmate victimization are several times higher than indicated by official data (Cooley 1992).

One survey of Canadian inmates found that most of those surveyed had no personal experiences with victimization, while one-third had been threatened with assault, one-fifth had been assaulted, and a small group had been repeatedly threatened or physically assaulted (Chubaty 2002). In actuality, it is a relatively small percentage of any inmate population that is a threat to others.

Sexual Coercion and Rape

Sexual coercion and rape are two brutal realities of prison life, yet there is very little information on the perpetrators and victims of this type of violence or on its prevalence in Canadian institutions. The reluctance of inmate victims to report victimization, combined with the assumption by many correctional observers that most inmate sexual activity is consensual, has hindered an understanding of this very important area of institutional corrections

Federal correctional officer in Quebec shows a display of homemade weapons seized from inmates.
CP PHOTO/Paul Chiasson

(Jones and Pratt 2008). More attention has been given to this topic in the United States (visit, for example, the website of Stop Prisoner Rape at http://www.spr.org). A survey of federal and state inmates in the United States found that 4.5 percent reported having experienced some form of sexual violence, ranging from unwanted touching to nonconsensual sex (Kaufman 2008). Younger inmates and inmates who are intellectually impaired or mentally ill may be at greater risk of victimization (Austin et al. 2006).

Perpetrators use a variety of tactics in cases of sexual coercion, including inflicting physical harm or threatening violence, intimidating the target with physical size and strength, and applying persuasion. An inmate may succeed in taking another inmate as his "punk"—an exploitative relationship that nevertheless provides a measure of security and protection for the weaker inmate. Depending on the circumstances of the incident, such as whether there are multiple perpetrators, the target can often prevent the attack by avoiding the perpetrators, consistently refusing, using defensive threats, or fighting:

> *He was always winking, blowing kisses and always trying to talk me into letting him give me a blow job. Until one day when he grabbed ahold of my penis and said I want you. Up until then I let it ride but after dinner that night I caught him by the tennis court where no guards could be and I*

smiled and said so you want me and when he said yes I plant my foot upside his jaw and left him laying on the ground and that put an end to it. (in Struckman-Johnson et al., 1996:73)

Such tactics of resistance, however, may not work if the target inmate is vulnerable to attack, for example, because of physical weakness or lack of a protective friendship group. There are, however, a number of factors that mitigate against inmates sexually assaulting even weaker inmates in the prison, including being investigated by prison authorities, the threat of disciplinary sanctions, and potential criminal and civil charges. As well, American studies have found that prison rapists are viewed by inmates as undermining order in the prison (Austin et al. 2006).

Inmate Strategies for Avoiding Violence and Victimization

Because institutional staff cannot guarantee an inmate's safety, inmates use a variety of strategies or avoidance behaviours to reduce the risk of violence and victimization. These strategies can be grouped into **passive precautions** and **aggressive precautions.** Passive precautions, which tend to be used by older, socially isolated inmates who are serving longer periods of confinement and who have been victimized in the past, include keeping to oneself; avoiding certain areas of the institution where there is a high risk of attack, such as the dining hall, recreation areas, and the yard; and spending more time in one's cell. Aggressive precautions tend to be adopted by younger inmates and include developing a tough attitude, lifting weights, and keeping a weapon (McCorkle 1992a, 1992b).

INMATES AS PARTNERS AND PARENTS

Discussions of corrections often overlook the fact that many inmates are fathers, mothers, and spouses. Little attention has been given to the dynamics and needs of the inmate family, both during the inmate's confinement and following release. This is somewhat surprising, given that nearly half of offenders in confinement are married at the time of admission and that most have children or stepchildren. Furthermore, inmate mothers are likely to be the sole caregiver for their children.

Systems of correction have generally not been designed to consider the needs of inmate families, and family members may feel isolated and neglected by correctional authorities. Other concerns relate to finances, housing, isolation from the community, and fears related to the offender's return to the community (Carr 1995). Children whose parents are incarcerated can suffer from emotional, behavioural, and academic problems, the type and severity of which vary with the child's age, gender, and length of separation from parents (Caddle and Crisp 1997; Gabel 1995). The symptoms can mirror those evidenced by children who have experienced the death of a parent. The children of inmates may also feel responsible for their parents' incarceration, be embarrassed among their peers, and worry that they may be sent to prison one day.

For the inmate, the loss of regular family contact is one of the pains of imprisonment. An offender incarcerated for a white-collar crime describes this difficulty:

> *I was fortunate to have a strong family and loving wife that stayed with me. I also have a good education and the belief in myself that I have a future. My situation was unique. I constantly received mail from friends, talked to friends on the phone, and enjoyed their frequent visits. I was so lucky to have friends who still cared about me and my family and who allowed me to vent through the many days of intense loneliness and frustration. Most who enter prison lose their family, have no education, and … cannot see a future. They receive no mail, no visits, and have no one to call. Time crawls in an atmosphere of little hope. (Hubbell 1997, 6)*

A number of factors hinder efforts to maintain and strengthen the family ties of incarcerated offenders, including the obstacles imposed by distance of the correctional facility from the family's home community and the difficulties of maintaining family ties over the course of a long-term sentence.

The Dynamics of Inmate Families

Many inmates lack parenting skills that would help them develop and sustain a positive relationship with their spouses and children while incarcerated. This lack of skills is a consequence of being raised in dysfunctional family environments characterized by poverty and violence, of living in foster homes, or of spending lengthy periods of time in youth correctional facilities.

As well, there are high levels of sexual, physical, and psychological abuse in many inmate families. The rates are especially high in the families of Aboriginal inmates. Most often it is female partners who are the victims of this violence and abuse, with children being victimized much less frequently. Most inmates who are violent toward family members were abused themselves as children (Robinson 1995).

Female Inmates and Their Children

> *"Mother's Happiness"*
>
> *Completely numb…*
>
> *They were gone, I could not breathe*

The walls closing around me
It was dark, It was cold
As a mother, I lost my soul
Let there be nothing but love for my kids
Inside their walls let there be nothing
But love from mommy to help them live
Let their dark turn to sunshine
Let there be no more blame
Let there be no more shame
Let there be no more of Satan's games
I can now breathe …

—Helenann Young 2008. Reprinted with permission.

Source: http://www.pasan.org/Cell_Count/Issue_49.pdf

This poem describes the pain that a female offender experienced with her incarceration and loss of contact with her two children, ages three and four. Female inmates are likely to be the sole custodial parent of their children. When they are incarcerated, their children are usually cared for by relatives, most commonly grandparents. When no surrogate caretaker is available, the children may be taken in by provincial/territorial child welfare authorities and placed in foster care. If the period of incarceration is long and the children are young, they may be candidates for adoption. Because of these factors, the incarceration of a mother typically results in greater disruption in the lives of children than is the case if a father is incarcerated.

Inmate mothers have varying levels of contact with their children, including contact visits, overnight family visits, on-site part-time residency, and live-in programs that allow the inmate-mother to have her child stay in the institution. Private family visits are generally available only in federal facilities. These visits, which allow the spouse and family members to spend up to seventy-two hours in a trailer unit or small house on prison grounds, provide the opportunity for more normal parent–child interaction than is possible on a four-hour day visit.

Mother–child programs generally allow infants to reside with their mothers in open living units. The first Canadian mother–child programs were developed in provincial institutions in British Columbia and Manitoba. The regional correctional institutions that have been developed for federally sentenced women include bedrooms for children. For example, there are ten

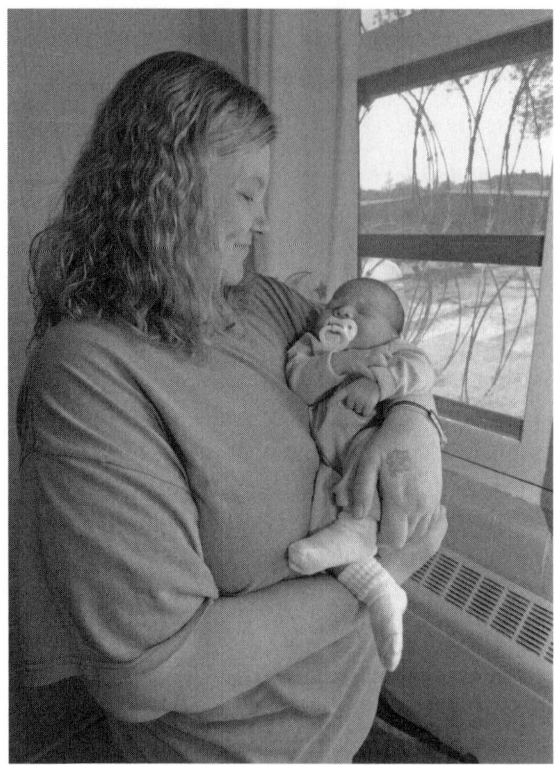

Inmate mother holds her baby inside a women's prison.
CP PHOTO/AP Photo/Michael Conroy

bedrooms at Grand Valley Institution in Kitchener, Ontario; and the Okima Ohci Healing Lodge for Aboriginal women in Saskatchewan can accommodate eight to ten children up to the age of four. A daycare has also been built at the healing lodge.

Mother–child programs can involve regular part-time visits, such as weekends, or full-time residency in the institution, which is generally available only for preschool-aged children. To participate in the program, the inmate-mother must have a positive relationship with her child or be able to demonstrate that such a relationship is possible. The determining factor in deciding whether an inmate-mother can participate in the program is the best interests of the child. As well, federal female offenders who have been convicted of violent offences are not allowed to participate in mother–baby/child programs. Despite support for mother–child programs by the CSC and various provincial/territorial correctional systems, implementation has been slow and uneven across the country. In 2008, B.C. cancelled a program that allowed female offenders who gave birth while incarcerated to keep their babies in jail with them. Provincial corrections authorities cited a number of reasons for cancelling the program, including lack of adequately trained staff (Canadian Press 2008). A number of issues have been raised by these programs. Share your thoughts on "At Issue 6.3: Should There Be Mother–Child Programs in Correctional Institutions?" presented at the end of the chapter.

THE CARCERAL EXPERIENCE: IN THE WORDS OF INMATES

> *It is a cold, dark, gloomy place. It has the stink of tobacco, the foul smell of body odour at night, and the smell that you find in a basement filled with dust and cobwebs. In prison, existence is slow, tense, and gloomy, and everybody feels everything intensely, and yet these things are small, meaningless and often trivial. You wouldn't believe how many fights I've seen in a meal line and often just because one person accidently bumped into another. Why is that? Well, our past is dead and gone, our future is non-existent and the present is all we have, causing great pain. (inmate's description of Kingston Penitentiary, in Thompson 2002, 124)*

It is difficult if not impossible for those of us who have never been confined in a correctional institution to understand the carceral experience. The closest we can get is the writings of inmates about their experiences doing time (see, for example, Thompson 2002). Inmate-authored poems are another expression of the carceral experience.

> *"Locked Away"*
>
> *Cold & barren, unforgiving*
>
> *Deadly quiet, nothing living*
>
> *Hostility, anger, lost in fear*
>
> *Nothing but darkness dare to come near*
>
> *The violence of a life-long fight*
>
> *The silence of eternal night*
>
> *Unwanted, abandoned, a little boy*
>
> *Becomes the darkside's unwitting toy*
>
> *A life of drugs, a life of crime*
>
> *At the age of 30, he's doing time*
>
> *Growing up devoid of love*

A wall of hate grows high above
A vicious circle of poverty
He's trapped & cannot be set free
—Ted Meyers, Joyceville Institution, Kingston 2008. Reprinted with permission.

Source: http://www.pasan.org/Cell_Count/Issue_49.pdf

INMATE COMPLAINTS, GRIEVANCE SYSTEMS, AND INVESTIGATIONS

For inmates confined in federal institutions, Sections 90 and 91 of the Corrections and Conditional Release Act set out the procedures for ensuring that any complaints are dealt with in a fair and equitable manner. Grievances are to be handled fairly, in a timely fashion, and effectively. Inmates must make every attempt to resolve their grievance through the internal grievance procedure in the institution before filing a written complaint with the Correctional Investigator. Similar grievance procedures and requirements are in place for inmates confined in provincial/territorial institutions. The recommendations of both the federal Correctional Investigator and provincial ombudsmen are nonbinding, though there is an attempt to reach a solution to identified problems.

Thousands of complaints or grievances are filed every year by inmates in federal and provincial correctional facilities. As little as 5 percent of the inmate population is responsible for nearly 70 percent of the complaints and grievances that are filed. The most common complaints received centre on health care and staff conduct. Contribute your thoughts on "At Issue 6.2: Should inmates have the full benefit of the Charter of Rights and Freedoms?" presented at the end of the chapter.

Following is an illustration of the types of cases investigated and resolved by provincial ombudspeople:

- Two inmates complained that COs had interrupted an Aboriginal pipe ceremony during which sage and sweetgrass had been burned and a pipe was being smoked. The officers accused the participants of smoking marijuana. An elder who was present at the ceremony denied the allegation and offered to let the officers inspect his medicine bundle. Despite this, the officers terminated the ceremony. The inmates felt that the actions of the COs demonstrated a lack of respect toward the elder and the pipe ceremony. The resolution of the case involved arrangements for an elder to provide Aboriginal Spiritual

Awareness sessions to correctional staff and an apology by the officers involved in the incident (Saskatchewan Provincial Ombudsman 2001, 18-19).

- Acting on complaints from a number of female inmates and an advocacy group, investigators from the ombudsman's office conducted a surprise inspection of the Central East Correctional Centre (CECC). The inspection found no evidence of overcrowding; there was, however, evidence that female inmates with a history of sexual abuse and mental illness had been placed in the men's unit on several occasions the previous year. The inspection also revealed that the emergency call buttons in the women's unit had been disabled.

  Correctional officials in CECC indicated that the number of women's beds had been increased and that overcrowding rarely occurred. However, they were unable to make assurances that female offenders would no longer be placed in the men's unit. Corrections officials also indicated that the emergency call buttons had been disabled because they were unnecessary since the units were regularly patrolled by COs. However, the ombudsman investigators found that it was nearly impossible for a CO to hear a voice from within the cells.

  The ombudsman's investigation and subsequent discussions with corrections officials resulted in the reactivation of the emergency call buttons. There was also agreement that female inmates would only be housed in the men's unit as a last resort and only with the prior approval of the regional director of corrections.

Source: Ontario Provincial Ombudsman 2008.
http://www.ombudsman.on.ca/media/18971/ar08_eng.pdf

There are times when the ombudsman is unable to resolve the issue at hand. This is illustrated by the following case from Saskatchewan:

Issue: The ombudsman in Saskatchewan conducted a review of the way in which methadone was being administered in the correctional centre environment and whether it afforded participants sufficient privacy. Daily treatments of methadone lessen the withdrawal symptoms of some drug-addicted inmates. In the prison environment, if inmates are known to be on the methadone treatment program, they may be targeted by other inmates, either for illicit drug sales or for receipt of the methadone itself.

Findings: When methadone is administered, the patient must be observed for at least twenty minutes to ensure that the methadone has been ingested. Typically, a number of inmates are dosed and observed at one time. This treatment is not private, and even it if was, it would not be hard for the other inmates to guess why an individual was being taken to the medical unit each day. The greatest difficulty in administering methadone privately is the twenty minutes' observation time. If this were done separately for each inmate, a dramatic increase in nursing staff would be required—and at a time when there is already a nursing shortage in correctional centres and elsewhere.

Another consideration is that, even though a risk exists in the lack of privacy of methadone treatments, it has not resulted in any serious problems. Correctional centres in other provinces operate similarly and have not had complaints about the process.

Conclusion: Ideally, methadone dosages should be administered privately, but there is no practical way to make this happen. No appropriate remedy seems to be available (Saskatchewan Provincial Ombudsman 2007. http://www.ombudsman.sk.ca/pdf/ar2006.pdf).

FAILING TO COPE WITH CONFINEMENT: SELF-INJURIOUS BEHAVIOUR AND SUICIDE

The prison suicide rate is more than twice that of the general Canadian population. Suicide is the most common cause of death among male inmates in federal correctional institutions, followed by homicides and accidents. The most common suicide methods are hanging, followed by drug overdoses and self-inflicted wounds. Many male inmates are at risk of suicide; female offenders tend more to engage in self-injurious behaviour, including slashing and self-mutilation. For female offenders, self-harm is a way to cope with emotional pain, distress, and isolation (Dell and Beauchamp 2006; Gabor 2007).

Assessing the Risk of Suicide

It is often difficult to predict inmate suicides and to identify causal factors that may place an inmate at increased risk. Though prison psychologists are often able to determine that an inmate is at risk of suicide, the techniques are not sufficiently developed to predict the likelihood of a suicide. The task is made even more difficult by the wide variety of behaviours that may or may not be related to future suicide. These include certain gestures, self-injury, and attempted suicides.

Among the risk factors found to be associated with completed suicides among inmates in institutions and offenders being supervised in the community are age (young, male inmates and elderly inmates are at greater risk); alcohol abuse (alcoholics have five times the risk of nonalcoholics); prior suicidal behaviour; depression; and mental illness (Polvi 1997; Rosine 1995). There is some evidence that self-injurious behaviour among female offenders is linked to childhood abuse, pre-prison psychological difficulties, and involvement in institutional incidents (Snow 1997). The risk of suicide may be higher for women who are placed in segregation (Martel 1999). The female offender profiled in Box 6.7 was in segregation at the time of her death.

In recent years, correctional systems have given increasing attention to developing screening protocols to identify inmates who may be at risk of suicide. There are primary suicide prevention efforts, designed to address factors in the institutional environment that may precipitate suicides, and secondary prevention efforts, which focus on individual inmates who have been identified as at risk of suicide. In an attempt to reduce the incidence of suicide and self-harm, the CSC has implemented inmate peer support programs in all maximum- and medium-security institutions. The Samaritans program, which operates in several federal facilities, is a peer support program through which a community-based organization provides suicide-prevention training for inmate peer counsellors.

BOX 6.7

The Death of Ashley Smith

On October 19, 2007, nineteen-year-old Ashley Smith was found unconscious in her segregation cell at the Grand Valley Institution for Women. She died later that day. The official cause of death was self-initiated asphyxiation.

At the time of her death, Ms. Smith was serving a sentence of six years and one month for a variety of weapons and assault offences that she had committed as a youth.

As a young offender, Ms. Smith was initially sent to the New Brunswick Youth Centre. During her stay in this facility, before being transferred to the Saint John Regional Correctional Centre, she accumulated more than 800 incident reports, more than 500 institutional charges, and 168 self-harm incidents.

Ms. Smith was transferred to the penitentiary at age nineteen and was subsequently moved seventeen times between nine different federal correctional facilities. She was in segregation during her entire confinement in the federal system.

The final report of the Correctional Investigator found that Ms. Smith's mental-health issues had not been addressed either in the youth facility or in the federal institutions in which she was confined. There had been no psychological assessment. The Correctional Investigator concluded that Ms. Smith's death might have been prevented had she been provided with proper care.

(continued)

Among the recommendations in the Correctional Investigator's final report were that the CSC comply with the law and policy in its operations; improve the response to medical emergencies; review segregation policy and practices; and ensure the delivery of adequate health care, including mental-health services (Office of the Correctional Investigator 2008). At this writing, the final report of the Correctional Investigator has not been released owing to the ongoing criminal proceedings. A report on Ms. Smith's confinement in youth facilities in New Brunswick was also completed by the New Brunswick Ombudsman and Child and Youth Advocate (2008).

An investigation of the incident by the Waterloo Regional Police Services resulted in the police laying charges of criminal negligence causing death against three COs and a supervisor. Police documents filed in court allege that the guards and supervisor "did, by criminal negligence, fail to come to the aid of Ashley Smith, thereby causing her death" (CBC 2008). These four correctional personnel were fired and four other COs were suspended without pay for sixty days. The acting warden and deputy warden were also fired. At this writing (late 2008), the cases of the three COs and the supervisor are still before the courts.

Sources: CBC 2008; New Brunswick Office of the Ombudsman & Child and Youth Advocate 2008. Office of the Correctional Investigator 2008.

AT ISSUE

ISSUE 6.1: Should there be limits on sexual relationships in prison?

"Joliette Institution Anti-sex Policies for Inmates Have Regressed Into the Dark Ages . . ." [Note: Joliette Institution is a federal prison for female offenders]

Joliette Institution is suppressing the inmates' need to express themselves freely through making physical love with each other. Sexual acts by inmates are frowned upon and discouraged by Joliette Institution. In most cases inmates who are caught by staff engaging in making love are punished with disciplinary charges.

Joliette Institution has eroded the inroads made by society, that practicing love making is a healthy and fundamental act necessary for the balanced mental and physical well-being of a person.

It is rather ironic that Joliette Institution issues to inmates condoms and rubber dental dams to encourage them to practice safe sex in order to lessen the chance of acquiring a communicable disease from their partner who may be infected. In the Joliette Institution Inmate Handbook, the Warden states "it is forbidden to show overly intimate or indecent behavior in public places of the Institution. Example: walking hand in hand is acceptable, kissing lasciviously is not."

In other words, inmates must hide from the view of others in order to express themselves in an affectionate manner. The possession by inmates, at Joliette Institution, of store-bought sexual toys such as dildos and vibrators is prohibited. This denial forces inmates to unlawfully make and use their own sexual toys.

Despite the Joliette Institution anti-love making policies against inmates, inmates still continue to make love and show their affections for each other in public areas of the Institution.

Sexologists, physicians and psychologists encourage persons to enter into relationships and to perform love making, as the benefits keep the human body and mind in balance and harmony. The entire spectrum of emotional and physical love permits the body and brain to manufacture chemicals and hormones which create a sense of well being and relaxation, thus increasing the quality of life.

Love can be expressed in many manners such as caressing, touching, hugging, kissing and looking someone into their eyes affectionately.

However, a more sensual communication and sharing of emotional and physical love with another person, occurs during nude body contact and genitalia stimulation with the ultimate expressing of having an orgasm.

Correctional Services Canada in their Dialectical Behaviour Therapy encourages inmates to maintain a happy emotional balance. The program states "Intensify certain positive emotions (those which create feelings of self-esteem and confidence) transform sad emotions by doing something opposite."

We are all born with the use of approximately 10 emotions. Sadness, happiness, pain, shame, suffering, fear, interest, guilt, anger, love. One of our more powerful emotions which we use is love.

For the majority of people our life evolves around love, which could be a sharing of smiles or the ultimate expression such as the sexual physical act.

In Canada, citizens have certain guaranteed fundamental freedoms such as set out in the Canadian Charter of Rights and Freedoms "s.2 FUNDAMENTAL FREEDOMS – Everyone has the following fundamental freedoms (b) freedom of thought, belief, opinion and expression including freedom of the press and other media of communication."

Inmates freedom to express love is suppressed by Joliette Institution causing inmates to practice love in fear, shame, and guilt. Joliette Institution should be encouraged to compare their policies about, and attitude towards inmates practicing love and sex and follow those policies in effect at other Canadian Penitentiaries, both for women and for men. Joliette Institution should make changes to their current practices and attitudes in order to reflect the current social norms and recommendations made by the medical profession that practicing love and safe sex should be tolerated and encouraged.

Source: Article by Christine White, in *Constellation*, volume 9, no. 1, winter 2005. Reprinted by permission from Stella (www.chezstella.org)

What do you think?

1. Do you agree or disagree with the arguments made in this selection? What is the basis for your position?

AT ISSUE

ISSUE 6.2: Should inmates have the full benefit of the Charter of Rights and Freedoms?

Consider the following opinion piece about the rights of inmates and then offer your views on this person's perspective.

"Inmates and Civil Rights: Their New Country Club"

It is something that I can not help but feel strongly about having worked in my current industry of retail loss prevention over 7 years. It is an opinion that you may not share so I have included references for you to access further information if you choose to do so.

In my opinion inmates should not be given the full spectrum of rights offered to other citizens during the incarceration phase of their punishment. The incarceration phase of a sentence should be for punishment and punishment only. The rights that are cherished to law abiding citizens living free and honestly in Canada should not be offered to those within the walls of our prison institutions. Incarceration is used by the courts as a last resort for the most serious of crimes and for repeat offenders. If Canadians are going to regain trust in the Correctional Services of Canada (and other branches of the criminal justice system) then it is important that we begin to once again punish those that are threatening our way of life through both specific and general deterrence.

The Canadian Charter of Rights is the basic rights that are available for every citizen living in Canada. The written legislation is 34 paragraphs and only a few pages long. On the other hand there is a section of the International Prison Policy Development document from July 2001 (taken from the UBC law website) that is the equivalent of the Charter for inmates. This document on inmate rights (section III only) is considered a guideline for Canadian correctional institutions. This section III document is the primary section that focuses on inmate rights but refers the reader often to other sections of the document. It is just short of being 100 pages compared to the Charter's measly few pages.

I am forced to ask myself then; "why do inmates essentially have more rights in Canada than the average citizen?" Why do they have rights that are not in the nature of punishment but can be construed as more of a privilege than a fundamental right? Why do they have rights that allow them to continue to be a threat to the rest of society?

The Charter of Rights says that everyone has the right to free association and peaceful assembly. In prison they have another way to phrase these rights. Inmates call prison "con college." Prison has become a place to meet up with old friends and forge new ones. It is a place to develop alliances and establish business arrangements both inside and outside of the facility. Prison also gives the criminal much more than a means to a social network. Serving any type of sentence gives the criminal street status.

Corrections often use reoffending as a yardstick as to whether or not a criminal has committed a new crime or series of crimes. The reality of the situation is that while providing inmates with restaurant like eating facilities, libraries, outdoor gardens and a wide array of recreational activities, the inmate is given an opportunity to interact with fellow inmates. It is well documented that inmates exchange information on law evasion and illegal profit enhancement in a swap meet of ideas. This mockery of Canadian Justice needs to stop and it should not be tolerated by law abiding citizens.

Incarceration should be about punishment, while community release programs and halfway houses should be used for the rehabilitation phase of a sentence. There is no legitimate reason that there should be a fundamental right to be social in a correctional facility. It is time that Canadian prisons stopped being summer camps.

What do you think?

1. What is your reaction to this opinion piece?

Source: Fenske, 2007. "Inmates and Civil Rights: Their New Country Club." October 22. http://huntersofthedamned.blogspot.com/2007/10/inmates-and-civil-rights-their-new.html.

AT ISSUE

ISSUE 6.3: Should there be mother–child programs in correctional institutions?

The development of mother–child programs in federal and provincial/territorial correctional institutions attempts to address one of the most critical issues facing women in prison. These programs, however, have also been criticized.

Proponents of mother–child programs in correctional institutions make these arguments:

- The programs create or strengthen the bonds between mothers and their children.
- Mothers have the opportunity to provide early childhood nurturing.
- The programs allow closer monitoring of the health and safety of children than would be possible in the community.
- Inmate-mothers have the chance to learn parenting skills.
- Inmate-mothers are more likely to maintain family ties on release.
- The programs assist inmates in developing prosocial attitudes and behaviours.

Critics of mother–child programs counter that such programs are not in the best interests of children, for these reasons:

- The prison environment, with its attendant illicit activities such as drug use, is no place for young children.
- Inmate-mothers should address their own problem behaviour before becoming involved in child care.
- Young children who reside in correctional institutions are stigmatized.
- The prison is an artificial environment that bears little resemblance to the outside community in which the inmate-mother and her child will ultimately have to adjust.
- It is unfair and disruptive to children to place them in a correctional facility, only to remove them at a later date if the inmate-mother is serving a lengthy sentence.
- Mother–child programs are discriminatory toward inmate fathers, who are not allowed similar access to their children.

The Research Evidence

To date, there have been no published studies on mother–child programs in Canadian correctional institutions; thus, it is impossible to determine whether the arguments made by proponents of these programs are valid or whether the concerns of critics are justified. It is not known, for example, what impact living in a correctional institution has on children; whether programs strengthen mother–child bonds; and whether women who participate in these programs have higher rates of success on release. Further, and importantly, there have been no studies that have examined the impact of these programs on children.

What do you think?

1. **Should criminal court judges consider whether a female offender has children in determining whether a period of incarceration is imposed? Why or why not?**
2. **Are you generally supportive of mother–child programs in correctional institutions? Why or why not?**
3. **What would be your position if it were proposed that father–child programs be developed in correctional institutions?**

Sources: Teather, Evans, and Sims 1997; Watson 1995.

KEY POINTS REVIEW

1. Persons confined in correctional institutions tend to be marginal in education and employment skills, to have addiction issues, and to be disproportionately Aboriginal and Black.
2. The specific impact that entry into prison will have on an individual offender will vary with a number of factors, including personality, offence history, and previous incarcerations.
3. The pains of imprisonment may be more severe for female offenders, as many are far from their home community and most are the primary caregiver for their children.
4. A major challenge confronting correctional systems is to prevent offenders from becoming so immersed in the culture of the prison that change is not possible.
5. While most inmates pay lip service to the tenets of the inmate code, it appears that it is no longer the behavioural guide that it was in the past.
6. Inmates spend a considerable part of their time attempting to reduce the pains of imprisonment and to protect themselves inside the prison.
7. There is no empirical evidence that long-term confinement leads to mental and physical deterioration in inmates or to an impairment of coping abilities, though it may affect the ability of the inmate to reenter the community.
8. The degree to which an inmate is vulnerable to attack and exploitation by other inmates depends in large measure on his or her status, power, and friendship networks.
9. There are a number of factors that put strains on inmate families.

10. Provincial/territorial and federal correctional systems have formal inmate grievance procedures. They also have ombudspersons who may investigate inmate complaints.
11. The prison suicide rate is more than twice that of the general Canadian population. That said, it is often difficult to predict inmate suicides and to identify the causal factors that place inmates at increased risk of suicide.
12. Among the factors that have been identified as placing male inmates at risk are age (young or elderly), a history of alcohol abuse, prior suicidal behaviour, depression, and mental illness.
13. Self-injurious behaviour among female inmates seems to be associated with childhood abuse, pre-prison psychological difficulties, and involvement in institutional incidents.

KEY TERM QUESTIONS

1. Define and then discuss the importance of the following concepts for the study of corrections and life inside correctional institutions: (1) **mortification;** (2) **status degradation ceremonies;** and (3) **pains of imprisonment.**
2. Discuss the attributes of the **inmate subculture/inmate social system** and then discuss what is known about its existence in correctional institutions.
3. Describe and contrast the **importation theory** of the inmate social system and the **deprivation theory** of the inmate social system.
4. Discuss the concept of **prisonization** and describe what is meant when it is said that an inmate has become **institutionalized.**
5. Identify the basic tenets of the **inmate code** and discuss whether the code still exists among inmates in correctional institutions.
6. What role do **niches** (of inmates) and **social** (or **argot**) **roles** play inside correctional institutions?
7. Describe what is meant by **mature coping** by inmates, identify the components of mature coping, and note the obstacles that inmates may encounter in their efforts engage in this practice.
8. Discuss the challenges faced by **state-raised offenders.**
9. Define, compare, and contrast **expressive violence** and **instrumental violence** among inmates in correctional institutions.

10. Define, compare, and contrast **passive precautions** against violence and **aggressive precautions** against violence among inmates in correctional institutions.

REFERENCES

Anonymous. 2007–8. "Where'd All the Cons Go?" *Cell Count* 48. http://www.pasan.org/Cell_Count/Issue_48.pdf

Ault, F.A.W. 1997. "Imprisoned by an Uncaring Public," *Globe and Mail*, April 21, A14.

Austin, J., T. Fabelo, A. Gunter, and K. McGinnis. 2006. *Sexual Violence in the Texas Prison System.* Washington: National Institute of Justice. http://www.ncjrs.gov/pdffiles1/nij/grantas/215774.pdf

Caddle, D., and D. Crisp. 1997. *Mothers in Prison, Research Findings no. 38.* London: Research and Statistics Directorate, Home Office. http://www.homeoffice.gov.uk/rds/pdfs/r38.pdf

Canadian Press. 2008. "Critics Condemn B.C. Decision to Separate Moms from Babies in Jail" August 13. http://www.prisonjustice.ca/starkravenarticles/babies_jail_0808.html

Carr, C. 1995. "A Network of Support for Offender Families." *Forum on Corrections Research* 7(2): 31–33.

CBC. 2008. "Guards Accused of Criminal Negligence Back in Court in March." February 6. http://www.cbc.ca/canada/new-brunswick/story/2008/02/06/smith-court.html

Chubaty, D.E. 2002. "Victimization, Fear, and Coping in Prison." *Forum on Corrections Research* 14(1): 13–15.

Clemmer, D. 1940. *The Prison Community.* Boston: Christopher.

Cloward, R.A. 1969. "Social Control in the Prison." In *Prison within Society: A Reader in Penology*, ed. L. Hazelrigg. Garden City: Doubleday. 78–112.

Cooley, D. 1992. "Prison Victimization and the Informal Rules of Social Control." *Forum on Corrections Research* 4(3): 31–36.

Correctional Service of Canada. 2000. "Profile of an Aboriginal Woman Serving Time in a Federal Correctional Institution." http://www.csc-scc.gc.ca/text/prgrm/abinit/know/5-eng.shtml

Dell, C.A., and T. Beauchamp. 2006. "Self-Harm Among Criminalized Women." *Fact Sheet.* Canadian Centre on Substance Abuse. http://ccsa.ca?CCSA.EN/Publications

Dube, R. 2002. *The Haven: A True Story of Life in the Hole.* Toronto: HarperCollins.

Faulkner, P.L., and W.R. Faulkner. 1997. "Effects of Organizational Change on Inmate Status and the Inmate Code of Conduct." *Journal of Crime and Criminal Justice* 20(1): 55–72.

Gabel, S. 1995. "Behavioural Problems in the Children of Incarcerated Parents." *Forum on Corrections Research* 7(2): 37–39.

Gabor, T. 2007. *Deaths in Custody: Final Report.* Ottawa: Office of the Correctional Investigator. http://www.oci-bec.gc.ca/reports/custody_e.asp

Goffman, E. 1961. *Asylums: Essays on the Social Situation of Mental Patients and Other Inmates.* Garden City: Doubleday.

Harris, M. 2002. *Con Game: The Truth About Canada's Prisons.* Toronto: McClelland & Stewart.

Hubbell, W. 1997. "Light from Darkness." *George Magazine*. August. http://www.ncianet.org/george.html (webpage has been deleted)

Hughes, the Honourable E.N. (Ted) (chair). 1996. *Report of the Independent Review of the Circumstances Surrounding the April 25–26, 1996 Riot at the Headingley Correctional Institution.* Winnipeg: Ministry of Justice, Province of Manitoba.

Ireland, J., and J. Archer. 1996. "Descriptive Analysis of Bullying in Male and Female Adult Prisoners." *Journal of Community and Applied Social Psychology* 6: 35–47.

Irwin, J., and D.R. Cressey. 1962. "Thieves, Convicts, and the Inmate Culture." *Social Problems* 10(1): 142–55.

Johnson, R. 1996. *Hard Time: Understanding and Reforming the Prison.* Belmont: Wadsworth.

Jones, T.R., and T.C. Pratt. 2008. "The Prevalence of Sexual Violence in Prison." *International Journal of Offender Therapy and Comparative Criminology* 52(3): 280–95.

Kaufman, P. 2008. "Prison Rape: Research Explores Prevalence, Prevention." *NIJ Journal.* 259: 24–29. http://www.ojp.usdoj.gov/nij/journals/259/prison-rape.htm

Lamb, W. 2007. *I'll Fly Away: Further Testimonies from the Women of York Prison.* New York: HarperCollins.

———. 2004. *Couldn't Keep it to Myself: Wally Lamb and the Women of York Correctional Institution.* New York: HarperCollins.

Landry, L., and M. Sinha. 2008. "Adult Correctional Services in Canada, 2005/2006." *Juristat* 28(6). Cat. no. 85-002-XIE. Ottawa: Minister of Industry. http://www.statcan.gc.ca/english/freepub/85-002-XIE/85-002-XIE2008006.htm

Lawson, D.P., C. Segrin, and T.D. Ward. 1996. "The Relationship Between Prisonization and Social Skills Among Prison Inmates." *Prison Journal* 76(3): 293–309.

Leschied, A.W., A. Cunningham, and N. Mazaheri. 1997. *Safe and Secure: Eliminating Peer-to-Peer Violence in Ontario's Phase II Secure Detention Centres.* London: London Family Court Clinic.

Martel, J. 1999. *Solitude and Cold Storage: Women's Journeys of Endurance in Segregation.* Edmonton: Elizabeth Fry Society of Edmonton.

McCorkle, R.C. 1992a. "Institutional Violence: How Do Inmates Respond?" *Forum on Corrections Research* 4(3): 9–11.

———. 1992b. "Personal Precautions to Violence in Prison." *Criminal Justice and Behavior* 19(2): 160–73.

Murphy, P.J., and L. Johnsen. 1997. *Life 25: Interviews with Prisoners Serving Life Sentences.* Vancouver: New Star.

Murphy, P.J., L. Johnsen, and J. Murphy. 2002. *Paroled for Life: Interviews with Parolees Serving Life Sentences.* Vancouver: New Star.

National Parole Board. n.d. "Inmate Jargon." Abbotsford: NPB Pacific Region.

New Brunswick Office of the Ombudsman & Child and Youth Advocate. 2008. *Ashley Smith: A Report of the New Brunswick Ombudsman and Child and Youth Advocate on the Services Provided to a Youth Involved in the Youth Justice System.* Fredericton. http://www.gnb.ca/0073/PDF/AshleySmith-e.pdf

Office of the Correctional Investigator. 2008. "Correctional Investigator Submits Final Report to Minister Stockwell Day on Death of Ms. Ashley Smith at Grand Valley Institution, Kitchener." *News Release.* June 24. Ottawa. http://www.oci-bec.gc.ca/newsroom/releases/20080624_e.asp

Ontario Provincial Ombudsman. 2008. *Annual Report, 2007/2008.* Toronto: Legislative Assembly, Province of Ontario. http://www.ombudsman.on.ca/media/18971/ar08_eng.pdf

Paulus, P.B., and M.T. Dzindolet. 1992. "The Effects of Prison Confinement." In *Psychology and Social Policy,* ed. P. Seudfeld and P.E. Tetlock. New York: Hemisphere. 327–41.

Plourde, C. 2002. "Consumption of Psychoactive Substances in Quebec Prisons." *Forum on Corrections Research* 14(1): 16–18.

Polvi, N.H. 1997. *Inmate Suicides and Prisoner Suicide: A Review of the Literature.* Ottawa: Correctional Service of Canada. http://www.csc-scc.gc.ca/text/pblct/health/toc-eng.shtml

Porporino, F.J. 1991. *Differences in Response to Long-Term Imprisonment: Implications for the Management of Long-Term Offenders.* Ottawa: Correctional Service of Canada. http://www.csc-scc.gc.ca/text/rsrch/reports/r10/r10e-eng.shtml

Public Safety Canada Portfolio Corrections Statistics Committee. 2007. *Corrections and Conditional Release Statistical Overview.* Ottawa: Public Works and Government Services Canada. http://www.publicsafety.gc.ca/res/cor/rep/ccrso2007-eng.aspx

Robinson, D. 1995. "Federal Offender Family Violence: Estimates from a National File Review Study." *Forum on Corrections Research* 7(2): 15–18.

Rosine, L. 1995. "Assessment of Suicides in Incarcerated Populations." In *Forensic Psychology—Policy and Practice in Corrections,* ed. T.A. Leis, L.L. Motiuk, and J.R.P. Ogloff. Ottawa: Correctional Service Canada. 150–63.

Saskatchewan Provincial Ombudsman. 2001. *Annual Report, 2001.* Regina: Legislative Assembly. http://www.ombudsman.sk.ca/pdf/ar2001.pdf

———. 2007. *Annual Report, 2006.* Regina: Legislative Assembly. http://www.ombudsman.sk.ca/pdf/ar2006.pdf

Shephard, M. 1997. "'Imagine the Worst': Inmates Soon Learn that to Be Sent to a Canadian Prison Is to Be Condemned to a Term of Fear, Pain, Even Torture." *Toronto Star,* August 31, F1.

Snow, L. 1997. "A Pilot Study of Self-Injury Amongst Women Prisoners." *Issues in Criminological and Legal Psychology* 28: 50–59.

Struckman-Johnson, C., D. Struckman-Johnson, L. Rucker, K. Bumby, and S. Donaldson. 1996. "Sexual Coercion Reported by Men and Women in Prison." *Journal of Sex Research* 33(1): 67–76.

Sykes, G.M. 1958. *Society of Captives—A Study of a Maximum Security Institution.* Princeton: Princeton University Press.

Sykes, G.M., and S.L. Messinger. 1960. 'The Inmate Social System." In *Theoretical Studies in the Social Organization of the Prison*, ed. R.A. Cloward, D.R. Cressey, G.H. Grosser, R. McCleery, L.E. Ohlin, G.M. Sykes, and S.L. Messinger. New York: Social Science Research Council. 5–19.

Teather, S., L. Evans, and M. Sims. 1997. "Maintenance of the Mother–Child Relationship by Incarcerated Women." *Early Childhood Development and Care* 131(1): 65–75.

Terry, C.M. 1997. "The Function of Humor for Prison Inmates." *Journal of Contemporary Criminal Justice* 13(1): 23–40.

Thompson, S. 2002. *Letters from Prison: Felons Write About the Struggle for Life and Sanity Behind Bars.* Toronto: HarperCollins.

Union of Canadian Correctional Officers. 2007. "Rewards and Consequences: A Correctional Service for the 21st Century." Brief to the Independent Review Panel studying the future of the Correctional Service Canada. Montreal. http://www.ucco-sacc.csn.qc.ca

Watson, L. 1995. "In the Best Interests of the Child: The Mother–Child Program." *Forum on Corrections Research* 7(2): 25–27.

Welch, M. 1996. *Corrections: A Critical Approach.* New York: McGraw-Hill.

Yates, J.M. 1993. *Line Screw: My Twelve Riotous Years Working Behind Bars in Some of Canada's Toughest Jails.* Toronto: McClelland & Stewart.

Zamble, E., and F.J. Porporino. 1988. *Coping, Behavior, and Adaptation in Prison Inmates.* New York: Springer-Verlag.

WEBLINKS

Canadian Family and Corrections Network

http://www.cfcn-rcafd.org/#story3
Designed for families of offenders, this site contains links to a variety of programs and services, including for children of prisoners and parenting programs for inmates.

prisonjustice.ca

http://www.prisonjustice.ca
A website in support of prisoners and prison justice activism in Canada. Contains recent news, resources, and links to other corrections sites.

Cell Count

http://www.pasan.org/index.html?Cell_Count.htm~mainFrame
The newsletter of the Prisoner's HIV/AIDS Support Action Network (PASAN), which contains inmate poetry and writings, as well as discussions on corrections

policies and initiatives, with particular reference to HIV/AIDS and corrections activism.

prisontalk.com

http://www.prisontalk.com
This site has online forums for inmate families and friends as well as links to various prison topics.

enterprison.com

http://www.enterprison.com
This site contains interactive inmate websites and blogs.

Prison Resources and Links

http://www.prisonlinks.com
This site contains a number of links, including prison art, and discussions of prison rape and abuse.

Thai Prison Life

http://www.thaiprisonlife.com
For those students and professors planning a trip to Thailand: an interesting look inside the Thai prison system, as well as links to blogs

CHAPTER 7

CLASSIFICATION, CASE MANAGEMENT, AND TREATMENT

CHAPTER OBJECTIVES

After reading this chapter you should be able to:

- *Discuss the process of classification.*
- *Discuss the tools and techniques used in classifying inmates.*
- *Describe the various types of treatment programs offered in correctional institutions.*
- *Identify and discuss the principles of effective correctional treatment.*
- *Discuss what is known about the effectiveness of various types of correctional treatment programs.*
- *Discuss the difficulties that surround attempts to assess the effectiveness of correctional treatment programs.*
- *Identify and discuss the potential obstacles to effective correctional treatment.*
- *Discuss the issues that surround the question as to whether prison inmates should have the right to refuse treatment.*
- *Set out the arguments offered in support of, and in opposition to, private-sector industry in Canadian correctional facilities.*

KEY TERMS

Classification
Static risk factors
Need or dynamic factors
Criminogenic risk factors
Case management
Correctional plan
Risk principle
Need principle
Responsivity principle
Differential treatment effectiveness
Differential amenability to treatment
Recidivism rates
Differential treatment availability
Program fidelity
Program drift

PERSPECTIVE

Treatment Therapist

In discussing treatment, I will always separate out sex offenders in terms of the dynamics of offending and treatment intervention. But, with the general offender population, you will find a lot of commonalities in their histories. There are childhood disturbances, coming from a dysfunctional family, and a lot of what I have seen throughout the years is the increasing involvement in drugs; many offenders are addicted in some way. And you see that within the population of women offenders as well. Often, the violence that is committed can be traced back to a childhood of abuse and to anger that has never been resolved. There is often an abuse history that is a precursor to crime for both male and women offenders.

In doing treatment intervention, it is really important to look at the past and see how that past is influencing today's behaviour. That is an issue that everyone needs to have some recognition of. You can't change the past and no amount of sitting and talking about it is going to change it. But, what it can do is to help put it into perspective. I'm very much a person who looks at risk factors; how the person got to where they are and why they made the decisions they did. You've got to go back to the past to look at that. I call it the criminal behaviour cycle: how you got to the point where you gave yourself permission to commit that offence. There is a point at which offenders have to acknowledge what happened and to answer the question: "What are you going to do today?" And that's a hard one. And I get myself into trouble when I say this, but it's particularly true with women offenders: we have encouraged them to be victims, we've encouraged them to believe that they have no control over their lives; that they have no control over the decisions that they have made, and we have to get them past that stage. And they *have* been victims—don't get me wrong. But we have to help all offenders to get past the victim stage and take responsibility for what they did. Women offenders do generally come from very dysfunctional backgrounds. There has been a lot of abuse. Many are addicted. And there is difficulty in accepting the fact that they have committed a criminal offence.

Embarrassment and shame are two major issues you have to deal with. And denial. And wanting to blame others: "It's not really my fault. If I hadn't been dating Joe, this would never have happened." Accepting responsibility for what they did, and the fact that they made choices to deal drugs, or whatever, is important. Yes they were involved in prostitution. Yes they were abused and addicted. But that does not give them permission to hurt somebody, to do a home invasion.

Sex offenders are the ones who have the greatest difficulty taking responsibility for what they have done. Groups are a good way to get to them. When you facilitate a group of sex offenders, there is a certain dynamic that goes on. A sex offender might say that the only reason that they fondled the five-year-old is because they were drunk; another sex offender across the room will say, "I wasn't drunk when I fondled my victim." Sex offenders in the group have an understanding of behaviour that I will never have. With sex offenders, the biggest strength of the group was their being able to help each other accept responsibility for their behaviour. Sometimes it would get very intense in the groups and the language would be very colourful. They would get into each other's faces and say, "You are lying to yourself. You can lie to us, but don't lie to yourself."

These are the issues that a treatment therapist deals with.

Source: Female treatment therapist with 20 years' experience working with sex offenders and female offenders.

This chapter distills the massive amount of information that has been published on classification, case management, and treatment programs for incarcerated offenders. There are three major trends in offender classification and treatment: (1) the increasing use of sophisticated risk/needs assessment instruments; (2) the increasing domination of treatment research, policy, and programs from a psychological perspective—in particular, a cognitive-behavioural approach; and (3) a differentiated treatment approach for women, Aboriginals, and specific categories of offenders such as sex offenders.

CLASSIFICATION AND RISK ASSESSMENT

Classification is the process by which inmates are subdivided into groups based on a variety of factors. In each region of the Correctional Service of Canada (CSC) there are reception centres where offenders spend a period of time after sentencing. Classification is used to determine the appropriate custody and security level, program placement, and assignment to housing units within the institution.

This process involves gathering existing documentation on the offender from a variety of sources, including the family, corrections, the court, the police, and the victim. At the reception centre the following are conducted: health, mental-health, security, and suicide screening; a risk and needs assessment; and a security classification. On the basis of these, an institutional placement is decided on and programming recommendations are made. The classification of offenders, with particular emphasis on their risk and needs, is a core component of correctional treatment.

Various instruments are used to conduct psychological, substance-abuse, vocational and educational, and family-violence assessments. The assessment process continues throughout the offender's sentence, from intake to incarceration to release from custody and up to sentence expiry. Inmates are reclassified periodically during the course of their confinement, based on their progress and performance in treatment programs and work assignments and on their behaviour in the institution. Both at the initial classification stage and in later classification decisions, correctional personnel consider security and risk concerns, as well as the inmate's abilities and program needs.

Offenders have a variety of criminogenic needs that must be addressed both within the institution and later in the community. Treatment services should address the following criminogenic needs: education, mental health, social networks, employment, accommodation, drugs and alcohol, attitudes, and cognitive skills. All of these criminogenic needs are *dynamic* risk factors—that is, they are amenable to change and have been found to be important factors to address in order to reduce the likelihood of reoffending (Harper and Chitty 2005).

Classification Tools and Techniques

The classification systems used by federal and provincial/territorial corrections generally include psychological, personality, and behavioural inventories that attempt to categorize offenders. At the federal level this procedure is referred to as the Offender Intake Assessment (OIA), during which extensive information on the offender's criminal history and pattern of victimizations is gathered (see Figure 7.1). Among the documents that form the OIA are the preliminary assessment, the postsentence community assessment (the result of interviews with key community contacts), and a summary of the various inmate risk factors. Note that many of the assessment instruments are used only for male, non-Aboriginal offenders. For a variety of reasons, the instruments are deemed inappropriate for assessing female offenders and Aboriginal offenders.

Figure 7.1

Offender Intake Assessment Process

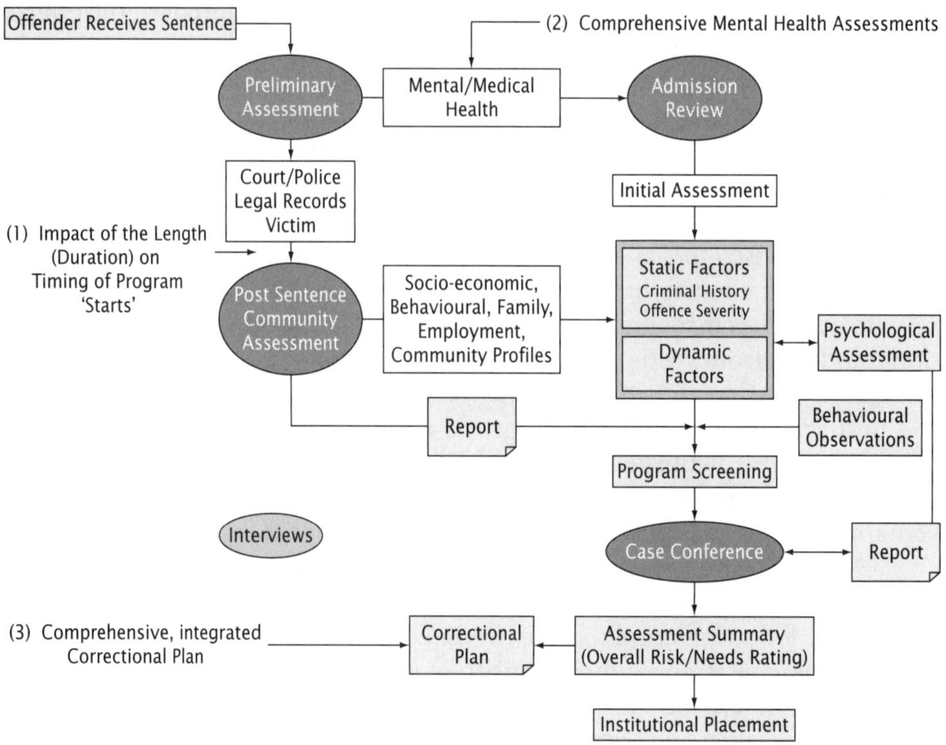

Source: Sampson 2007, 35.

The factors considered in determining the inmate's security level during the initial classification process include the following:

- seriousness of offence
- outstanding charges
- inmate's performance and behaviour while under sentence
- inmate's social, criminal, and (where available) young offender history
- any physical or mental illness or other disorder
- the inmate's potential for violence
- the inmate's continued involvement in criminal behaviour

The principal tool used by the federal CSC to assess male offender risk and to determine security classification is the Custody Rating Scale (CRS). Evaluation research has revealed that the CRS is an effective classification instrument (Luciani 1997). For federal female offenders, the Security Reclassification Scale for Women is used (Gobeil and Blanchette 2007). This instrument is based on research that indicates not only that there are measurable differences among offenders, but also that offenders can be categorized in terms of adjustment to confinement, risk of escape, and risk to the community should they escape. The scale consists of a number of items that attempt to measure these differences.

In Ontario the Level of Service Inventory—Ontario Revision (LSI-OR) is the primary classification/assessment instrument. This is a standardized interview that includes a range of questions relating to the offender, including offence history, substance abuse, and employment history. For each of the 43 items in the inventory, the offender is scored either 0 or 1. The higher the total score of the inmate, the greater the likelihood that the inmate will have difficulties in the institution and upon release. Evaluations of the LSI-OR indicate that it is an acceptable tool for predicting the performance of inmates in both institutional and community-based programs (Gendreau, Little, and Goggin, 1996).

Another widely used assessment instrument is the Static-99, profiled in Box 7.1. Research studies in a number of countries have found that the Static-99 offers moderate accuracy in predicting sexual and violent recidivism (see Ducrol 2006; Hanson and Thornton 1999).

Risk and Need Profiles of Offenders

The assessment of risk is a key component of classification and case management. Risk assessments are designed to identify those offenders who are most likely to reoffend upon release from the institution if no treatment intervention occurs (Taylor 1997). Risk analysis is used to determine which facility the offender should be confined in or moved to; to identify the offender's treatment

BOX 7.1

The Static-99: A Risk Assessment Instrument for Sex Offenders

The Static-99 is designed to estimate the probability of sexual and violent recidivism among men who have been convicted of at least one sexual offence against a child or non-consenting adult. The scale contains 10 items and must be completed by a psychologist.

STATIC-99 Coding Form

Question Number	Risk Factor	Codes		Score
1	Young (S9909)	Aged 25 or older		0
		Aged 18–24		1
2	Ever Lived With (S9910)	Ever lived with lover for at least two years?		
		Yes		0
		No		1
3	Index non-sexual violence - Any Convictions (S9904)	No		0
		Yes		1
4	Prior non-sexual violence - Any Convictions (S9905)	No		0
		Yes		1
5	Prior Sex Offences (S9901)	Charges	Convictions	
		None	None	0
		1-2	1	1
		3-5	2-3	2
		6+	4+	3
6	Prior sentencing dates (excluding index) (S9902)	3 or less		0
		4 or more		1
7	Any convictions for non-contact sex offences (S9903)	No		0
		Yes		1
8	Any Unrelated Victims (S9906)	No		0
		Yes		1
9	Any Stranger Victims (S9907)	No		0
		Yes		1
10	Any Male Victims (S9908)	No		0
		Yes		1
	Total Score	**Add up scores from individual risk factors**		

TRANSLATING STATIC 99 SCORES INTO RISK CATEGORIES

Score	Label for Risk Category
0,1	Low
2,3	Moderate-Low
4,5	Moderate-High
6 plus	High

Source: Harris, et al. 2003, 67

needs; to identify those offenders who require higher levels of support, intervention, and supervision upon release; and to assist in release decisions. Since an inmate's criminal history is strongly related to failure on conditional release, the combined assessment of both risks and needs improves the ability to predict which offenders will recidivate.

In assessing the degree of risk posed by an offender, corrections personnel generally consider the following:

- **static risk factors**: The offender's criminal history, including prior convictions, seriousness of prior offences, and whether the offender successfully completed previous periods of supervision in the community.
- **dynamic risk factors**: Those attributes of the offender that can be altered through intervention (e.g., level of education and cognitive thinking abilities). Unlike the static criminal-history factors, the needs of the offender can change (for the better or, if not addressed, for the worse). Many risk/need factors are **criminogenic**—that is, if they are not addressed, future criminal behaviour may occur.

The risk determination, then, is the result of combining static criminal history information with dynamic (or criminogenic need) factors. This determination also plays a role in decisions to release offenders from confinement (see Chapter 8). Systems of corrections have often been criticized for their tendency to "overclassify"—that is, to assign inmates to higher security than their actual risk warrants. There is, however, no evidence that this is a widespread practice for either male or female offenders (Irving and Wichmann 2001).

CASE MANAGEMENT

Correctional **case management** is the process by which the needs and abilities of offenders are matched with correctional programs and services. The primary goals of case management are (1) to provide for systematic monitoring of the offender during all phases of confinement; (2) to facilitate the graduated release of offenders into the community; and (3) to prevent reoffending by the inmate upon release into the outside community.

A properly operated case management process (1) ensures that the inmate is provided with the level of structure and supervision required while addressing identified offender needs; (2) balances the need for rehabilitative intervention with community protection; (3) prepares the inmate for successful reintegration into the community; and (4) contributes to effective supervision of the offender in the community.

An overview of the case management process is presented in Box 7.2. Note that case management is carried out both during the inmate's confinement and following release from the institution. Note also that the process outlined in Box 7.2 is intended only as a general description of the various phases of case management. The number of phases and their specific titles may vary across systems of corrections.

The Correctional Plan

At the core of the case management process is the **correctional plan,** which is developed for most inmates, the exception being those serving short sentences. This plan determines the offender's initial institution placement, specific training or work opportunities, and release plan. The correctional plan is based on the risk/needs profile of the inmate and is used to guide all decisions made about the inmate. The plan identifies program needs, based in part on the dynamic factors discussed above. For example, if substance abuse is a contributing factor to the

BOX 7.2

The Five Phases of the Case Management Process

I. Initial Assessment and Institutional Placement
- identification of inmate risks/needs
- development of correctional plan

II. Correctional Planning and Institutional Supervision
- correctional plan initiated
- institutional programs (work, treatment, skills upgrading)
- institutional transfers
- institutional releases (temporary absences, work releases)
- ongoing monitoring of inmate progress

III. Preparing Cases for Release Decisions
- institutional progress reports
- community assessments

IV. Parole Board Decision and Release
- temporary absences, day/full parole, statutory release

V. Community Supervision

inmate's pattern of criminality, then the offender should be referred to a substance-abuse program. The correctional plan also sets out benchmarks, including parole eligibility dates and likely program entrance dates.

The informational heart of the case management process in federal institutions is the Offender Management System (OMS), a centralized database on offenders that is used to improve efficiency in the gathering and sharing of information on offenders across the country. Such information will be helpful, for example, if a parolee from the Vancouver area absconds and is arrested in Halifax. The Halifax district parole office will have immediate access to the accumulated file information.

Provincial/territorial correctional systems also have means for gathering information on inmates on an ongoing basis, though again, the relatively short period that offenders are confined reduces the time spent on information gathering. Ontario uses the Offender Tracking Information System (OTIS).

Since only a small percentage of inmates in provincial/territorial correctional systems spend more than a year in confinement, the primary focus of case management is release planning. In federal institutions, by contrast, the case management process generally involves a much longer time frame. Regular reviews are conducted during which program requirements are identified and decisions are made about transferring inmates from one institution to another and, eventually, releasing them.

The Role of Federal Institutional Parole Officers

In federal corrections, institutional parole officers (IPOs) have primary responsibility for case management and work as part of a team that includes correctional officers, psychologists, and the offender, among others. Their duties include assessing offender needs, as well as behaviours or attitudes that have contributed to their criminal behaviour; developing intervention plans to address these attitudes and behaviours; and helping offenders undertake and complete these intervention plans. The IPOs also make recommendations concerning offender transfers, temporary absences, and other forms of conditional release, including parole. In many institutions, IPOs spend most of their time completing paperwork rather than supervising and counselling inmates.

INSTITUTIONAL TREATMENT PROGRAMS

The most common types of treatment programs in federal and provincial/territorial institutions focus on living skills, anger management, substance abuse, family violence, basic education, and vocational training. There is considerable variation among institutions in the specific types of programs offered.

The CSC offers a number of core programs that are designed to address specific need areas and to prepare inmates for reentry into the community. Many of these programs are also available in provincial/territorial institutions, albeit in a compressed form owing to the short periods of time that inmates are confined.

Living Skills Programming

Living skills programs generally include parenting skills training, anger and emotion management, critical thinking, interpersonal problem solving, living without violence, and leisure education. Cognitive skills training focuses on the development of skills for effective thinking, decision making, problem solving, and goal setting, as well as interpersonal skills. Many criminal offenders lack self-control and are unable to regulate their own behaviour. They also lack interpersonal and problem-solving skills as well as critical reasoning and planning skills. Cognitive skills training is designed to change the way offenders think in order to change the way they act (Fabiano, Porporino, and Robinson 1990).

Violence Prevention Program (VPP)

The VPP program is directed toward those inmates who have been assessed as at high risk to commit violent offences. The program consists of 120 two-hour sessions delivered over four months to a group of no more than 12 offenders. The program uses a cognitive-behavioural and skills-set approach and is presented in a number of modules, including these: violence awareness, anger control, problem solving, positive relationships, resolving conflicts, self-control, and violence prevention. Each participant is required to develop, articulate, and manage a comprehensive violence-relapse prevention plan.

Substance Abuse Intervention

A high percentage of inmates have a history of substance abuse, and for many, alcohol and drugs are directly related to their criminal history. To address these issues, substance-abuse programs are offered in most federal and provincial/territorial institutions. The CSC uses the Computerized Lifestyle Assessment Instrument (CLAI) to identify inmates with substance-abuse problems and to determine their specific treatment needs. This instrument is a valid assessment tool for both non-Aboriginal and Aboriginal inmates.

The core program offered by the CSC is the Offender Substance Abuse Pre-Release Program (OSAP). OSAP uses behavioural and cognitive-behavioural approaches in an attempt to alter patterns of substance abuse and to reduce the likelihood that the inmate will abuse drugs or alcohol upon release from the institution. Among the program components are cognitive and behavioural skills, problem-solving skills, alcohol and drug education, and techniques of relapse prevention. Similar programs are offered in many provincial/territorial institutions. The Women Offender Substance Abuse Program (WOSAP) is a gender-responsive, multidimensional model that offers a continuum of interventions and support from the time of admission to a correctional facility to Warrant Expiry Date.

Family Violence Programs

In Chapter 6 it was noted that inmate family life is often characterized by a considerable amount of conflict and violence. This program, which has information and skill-building components, is directed toward inmates who either have a history of violence or are at risk of becoming abusive. The program offered by the CSC takes a feminist-informed cognitive-behavioural approach. It teaches participants about the power and control dynamics that underlie their abusive behaviour toward partners and children.

Literacy and Education Programs

As many as two-thirds of the inmates admitted to correctional institutions test at or below grade eight levels in math and language. The education programs in correctional facilities focus on general literacy and Adult Basic Education (ABE). Most provincial/territorial facilities and all federal institutions also offer secondary education (grades eleven and twelve) as well as vocational training. Inmates in federal institutions can also access university-level courses via correspondence, though the inmate generally assumes the cost of these courses.

Sex Offender Treatment Programs

The treatment of sex offenders has become a focal point of correctional systems, in large measure because of increasing public and political concern about this group of offenders and their growing numbers in institutional populations.

As a group, sex offenders are difficult to treat, especially those classified as high risk. The patterns of deviance are often deeply entrenched. Furthermore, to a greater extent than other offender groups, sex offenders tend to deny having committed an offence, to minimize the impact of the crime on the victim(s), and to attribute their behaviour to the actions and wishes of the victim(s). Sex offenders may not be motivated to participate in treatment programs and to engage in the process of self-change (Nunes et al. 2007).

Most treatment interventions for sex offenders take a multidisciplinary team approach, one that involves psychiatrists, psychometrists, social workers, physicians, nurses, chaplains, recreational staff, and volunteers. These programs are designed to reduce the likelihood that sex offenders will recidivate upon release from the institution. Programs focus on identifying the nature and pattern of the offender's behaviour, as well as on providing skills in self-management and self-control. Many treatment programs for sex offenders use a cognitive-behavioural approach and emphasize relapse prevention.

In Ontario there are a number of specialized treatment facilities for sex offenders under provincial jurisdiction, including Millbrook Correctional Centre. That centre operates a variety of treatment interventions for sex offenders, including a relapse prevention program, which teaches inmates techniques for avoiding cues that are likely to result in reoffending, as well as various alternative coping strategies. Relapse prevention programs for sex offenders centre on having the offender identify the patterns of his offences and the distorted rationalizations used to justify them. The offender is then taught to avoid the situations in which he is most likely to reoffend, especially those sequences of events that, once started, he may not be able to stop. For example, if an offender has a history of befriending prepubescent boys in parks, he must learn never to go to parks and to resist the sometimes convoluted thinking that can lead him to think he absolutely has to go to the park today on his way home from the local parole office.

A program for federal sex offenders is outlined in Box 7.3.

Vocational and Work Programs

Prison work has a long and somewhat inglorious history in Canadian corrections, and it is only in the past few decades that vocational and work programs have been viewed as part of the rehabilitation regimen. The federal government agency CORCAN has as its primary mandate the production and marketing of prison-made goods. The objective of CORCAN is to provide offenders with training and work experiences in an institutional setting that they can transfer to the private sector in the outside community. Under provisions of the CCRA, goods and services produced by inmates can be sold only to federal, provincial, and municipal governments or to charitable, religious, and not-for-profit organizations.

Despite the recommendations of numerous commissions of inquiry, prison industry programs continue to be afflicted by poorly defined and conflicting program objectives, dull work assignments, outdated equipment, and a lack of programs that provide realistic prospects for inmates to secure employment

BOX 7.3

Institut Philippe Pinel de Montréal Treatment Program for Sex Offenders

This is an intensive 12-month treatment program for sex offenders, including sex murderers who have been diagnosed with several deviance disorders. The program takes a cognitive-behavioural approach. Program components include sex education, social-skills training, stress and anger management, aversion therapy, and orgasmic reconditioning. An attempt is made to match specific program modules to individual offenders. Service delivery is 80 percent group and 20 percent individual, with groups ranging in size from six to eight. Program therapists include a criminologist-sexologist, a psychiatrist, and a psychologist. A number of pre- and post-treatment assessments and evaluations are used to determine whether the objectives of the treatment program—including improving social skills, understanding the aggression cycle, increasing empathy, modifying sexual preferences, and formulating strategies for relapse prevention—have been achieved. The program, which is operated under contract with the CSC, can accommodate 15 offenders.

Source: Carter and Lefaive 1995, 44–45.

upon release. The fact that inmate pay scales provide for remuneration of less than $10 per day for most jobs further reduces incentives for inmate participation and diminishes the value of work performed. Successive reports of the Auditor General of Canada have documented CORCAN's failure to become a sustainable enterprise.

The failure of correctional systems to develop meaningful and productive work and vocational programs for inmates is even more unfortunate when one considers the vast untapped source of creativity and energy in inmate populations and the positive impact that meaningful employment programs could have on life inside correctional institutions. One option to improve prison industry and vocational programs in Canadian institutions is to involve the private sector. This approach is widespread in the United States, where most state systems of corrections and the federal prison system have partnerships with the private sector. The question of whether such partnerships should be developed in Canada is likely to become a topic of discussion in the near future. Contribute your thoughts on this topic in the "At Issue 7.1: Should there be private-sector industry in Canadian correctional institutions?" presented at the end of this chapter.

Religious Programs and the Chaplaincy

Religion has been a key component of institutional life ever since the first prisons were built in the early 1800s. Though there is no Canadian data on how many inmates participate in religious programs and services in Canadian institutions, figures from the United States indicate that one in three inmates is involved in religious programs. One can assume that the numbers are much the same in Canada. Across Canada, a wide range of religious groups and organizations offer programs to inmates on a volunteer basis.

Community Involvement in Institutional Programs

Community volunteers are involved in a wide range of activities in federal and provincial/territorial institutions. Many volunteers represent community service clubs and organizations; others work one-on-one with inmates both during confinement and following release. The most active programs of this type are M2 (Man to Man) and W2 (Woman to Woman). In these programs a citizen from the community is matched with an offender. Across the country, college and university students are also actively involved in institutional programs.

FEMALE INMATES AND TREATMENT

A number of task forces have identified the need for a women-centred approach to treatment, one that centres on empowerment and that recognizes the broader, systemic barriers facing women in general: poverty, unemployment, lack of education, and sexism (see Glube 2006; Task Force on Federally Sentenced Women 1990). Women's offences are generally less serious than those of male offenders; at the same time, female inmates generally have higher levels of health and mental-health needs than male inmates and are more likely to have experienced sexual or physical victimization prior to incarceration (Raj, 2008). They are also more likely to be taking care of children (Brown, Miller, and Maguin 1999). Finding employment may be even more challenging for women than it is for men, because women are less likely to have completed their education, often have little job experience, and may have to find and pay for daycare (Glube 2006; Sampson 2007).

ABORIGINAL INMATES AND TREATMENT

> *So, prison is no place to recover. From anything, either the grief of memory, or loss, or abuse, or the diseases of addiction. But if you're Native and you can get the help to seek and find and claim your spiritual name, a lot can be*

> *changed. You can discover your destiny. Your life can bridge back to the origins of your family and people, you can seek out your colours, your clan, your spirit keepers. You may find the self you never knew you were. (Yvonne Johnson, as told to Rudy Wiebe 1998, 387)*

The special treatment needs of Aboriginal inmates have received increasing attention by systems of corrections, largely because of the high rates of incarceration of Aboriginal offenders. This is reflected at Pe Sakastew Institution, a minimum-security facility for Aboriginal male offenders on the Samson Cree Nation in Alberta. Aboriginal elders were directly involved in developing the treatment programs, which focus on healing and include a sweat lodge. Inmates in the minimum-security facility are called Owiciiyisiwak, which in the Cree language means "here to learn." Offenders are screened carefully before being sent to the institution and must have demonstrated an interest in rehabilitation programs and a history of positive interaction with correctional staff.

A wide variety of Aboriginal-specific programs can be found in federal and provincial/territorial institutions. Many of these programs are operated by correctional systems, while others are sponsored by outside Aboriginal organizations and agencies. In an attempt to address the security-threat and reintegration needs of the estimated 300 Aboriginal gang members who are incarcerated in federal institutions in the Prairie Region, the CSC has developed the Aboriginal Gang Initiative (AGI). The AGI team includes five Aboriginal facilitators guided by Aboriginal elders. An effort is made to help gang members find new identities in their Aboriginal culture and to provide them with a positive foundation with which to reenter the community (Phillips 2002).

Among the more common Aboriginal-specific programs found in correctional institutions across the country are sweat lodges, healing circles, and modules that focus on cultural awareness, substance abuse, and family violence. There are also Pathways units in several federal facilities, which are led by teams composed of Aboriginal elders and correctional staff. The approach these units take is grounded in Aboriginal culture and spirituality. They address issues related to residential schools, reserve life, and broken families through individual counselling, sweat lodge ceremonies, and other culturally based activities (Amellal 2006). The Okimaw Ohci Healing Lodge for federal Aboriginal female offenders in Saskatchewan follows a healing model that incorporates Aboriginal culture and spirituality. The In Search of Your Warrior program is an intensive intervention program for federally incarcerated Aboriginal offenders with a history of violence. That

Inmates at the Aboriginal Healing Range at Stony Mountain Institution participate in a drum circle.
CP PHOTO/Winnipeg Free Press/Ken Gigliotti

program combines Western treatment approaches with traditional Aboriginal spirituality in an attempt to break the cycle of violence. The Ma Mawi Wi Chi Itata Family Violence Program in Stony Mountain Institution is profiled in Box 7.4.

BOX 7.4

The Ma Mawi Wi Chi Itata Family Violence Program, Stony Mountain Institution (Manitoba)

This program for Aboriginal inmates is designed to address the issues related to violent behaviour and attempts to alter inmates' patterns of violent behaviour toward spouses and family members, as well as disruptive behaviour in the institutional setting. The program focuses on education, counselling, healing, and prevention and incorporates contemporary and traditional treatment approaches.

The program has four sections, each representing a geographical direction on the Medicine Wheel:

- *The East.* Represented by the eagle. The primary objective is "to see." The focus is on the cycle of violence, the role of socialization in committing violence, and the relationship between violence and substance abuse.
- *The South.* Represented by the mouse. The primary objective is "to do." The focus is on the offender's expressing negative emotions, including those related to childhood experiences and family origin; and on exploring feelings of shame and guilt for past behaviour, which includes discussion of the inmate's most violent incident.
- *The West.* Represented by the bear. The primary objective is "to think." The focus is on the impact of violence on children and families. Also addressed are the various dimensions of relationships, as well as skills in substituting assertiveness for aggression.
- *The North.* Represented by the buffalo. The primary objective is "to know." The focus is on taking the middle way. Inmates meet in sharing circles to establish goals, share stories, and relate feelings.

On completion of the program, there are a number of ceremonies, including a sweat lodge ceremony and a feast. These ceremonies and the program itself are designed to provide the Aboriginal inmate with a new identity.

Source: Proulx and Perrault 1996.

COMMUNITY SERVICE PROJECTS AND ACTIVITIES

The media's focus on the more sensational events in corrections, such as escapes, riots, and heinous crimes committed by offenders under supervision in the community, tends to obscure the extensive involvement of inmate populations in community-service projects. These activities benefit various groups of community residents; they also provide an outlet for the energies and talents of inmates while engaging them in community-focused endeavours. Participation in community projects may also help inmates develop prosocial attitudes and behaviours. Federal inmate community-service initiatives are coordinated under the Giving Back to the Community program. At Westmorland Institution in Dorchester, New Brunswick, inmates have raised more than $34,000 for the Children's Wish Foundation. Inmates at Joliette Institution for Women in Quebec operate a toys-for-tots program, repairing donated toys to be distributed to children at Christmas. Inmates at Stony Mountain Institution have made playhouses, which have then been raffled to raise money for Habitat for Humanity.

Inmates watch as a developmentally challenged boy high jumps as part of an inmate-sponsored event within the confines of the Leclerc Institution, a medium-security penitentiary in Laval, Quebec.
CP PHOTO/Paul Chiasson

PRINCIPLES OF EFFECTIVE CORRECTIONAL TREATMENT

Five core principles provide the basis for effective correctional treatment. Research studies indicate that when these principles are addressed effectively, especially in a community setting, there can be significant reductions in rates of reoffending (Andrews and Bonta 2003; Bonta and Andrews 2007).

The Risk Principle

The **risk principle** holds that treatment interventions have a greater chance of success when they are matched with the risk level of the offender. Higher levels of service are reserved for higher risk inmates; lower risk inmates do not require the same level of service to benefit from treatment interventions and may, in fact, be negatively affected by intensive service delivery. Among the risk factors that have been identified are antisocial attitudes, values, beliefs, rationalizations, and cognitive-emotional states (such as anger, resentment, defiance, and despair); a lack of problem-solving and self-management skills, and impulsiveness (Andrews 1995; Andrews and Bonta 2003). Note that this list includes both static risk factors and dynamic risk factors (or criminogenic needs).

An extensive body of evaluation research indicates that treatment programs have little impact on reoffending among low-risk offenders and that higher risk inmates benefit from treatment programs that focus on criminogenic factors (Smith and Gendreau 2007). This principle may prove a challenge for treatment staff. One observer has noted that "clinicians and front-line workers . . . often become frustrated by having to work with the high-risk, poorly motivated and disruptive offender who is taking up valuable treatment space" (Wormith 2007, 3).

The Need Principle

The **need principle** holds that to be effective, treatment interventions must also address the criminogenic needs of inmates. These include such attributes as alcohol or substance abuse, relations with peers, and attitudes toward and experiences with employment. The objective of targeting criminogenic needs is to alter personal attributes of the offender so as to reduce the likelihood of reoffending.

The Responsivity Principle

The **responsivity principle** states that treatment interventions must be matched to the learning styles and abilities of individual inmates. This presents challenges to correctional systems, as many offenders have disabilities that may present obstacles to learning.

Professional Discretion

Effective treatment interventions require that corrections personnel consider the unique attributes of individual inmates and apply the above three principles in an appropriate manner. There is considerable heterogenity even among inmates convicted of the same crimes, such as sex offenders, or with similar histories, such as substance abuse, and these must be considered by the treatment professional.

Program Integrity

According to this principle, efforts must be made to ensure that treatment programs are designed and delivered by qualified professionals whose adherence to the treatment model is monitored.

CREATING THE CONDITIONS FOR EFFECTIVE CORRECTIONAL TREATMENT

Besides the above principles for designing and delivering correctional treatment programs, a number of additional factors may enhance treatment effectiveness.

Correctional Officers and Correctional Staff

Effective program interventions require COs and staff who understand and support the objectives of correctional treatment. Means must be found to ensure that institutional staff reinforce treatment efforts instead of undermining them. Recall from Chapter 5 that compared to other institutional staff, COs are more punitive in their attitudes toward inmates as well as less supportive of rehabilitation programs. Yet at the same time, COs are well positioned to provide various types of assistance to inmates and, in so doing, to act as change agents. The training, experience, motivation level, and other attributes of correctional staff and treatment personnel all have a strong effect on successful treatment interventions (Lösel 1995).

Other correctional personnel within institutions, including civilians who supervise industrial and agricultural programs, may also have an impact on the attitudes and behaviours of inmates. A study of the CSC industry program, CORCAN, found that shop instructors who had dynamic leadership styles and who encouraged inmates had a significant impact on inmate behaviour in the institution (Gillis et al. 1998).

Matching Inmate Needs with Programs

One of the challenges confronting systems of corrections is how to address the needs of a client population that is marginal in terms of lifestyle skills and abilities. In the past, treatment programs were delivered to inmate populations within a "one size fits all" framework, the assumption being that all inmates would benefit equally from exposure to a specific intervention.

Though inmate populations share some general attributes—for example, low levels of education and skills development and histories of alcohol and substance abuse—each inmate is first and foremost an individual with unique needs and requirements. Heterogeneity, rather than uniformity, characterizes inmates, even those who have committed the same type of offence. To be effective, treatment interventions must be multifaceted and matched to the specific needs of individual offenders. This is the idea underlying **differential treatment effectiveness.** Classification and case management are designed to assist in determining the needs of individual offenders.

Inmate Amenability to Treatment

The inmate is a key component of the treatment process. For any program to have a significant impact on the attitudes and behaviour of the inmate, the offender must be amenable to treatment. Among the inmates in any institutional population there is a **differential amenability to treatment.** That is, for a variety of reasons, including mental deficiency or learning disability, a deeply rooted attitudinal and behavioural pattern centred on a criminal lifestyle, an extensive history of confinement in institutions, and/or a general lack of interest in making the effort to change, not all inmates are receptive to treatment. Many offenders are in a state of denial about the offence for which they have been convicted, and this frame of mind may make effective treatment intervention more difficult.

Until recently, offenders were generally excluded from having input into determining the specific treatment programs they would take part in while in the care and control of the correctional system. It is now an accepted principle of correctional practice that inmates must participate actively in the development of their treatment plan. A challenge for systems of corrections and treatment personnel is to develop strategies that will interest and motivate inmates to become involved in treatment programs as part of a concerted effort to alter their attitudes and values.

Continuity of Treatment Interventions from Institution to Community

A long-standing challenge to correctional systems has been to ensure continuity between treatment interventions in institutional settings and those in the community following release. The absence of resources, the lack of communication between institutional treatment personnel and their community-based counterparts, and the loss of eligibility to participate in community-based programs on warrant expiry have all contributed to the lack of treatment continuity. There is evidence, for example, that when institutional treatment interventions for substance abusers are part of a continuum with community-based treatment following release, there are higher rates of long-term abstinence (Inciardi 1996). Continuity of treatment is a major issue when Aboriginal inmates return to northern or remote communities. This issue is discussed further in chapter 9.

THE EFFECTIVENESS OF CORRECTIONAL TREATMENT

Since the introduction of treatment programs into correctional institutions in the 1950s, there has been an ongoing (and still unresolved) debate over their effectiveness. That debate has involved politicians, community interest groups, correctional scholars, and senior and line-level corrections personnel.

"Nothing Works" versus "Some Things Work": The Legacy of Robert Martinson

For the past three decades, no discussion of the effectiveness of correctional treatment programs has been complete without mention of Robert Martinson, a scholar who conducted a survey of more than two hundred treatment programs and concluded that "with few and isolated exceptions, the rehabilitative efforts that have been reported so far have had no appreciable effect on recidivism" (1974, 25). The "nothing works" finding, as it became known, had a significant impact on correctional policy for many years, even though, in a less publicized effort, Martinson (1979) himself reevaluated the treatment programs five years later using more valid criteria and concluded that some treatments did have an effect on recidivism.

Martinson's name and study continue to be invoked by those correctional observers who contend that rehabilitation programs are ineffective in altering the attitudes and behaviours of inmates and in reducing rates of reoffending. The general consensus among researchers, however, is that some programs work to reduce reoffending of some offenders; that direct treatment services are more likely than criminal sanctions to reduce recidivism; that effective treatment programs follow the principles of risk and need; and that treatment programs using a cognitive-behavioural approach have considerable promise (Bonta 1997; Lösel, 1995; Sherman et al., 1997).

A review of the effectiveness of selected treatment interventions is presented in Box 7.5.

BOX 7.5

Research Summary: The Effectiveness of Selected Treatment Interventions

Adult basic education. A significant relationship exists between program completion and reduced likelihood of recidivism upon release, even among high-risk inmates. Effectiveness may be improved with more continuity between prison education and postrelease follow-up and support (John Howard Society of Alberta 2002).

Vocational and work programs. There is some Canadian evidence that participation in vocational and work programs reduces levels of misconduct in the institution, increases the likelihood that the offender will find employment when released, and increases the chances of success in the community (Gillis, Motiuk, and Belcourt 1998). Evaluations in the United States have found that inmates who worked in private industries while in prison obtained employment more quickly and had lower recidivism rates than those who did not (Moses and Smith 2007; Smith et al. 2006).

Cognitive skills programs. These are promising correctional interventions that have, nevertheless, produced mixed results. Canadian research using control and experimental groups found that cognitive skills programs can increase critical reasoning skills, the capacity for optional thinking, and interpersonal problem solving; they can also reduce rates of recidivism upon release. Moreover, such programs are effective for offenders under supervision in the community (Robinson 1995; Vennard, Sugg, and Hedderman 1997). British researchers, however, found no statistically significant differences in one- and two-year reconviction rates between female and male offenders who participated in cognitive skills programs while confined and matched comparison groups of offenders who did not participate in these programs. Limitations in program implementation and evaluation methodology were identified as possible contributors to these findings (Canin 2006; Falshaw et al. 2003).

Substance abuse programs. Participants in the federal Intensive Supervision Unit (ISU) programs (see Chapter 4) were 36 percent less likely to be returned to custody than offenders in a matched comparison group and they were less likely to be returned to custody for a new offence (Varis, Lefebvre, and Grant 2006). An evaluation of the High Intensity Substance Abuse Program (HISAP) for severely addicted inmates found that HISAP participants were less likely to be readmitted within six months of their release and less likely to have their conditional release revoked as the result of a new offence as compared to a matched sample (Grant et al. 2003). Studies in the United States have found that participation in drug treatment programs can reduce rates of reoffending upon release (Pelissier et al. 2000). In particular, long-term, residential "coercive" programs—that is, programs offered in the context of the criminal justice system, in which the offender has little or no choice but to participate—have been found to reduce rates of reoffending among high-risk offenders who have substance-abuse issues. The same has been found for multistage residential programs that provide a bridge between the prison and the community (Belenko et al. 2004; see also Inciardi, Martin, and Butzin 2004).

Sex offender treatment programs. While the treatment of sex offenders has often been subjected to the "nothing works" criticism, there is research evidence that some treatment approaches work. Programs that focus on high-risk sex offenders, use a group format, focus on anger management and the development of cognitive-behavioural skills, and have a relapse prevention component, have been successful in reducing rates of sexual reoffending (Gordon and Nicholaichuk 1996). These findings reaffirm that it is high-risk offenders who are most likely to benefit from treatment interventions. The serious consequences of sex offences for victims and community perceptions of safety mean that the rates of recidivism among this offender group remain a concern at any level.

Violent offender programs. The Violence Prevention Program offered in federal correctional institutions reduces institutional misconduct as well as violent reoffending among high-risk/high-need violent offenders (Cortoni, Nunes, and Latendresse 2006).

(continued)

Religious programs. Findings from the United States suggest that participation in religious programs has a positive impact on the attitudes, values, and behaviour of inmates, resulting in fewer incidents of institutional misconduct and a reduced likelihood of recidivism upon release (Fabelo 2003). American research suggests that inmates who are committed to their religious beliefs and who participate extensively in religious programs have fewer institutional infractions than inmates who have little or no involvement in prison fellowships. They are also significantly less likely to be rearrested at two and three years following release (Johnson, Larson, and Pitts 1997; Johnson, 2004).

Women-centred treatment programs. Correctional systems are focusing more and more on gender-specific programming. However, there is a lack of evaluation research on the related treatment outcomes. Specifically, though the unique needs of female offenders have been identified, it is not clear whether current programming efforts have reduced rates of reoffending. Information on rates of reoffending is, at best, anecdotal. Interim research conducted on the Woman Offender Substance Abuse Program (WOSAP) found high rates of program completion, increased knowledge and skills among participants, and high levels of participant satisfaction with the program. However, reoffending upon release has not been studied (Furlong and Grant 2006).

Aboriginal-focused treatment programs. The lack of evaluations of treatment outcomes of Aboriginal-specific programs precludes a determination of whether these programs are more effective than generalist programs (i.e., ones that are offered to both Aboriginal and non-Aboriginal inmates). There is a widespread belief that Aboriginal-specific treatment interventions such as the Pathway units are more effective than general programs; however, LaPrairie notes that "the evidence for this is often anecdotal and often put forward by the people who write policy or deliver programs (1996, 82)." An evaluation of the Ma Mawi Wi Chi Itata family violence program in Stony Mountain Institution (see Box 8.6) found high levels of inmate and staff satisfaction with the program and a widely shared view among inmate participants that the program had significantly affected their behaviour, attitudes, and emotions. An evaluation of the Okimaw Ohci Healing Lodge for Aboriginal federal female inmates identified a number of issues related to the program's operations that were limiting its effectiveness. No attempt was made to measure postrelease outcomes in either of these programs (Correctional Service of Canada 2002; Proulx and Perrault 1996). An evaluation of the In Search of Your Warrior program found that a significantly smaller number of offenders who had participated in the program were returned to prison within a year for committing a new violent offence, though the rates of readmission were not significantly different from those of Aboriginal offenders who did not participate in the program (Trevethan, Moore, and Allegri 2005).

MEASURING THE EFFECTIVENESS OF CORRECTIONAL TREATMENT

Efforts to assess the effectiveness of treatment programs have encountered a number of difficulties.

The Absence of and Poor Quality of Program Evaluations

A major obstacle in determining "what works" is the absence of a standardized evaluative framework. This makes it difficult to determine whether offenders who participate in a particular treatment program benefit from the experience (Lane et al. 2002).

Studies of the effectiveness of treatment interventions in provincial/territorial institutions are virtually nonexistent. These correctional systems face the added difficulty of high inmate turnover—an obstacle not only to the delivery of treatment programs but also to any attempts to determine program success.

Measuring Treatment Success: A Difficult Task

The traditional method used to determine success is **recidivism rates**—that is, the number of offenders who, once released from confinement, are returned to prison either for a technical violation of their parole or statutory release or for the commission of a new offence. The use of recidivism rates as a measure of program effectiveness has been criticized on a number of counts:

- Using legal criteria of subsequent contact with the criminal justice system makes no provision for the "relative" improvement of the offender. Offenders who previously committed serious crimes and are subsequently returned to confinement for a relatively minor offence might be viewed as a "relative success" rather than as a failure.
- The question of how long after release from confinement the offender's behaviour is to be monitored is undecided. Many types of sex offenders, for example, remain a high risk to reoffend for a decade or longer following release.
- Recidivism rates are a result of detection of the released offender by parole or police officers. In fact, the offender may have returned to criminal activity and not have been detected—a not unlikely scenario, given that clearance rates of the police for most nonviolent offences are less than 20 percent and often as low as 5 percent.

- The success or failure of an offender upon release may be due in large measure to the level and type of supervision he or she receives. Among parole officers there are a variety of supervision styles, ranging from officers who have a more punitive orientation to those who focus on providing services and assistance (see Chapter 9).
- It is difficult to relate the offender's behaviour upon release to specific treatment interventions that he or she received while incarcerated. There are many reasons why an individual may cease violating the law, including the efforts of a supportive family and/or spouse, success in securing stable employment, and maturation.

The use of control groups within an experimental design eliminates many of the problems associated with using recidivism as an outcome measure.

The Notion of "Relative" Success on Release

In an attempt to address many of these difficulties with using recidivism rates to measure the effectiveness of treatment interventions, several observers have suggested the use of more refined indicators of post-institution behaviour, including the following:

- *Clear reformation.* Offenders have been on parole, have stable employment, and are not associating with persons involved in criminal activity.
- *Marginal reformation.* Offenders have not been returned to a correctional institution but have failed to maintain employment, are associating with persons involved in criminal activities, and/or have committed minor offences.
- *Marginal failures.* Offenders are returned to correctional institutions for violating the conditions of their release or for minor crimes.
- *Clear recidivists.* Offenders commit a major crime and are returned to prison (Glaser 1964, 31–58).

This scheme was proposed nearly five decades ago. In recent years, correctional researchers and systems of corrections have been distinguishing between those offenders returned to institutions for violations of release conditions and those who committed new offences.

POTENTIAL OBSTACLES TO EFFECTIVE CORRECTIONAL TREATMENT

There are a number of potential obstacles to the delivery of effective treatment programs in correctional institutions. These include the following:

Punishment versus Treatment

The primary mandate of correctional institutions—to securely confine offenders—often undermines the objectives of treatment programs. You will recall from the discussion in Chapter 4 that a defining attribute of correctional institutions is that they are public and political. The availability of treatment resources may be restricted by politicians, legislatures, and community interest groups. In recent years, community interest groups and politicians have voiced concerns about the living conditions in correctional institutions and the privileges accorded to inmates, often referring to federal institutions as "club feds."

Doing Time and Doing Treatment

The discussion in Chapter 6 revealed that inmates are confronted with a variety of pains of imprisonment, as well as with the need to develop coping and survival strategies for doing time. Though inmate adherence to the convict code has eroded in recent years, the inmate social system, with its attendant activities in securing illicit goods and services, and the violence and coercion that exist in many institutions may be a major obstacle to treatment within the system. For those inmates who must spend a considerable portion of their time and energy coping with confinement and avoiding victimization, pursuing self-change through participation in treatment programs may be difficult. It is not hard to imagine the challenges to doing treatment that confronted inmates in the Headingley Institution at the time the riot occurred (see Chapter 4). Inmates may also be intimidated by other inmates not to participate in correctional programming (personal communication with deputy warden, federal correctional institution). Ironically, then, one of the biggest potential obstacles to the delivery of effective correctional treatment may be the institution itself and the dynamics of life inside correctional institutions.

Inmate Access to Programs and Inmate Attrition

How treatment programs are delivered, including the timeliness of program offerings and the extent to which programs attract and retain inmate participants, can affect treatment outcomes. For treatment interventions to be effective, the inmate must have the opportunity to participate in and complete the particular program. Generally, treatment programs operate on one of two types of schedules: "closed group," which means that the program begins and ends on specified dates and that inmates must participate in all of the sessions; and "open group" (or continuous intake), which allow inmates to join the program at any time if space is available. Most treatment programs are of the closed variety, which often makes it difficult to match offenders with programs. These

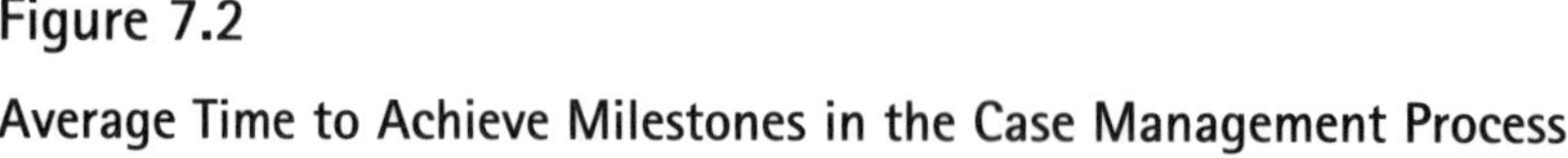

Figure 7.2

Average Time to Achieve Milestones in the Case Management Process

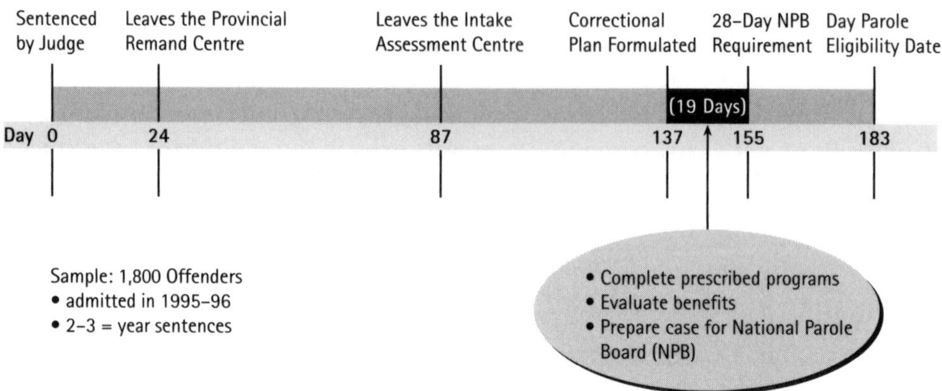

Source: Auditor General of Canada 1996, 16. Reproduced with the permission of the Minister of Public Works and Government Services Canada. 2008.

designations do not apply to treatment programs that involve one-on-one interventions with inmates. A lack of space and program resources often results in inmates waiting months or even years to gain access to specific programs. Figure 7.2 illustrates the "timeline" problems encountered by a large sample of federal inmates. It reveals a very small window for completing treatment programs, for staff evaluation of the benefits of the program, and for preparation of a plan for the parole board.

Inmate attrition can also limit the effectiveness of treatment programs. Those inmates who complete treatment programs have higher rates of success in terms of successful reintegration (Griffiths, Dandurand, and Murdoch 2007). Though the classification process is able to determine the programming needs of inmates, many offenders either never enroll in programs or fail to complete the ones that have been recommended. Noncompletion rates appear to be higher among Aboriginal inmates, higher risk inmates, and inmates with less education (Nunes and Cortoni 2006; Wormith and Olver 2002).

The short period of time that inmates are confined in provincial/territorial correctional facilities often precludes or limits participation in treatment programs. Yet offenders in these facilities face many of the same deficiencies as federal inmates, including low levels of education, anger management problems, a propensity to violence, mental disabilities, and substance-abuse problems.

One of the only published studies on treatment programs in provincial institutions found that the programs in a women's facility fell short of providing programs that met the inmates' needs. Provincial fiscal constraints, the isolated location of the facility, and the difficulty of attracting professional staff resulted in the women being deprived of treatment programs that would have addressed their criminogenic and noncriminogenic needs (Monster and Micucci 2005). Overcrowding may limit inmate access to treatment programs (see Chapter 4).

Levels of program participation are another potential obstacle to treatment success, especially for Aboriginal inmates. One possible explanation for the low participation rates of Aboriginal offenders is that a higher proportion of them are classified as high-risk (i.e., relative to non-Aboriginal offenders) because they have a higher number of risk factors as measured by risk prediction instruments. A higher risk score usually results in a higher security classification, which in turn results in placement in a maximum-security institution where appropriate programming is less likely to be offered. As a consequence, high-risk Aboriginal offenders are unable to participate in Aboriginal-specific treatment approaches such as healing lodges (Rugge 2006).

There is also the issue of **differential treatment availability**, both across provincial/territorial jurisdictions and among the various regions of the CSC. This results in situations, for example, where a high-risk sex offender might receive a year of treatment in a specialized program in one CSC region, while a sex offender in another region might complete only a six-month nonresidential program. The CSC spends less than 10 percent of its budget on treatment programs.

Program Fidelity and Program Drift

A key factor in the development of effective correctional treatment programs is program implementation (Gendreau, Goggin, and Smith 1999; Lowenkamp, Latessa, and Smith 2006). Correctional authorities must ensure that there is **program fidelity**—that is, that a treatment program is delivered in the way it was originally designed. Program fidelity can be assured by providing a clear program manual as well as appropriate training and supervision to treatment staff. This is closely related to the principle of program integrity noted earlier.

One federal inmate commented on the problem of program fidelity:

The Substance Abuse Program I attended involved nothing more than watching a series of videotapes two days a week for 10 weeks. Our group

> *viewed the tapes, then were dismissed. There was no discussion; there was no interaction between facilitator and group; there was no attempt to talk about anything. After the program was over I had an idea what abuse of drugs and alcohol would do to my body, but I had no idea why I ever wanted to use them. (Kowbel 1995, A20)*

Program fidelity may also be compromised in institutions where correctional officers are involved in facilitating core treatment programs, as in some provincial institutions in British Columbia. It is also important to use outcome measures that can detect **program drift**. For example, if it is known that a substance-abuse program reduces levels of substance abuse among released offenders, then an increase in substance use among program completers may indicate that program delivery is drifting, and steps can be taken to correct this.

Lack of Continuity Between Prison Treatment Programs and Community Treatment Programs

As noted earlier, continuity in treatment from the institutional to the community setting enhances treatment effectiveness. However, the absence of resources and the lack of coordination between correctional systems and social service systems often results in offenders who have been incarcerated leaving prison without any connection to support services. Studies have found that the effectiveness of institution-based treatment programs is enhanced when there is a "seamless" transition to community-based treatment when the offender is released from confinement (Solomon et al. 2004). More on this in chapter 9.

THE ETHICS OF CORRECTIONAL TREATMENT

Historically, inmates had no power to resist the sanctions imposed on them, and a wide variety of punishments have been inflicted on inmates under the guise of treatment. At one time, these punishments included electroshock "therapy," which was administered to many inmates without their consent until the 1980s. Inmates were also used as subjects in a variety of experiments, including studies of the effects of LSD. The inmates in this series of studies did provide "consent"; the issue is whether a captive person is able to provide informed consent. The Canadian Charter of Rights and Freedoms (1982) has provided inmates with some degree of legal protection. Examples of mandatory treatment in Canada are the Heroin Treatment Act in B.C., which forced addicts to participate in a government heroin-treatment program, and the Protection of Children Abusing Drugs Act in Alberta, which requires youth under 18 who have alcohol or drug problems to participate in treatment (Mugford and Weekes 2006).

Contribute your opinion to the debate over mandatory treatment in the "At Issue 7.2: Should prison inmates have the right to refuse treatment?" presented at the end of the chapter.

"It's interesting—with each conviction I learn a little more about myself."

AT ISSUE

ISSUE 7.1: Should there be private-sector industry in Canadian correctional institutions?

There are a variety of ways in which the private sector can become involved in developing and operating prison-based industries. These industrial programs could be developed in federal and provincial/territorial facilities, in privately operated prisons, or in the community.

Proponents of involving the private sector in prison industries make these arguments:

- The correctional-system/private-sector partnership is a "win–win" situation: industry secures access to a motivated, reliable workforce, while prisons have access to private-sector expertise and inmates develop skills that will make them employable in the outside community.
- Inmates who work in private-sector industries and earn a wage similar to their "free world' counterparts can use this money to support their families, pay restitution to victims, pay room and board, and save money for release.
- Private-sector industries reduce inmate idleness, lessen the frequency of behavioural disruptions, and create a positive institutional environment.
- Participating in prison industries teaches inmates responsibility as well as a skill set; both will be assets in the free community.

Opponents of private-sector prison industries make these points:

- The "in-kind" subsidies for private-sector businesses, including nominal rents and security, are too generous and should not be paid for by taxpayers.
- Business and labour groups in the outside community would oppose private-sector prison industries and would try to prevent the goods produced by these industries from being sold on the open market.
- Inmates would be susceptible to exploitation by private industry.
- Private-sector industries would take jobs from workers in the outside community.
- It is immoral to profit from inmates, who are a disadvantaged group in society.
- Participation in prison industries may prevent an inmate from completing essential treatment programs.

The Research Evidence

There is no current research on the viability of private-sector prison industries in Canada. There has been some friction between the private sector and unions and correctional systems in the United States over prison industries.

What do you think?

1. Would you support the development of private-sector industries in Canadian correctional institutions on a trial basis? Why or why not?

2. If yes, which criteria would you use to determine whether such an initiative was successful?
3. If yes, would you require inmates who worked in prison industries to contribute to the costs of their room and board? Pay victim compensation?

Sources: Cholodofsky 2005; insideprison.com 2006; Light 1999; Sandberg 2008.

AT ISSUE

ISSUE 7.2: Should prison inmates have the right to refuse treatment?

Consider the following scenario: An inmate convicted of a sex offence is sentenced to 15 years in prison. During confinement, he refuses to participate in treatment programs. As a consequence, he does not receive any form of conditional release, is denied statutory release after having served two-thirds of the sentence, and serves his entire sentence in prison. On his warrant expiry date, he is released, untreated, from the correctional institution, at high risk of reoffending.

This raises the issue of whether inmates have a legal right to refuse treatment. A provision of the CCRA states that inmates must provide informed consent, both at the outset and during treatment, and that the inmate has the right to refuse treatment or to withdraw from a treatment program at any time. The Canadian Charter of Rights and Freedoms also guarantees that all persons have the right to life, liberty, and security of the person, rights that would most likely be violated by any provision of mandatory treatment (McKinnon 1995).

What do you think?

1. What is your position on the right of inmates to refuse treatment? Would you, for example, support an attempt to impose mandatory treatment on certain categories of offenders, such as sex offenders and violent offenders?
2. Inmates who refuse treatment may have applications for conditional release denied and may also be prohibited from being released on their statutory release date. This means they will serve their entire sentence in confinement and be released with no conditions or supervision. Given this, would you support the release of serious offenders on either conditional release or statutory release even if they have refused to participate in treatment programs?

KEY POINTS REVIEW

1. Three major trends in offender classification and treatment are the increasing use of risk assessment instruments, the use of psychological approaches to treatment, and the development of differentiated

treatment approaches for women, Aboriginals, and specific categories of offenders.

2. The Static-99 is an assessment instrument that is used with moderate success, to predict sexual and violent reoffending.
3. The assessment of risk is a key component of classification and case management.
4. The most common types of treatment programs inside correctional institutions focus on living skills, anger management, substance abuse, family violence, basic education, and vocational training/industries.
5. As a group, sex offenders are difficult to treat. Programs for them focus on identifying the nature and pattern of offending and providing skills in self-management and self-control.
6. Female offenders generally have greater health and mental-health needs than male inmates and are more likely to have experienced sexual or physical victimization prior to incarceration.
7. The special treatment needs of Aboriginal offenders have received increasing attention from correctional systems.
8. Research studies indicate that when the principles of effective correctional treatment are applied, there can be significant reductions in rates of reoffending.
9. The conditions required for effective correctional treatment include supportive correctional officers and staff, the matching of inmates needs/amenability with programs, and continuity of treatment from the institution to the community.
10. The general consensus among corrections researchers is that some programs work to reduce reoffending among some offenders and that higher-risk inmates are more likely to benefit from correctional treatment than low-risk inmates.
11. The absence of controlled evaluations precludes a determination of whether women-centred and Aboriginal-centred treatment programs reduce rates of reoffending.
12. The difficulties of assessing the effectiveness of correctional treatment programs include an absence of (or poor-quality) program evaluations and the challenges of measuring treatment success.
13. Among the potential obstacles to effective correctional treatment are the conflicts between punishment and treatment, the dynamics of life inside prisons, inmate access to programs and inmate attrition, and the lack of continuity between prison treatment programs and community treatment programs.

KEY TERM QUESTIONS

1. Define **classification** and its role in corrections.
2. Compare and contrast **static risk factors** and **need** (or dynamic) **risk factors**, and note the role of each type of factor in the classification process.
3. What are **criminogenic risk factors**?
4. Define and discuss the goals of correctional **case management.**
5. What is the **correctional plan** and what role does it play in correctional treatment?
6. Define (a) the **risk principle,** (b) the **need principle,** and (c) the **responsivity principle,** and then discuss the role that each plays in creating the conditions for effective correctional treatment.
7. What is meant by (a) **differential treatment effectiveness** and (b) **differential amenability to treatment**, and how does each of these notions contribute to our understanding of correctional treatment for inmates?
8. What are the issues that surround the use of **recidivism rates** as a measure of the success of correctional treatment programs and what alternatives have been suggested that may more accurately reflect treatment success?
9. What is meant by **differential treatment availability?**
10. Define the concepts of **program fidelity** and **program drift** and discuss why these concepts are important in the study of correctional treatment.

REFERENCES

Amellal, D. 2006. "The Pathways Unit at La Macaza Institution: The Path to Personal Growth and Healing." *Let's Talk* 31(1). http://www.csc-scc.gc.ca/text/pblct/lt-en/2006/31-1/6-eng.shtml

Andrews, D. 1995. "The Psychology of Criminal Conduct and Effective Treatment." In *What Works: Reoffending—Guidelines from Research and Practice*, ed. J. McGuire. Chichester: Wiley. 35–62.

Andrews, D.A., and J. Bonta. 2003. *The Psychology of Criminal Conduct*, 3rd ed. Cincinnati: Anderson.

Auditor General of Canada. 1996. *Annual Report of the Auditor General of Canada.* Ottawa: Minister of Public Works and Government Service of Canada. http://www.oag-bvg.gc.ca/internet/English/parl_oag_199611_30_e_5061.html

Belenko, S., C. Foltz, M.A. Lang, and H-E. Sung. 2004. "Recidivism Among High-Risk Drug Felons: A Longitudinal Analysis Following Residential Treatment." *Journal of Offender Rehabilitation* 40(1/2): 105–32.

Bonta, J. 1997. *Offender Rehabilitation: From Research to Practice.* Ottawa: Department of the Solicitor General of Canada. http://ww2.ps-sp.gc.ca/publications/corrections/pdf/199701_e.pdf

Bonta, J., and D.A. Andrews. 2007. *Risk-Need-Responsivity Model for Offender Assessment and Rehabilitation.* Ottawa: Public Safety Canada. http://www.ps-sp.gc.ca/res/cor/rep/_fl/Risk_Need_2007-06_e.pdf

Brown, A., B. Miller, and E. Maguin. 1999. "Prevalence and Severity of Lifetime Physical and Sexual Victimization Among Incarcerated Women." *International Journal of Law and Psychiatry* 22: 301–22.

Canin, J. 2006. *Cognitive Skills Programmes: Impact on Reducing Reconviction Among a Sample of Female Prisoners.* London: Research, Development, and Statistics Directorate, Home Office. http://www.homeoffice.gov.uk/rds/pdfs06/r276.pdf

Carter, W., and P. Lefaive. 1995. *Sex Offender Programs in CSC. Program Inventory and Description, Resourcing and Capacities.* Ottawa: Sex Offender Programs, Correctional Service of Canada.

Cholodofsky, R. 2005. "Prison Industry Thriving." *Pittsburgh Tribune-Review,* May 1. http://www.pittsburghlive.com/x/pittsburghtrib/s_329746.html

Cortoni, F., K. Nunes, and M. Latendresse. 2006. *An Examination of the Effectiveness of the Violence Prevention Program.* Ottawa: Correctional Service of Canada. http://www.csc-scc.gc.ca/text/rsrch/reports/r178/r178_e.pdf

CSC (Correctional Service of Canada). 2002. *Report on the Evaluation of the Okimaw Ohci Healing Lodge.* Ottawa. "http://www.csc-scc.gc.ca/text/pa/ev-oohl-294-2-020/oohl_eval_e.pdf

Ducrol, C. 2006. "Evaluation of the SORAG and the Static-99 on Belgian Sex Offenders Committed to a Forensic Facility." *Sexual Abuse: A Journal of Research and Treatment* 18(1): 15–26.

Fabelo, T. 2003. *Initial Process and Outcome Evaluation of the InnerChange Freedom Initiative: The Faith-Based Prison Program in TDCJ.* Austin: Criminal Justice Policy Council. "http://www.pfm.org/media/ifi/Docs/IFIInitiative%20texas%20study.pdf

Fabiano, E.A., F.J. Porporino, and D. Robinson. 1990. *Rehabilitation Through Clearer Thinking: A Cognitive Model of Correctional Intervention.* Ottawa: Research and Statistics Branch, Correctional Service of Canada. "http://www.csc-scc.gc.ca/text/rsrch/briefs/b4/b04e-eng.shtml

Falshaw, L., C. Friendship, R. Travers, and F. Nugent. 2003. *Searching for 'What Works': An Evaluation of Cognitive Skills Programmes.* London: Research, Development, and Statistics Directorate, Home Office. http://www.homeoffice.gov.uk/rds.pdfs2/r206.pdf

Furlong, A., and B.A. Grant. 2006. "Women Offender Substance Abuse Programming: Interim Results." *Forum on Corrections Research* 18(1). http://www.csc-scc.gc.ca/text/pblct/forum/e181/e181k-eng.shtml

Gendreau, P., T. Little, and C. Goggin. 1996. "A Meta-Analysis of the Predictors of Adult Offender Recidivism: What Works!" *Criminology* 34(4): 575–95.

Gendreau, P., C. Goggin, and P. Smith. 1999. "The Forgotten Issue in Effective Correctional Treatment: Program Implementation." *International Journal of Offender Therapy and Comparative Criminology* 43(2): 180–87.

Gillis, C.A., L.L. Motiuk, and R. Belcourt. 1998. *Prison Work Program (CORCAN) Participation: Post-Release Employment and Recidivism.* Ottawa: Research Branch, Correctional Service of Canada. http://www.csc-scc.gc.ca/text/rsrch/reports/r69/r69_e.pdf

Glaser, D. 1964. *The Effectiveness of a Prison and Parole System.* Indianapolis: Bobbs-Merrill.

Gobeil, R., and K. Blanchette. 2007. "Revalidation of a Gender-Informed Security Reclassification Scale for Women Inmates." *Journal of Contemporary Criminal Justice* 23(4): 296–309.

Glube, C. (chair). 2006. *Moving Forward with Women's Corrections.* Ottawa: Correctional Service of Canada. http://www.csc-scc.gc.ca/text/prgrm/fsw/wos29/wos29-eng.shtml

Gordon, A., and T. Nicholaichuk. 1996. "Applying the Risk Principle to Sex Offender Treatment." *Forum on Corrections Research* 8(2): 36–38.

Grant, B.A., D. Kunic, P. MacPherson, C. McKeown, and E. Hansen. 2003. *The High Intensity Substance Abuse Program (HISAP): Results from the Pilot Programs.* Ottawa: Correctional Service Canada. http://www.csc-scc.gc.ca/text/rsrch/reports/r140/r140_e.pdf

Griffiths, C.T., Y. Dandurand, and D. Murdoch. 2007. *The Social Reintegration of Offenders and Crime Prevention.* Ottawa: National Crime Prevention Centre, Public Safety Canada. http://www.publicsafety.gc.ca/res/cp/res/soc-reint-eng.aspx

Hanson, R.K., and D. Thornton. 1999. *Static 99: Improving Actuarial Risk Assessments for Sex Offenders.* Ottawa: Solicitor General. http://ww2.ps-sp.gc.ca/publications/corrections/199902_e.pdf

Harper, G., and C. Chitty. 2005. *The Impact of Corrections on Re-Offending: A Review of "What Works."* Home Office Research Study 291. London: Development and Statistics Directorate, Home Office. http://www.homeoffice.gov.uk/rds/pdfs04/hors291.pdf

Harris, A., A. Phenix, R.K. Hanson, and D. Thornton. 2003. *STATIC-99 Coding Rules, Revised—2003.* Ottawa: Corrections Directorate, Solicitor General. http://ww2.ps-sp.gc.ca/publications/corrections/pdf/Static-99-coding-Rules_e.pdf

Inciardi, J.A. 1996. *A Corrections-Based Continuum of Effective Drug Abuse Treatment.* National Institute of Justice Research Preview. Washington: Office of Justice Programs, U.S. Department of Justice. http://www.ncjrs.gov/pdffiles/contdrug.pdf

Inciardi, J.A., S.S. Martin, and C.A. Butzin. 2004. "Five-Year Outcomes of Therapeutic Community Treatment of Drug-Involved Offenders After Release from Prison." *Crime and Delinquency* 50(1): 88–108.

insideprison.com. 2006. "A Brief History of Prison Industry" (April). http://www.insideprison.com/prison-industry-labor.asp

Irving, J., and C. Wichmann. 2001. *An Investigation into the Factors Leading to Increased Security Classification of Women Offenders.* Ottawa: Research Branch, Correctional Service of Canada. http://www.csc-scc.gc.ca/text/rsrch/reports/r98/r98_e.pdf

John Howard Society of Alberta. 2002. *Inmate Education.* Edmonton. http://www.johnhoward.ab.ca/PUB/respaper/educa02.htm

Johnson, B.R. 2004. "Religious Programs and Recidivism Among Former Inmates in Prison Fellowship Programs: A Long-term Follow-up Study." *Justice Quarterly* 21(2): 329–54.

Johnson, B.R., D.B. Larson, and T.C. Pitts. 1997. "Religious Programs, Institutional Adjustment, and Recidivism Among Former Inmates in Prison Fellowship Programs." *Justice Quarterly* 14(1): 145–66.

Kowbel, R.D. 1995. "Self-Help Programs Are Part of Jailhouse Games." *Globe and Mail*, January 13, A20.

Lane, P., M. Bopp, J. Bopp, and J. Norris. 2002. *Mapping the Healing Journey: The Final Report of a First Nation Research Project on Healing in Canadian Aboriginal Communities.* Ottawa: Solicitor General and Aboriginal Healing Foundation. http://ww2.ps-sp.gc.ca/publications/abor_corrections/pdf/apc2002_e.pdf

LaPrairie, C. 1996. *Examining Aboriginal Corrections in Canada.* Ottawa: Solicitor General, Aboriginal Corrections. http://ww2.ps-sp.gc.ca/publications/abor_corrections/199614_e.pdf

Light, J. 1999. "The Prison Industry: Capitalist Punishment." *CorpWatch*. http://www.corpwatch.org/article.php?id=853

Lösel, F. 1995. "The Efficacy of Correctional Treatment: A Review and Synthesis of Meta-Evaluations." In J. McGuire (ed.), *What Works: Reducing Reoffending—Guidelines from Research and Practice*, ed. J. McGuire. Chichester: John Wiley. 79–111.

Lowenkamp, C.T., E.J. Latessa, and P. Smith. 2006. "Does Correctional Program Quality Really Matter? The Impact of Adhering to the Principles of Effective Intervention." *Criminology & Public Policy* 5(3): 575–94.

Luciani, F. 1997. "Tried and True: Proof That the Custody Rating Scale Is Still Reliable and Valid." *Forum on Corrections Research* 9(1): 13–17.

Martinson, R.M. 1974. "What Works? Questions and Answers About Prison Reform." *Public Interest* 35: 22–54.

———. 1979. "New Findings, New Views: A Note of Caution Regarding Sentencing Reform." *Hofstra Law Review* 7: 243–58.

McKinnon, C. 1995. "The Legal Right of Offenders to Refuse Treatment." *Forum on Corrections Research* 7(3): 43–47.

Monster, M., and A. Micucci. 2005. "Meeting the Rehabilitative Needs at a Canadian Women's Correctional Centre." *Prison Journal* 85(2): 168–85.

Moses, M.C., and C.J. Smith. 2007. "Factories Behind Fences: Do Prison 'Real Work' Programs Work?" *National Institute of Justice Journal* 257: 32–35. http://www.ojp.usdoj.gov/nij/journals/257/real-work-programs.html

Mugford, R., and J. Weekes. 2006. "Mandatory and Coerced Treatment." *Fact Sheet*. Canadian Centre on Substance Abuse. http://www.ccsa.ca/CCSA/EN/Publications

Nunes, K.L., and F. Cortoni. 2006. *The Heterogeneity of Treatment Non-Completers.* Ottawa: Correctional Service of Canada. http://www.csc-scc.gc.ca/text/rsrch/reports/r176/r176_e.pdf

Nunes, K.L., R.K. Hanson, P. Firestone, H.M. Moulden, D.M. Greenberg, and J.M. Bradford. 2007. "Denial Predicts Recidivism for Some Sexual Offenders." *Sexual Abuse: A Journal of Research and Treatment* 19(2): 91–105.

Pelissier, B., W. Rhodes, W. Saylor, G. Gaes, S. Camp, S. Vanyur, and S. Wallace. 2000. *TRIAD Drug Treatment Evaluation Project Final Report of Three-Year Outcomes: Part 1.* Washington: Office of Research and Evaluation, Federal Bureau of Prisons. http://www.bop.gov/news/PDFs/TRIAD/TRIAD_pref.pdf

Phillips, D. 2002. "The Aboriginal Gang Initiative." *Let's Talk* 27(2): 1–4.

Proulx, J., and S. Perrault. 1996. *An Evaluation of the Ma Mawi Wi Chi Itata Centre's Family Violence Program Stony Mountain Project.* Ottawa and Winnipeg: Ma Mawi Wi Chi Itata Family Violence Program.

Raj, A., J. Rose, M.R. Decker, C. Rosengard, M.R. Hebert, Ms. Stein, and J.G. Clarke. 2008. "Prevalence and Patterns of Sexual Assault Across the Life Span Among Incarcerated Women." *Violence Against Women* 14(5): 528–41.

Robinson, D. 1995. *The Impact of Cognitive Skills Training on Post-release Recidivism Among Canadian Federal Offenders.* Ottawa: Correctional Service of Canada. http://www.csc-scc.gc.ca/text/pblct/forum/e083/e083b-eng.shtml

Rugge, T. 2006. *Risk Assessment of Male Aboriginal Offenders: A 2006 Perspective.* Ottawa: Public Safety and Emergency Preparedness Canada. http://www.publicsafety.gc.ca/res/cor/rep/_fl/ramao-e.pdf

Sampson, R. (chair). 2007. *Report of the Correctional Service of Canada Review Panel.* Ottawa: Minister of Public Works and Government Services Canada. http://www.publicsafety.gc.ca/csc-scc/cscrpreport-eng.pdf

Sandberg, L. 2008. "Critics: Prison Labor Hurts Free-World Jobs." November Coalition. http://www.november.org/stayinfo/breaking08/TX-PrisonLabor.html

Sherman, L.W., D. Gottfredson, D. MacKenzie, J. Eck, P. Reuter, and S. Bushway. 1997. *Preventing Crime: What Works, What Doesn't, What's Promising.* Washington: Office of Justice Programs, U.S. Department of Justice. http://www.homeoffice.gov.uk/rds/pdfs06/r276.pdf

Smith, C.J., J. Bechtel, A. Patrick, R.R. Smith, and L. Wilson-Gentry. 2006. *Correctional Industries Preparing Inmates for Reentry: Recidivism & Post-Release Employment.* Washington: National Institute of Justice, U.S. Department of Justice. http://www.ncjrs.gov/pdffiles1/nij/grants/214608.pdf

Smith, P., and P. Gendreau. 2007. "The Relationship Between Program Participation, Institutional Misconduct, and Recidivism Among Federally Sentenced Adult Male Offenders." *Forum on Corrections Research* 19(1). http://www.csc-scc.gc.ca/text/pblct/forum/Vol19No1/v19n1-eng.shtml

Solomon, A.L., K.D. Johnson, J. Travis, and E.C. McBride. 2004. *From Prison to Work: The Employment Dimensions of Prisoner Reentry.* Washington: Justice Policy Center, Urban Institute. http://www.urban.org/UploadedPDF/411097_From_Prison_to_Work.pdf

Task Force on Federally Sentenced Women. 1990. *Creating Choices: The Report of the Task Force on Federally Sentenced Women.* Ottawa: Correctional Service of Canada. http://www.csc-scc.gc.ca/text/prgrm/fsw/choices/toce-eng.shtml

Taylor, G. 1997. "Implementing Risk and Needs Classification in the Correctional Service of Canada." *Forum on Corrections Research* 9(1): 32–35.

Trevethan, S., J.-P. Moore, and N. Allegri. 2005. *The 'In Search of Your Warrior' Program for Aboriginal Offenders: A Preliminary Evaluation.* Ottawa: Correctional Service of Canada. http://www.csc-scc.gc.ca/text/rsrch/reports/r172/r172-eng.shtml

Varis, D.D., D. Lefebvre, and B.A. Grant. 2006. "Intensive Support Units for Federal Offenders with Substance Abuse Problems: An Impact Analysis." *Forum on Corrections Research* 18(1). http://www.csc-scc.gc.ca/text/pblct/forum/e181/e181g-eng.shtml

Vennard, J., D. Sugg, and C. Hedderman. 1997. *Changing Offenders' Attitudes and Behaviour: What Works?* Home Office Research Study 171. London: Home Office Research and Statistics Directorate. http://www.unisa.edu.au/hawkeinstitute/sprg/documents/What-works.pdf

Wiebe, R., and Y. Johnson. 1998. *Stolen Life: The Journey of a Cree Woman.* Toronto: Vintage Canada.

Wormith, J.S. 2007. "Adhering to Principles of Effective Correctional Treatment: Musings of a Former Clinician and Administrator." *Forum on Corrections Research* 19(1). http://www.csc-scc.gc.ca/text/pblct/forum/Vol19No1/v19n1a-eng.shtml

Wormith, J.S., and M.E. Olver. 2002. "Offender Treatment Attrition and Its Relationship with Risk, Responsivity, and Recidivism." *Criminal Justice and Behavior* 29(4): 447–71.

WEBLINKS

United Kingdom Home Office

Research, Development, Statistics
http://www.homeoffice.gov.uk/rds/index.html
An excellent site containing research reports and crime data on a variety of topics, including corrections treatment programs.

National Institute of Corrections Library

http://www.nicic.org/features/Library
An extensive collection of materials on all facets of corrections and correctional practice, including evaluations of correctional treatment interventions and programs in North America.

CHAPTER 8

RELEASE FROM PRISON

CHAPTER OBJECTIVES

After reading this chapter you should be able to:

- *Discuss the purpose and priciples of conditional release.*
- *Identify the types of conditional release.*
- *Discuss the release options for provincial/territorial and federal inmates.*
- *Discuss accelerated parole review and the issues that surround its use.*
- *Describe how judicial review (Section 745, the so-called "faint hope clause" of the Criminal Code) works, what the statistics indicate about its use and outcomes, and the major arguments of proponents and critics of this practice.*
- *Define statutory release and discuss the issues surrounding this release option.*
- *Discuss the detainment practice known as detention during the period of statutory release.*
- *Describe the dynamics of parole board decision making and the issues that surround parole board decision making.*

KEY TERMS

Temporary absence
Day parole
Full parole
remission/discharge
Statutory release
Cold turkey release
Warrant expiry date
Accelerated parole review (APR)
Judicial review (faint hope clause)
Detention during the period of statutory release
Community assessment

PERSPECTIVE

A Journalist's Observations of the National Parole Board, Ontario Region

Like Santa, a parole board is supposed to know who's been good or bad, and so by the time the hearing arrives parole panelists (called directors) already know more about the prisoner than they perhaps care to—and a lot of it is not very nice.

On this particular day, three board directors—former prison warden Kenneth Payne, career correctional-service employee Sheila Henriksen and social worker John Brothers—have the final say.

Armed with documents describing the parole-seeker's criminal history, psychological assessments, education, family situation, other relationships, behaviour while in prison and the recommendation from Correctional Services Canada, the members try to evaluate what risk these individuals pose to society and determine if that risk is manageable in the community.

The first up to bat on this day is a 36-year-old Kingston man who was sentenced to life on a charge of second-degree murder for killing a friend in a dispute over a woman.

At 8:30 a.m., the slight, frail-looking man is waiting outside the hearing with his case management officer and a university law student as the morning announcements play over the intercom. The atmosphere is weirdly like high school.

When the door to the hearing room opens, the brief window of opportunity has arrived that the convict has been waiting for—make-or-break time. The parole panel will soon begin its grueling interview. No holds are barred, and no part of a convict's life is off limits.

Sitting a couple of metres from the convicts, looking them in the face, panel members have to sift through what they're hearing and judge what is sincere and what is contrived, remembering that people seldom get to this point in their lives by being totally honest.

The members take in the convict's appearance and mannerisms, dissect his answers, ask questions in different ways to get a better read and compare the answers to facts provided by the professions.

They often caution the convicts against lying, because their replies must be consistent with what's in their files.

This morning, the murderer from Kingston slouches, his hair slicked back tightly like people wore in the 1950s. He is wearing dark clothes, a tweed sports jacket and unmatching light-coloured socks.

The case management officer sits at a table to his left. Right as the hearing starts, the convict withdraws his application for full parole. He says day parole will suffice.

The man has spent time in a number of jails and prisons since the murder. He stares straight ahead as the case management officer outlines his criminal record, all of it minor and non-violent up to the killing. He also relates how the convict was granted full parole twice, in 1992 and again in 1995, and violated it both times.

A doctor's report rates the probability he will reoffend within a year of release at 40 per cent, saying he suffers from an anti-social personality disorder.

A panel member asks why he withdrew his application for full parole. In a low, frail voice, the convict states the obvious: "In a realistic view, I don't think you guys would send me to full parole."

A member jokes, "You have already done some of our work for us." Mr. Payne asks the convict about the bad choices he has made through his life, and there are many. The convict says his worst was getting involved in a relationship with the woman he killed for and, as he puts it, his "negative thinking."

The focus shifts to what he might have learned from his failures. "I needed to change the way I view things," the convict says. "I used to go through distorted thinking patterns. I have a problem over-complicating things. I used to take on other people's problems and make them my own."

In discussing an anger-management course he has just repeated, he is asked: "When was the last time you felt really angry?" "When I got the letter from the parole board that media would be at my hearing," he answers. He adds, "Nothing personal," as he turns toward the observers behind him.

Asked about the killing, the convict says he doesn't recognize the man who did it, that there are "some pretty blank spots surrounding that time."

Ms. Henriksen questions his integrity. "I have got a sense you have an ability to fool people," she says. He replies: "Sitting in the position I am in, it doesn't seem right for me to say, 'Trust me.'"

But the board chooses to trust him anyway. Following brief deliberations it grants the man once-a-month [unescorted temporary absences]. If he does well on those, the next step will be day parole and then full parole without any further hearing.

"The board is satisfied you have benefited from our programs," says Mr. Payne.

The convict thanks the directors and, as he leaves, passes the bank robber waiting outside. And the process repeats itself.

The day ends with the case of the Stratford father, a 29-year-old first time offender who smashed up his truck after a night of partying and nearly killed his passenger. His sentence was two years for criminal negligence causing bodily harm. He has served about a year.

If there is a common thread among these convicts it is the way they handle stress: Drugs and alcohol are their mainstays.

Oddly enough, the convict doesn't do a very good job of selling his case. Lucky for him it sells itself.

The case management officer gives an exemplary report on his prison behaviour, noting he attends night school and wants to pursue a trade in college.

The convict shakes as he appears before the panel members, who at times try to relax him.

One thing that works against him is a compelling victim impact statement. The victim is suing the convict. "I know he's mad but I have gone and tried to talk with him and all he does is yell at me or make rude gestures when he drives by," the convict explains. "I just wish it was me who got injured that night."

"All I know is I have two young kids I haven't seen in a month and I want to get back to them," says the man. "I can't wait."

Another quick verdict: immediate full parole. The directors deliver their judgment. And then they just hope.

Source: Campbell 1997, A3. Reprinted by permission of the Ottawa Citizen, Don Campbell.

As noted in the opening pages of this text, nearly everyone who is sent to a correctional institution will eventually be released. Most inmates are released sooner, rather than later, in their sentence. It is the small percentage of offenders who receive sentences of two years or more who present the greatest challenges. This chapter examines the decisions surrounding the timing and conditions of conditional release. Chapter 9 will consider the issues related to the reentry of offenders into the community.

THE PURPOSE AND PRINCIPLES OF CONDITIONAL RELEASE

Section 100 of the Corrections and Conditional Release Act states:

> *The purpose of conditional release is to contribute to the maintenance of a just, peaceful and safe society by means of decisions on the timing and conditions of release that will best facilitate the rehabilitation of offenders and their reintegration into the community as law-abiding citizens.*

The act also sets out a number of principles to be followed by the parole boards (as well as by the CSC when that agency makes release decisions) in pursuing the objectives of conditional release:

- The protection of society is the primary consideration in every case.
- Parole boards are to consider all available information that is relevant to the case, including recommendations from the sentencing judge, the results of assessments completed during the case management process, and information from victims and the offender.
- Parole boards can enhance their effectiveness by sharing information with other criminal justice agencies and by ensuring that information on policies and programs is communicated to offenders, victims, and the public.
- Parole boards should, in their decision making, make the least restrictive determination required to ensure the protection of society.
- Parole boards are to be guided by appropriate policies and to ensure that members receive sufficient training to implement these policies effectively.
- Offenders are to be provided with all relevant information relating to the decisions of parole boards, the reasons for the decision, and the conditions of any conditional release.

Release on parole is not a statutory right—it is a privilege. Though inmates have the right to apply for parole when eligible, there are no guarantees of a successful application.

With respect to the conditional releases decided by parole boards, Section 102 of the Corrections and Conditional Release Act states:

> *The [National Parole] Board or a provincial parole board may grant parole to an offender if, in its opinion,*
>
> *(a) the offender will not, by reoffending, present an undue risk to society before the expiration, according to law, of the sentence the offender is serving; and*
>
> *(b) the release of the offender will contribute to the protection of society by facilitating the reintegration of the offender into society as a law-abiding citizen.*

In practice, this means that conditional release can be granted under either of two conditions:

- the applicant is unlikely to reoffend between the release and warrant expiry, *or*
- there is a risk of reoffending but that risk can be managed by the specific interventions, such as a residential treatment program, that would be unavailable except as part of a conditional release.

The specific conditional release options available to inmates depend on the length of the offender's sentence and on whether he or she is under the supervision and control of provincial/territorial or federal systems of corrections. Generally, conditional release is granted when it can be demonstrated that the community will not be placed at risk by the release of the inmate from confinement. For some offenders, the risk of reoffending is rated as low because of their particular sociobiographical backgrounds and absence of previous convictions. Other offenders—those who are at a high risk to reoffend—must demonstrate that they have taken steps to address those aspects of their lives (criminogenic risk factors) that would increase their likelihood of reoffending. However, parole board members have considerable discretion in making decisions to grant or deny parole and may choose to disregard risk assessments.

The underlying premise of conditional release programs is that the likelihood of recidivism is reduced. More specifically, the following arguments are made: the prospect of early release serves as an incentive for inmates to participate in institutional programs; the threat of being returned to confinement helps deter criminal behaviour; conditional release programs help minimize the negative impact of incarceration; and supervision by a parole officer will be beneficial for the inmate. The absence of research studies, however, makes it difficult to determine the validity of these assumptions. The discussion in Chapter 6, for example, revealed that not all inmates are equally, or negatively, affected by the carceral experience, and the examination of correctional treatment in Chapter 7 illustrated the difficulties of connecting participation in institutional treatment programs with postrelease behaviour.

THE TYPES OF CONDITIONAL RELEASE

The release of an offender from custody can occur at one of three points in the sentence:

- The parole eligibility date, for either day parole or full parole.
- The "discharge possible" date, which generally occurs at the two-thirds point in a sentence.
- The warrant expiry date, which marks the end of the sentence imposed by the court.

The following types of conditional release are available to inmates incarcerated in federal and provincial/territorial correctional institutions:

- **Temporary absence (TA),** which may be escorted or unescorted. Also, it may begin very soon after admission and extend to the end of the sentence, and it may involve the offender being placed under electronic monitoring.
- **Day parole,** generally at the one-sixth point in a sentence.
- **Full parole,** available at the one-third point in a sentence.
- **Remission/discharge** for provincial inmates, available at the two-thirds point.
- **Statutory release** for federal inmates, available at the two-thirds point.

Inmates may also be released from confinement without any conditions and/or supervision. This is often referred to as **cold turkey release**, and it occurs when:

- provincial inmates are discharged from confinement at the two-thirds point of their sentence; *or*
- federal inmates are released at their warrant expiry date at the end of their court-imposed sentence.

Figure 8.1 illustrates the Sentencing Milestones for Federal Offenders.

Figure 8.1

Sentencing Milestones

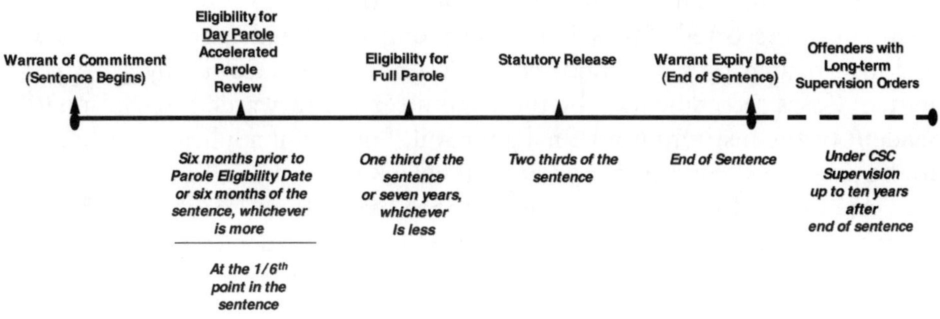

Source: Sampson, 2007:108. © Public Safety Canada

RELEASE OPTIONS FOR PROVINCIAL/TERRITORIAL INMATES

Except in Ontario, provincial inmates are released before their **warrant expiry date** in one of three ways: temporary absence, parole, or remission/discharge. Temporary absences and parole are forms of conditional release, whereas remission/discharge is automatic and does not involve conditions. In Ontario, inmates may be incarcerated until their warrant expiry date. Under the province's Corrections Accountability Act, inmates must earn the privilege of early release by participating in institutional programs and abiding by the rules of the facility. There is zero tolerance for acts of violence. Inmates who do not meet these criteria will fail to earn remission, also known as "good time."

Temporary Absences

Temporary absences (TAs) are the most common type of conditional release for provincial offenders. Each province/territory has its own form of TA program. A TA can be an escorted pass of a few hours' duration to attend a family funeral or a college class, but it can also span almost the full length of a provincial sentence, strung back-to-back in intervals that can run as long as 60 days. There may be a waiting period before eligibility, often one-sixth of the sentence, but inmates in some jurisdictions can apply for a TA immediately after entering the correctional system. In Ontario, for example, there are three types of temporary absence: (1) humanitarian; (2) medical; and, (3) rehabilitation/reintegration, such as work, school, or program attendance. In Ontario, all provincial inmates, including fine defaulters, are eligible to apply for a TA as long as (a) they are not facing outstanding charges for which they have been denied bail, (b) they have served one-sixth of their sentence, and (c) they have exhibited exemplary behaviour while serving their time. Decisions on escorted and unescorted TAs of up to 72 hours are made by the superintendents of correctional facilities. The Ontario Parole and Earned Release Board has responsibility for unescorted TAs of 72 hours or longer. All applications are reviewed and investigated by a TA coordinator, and most are reviewed by a TA committee. Cases recommended by the committee are forwarded to the superintendent of the institution for final approval. Successful applicants must agree to the prescribed conditions and carry their TA permits at all times.

An assumed benefit of TAs is that it is better for a qualifying inmate to serve his/her sentence in a community setting rather than in confinement. Also, TAs may help control overcrowding and reduce operational costs.

Electronic Monitoring and TAs

Electronic monitoring (EM) can be used as an alternative to confinement (see Chapter 3). But it can also be used as a condition of temporary absences (back-end EM) or as a sentencing option ordered by the sentencing judge (front-end EM). There is considerable variation among the provinces in how EM is used. In British Columbia, the use of EM is limited to offenders on day parole or full parole. In Ontario, EM may be a requirement for offenders on TAs.

Offenders who have EM as a condition of release are required to abide by a curfew and to be at their residence during specified hours. Compliance is monitored by random, computer-generated telephone calls made to the residence. In addition, correctional staff make random visits and telephone calls. The frequency of these is determined by a risk/needs assessment of the inmate.

Provincial Parole

Parole is a form of conditional release granted at the discretion of a parole board. Provincial inmates may apply for day parole consideration after serving one-sixth of their sentence and for full parole consideration after serving one-third of their sentence.

Inmates who appear before a parole board present a release plan and explain to board members why they would be good candidates to reenter the community, subject to monitoring by a parole officer. In accepting parole, provincial inmates forfeit all accumulated remission and so are subject to supervision until warrant expiry (the end of their sentence). Successful applicants agree to abide by a set of general and—depending on the case—specific conditions and to report to a parole supervisor.

The number of provincial offenders on parole has steadily declined over the past decade. The greatest decline has occurred in Ontario, where, over the past decade, the parole grant rate has dropped from approximately 60 percent to 26 percent in 2006–2007. This precipitous decrease has been due in large measure to the provinces' "get tough" approach to corrections, which places a premium on public safety and security (see Chapter 2). Also contributing to the overall decline in the numbers of inmates on parole is the fact that most parole-eligible inmates do not apply for parole, mainly because of their relatively short custodial sentences. As one parole-eligible provincial inmate commented to your author: "Why would I apply for parole and subject myself to supervision and control for the remainder of my sentence, when I can stay here in the prison and walk out at two-thirds of my sentence with no supervision? What's an extra couple of months in prison?"

Most provincial parolees are in the two provinces that have their own parole boards: Quebec and Ontario. These boards, like their federal counterpart, the NPB, are independent of the correctional system and have full-time and part-time members. Board members in Ontario are paid a per diem rate of $355 for each 24-hour period and a half-day per diem for working less than three hours. Board members are also able to claim travel and accommodation costs to the OPERB.

In Ontario, offenders who are serving sentences of six months or longer are automatically scheduled for an in-person hearing before the parole board, whereas those offenders serving sentences of less than six months must apply, in writing, to appear before the board. In Quebec, the parole board automatically reviews the cases of all offenders (even those who do not apply for parole) once they have served one-third of their sentence.

Outside of Quebec and Ontario, parole applications from provincial/territorial inmates are considered by a single member of the federal National Parole Board (NPB), usually without a hearing with the offender. If the applicant's parole is likely to be denied or revoked, the parole applicant will have a hearing with one board member. If the provincial parole applicant is serving a sentence for a violent crime that resulted in someone's death, two board members will conduct a hearing with the offender. The extensive reliance on "paper" decisions (no hearing) by the NPB raises the concern that provincial inmates are being denied an opportunity to present their case in person. As well, the NPB may be denying family members and crime victims the opportunity to speak directly to board members. Table 8.1 compares the provincial parole boards in Quebec and Ontario with the NPB on a number of items.

Table 8.1 Comparison of Two Provincial Parole Boards and the National Parole Board

	National Parole Board	**Ontario Parole and Earned Release Board**	**Commision québécoise des libérations conditionelles**	**NPR Hearing Applications from Provincial Inmates***
Qualification for day parole	One-sixth	Not available (inmates may apply for a temporary absence after one-sixth)	Not available	One-sixth
Qualification for full parole	One-third	One-third	One-third	One-third
Victim observation of parole hearing	Yes	Yes	No	Yes
Victim allowed to make oral statement	Yes	Yes	No	Yes
Grant rate, full parole	40% (2006–07)	26% (2006–07)	48.4% (2006–07)	71% (2006–07)

*Except in Ontario and Quebec.

Sources: Commission québécoise des libérations conditionnelles (www.msp.gouv.qc.ca); National Parole Board (www.npb-cnlc.gc.ca); Ontario Parole and Earned Release Board (www.operb.gov.on.ca).

Provincial inmates who are granted parole by the NPB are supervised by CSC parole officers. In Ontario and Quebec, probation officers are responsible for parole supervision.

Remission/Discharge

Another option for provincial inmates is to serve their entire sentence in confinement, minus remission, which is earned at a rate of one day for every two days served. This type of release can occur by default (because the sentence was so short), by choice (because the offender did not seek conditional release), or because all applications for TAs and parole were denied. Except in Ontario, as long as the inmate does not lose remission because of institutional misconduct, he or she is released from confinement after serving two-thirds of the sentence and is not subject to supervision by a parole officer. This type of release is often referred to as **cold turkey release**, though some provincial offenders will have been sentenced to complete a period of probation following confinement, with the probation to begin at discharge.

VICTIMS AND THE RELEASE OF PROVINCIAL INMATES

Despite public education campaigns aimed at both victims and the general population, there are many gaps and inaccuracies in Canadians' knowledge of the correctional process. It is unlikely, for example, that most crime victims and community residents are aware that a provincial offender can be released on a TA. This lack of awareness has resulted in situations where crime victims encounter their perpetrators in public only weeks, or days, after witnessing the sentencing in court. Even worse, victims may have their feelings of safety shattered when the perpetrator shows up on their doorstep. Also, crime victims may not understand the parole process and the criteria that are used by parole board members in making release decisions. Attending a parole hearing and being in the same room as the offender can be a difficult experience for crime victims.

Correctional authorities in several provinces have taken a number of steps to minimize the likelihood of revictimization, especially in cases where the offender and the victim are acquainted (which is most of the cases in the justice system). Some examples:

- Offenders convicted of interpersonal crimes are often disqualified from applying for extended or unescorted TAs.
- The offender may be required to complete certain programs before being considered for a TA.
- The directive that the offender not contact the victim is a near-universal condition of all types of conditional release.

- Crime victims are often able to contact the parole board and/or corrections officials and ask to be informed about the timing and specifics of any release.
- Crime victims can express their concerns to correctional authorities and/or the parole board.
- Except in Quebec, crime victims can ask to observe and make a written or oral submission at the parole hearing (see Table 8.1).

In Manitoba, corrections officials are proactive—that is, they attempt to locate and contact victims who may be at risk of revictimization. In Ontario, qualifying victims who register with the Victim Notification Service (VNS) are given a personal identification number, which allows them to access, via telephone, case-specific information about an offender in the provincial correctional system.

RELEASE OPTIONS FOR FEDERAL INMATES

Early in the federal inmate's sentence, a reintegration-potential rating is established, based on information gleaned from various risk-assessment instruments and other static and dynamic risk factors (see Chapter 7). This rating places the individual inmate into one of three categories: high, medium, or low reintegration potential. Most of the inmates with high reintegration potential will not require core programming. The existence of this category reflects the concern that some inmates are being steered into programs unnecessarily, wasting their time and the system's resources. For members of this group, any programs that are required can be accessed in the community. Accordingly, these inmates are viewed as candidates for conditional release as soon as they meet the eligibility criteria.

Federal inmates with medium reintegration potential are directed to core programs in the institution (see Chapter 7) and to follow-up programs in the community once they are released. (High-risk inmates are required to complete an extensive program of treatment intervention and are viewed cautiously by both correctional personnel and the parole board).

Federal inmates, who are incarcerated for longer periods of time compared to their provincial counterparts, tend to be released in gradual stages. This begins with escorted or unescorted temporary absences, decisions about which are usually made at the institutional level (for a discussion of federal temporary absences, see Grant and Johnson 1998; Grant and Millson 1998). They are also eligible for work releases and community development releases. Two types of conditional release—day parole and full parole—are discretionary; one—statutory release—is not. These release options are described in Box 8.1.

BOX 8.1

Release Options for Federal Inmates

Temporary Absences

- TAs are usually the first type of release an offender may be granted.
- TAs may be escorted (ETA) or unescorted (UTA).
- TAs are granted so that offenders may receive medical treatment; have contact with family; undergo personal development and/or counselling; and participate in community service work projects.

Eligibility

- Offenders may apply for ETAs at any time throughout their sentence.
- UTAs vary with the length and type of sentence. Offenders classified as maximum security are not eligible for UTAs.
- For sentences of three years or more, offenders are eligible to be considered for UTAs after serving one-sixth of their sentence.
- For sentences of two to three years, UTA eligibility is at six months into the sentence.
- For sentences under two years, eligibility for temporary absence is under provincial jurisdiction.
- Offenders serving life sentences are eligible to apply for UTAs three years before their full-parole eligibility date.

Day Parole

- Day parole prepares an offender for release on full parole or statutory release by allowing the offender to participate in community-based activities.
- Offenders on day parole must return nightly to an institution or a halfway house unless otherwise authorized by the NPB.

Eligibility

- Offenders serving sentences of three years or more are eligible to apply for day parole six months prior to full parole eligibility.
- Offenders serving life sentences are eligible to apply for day parole three years before their full-parole eligibility date.
- Offenders serving sentences of two to three years are eligible for day parole after serving six months of their sentence.

(continued)

Full Parole

- The offender serves the remainder of the sentence under supervision in the community.
- The offender must report to a parole supervisor on a regular basis and must advise on any changes in employment or personal circumstances.

Eligibility

- Most offenders (except those serving life sentences for murder) are eligible to apply for full parole after serving either one-third of the sentence or seven years.
- Offenders serving life sentences for first degree murder are eligible after serving 25 years.
- Eligibility dates for offenders serving life sentences for second degree murder are set between 10 and 25 years by the court (at the time of sentencing).

Statutory Release

- By law, most federal inmates are automatically released after serving two-thirds of their sentence if they have not already been released on parole. This is called statutory release.
- Statutory release is not the same as parole because the decision for release is not made by the NPB.

Eligibility

- Offenders serving life or indeterminate sentences are not eligible for statutory release.
- The CSC may recommend that an offender be denied statutory release if they believe the offender is likely to:
  (a) commit an offence causing death or serious harm to another person;
  (b) commit a sexual offence against a child; or
  (c) commit a serious drug offence before the end of the sentence.

In such cases, the NPB may detain that offender until the end of the sentence or add specific conditions to the statutory release plan.

Source: NPB 2007; http://www.npb-cnlc.gc.ca/infocntr/factsh/release.htm

Long-term studies have shown that offenders who are gradually released from prison on conditional release are more likely to become law-abiding citizens than those offenders who stay in prison until the end of their sentence (http://www.npb-cnlc.gc.ca). Results from an NPB study determined that only 10 percent of offenders who were released on parole and who completed their sentences on parole supervision were readmitted to federal penitentiaries with new offences during the 12-year follow-up period. In contrast, 50 percent of offenders who were released directly from prison without supervision were readmitted to a federal penitentiary with new offences over the course of the 12-year follow-up period (http://www.npb-cnlc.gc.ca/infocntr/myths_reality_e.htm).

The National Parole Board

The National Parole Board (NPB) was created in 1959 following the report of the Fauteux Committee (1956), which found that the ticket-of-leave system (see Chapter 2) was prone to political interference. The NPB is a division within Public Safety Canada, but it is independent of the CSC and can authorize conditional release of federal offenders. Parole board members are order-in-council appointments who serve for limited terms and are paid a per diem. Members are centralized in five regional offices and travel to the institutions for in-person hearings with parole applicants.

The NPB's conditional release program comprises seven operational areas and the following six components: (1) temporary absence, (2) day parole, (3) full parole, (4) statutory release, (5) detention, (6) long-term supervision, and (7) appeal decisions. Over the past decade, the grant rates for day parole and full parole have hovered around 70 percent and 40 percent, respectively.

Temporary Absences

Temporary absences for federal offenders are generally granted for one of three reasons: medical, compassionate, or to facilitate participation in treatment programs. The decision to release an offender on an ETA or UTA is made by corrections officials rather than by the NPB. Statistics indicate that there has been a decrease in the number of ETAs and UTAs in recent years, even though nearly all offenders successfully complete their temporary absences, and even though inmates almost never commit crimes while on this type of release.

Day Parole

Federal inmates are eligible for day parole at either one-sixth of the sentence or six months, whichever is longer (with some differences for special categories of offenders, such as lifers). It appears that the use of day parole is decreasing, largely because of the increased use of accelerated parole review.

Most inmates on day parole live in a community residential facility, and most of them apply for full parole when they reach the one-third point in their sentences. Day parole is meant to aid transition and, therefore, is seen as a short-term option immediately prior to the granting of full parole. Day paroles are normally no longer than six months. Female offenders are more likely to be granted day parole than men, and there has been a steady decrease in the number of Aboriginal offenders granted day parole (NPB 2007). This, in large measure, reflects the fact that women are better risks on parole and that Aboriginal offenders, as a group, are higher risks on conditional release (see Chapter 9).

Full Parole

Full parole is the most common form of release for federal offenders. Most often, the full parolee lives at home with family or friends, or independently. With certain exceptions, the parole eligibility date (PED) of a federal offender is at the one-third point in the sentence (or seven years, whichever is less). Remember from Chapter 1 that the sentencing judge sometimes determines that the offender must serve half the sentence (but never more than 10 years) before being eligible to apply for parole.

Some first-time federal offenders who have been convicted of a nonviolent offence may have their parole expedited after serving one-third of the sentence though **accelerated parole review (APR)**. Unless there is evidence that the offender is likely to commit a violent offence prior to the warrant expiry date, the NPB must direct a release. Note that the criterion for risk is the commission of a violent offence; the risk of the offender committing a property or drug-related offence is not sufficient to prevent release on APR. In APR cases, one member of the NPB can grant parole after conducting an in-office review of the file. There is no hearing. Though these inmates must still serve one-third of the sentence before being eligible, the parole approval process is streamlined by flagging these cases early in the process and expediting the development of a release plan. If the decision is *not* to direct release, a full hearing is held, at which the offender is present.

The APR review process has come under increasing scrutiny. The limited research that has been conducted on readmission rates of offenders released on APR indicates that, while the rates are lower than those of offenders who were not released, 30 to 40 percent of offenders released on APR are readmitted within two years of release (Gibbs 1999; Grant 1998). The CSC Review Panel (Sampson 2007) has recommended that APR, along with statutory release, be eliminated and replaced by earned parole. The difficulties that APR presents corrections are illustrated in Box 8.2.

BOX 8.2

The Dirty Banker and APR

A former bank manager who defrauded the Bank of Montreal in Edmonton of $16 million was released on APR after serving 14 months of a seven-year, four-month sentence. Nick Lysyk had spent much of the money on luxury homes, sports cars, and prostitutes. As a first-time, nonviolent offender, Lysyk was eligible for automatic release on accelerated day parole after serving one-sixth of his sentence. This, even though the NPB had written in his file: "Your behaviour demonstrated your extremely manipulative, untrustworthy, and despicable nature given that you were so easily able to abuse your position of trust for many years within society." The board also noted that Lysyk was a high risk to reoffend should he visit massage parlours, have contact with his mistresses, or become lonely or depressed. But since the law allowed the board to consider only Lysyk's potential for committing a violent act, it had no choice but to release him. Lysyk had violated the conditions of his bail prior to his trial by contacting one of his mistresses and had been sent to jail. The bank recovered only $5 million of the stolen money in cash and assets.

Source: Purdy 2005. Material adapted with the express permission of Edmonton Journal Group Inc., a CanWest Partnership.

Provincial parole boards and the NPB may also issue a Parole to Deportation certificate. This decision is made when federal immigration authorities place a "hold" on an offender who is not a Canadian citizen and have secured the necessary approvals to remove the person from the country. In such cases the inmate applicant is released to the custody of immigration authorities for removal.

Judicial Review (Section 745)

Often called the **faint hope clause**, this provision allows murderers serving a life sentence with no eligibility for parole for at least 15 years to apply for a reduction of this ineligibility period. The offender must first convince a superior court judge that there is a "reasonable prospect of success." If the offender passes this hurdle, the case will be heard in front of a jury for a decision.

The offender can apply for judicial review only after serving 15 years of the sentence. The judicial review procedures thus apply to (1) offenders convicted of first degree murder, who are required to serve at least 25 years in prison before being eligible for parole, and (2) offenders who have been convicted of second degree murder and sentenced to life in prison, with parole eligibility set at 15 years or longer. Offenders who have been convicted of multiple murders are not eligible to apply.

The judicial review must take place in the community where the crime was committed. A jury of community residents determines whether the parole eligibility date should be reduced (not whether the offender should be released). A hearing is held during which information is presented by the applicant and by the Crown counsel; however, the onus is on the offender-applicant to convince the jury to reduce the parole eligibility date.

The hearing focuses on the offender's conduct during the 15 years of confinement and on assessments about the risk of future offences. Both the offender-applicant and the Crown counsel may call and question witnesses and experts. The offender-applicant must testify, and members of the victim's family have the option of doing so. All members of the jury must agree before the parole eligibility date can be reduced (though only a two-thirds majority is required in cases for offenders sentenced before 1997).

The decisions the jury can reach include the following:

- Make no change to the parole eligibility date, but set a date when another application can be made (at least two years hence).
- Reduce the period of parole ineligibility to less than what it was but more than 15 years.
- Reduce the period of parole ineligibility to 15 years, which generally makes the offender immediately eligible to apply for parole.

To date, only about one-quarter of all offenders eligible for judicial review have applied for a hearing. Nationwide, the period of parole ineligibility has been reduced in 83 percent of the cases heard. Note, however, that both the number of applications and applicant success rates have varied considerably across the country. Also, 86 percent of the offenders whose parole eligibility was reduced have subsequently been paroled (Public Safety Canada Portfolio Corrections Statistics Committee 2007). The recidivism rate of offenders who have had an eligibility date reduced and have been granted parole has been very low, yet Section 745 continues to stir controversy. Contribute your opinion to "At Issue 8.1: Should Section 745 of the Criminal Code—the 'faint hope clause'—be removed from the Criminal Code?" presented at the end of the chapter.

Statutory Release

Statutory release occurs when a federal inmate has served two-thirds of his/her sentence and is still in confinement. This situation arises when the inmate has chosen not to apply for parole, or has applied for parole but failed, or has had an earlier release revoked and has not been released again. Since 1969, first with mandatory supervision and now with statutory release, federal offenders have been released at the two-thirds point in their sentence but have been subject to parole supervision until warrant expiry. Statutory release is a fairly common means of release, accounting for 36 percent of the federal conditional release population in 2006–7. Statutory releases do not involve the NPB, but under the provisions of the Corrections and Conditional Release Act, the board may impose residency conditions on the offender when there is evidence that the offender is a high risk to reoffend prior to warrant expiry. The NPB is sometimes asked to consider denying a statutory release and to detain the offender (see below).

Statutory release has been routinely criticized, especially within the federal Conservative government. The CSC Review Panel (Sampson 2007) noted that 60 percent of offenders on SR successfully complete their period of supervision. At the same time, offenders on SR are responsible for nearly 80 percent of violent reoffending in the community, even though SR releases account for only 35 percent of offenders on conditional release. The committee concluded that SR had undermined discretionary release, had not proven as effective as discretionary release in determining which offenders are likely to reoffend violently, and was not working. The committee recommended that SR be replaced with earned parole. Contribute your thoughts to the "At Issue 8.2: Should statutory release be abolished?" presented at the end of the chapter.

Detention During the Period of Statutory Release

A small group of federal inmates (390 as of 2007) have been judged by the CSC to be so likely to reoffend if released that they should be confined for their entire sentence (to warrant expiry) (NPB 2007). In these cases, concern for community safety outweighs the many undesirable aspects of a cold turkey release. As the inmate's statutory release date draws near, the CSC applies to the NPB for a detention hearing. The NPB will order the inmate detained if it is certain that he or she will commit an offence that causes death or serious harm, a sexual offence involving a child, or a serious drug offence before warrant expiry. This detainment is called **detention during the period of statutory release.**

The NPB approves the CSC recommendation for detention about 90 percent of the time. The others may be released with special conditions such as one-chance statutory release, which means that if the release is revoked, the offender is ineligible for a subsequent statutory release prior to the warrant expiry date. Another option is to release the offender with the requirement that he or she live in a community facility with supervision.

Inmates referred for detention hearings tend to be serving longer sentences and are likely to have been convicted of a sexual offence and/or assault. Few female offenders have been subject to detention review; however, a significant number (30 percent in 2006–7) of reviews involve Aboriginal offenders.

The purpose of detention is public protection through incapacitation. The question is whether detention meets that goal. The limited research that has been conducted to date suggests that detention, as practised by the CSC and the NPB, may not be meeting the goal of public protection. One study found that offenders released on statutory release have higher rates of reoffending than offenders who are detained and then released at their warrant expiry date (Grant 1997). This suggests that the selection process for detention has not resulted in the highest risk offenders being detained in confinement.

VICTIM INVOLVEMENT IN FEDERAL PAROLE

Several provisions in the Corrections and Conditional Release Act are designed to increase the input and participation of crime victims in the federal parole process, as well as to provide victims with general and case-specific information. In response to the act's requirements, the NPB has undertaken the following initiatives.

Each regional office has community liaison officers on staff, who provide victims with services and information:

- At their request, victims can be advised of eligibility dates, parole board decisions, and release status.
- Victim impact statements and expressions of concern for postrelease safety are considered by the NPB.
- Victims may attend parole hearings and make oral presentations to the NPB.
- Interested parties can request written copies of NPB decisions from the Decision Registry.

A number of concerns have been raised about these policies. For example, it is feared that correspondence from victims could be accessed by the offender, thus placing those victims at risk of retaliation. Also, the lack of proactive contact by correctional authorities forces victims to learn on their own about their rights and to take steps to contact authorities. This latter point has been addressed in part by public education campaigns as well as by toll-free numbers for questions and requests.

PAROLE AND THE LONG-TERM OFFENDER

As noted in Chapter 1, sentencing judges have the option to designate certain offenders as long-term offenders. This involves appending a long-term supervision order to the end of a federal sentence. Such an order can run as long as 10 years, beginning at warrant expiry, with the specific period determined by the sentencing judge. As such, it does not affect the inmate's parole eligibility.

The CSC is responsible for supervising long-term offenders. The NPB can set standard and special conditions for the offender, which must be adhered to during this period. An offender who violates a condition of the order may be readmitted to custody for a period not longer than 90 days or admitted to a halfway house or to a mental health facility. The CSC can also refer the matter to the NPB, which can cancel the suspension (and release the person), cancel the suspension and add new conditions, or recommend (with the approval of the provincial attorney general) that the offender be charged with "breaching long-term supervision" without reasonable excuse. This offence carries a maximum penalty of 10 years imprisonment.

This measure had as its origin the observation that the ability to detain offenders during the period of statutory release leaves the most dangerous offenders with the least supervision at the time of release. Note that this designation cannot be applied retroactively and is available only at the time of sentencing. As of 2006–7, 169 offenders were under long-term supervision. This offender population is expected to increase in the near future; 252 federal offenders are scheduled to be subject to long-term supervision orders once they reach warrant expiry (NPB 2007).

THE RELEASE OF DANGEROUS OFFENDERS

Inmates who have been designated as dangerous offenders (see Chapter 1) by a criminal court serve indeterminate sentences of imprisonment and can be released only by the NPB. Since 1978 there have been 427 dangerous offender designations (all but two of them men). At present, there are 370 offenders with an active dangerous offender designation (none of them are women). About 80 percent of all dangerous offenders have at least one previous conviction for a sexual offence, and many have been diagnosed with antisocial personality disorder (Bonta et al. 1996; Bonta et al. 1998; Public Safety Canada Portfolio Corrections Statistics Committee 2007).

Statutory release is not available to dangerous offenders. These inmates can, literally, spend the rest of their lives in prison, repeatedly being denied release at successive parole board hearings. The NPB is not to release a dangerous offender unless it is certain that the community will not be placed at risk. In practice, release is rarely granted.

THE PAROLE FILE

In its deliberations, the parole board considers a number of documents contained in the inmate-applicant's parole file. These generally include, but are not limited to, the following:

- *Institutional reports,* which provide information on work performance, rule infractions, attitudes toward and interactions with staff and other

"Bad news. The mailman is going to attend the parole-board hearing."

inmates, and participation in core programs. They also include assessments prepared by treatment staff and case managers.

- *Victim impact statements*, which are prepared for the sentencing judge and for the parole hearing.
- *Court transcripts*, including the comments of the judge at sentencing.
- *Police reports.*
- *Presentence reports*, which are prepared by probation or parole officers for the sentencing judge.
- *Official offence records*, from the Canadian Police Information Centre and/or the federal and provincial/territorial justice system records systems.
- *Materials prepared by the inmate-applicant*, including—for sex offenders—a relapse prevention plan and the proposed release plan.
- *Letters of support submitted on behalf of the inmate-applicant* from family, friends, community support people, and employers (among others).
- *A community assessment* prepared by probation or parole officers.

Historically, problems have arisen assembling the relevant documentation and ensuring that the offender's parole file is complete. In particular, provincial parole boards often find it difficult to secure records from the CSC and the NPB in cases where the offender has served federal time in the past. This information is vital to provincial parole board members when it comes to assessing the risk posed by the inmate-applicant and to making a decision on conditional release and the conditions that will be attached to any form of release.

A key document in the parole file is the **community assessment** (in Ontario, the Pre-Parole Report), which is prepared by parole officers (probation/parole officers in Quebec and Ontario). The community assessment is best described as an investigation designed to evaluate the feasibility of the inmate-applicant's proposed community plan in terms of the level of supervision required and the availability of community resources. The standard areas addressed by the Community Assessment or Pre-Parole Report include the following:

Police Information

- Opinion of the police regarding the potential release of the offender.

Assessment of the Proposed Plan

- Proposed residence (location, suitability, availability of placement in a community-based resource, etc.).
- Education and/or employment activities (i.e., verification of availability, suitability to inmate, confirmation of acceptance).
- Proposed treatment or counselling programs.

Community Information

- Significant relationships (family, friends, others).
- Financial situation (expected income, major assets, debts and obligations).
- Support services available to the inmate.
- Community reaction (including police opinion) to the release of the inmate.

Response to Previous Corrections

- Performance and compliance on supervision in the community, including probation, conditional sentences, and provincial/federal day parole.

Victim Information

- Victim impact and concerns.
- Results of Protection Order Registry check.

Areas of Risk and Supervision Issues

- Factors that support, and weigh against, the offender's release.

Recommended Special Conditions

- Special conditions on the parole certificate (discussed later in the chapter) that address risk/need factors and that provide for the level of supervision required to access appropriate community resources.

Though the community assessment is intended to be an assessment of the inmate's plan, the probation officer or parole officer preparing the report may sometimes express an opinion as to whether release should be granted.

DYNAMICS OF PAROLE BOARD DECISION MAKING

The decision of a parole board to release an inmate back into the community is, along with the verdict of the criminal court, perhaps the most important decision that is made in the correctional process. Despite this, little attention has been given to the composition of parole boards, the relationship between member characteristics and conditional release decisions, how board members use the information contained in offender case files, and the consequences of decisions for the offender, the victims, and the community.

Parole hearings are usually presided over by two board members and are generally held in the institution where the inmate is being held. In federal parole hearings the inmate-applicant is accompanied by his or her case manager, who serves as an assistant. Lawyers also may attend. The victim of the offence committed by the inmate-applicant may observe the hearing and can make a statement. The victim's presence is rare, in part because most people would have to travel great distances and bear the related costs. When victims do attend, an NPB staff member accompanies them into the hearing and debriefs them afterward.

Before the hearing, the board members review the parole file and make notes on key points. During the hearing, the board members ask the inmate about the release plan and other questions to ascertain suitability of release. The board may pay a great deal of attention to the inmate's version of the offence, looking for some insight into why it was committed and why it would not happen again. (The inmate's participation in treatment programs and skills/trades training, as well as any other positive steps taken while in custody, are key factors here.) Board members are interested in the insights the offender has gained about the offence, the decisions that led to the criminal behaviour, and the steps the offender has taken to address the issues that were associated with the criminal activity. Often, this involves addressing issues related to alcohol or drug abuse, anger management, or life skills. Indications of remorse and of empathy for the victim are considered important by board members. The file review and the interview are meant to determine whether the offender can be managed at an acceptable level of risk in the community.

Conducting an effective interview with the inmate applicant requires that board members be aware of their own biases and avoid moralizing. As well, board members must appreciate the pressure that is on the inmate-applicant. Most such applicants appear without assistants or family members present and may have limited verbal skills. Parole boards are administrative tribunals, not courts of law. That said, the onus is on such boards to be fair, and they must follow specific procedures (see the grounds for appeal, discussed below). Lawyers may attend hearings on the inmate's behalf, but there is no provision for the adversarial approaches found in criminal courts. Lawyers may provide additional information to the board and/or speak in support of the inmate's application.

After the interview the inmate is asked to wait outside the hearing room while the members deliberate and come to a decision. The inmate returns to the room to be told the outcome—whether the release has been granted, or denied, or deferred pending the gathering of additional information. If it has been denied, specific reasons must be given so that the inmate can understand how to increase the likelihood of success if another application is made—for example, by participating in a treatment program, completing a program already in progress, or developing a different release plan. For example, if the plan had been to live with friends who might not be a good influence, the board may recommend that the inmate secure alternative, more suitable accommodations. Provincial parole boards in Ontario and Quebec follow a decision-making process similar to that of the NPB, with the exception that victims who attend hearings of the provincial parole board in Quebec cannot make oral statements to the board.

If the parole board determines that the level of risk the inmate-applicant presents is not manageable in the community, the application for release on day parole or full parole will be denied. In such cases the inmate must wait a specified period of time before reapplying for release. However, given the relatively short sentences that provincial inmates serve in custody, the board may way waive the waiting period in order to encourage the inmate to prepare another application for conditional release. A decision of the Ontario Parole and Earned Release Board to grant parole is presented in Appendix 8.1.

Many provincial/territorial inmates do not apply for parole; instead, they serve out their sentences in custody. Under statutory release, these inmates are eligible to be released after serving two-thirds of their time in custody. In contrast to federal offenders, provincial/territorial inmates on statutory release are not supervised by parole officers. Provincial parole boards often must decide whether to release an offender on parole who may present a risk, and with a plan that is not optimal, or to have the inmate serve until the statutory date and then leave custody with no supervision or plan.

A virtual hearing of the NPB is available at http://www.npb-cnlc.gc.ca/hearing/index-eng.html

THE PAROLE CERTIFICATE

If parole is granted, a certificate of parole is prepared. The parole certificate contains both mandatory conditions and additional conditions. Mandatory conditions include reporting regularly to a parole officer, obeying the law, and securing permission from the supervising parole officer prior to leaving a specified geographic area.

There are mandatory release conditions for all federal offenders on conditional release:

- On release, travel directly to the offender's place of residence, as set out in the release certificate, and report to the parole supervisor immediately and thereafter as instructed.
- Remain at all times in Canada, within territorial boundaries prescribed by the parole supervisor.
- Obey the law and keep the peace.
- Inform the parole supervisor immediately if arrested or questioned by the police.
- Always carry the release certificate and the identity card provided by the releasing authority and produce them on request for identification to any peace or parole officer.
- Report to the police if and as instructed by the parole supervisor.
- Advise the parole supervisor of address of residence on release and thereafter report immediately:
  - any change in address of residence
  - any change in occupation, including employment, vocational or educational training, and volunteer work
  - any change in the family, domestic, or financial situation
  - any change that may reasonably be expected to affect the ability to comply with the conditions of parole or statutory release
- Not own, possess, or have the control of any weapon (NPB 1994, 14–15).

Additional conditions are applied to individual offenders. These are designed to reduce or manage specific risk factors. Frequently applied additional conditions for federal parolees include these: (1) avoid certain persons (either a specific person such as a coaccused or people with criminal records in general), (2) follow the treatment plan, (3) abstain from intoxicants, (4) take psychological counselling, and (5) avoid certain places (Solicitor General of Canada 1998). Other common additional conditions include the requirement that the parolee seek and maintain employment or schooling, remain in a defined area, and not contact the victim(s) of their crime. Offenders convicted of sexual offences against children are often prohibited from being in the company of anyone under 14 except when accompanied by an approved adult; they are also often forbidden to live near or be in the vicinity of schools, playgrounds, parks, or any other area where there is a reasonable expectation that children are present. The parole board can require that the offender live in a community residential facility or other approved residence.

A parole certificate issued by the Ontario Parole and Earned Release Board is presented in Appendix 8.2.

INMATE APPEALS

Section 147 of the Corrections and Conditional Release Act provides that an inmate-applicant who is denied parole may appeal on the grounds that, in making its decision, the parole board:

- failed to observe a principle of fundamental justice;
- made an error of law;
- breached or failed to apply a board policy;
- based its decision on erroneous or incomplete information; *or*
- acted without jurisdiction or beyond its jurisdiction, or failed to exercise its jurisdiction.

In considering those cases that meet one or more of the above-noted criteria, the appeal division of the parole board may (1) affirm the decision, (2) affirm the decision, but order a further review of the case by the board on a date earlier than the date otherwise provided for next review, (3) order a new review of the case by the board and order the continuation of the decision pending the review, or (4) reverse, cancel, or vary the decision. Few decisions of the NPB are appealed, and in the large majority of such cases (95 percent), the board's initial decision is affirmed. Comparable figures are not available from the provincial parole boards.

ISSUES IN PAROLE BOARD DECISION MAKING

A number of issues surround parole board decision making, including the following:

Boards May Be Subject to Public and Political Influence

Similar to correctional institutions parole boards can be described as public and political institutions, subject to influences from a variety of sources (see

Figure 4.1, p. 142). Indeed, criticism is often directed toward parole board members (especially members of the National Parole Board), and considerable controversy often surrounds their decisions, especially when an inmate on conditional release commits a heinous crime.

With respect to public criticisms of parole and parole boards, recall from Chapter 1 that the public at large knows very little about corrections, including parole. Surveys have found that the public overestimates the number of offenders who are released on parole, their revocation rates, and the recidivism rate generally (NPB 2007).

Potential political influence extends to the appointment of parole board members. Positions on parole boards have long been patronage appointments—that is, rewards for supporters of the federal government. Members are not required by legislation to have any special training or expertise in law, criminology, psychology, or corrections. In 2008 the federal Conservative government was accused of "politicizing" the NPB by filling 23 of 36 vacant NPB positions with retired peace officers. Critics argued that this represented a continuation of the federal government's "get tough" approach to crime (Naumetz 2008).

The Ontario Parole and Earned Release Board requires that persons applying to be board members have the following education and/or experience: a high school diploma or equivalent, preferably graduate or postgraduate education in behavioural sciences, education, law, or psychiatry; experience in social services programs; criminal justice system experience; and community service experience (Ontario Parole and Earned Release Board). The extent to which these credentials help board members make good parole decisions remains to be determined (see "Reflections of a Former Parole Board Member," Box 8.4, p. 326).

The Absence of Clearly Defined Release Criteria

One criticism often levelled against parole boards is that too much discretion has been vested in nonjudicial, unscrutinized decision makers. As noted near the beginning of this chapter, the Corrections and Conditional Release Act sets out two general criteria that are to guide decisions as to whether an offender should be released from confinement on conditional release. This generality has long been a source of difficulty for correctional staff, for inmates, and for parole board members themselves. Board members have access to a great deal of information on each inmate-applicant—including police reports, presentence reports, the presiding judge's reasons for the sentence, materials produced by case managers (including risk/needs assessments), and parole officers' community assessments—yet it is often difficult for them to prioritize this information. This lack of guidance, combined with the discretion exercised by board members, can result in individual styles of decision making. These styles may lead to disparity in decisions on applications for conditional release between boards as well as among board members, even within the same jurisdiction.

The Absence of Information Feedback to Parole Board Members

Few if any mechanisms are in place for parole board members to receive feedback on the outcomes of their decisions—that is, what happens to offenders while they are under supervision in the community and after warrant expiry and the end of supervision. Generally, parole board members learn of an inmate's behaviour on conditional release only when that person commits a high-profile crime or, by happenstance, reappears during a parole suspension hearing before one of the board members involved in the original decision. In other words, the only parolees that board members hear about after the decision to grant a conditional release are the ones who have failed. As a result, board members may develop a skewed perspective and may become more reluctant to grant inmates' applications for conditional release. Also hindering feedback is the practice of randomly assigning board members to parole hearings. This means that only rarely are the same board members involved in ongoing decisions about a given inmate-applicant. Thus the board members being asked to decide on an application for full parole will rarely have been involved in making the decision that released the inmate on day parole.

THE INMATE AND PAROLE HEARINGS

For inmates applying for conditional release, the appearance before the parole board can be stressful, intimidating, and anxiety-provoking. Even inmates who have previously appeared before a parole board are uncertain what questions will be asked and how individual board members will weigh the information contained in the parole file and the responses provided by the inmate during the interview. There are often great disparities between the socioeconomic levels of the board members and the inmates; there may also be cultural differences (including language barriers) that make it difficult for board members and the inmate to communicate. Many inmates have little or no understanding of the role of the parole board and may be intimidated by the more sophisticated language skills of board members. Parole board members, for their part, may not realize that the inmate-applicant is mentally disordered or is still in withdrawal following a relapse into drug use while on conditional release.

Inmates have only a short time to make their case to the board. Most likely, they have never seen the board members before and never will again.

Though inmate-applicants are allowed to have legal representation or other persons in attendance for support, parole board hearings are not a court of law, and the role of lawyers is limited. Current restrictions on legal aid have limited access to legal counsel in many provinces for all but those who can afford to pay their lawyers to attend. Most parole applicants appear on their own.

Board members can ask the inmate-applicant literally anything. The questions may relate to past criminal activities and convictions, the present offence, and participation in treatment programs. Also within bounds are more personal questions about family members and current friendships. For most inmates who plead guilty in criminal court, this is the first time they have been asked detailed questions about their crimes, their personal history, and their future intentions. The severe time constraints under which many parole boards operate place an added burden on both board members and the inmate-applicant, and this may lead to superficial coverage of some topics.

The difficulties inmates encounter at parole hearings are often reflected in the complaints or appeals filed by inmate-applicants who have been denied parole. Common complaints from inmates include these: they completed the required programs yet did not get parole; they were denied parole despite a parole plan; the case manager was unhelpful; and required classes were not available (West-Smith, Progrebin, and Poole 2000). The absence of specific release criteria contributes to a lack of predictability in parole board decision making that may undermine the credibility and effectiveness of case managers and treatment staff, who may have encouraged the inmate and written positive recommendations, only to have the parole board deny the application for conditional release.

Some inmate-applicants play the parole "game"—that is, they manipulate the system to create the impression that they addressing their issues and are committed to moving toward a law-abiding life. Good institutional conduct may not be a strong indicator of suitability for release (Greenspan, Matheson, and Davis 1998).

There is more knowledge of the role of the parole board and of the dynamics of parole hearings among federal offenders who have served multiple terms in custody. A lifer on parole who had appeared before the parole board on numerous occasions offered the following opinion:

> *Parole hearings for me now are old hat. I know how to present myself, what to do, what they want to hear, why they want to hear it. I have a good understanding of what their role is, and what they think their role is and how to approach that … I think they have a really difficult job in trying to gauge the threat to society of the people who are there. They're responsible for the decisions they make. Just looking at a file doesn't give you a very*

good indicator of who people are. But if you put a person in a stressful situation and crank them up a bit and see how they react and see how they handle a situation, then you get a pretty good view of who that person is. I think the board does that quite often ... If you're able to handle yourself in those situations and still be apply to supply the things that are necessary, and make them feel comfortable with the idea of actually letting the person out, then you've done your job as a presenter to the board of your case. (Murphy, Johnsen, and Murphy 2002, 93)

The importance of the parole hearing raises doubts about the large number of "paper" decisions that are made by the NPB in cases involving accelerated parole review and in cases of provincial inmate parole applications.

Aboriginal Inmates and the Parole Board

Aboriginal inmates are overrepresented in provincial/territorial and federal institutions. Moreover, they are less likely to succeed in their applications for conditional release and may choose not to apply at all. A number of factors have been identified as contributing to the difficulties that Aboriginal offenders experience on parole. These factors include a lack of understanding of the parole process, feelings of alienation, a lack of confidence in their ability to successfully complete conditional release, and a lack of assistance for Aboriginal inmates wishing to apply for parole. These inmates are more likely to be on statutory release than on other types of release, in part because of a high rate of waiving the right to a parole hearing.

There may be particular difficulties between Aboriginal inmate-applicants and parole boards. Across the country, there are very few Aboriginal parole board members, which raises the possibility of a lack of cultural sensitivity among non-Aboriginal board members and of inequities in the hearing process. These problems are reflected in the observations of a non-Aboriginal former member of the NPB in the Prairie region:

When I found myself sitting opposite Samuel Grey Hawk, or Amos Morning Cloud, or Joseph Brave Bear, or when I caught the shy, uncertain eyes of a Cree-speaking teenager from the far North attempting to follow, through an interpreter, our ritualistic procedures and answer our thoroughly white middle-class questions, I felt a little like a fraud. It seemed incalculably unfair that these men had the misfortune to have to depend upon the decisions of people who might as well have come from another planet, as far as the similarities in culture and lifestyle were concerned. (Birnie 1990, 195)

A number of initiatives have been undertaken in an attempt to address these difficulties. Federal Aboriginal offenders have the opportunity to participate in parole hearings involving an Aboriginal Cultural Advisor. That person may say a prayer or perform a ritual (such as smudging) to open and/or close the parole hearing. He or she may also provide board members with general information regarding Aboriginal experiences, traditions, and cultures as well as, hopefully, information specific to the culture of the Aboriginal parole applicant (NPB 2007, 81).

Particular difficulties may be encountered by Aboriginal inmate-applicants from northern and remote regions:

> *Sometimes the inmate was ready to go out, and if he was from a city, we would release him. Another inmate, just as ready, would be denied release simply because he was from a community in the Far North with no supports available to him—not only no work, but also no self-help group of former alcoholics, no local hospital with a mental health program, no drug counselors, no sex offender programs. (Birnie 1990, 196)*

PREDICTING REDCIDIVISM: A CHALLENGING TASK

The process of determining which inmates qualify for conditional release is forward-looking, asking two basic questions: (1) If released, will the inmate commit an offence that he or she would not have committed if kept in confinement? (2) Will conditional release with supervision reduce the risk for reoffending compared to a cold turkey release? To answer these questions, parole board members must know the factors that contribute to (and reduce) the probability of reoffending.

Predicting future behaviour is difficult at the best of times, yet parole board members are expected to do just that. Research studies have found that static risk factors, such as the number of prior offences, prior incarcerations, and offences involving violence are strong predictors of future behaviour. But they have also found that dynamic risk factors that are amenable to change, such as substance addiction and peer relationships, are also related to reoffending. In every case, board members must determine whether the inmate is amenable to change and has a release plan that will provide opportunities to alter his or her attitudes and behaviours.

WHEN BOARD DECISIONS GO BAD

> *The hardest job for a Parole Board is to divine the future, and the worst thing that can happen is for that prediction to be proven wrong. (Chair, NPB, in Houlahan 2007)*

All of the cases in which parole board members make decisions that have positive outcomes can be overshadowed by a case in which an offender on conditional release commits a heinous crime. See Box 8.3.

High-profile incidents such as the Ulayuk case have contributed to calls for more restrictive release policies for violent offenders.

BOX 8.3

A Death in Yellowknife

On October 6, 2004, at 10 a.m., Louise Pargeter, a 34-year-old CSC parole officer, went to the home of Eli Ulayuk, one of the parolees she supervised. She failed to return to her office as scheduled by 11:30 a.m., and her coworkers were unable to locate her. The following day, the RCMP made a gruesome discovery: they found Pargeter's body at Ulayuk's apartment. During the course of the trial, the court learned that Ulayuk had wanted to kill Pargeter since 2001 when she revoked his day parole. He finally acted out this desire. The court heard that Ulayuk struck Pargeter with a hammer five times, strangled her with twine, and had sex with her body. In February 2006, Ulayuk was found guilty of second degree murder and sentenced to life in prison, with the recommendation that he be ineligible for parole for 25 years. This is the first Canadian case of a parolee murdering his parole officer during a home visit.

A CSC inquiry into the incident identified a number of factors that may have led to Pargeter's death (CSC and National Parole Board 2006). Earlier, Ulayuk had been convicted of the murder of a woman in his home community of Igloolik, Nunavut, and had been diagnosed as a necrophiliac, a form of sexual deviance. The sentencing judge in that case commented that Ulayuk was one of the most dangerous offenders to come before the court. The Board of Investigation (BOI) found that while in confinement, the CSC had not completed sufficient clinical assessments of Ulayuk, nor had sufficient attention been given to his sexual deviancy in the treatment plan. The BOI stated that there had not been sufficient analysis of Ulayuk's case file prior to his release; it then made numerous recommendations with respect to the CSC information-gathering process, case preparation for NPB hearings, and the supervision of offenders in the community. The BOI also recommended that the NPB change the format of its decisions to make it more structured, with a focus on specific risk factors.

Source: http://www.nunatsiaq.com/archives/60324/news/nunavut/60324_11.html

REFLECTIONS OF A FORMER PAROLE BOARD MEMBER

To conclude the discussion of parole boards and parole board decision, the observations made by your author while serving as a community member of the British Columbia Board of Parole from 2000–2005 are presented in Box 8.4. (The board was disbanded by the provincial government in 2007 and its responsibilities assigned to the NPB.)

BOX 8.4

Reflections of a Former Parole Board Member

There was among the board members considerable variation in how hearings were conducted, the focus of their questions, and in the case file information deemed to be most important in reaching a decision. The provincial parole act provided no guidance on how to weigh the various items of information in the inmate's case file. Was the community/risk needs assessment more important than the materials presented in the community assessment document prepared by the probation officer? How much weight should be given to the victim impact statement? To letters of support written on behalf of the inmate? To the inmate's prior record? To the comments of the judge at sentencing? To the treatment programs that the inmate had completed inside (often more than once if the inmate had previously been incarcerated)? To behavioral reports written by correctional officers? How much weight should the inmate applicant's performance in the hearing room be given? Since parole boards have no capacity of independent information gathering, we had to rely on institution staff and community corrections personnel to develop the materials in the case file. Key information, such as the inmate's prior involvement in federal corrections, was often incomplete or missing entirely. There were ongoing challenges in securing information on offenders from federal corrections.

The large amount of discretion that we as board members had frequently resulted in members weighing information differently. Some board members would override the general consensus presented in the case file, based on a good showing by the inmate in the parole hearing. As a board member, I was reluctant to ignore the recommendations of institutional staff and community corrections personnel. In cases where there was contradictory or incomplete information in the case file, the hearing would be "stood down" while a telephone call was placed to secure the necessary information or to clarify points of information.

In the parole hearing interviews, some board members focused on substance abuse to the near-exclusion of other items of information. Others, particularly those with strong religious beliefs, tended to engage in moral "finger wagging" about the inmate's lifestyle choices. Board members with backgrounds in social work would often conduct lengthy casework-style interviews covering details of the inmate's childhood, including family life, peer relationships, and abuse. These interviews could take several hours. I was never certain as to how we could use this information in making a release decision, given that community-based resources and facilities for offenders who had been sexually abused, were suffering from mental disabilities, fetal alcohol spectrum disorder, and other challenges, were generally nonexistent. I often wondered about the wisdom of conducting a lengthy interview with an offender about their background, have them share their most private experiences with us, only to deny parole due to there being no community resources. Other board members completed hearings in as little as a half-hour.

Crime victims and/or their families rarely attended the hearings and special attention had to be given to those who did attend. Most knew nothing about parole, the role of the board, the procedure for parole hearings, the legislative framework within which we operated, or conditional release. For many victims, the parole hearing was the next forum, after criminal court, where they could express their anger, and grief, which was often directed toward my colleagues and me. In cases where the offender had committed a particularly heinous crime, the tension in the hearing room could be cut with a knife: the victim's family would interrupt the hearing, often shouting at the offender. On a few occasions, correctional officers would have to remove these persons from the hearing room.

In conducting parole hearings, I always tried to remain mindful of the extreme power differential between the inmate-applicant and myself as a parole board member. My colleagues and the inmate-applicant were from different worlds. I had to constantly remind myself (and often, my colleagues) to speak in "plain" English and to use non-technical language to ensure that the inmate applicant understood what was being asked of, or explained to them. Of course, the primary objective of all of the inmates that appeared before us was to get out of prison as soon as possible. One had to read between the lines and to determine, on a very subjective level, the sincerity of the inmate and the level of commitment to the release plan.

A primary focus of my interview questions as a board member was whether the inmate applicant "got it"—that is:

- Did they understand the reasons why they had become involved in the criminal behaviour that landed them in jail?

(continued)

- What did they identify as their "thinking errors" and what treatment programs had they participated in to address those?
- To what extent had they reflected on their behaviour and its impact on the victim and the community?

These types of questions were particularly important to ask sex offenders, who tended to deny responsibility for their behaviour, blame the victim, and/or minimize their behaviour and its impact on victims. Given that the majority of inmate-applicants who appeared before us had significant substance-abuse issues, we were constantly attempting to determine whether the person was an addict who resorted to criminal behaviour to support their addiction, or whether the applicant was immersed in the criminal lifestyle. There was no statutory guidance on how to make that assessment. To make good decisions as a board member, one must develop a sixth sense about the person who appears before you, and about any support persons that appear on the inmate's behalf. Call it a "bullshit" detector, if you will. With the exception of the clinical psychologist who was also a board member, none us had received training in how to determine whether the inmate was being less than honest with us or to determine their level of commitment to living a law-abiding life.

One of the most common responses that my colleagues and I received when the inmate was asked, "What do you understand about how you ended up here in prison?" was "Hanging around with the wrong crowd, I guess." Often, applicants were unable to offer any further insights into their behaviour and the reasons for it. Many of the offenders had simply not thought about it, even though they may have been involved in a criminal lifestyle for decades. For many, notions of accountability and accepting responsibility were foreign concepts. Nor had they considered that there might be options to the lifestyle they were living. My colleagues and I soon realized that part of the problem was that most offenders had never had the opportunity, or been required, to speak about their behaviour, to reflect on their lifestyle choices, or to understand the impact of their behaviour on themselves, their family, the victim, and the community. Most had simply pled guilty. For those of us on the board, it highlighted the need for a forum for inmates to discuss and address these issues. Such a forum does not generally currently exist in the justice system, although many of the restorative-justice approaches presented in Chapter 4 do provide such an opportunity. As a board member, I always felt that it was pretty late in the game to attempt to begin a conversation with the inmate about these very important issues.

As a board member, I developed a set of guidelines for my decision making. Two of these were: "If in doubt, deny parole" and "If I release this person and they violate the conditions of their release certificate, are they likely to do self-harm, that is, relapse into drug use, or are they likely to cause others harm?" If the likelihood was that they would only do self-harm, my tendency was to release them (often multiple times over the course of the five years I served on the board) to a residential treatment program.

When the decision was made to grant day parole or full parole, a major issue was what additional conditions would be attached to the parole certificate. Many board members routinely attached the requirement that the parolee abstain from alcohol or intoxicants, even if alcohol or drugs were not a component of their criminal behaviour. I often felt that some board members attached so many additional conditions that the inmate was likely to fail.

While the large majority of inmate-applicants had serious and often long-standing substance abuse issues and had social histories that included physical and/or mental abuse, there were the odd applicants who had stumbled into the justice system via a series of unfortunate events: the 45-year-old charter bus driver who, deep in gambling debts, had agreed to transport drugs into the United States in the cargo hold of his bus. And the two pre-med students who, in a chance meeting with an ex-offender at a bar, hatched a hair-brained scheme to rob a night accountant at a resort hotel and use the money to pay off their student loans.

Even after serving a number of years on the board, I and my fellow board members could be fooled. In one case, an inmate-applicant had a substance-abuse problem, but he appeared before us with a sterling case file, positive recommendations from institution staff, a solid community plan that involved going to residential drug treatment and recovery, and strong support from his girlfriend who was employed as a bank manager. Parole was granted. Immediately after being released from the facility two days later, he and his girlfriend shot up heroin in the parking lot and he went AWOL for two months before being apprehended. His parole was suspended and subsequently revoked.

A huge source of frustration for my colleagues and I was the absence of community resources for inmates. There were no programs for inmates with FASD or mental disabilities, and most of the residential treatment programs would not take inmates who were serving a sentence for a crime of violence. In these cases, we often had to deny parole, which meant that the offender would serve to the two-thirds point in their sentence and then be released with no supervision or assistance.

In retrospect: Did the fact that I had a Ph.D. in sociology, and that I taught corrections courses and a senior-level seminar in decision making in the School of Criminology at Simon Fraser University, help me make good decisions as a parole board member, decisions that provided assistance to the offender in moving toward a law-abiding life, while protecting the community? I still wonder. I'm not certain

(continued)

that it helped me prioritize the vast amount of information in an inmate applicant's case file; or "read" an inmate in a parole hearing to determine whether he or she was being truthful; or assess the extent to which wives, husbands, parents, and other support persons were being truthful and would be of assistance to the inmate if released into the community; or determine which inmates have benefited from core treatment programs in the prison; or predict which inmates would succeed in the community. The inmates who appeared before me during those years had so many issues, the time they were in confinement was so short, the institutional and community program resources so limited, and the opportunities for them to engage in self-reflection and change so fleeting, that success in the community was always, at best, a long shot.

AT ISSUE

ISSUE 8.1: Should Section 745 of the Criminal Code—the "faint hope clause"—be removed from the Criminal Code?

Section 745 was added to the Criminal Code in 1976 amidst the debate over the abolition of capital punishment. At that time, those serving life sentences for murder were eligible for parole after seven years. The increase to a mandatory 25 years was so dramatic that Parliament created the judicial review option.

Proponents argue that Section 745:

- reflects enlightened corrections policy;
- provides an incentive to offenders to participate in rehabilitation programs;
- helps corrections personnel manage long-term offenders;
- does not guarantee release, even if the application is successful, but rather makes the offender eligible for parole consideration; *and*
- provides that offenders whose applications are successful and who are granted parole must remain under supervision for the rest of their lives.

Critics of section 745, many of whom have argued that the section should be deleted in its entirety from the Criminal Code, counter that the provision:

- undermines the potential impact of life sentences as a general and specific deterrent to crime;
- results in the revictimization of crime victims and their families during the Section 745 hearing, during subsequent parole hearings, and when the offender is released on parole prior to the 25-year point;
- makes a mockery of the law (i.e., "life means life"); *and*
- results in violent offenders being released into the community

What do you think?

1. What is your position on Section 745 of the Criminal Code? Would you favour its abolition, or do you feel that the current provisions are adequate?
2. How would you respond to the criticisms that have been directed against Section 745?

AT ISSUE

ISSUE 8.2: Should statutory release be abolished?

The report of the Correctional Service Review Panel (Sampson 2007) recommended that statutory release be abolished and replaced with earned parole. The panel argued that, instead of being automatically released at the two-thirds point in their sentence (with the exception of the few offenders who are detained), offenders should have to earn their release. The panel further stated that:

- statutory release is not working and does not contribute to the rehabilitation of the offender;
- offenders who "play the clock" until the two-thirds mark of their sentence cause disruptions in the prison and are not motivated to participate in treatment programs;
- currently, offenders who wait until their statutory release date have all of the privileges of other inmates, even though they may not be making satisfactory progress with their correctional plan; *and*
- violent reoffending rates by offenders on statutory release are three times higher than for offenders on parole.

Proponents of statutory release counter that:

- ending statutory release would place more pressure on an already stressed system;
- there would be additional costs to taxpayers to house more offenders for longer periods of time; *and*
- there is no evidence that keeping offenders in prison for longer periods of time reduces the rate of reoffending.

For more serious offenders who are denied parole, statutory release provides for supervision in the community, whereas if an offender serves to his or her warrant expiry date in prison, there is no supervision upon release into the community.

What do you think?

1. Do you support the recommendation of the CSC Review Panel that statutory release be abolished? Why? Why not?

Sources: Bailey and Bronskill 2007; Sampson 2007

KEY POINTS REVIEW

1. The underlying premise of conditional-release programs is that the likelihood of recidivism is reduced when inmates are offered incentives to participate in institutional programs. This minimizes the negative impact of incarceration and ensures supervision by probation and parole officers.
2. Federal inmates, who are incarcerated for longer periods of time compared to their provincial counterparts, tend to be released in gradual stages, and long-term studies show that offenders who are gradually released from prison are more likely to become law-abiding citizens than offenders who remain in prison until the end of their sentence.

3. A number of initiatives have been developed to ensure that crime victims are informed and may participate in the conditional release process.
4. Parole certificates contain both mandatory and additional conditions to which the inmate must adhere.
5. Issues surrounding parole board decision making include these: boards may be subject to public and political influence; there is an absence of clearly defined release criteria; feedback on case decisions to parole board members is lacking; and inmate-applicants face difficulties arranging an appearance before the board.
6. Predicting which offenders will reoffend upon release is a difficult task.
7. The consequences of parole board decisions can be significant if the offender reoffends.

KEY TERM QUESTIONS

1. Define the following types of conditional release: **temporary absence, day parole, full parole, remission/discharge,** and **statutory release.**
2. What is **cold turkey release** and what issues does it raise?
3. What is **accelerated parole review** and why might it be controversial?
4. What is the **warrant expiry date?**
5. Describe the **faint hope clause (Judicial review).**
6. Describe the procedures and objectives of **detention during the period** of **statutory release.**
7. Discuss the role of the **community assessment** in the conditional-release process.

APPENDIX 8.1

Ontario Parole and Earned Release Board

Commission ontarienne des libérations Conditionnelles et des mises en liberté méritées

Parole Decision of Board
Décision de la Commission En matière de libération Conditionnelle

Surname/Nom de famille Given/Prénom Middle/Prénom	DOB/Date de naissance	Date of Decision/Date de décision
Institution/Établissement Monteith Correctional Centre	OTIS No./Numéro du SISC	FPS No./Numéro du service d'empreintes digitales

Hearing/Meeting/Location/Lieu de réunion ou d'audience	Parole Eligibility Date d'admissibilité à la libération conditionnelle	Discharge Possible Date Date possible de libération	Final Warrant Expiry Date Date d'échéance finale du mandat
Monteith Correctional Centre	09/15/2007	11/17/2007	16-Jan-08

After careful review of all available information about your case, the Ontario Parole and Earned Release Board has decided/Après avoir étudié attentivement tous les renseignements disponibles sur votre cause, la commission ontarienne des libération conditionnelles et des mises en libertés méritées a conclu la décision suivante.

☒	Parole Granted/ Libération conditionnelle accordée	☐	Parole Terminated/ Libération conditionnelle Terminée	☐	Hearing Denied/ Audience refusée
☐	Parole Denied/ Libération conditionnelle refusée	☐	Parole Continued/ Libération Conditionnelle prolongée	☐	Parole Granted Decision Rescinded Décision de libération conditionnelle annulée
☐	Parole Decision Deferred/ Décision ajournée	☐	Hearing Granted/ Audience accordée	☐	Conditions Varied/ Conditions modifiées
☐	Parole Revoked/ Libération conditionnelle révoquée	☐	Hearing Rescheduled/ Audience remise à une autre date	☐	Conditions Not Varied/ Conditions maintenues
Details/Détails Parole Garnted effective September 26, 2007				☐	Remission Recredited/ Remise de peine reportée au dossier
				☐	Remission Not Recredited/ Remise de peine non reportée au dossier

Reason for Decision/Raisons qui motivent la décision:

a) Risk to society by re-offending/Danger de récidive pour la société

Your custody sentence relates to a very serious assault offence that occurred while you were under the influence of alcohol after a lengthy period of consumption. You have no prior convictions and you have maintained a successful and lawful interim release period prior to coming into custody. It is apparent that the offence and related charge caused you to realize that you required assistance in dealing with personal issues which include alcohol consumption and anger management. In response to your issues, you have completed an anger management program and additional, more intensive, counselling sessions at the North of Superior Community Mental Health Programs. It is also noted by the Board that you have maintained institutional program involvement and institution work while in custody.

b) Protection of society through reintegration/Protection de la société grâce à la réinsertion sociale :

Your release plan includes sponsor support and your plans to return to your employment. You also intend to continue counselling sessions with the North of Superior Community organization. The Board believes that your plan contains sufficient support to ensure a successful parole release. Your request is granted to become effective September 26, 2007.

Standard Parole Conditions/Conditions générales de libération conditionnelle

You have agreed to the following standard conditions/Vous avez accepté les conditions générales suivantes:

Pursuant to Section 48 ss(a) to (e) of the Ministry of Correctional Services Act and Regulations (1990)/Conformément aux alinéas a) à c) de la *Loi de 1990 sur le ministère des Services correctionnels* et ses règlements.

48. It is a condition of every grant of parole, unless the Board orders otherwise that the parolee shall/ À moins d'avis contraire par la Commission, tout libéré conditionnel doit respecter les conditions suivantes:

    1) remain within Jurisdiction of the Board/vous devez rester dans la jurisdiction territoriale de la Commission

    2) keep the peace and be of good behaviour/vous ne devez pas troubler l'ordre public et vous devez vous conduire convenablement

    3) obtain the consent of the Board or the parole supervisor for any change of residence or employment/vous devez obtenir l'autorisation de la commission ou de votre surveillant de libération conditionnelle pour tout changement de domicille ou d'emploi

Ontario Parole and Earned Release Board

Commission ontarienne des libérations Conditionnelles et des mises en libérté méritées

Parole Decision of Board
Décision de la Commission En matière de libération Conditionnelle

4) report immediately upon release to your parole supervisor and the local police force. Report thereafter as required by your parole supervisor./ vous devez vous présenter au bureau de votre surveillant de libération conditionnelle et au poste de police immédiatement après liberation. Et par après vous presenter tel que convenu avec votre surveillant de liberation conditionelle.

5) refrain from associating with any person who is engaged in criminal activity or unless approved by the parole supervisor, with any person who has a criminal record/Il vous est interdit de fréquenter des personnes ayant des activités criminelles ou, sauf avec autorisation du surveillant de libération conditionnelle, des personnes ayant un casier judiciaire

6) carry your parole certificate at all times and present it to any police officer or probation and parole officer upon request./Porter sur vous,en tout temps, votre document de liberation conditionnelle et le presenter à tout agent de probation et liberation conditionnelle ou à tout agent de police qui vous le demande

Special Parole Conditions /Conditions spéciales de libération conditionnelle

You have also agreed to the following special conditions/Vous avez aussi accepté les conditions spéciales suivantes:

1. Upon release abide by your approved travel plan.

2. Abstain from the purchase, possession or consumption of alcohol or other intoxicating substances.

3. Not to enter or be found in any establishment whose primary source of business is the sale of alcohol.

4. Not to associate or hold any communication directly or indirectly with (named individual) except with in circumstances approved of by the parole officer in writing.

5. Abstain from owning, possessing or carrying any weapon as defined by the criminal code.

6. Continue to attend for and actively comply with any counselling program for anger management issues and substance use issues with the North of Superior Community Health Program and provide written verification of same to your Parole Officer, or any such programming as may be recommended by your Parole Officer and provide proof of same to your Parole Officer.

Release Plans/Plans de Libération

Residence/Domicile
Employment/Education/Other/Emploi, éducation et autre(s)

Vice Chair/ designate – Vice-président/ mandataire

Request for Review/Demande exigée pour une révision
If you would like Board to review the decision, contact your superintendent/designate/Si vous désirez que La Commission des libérations conditionnelles révise la décision, communiquez avec

Proviso
The Board's decision to grant parole is conditional upon your good behaviour and the continuation of your Board approved release plan./ La Commission accorde la libération à la condition que votre comportement demeure convenable et que vous vous conformiez à votre plan de libération approuvé par la Commission.

Distribution/Distribution:

- ☐ Inmate Parolee/Détenu en liberté conditionnelle
- ☐ Board Case File/Dossier de la Commission
- ☐ I.L.O./Parole Supervisor/Agent de liaison de l'établissement/surveillant
- ☐ Superintendent/Directeur

APPENDIX 8.2

Ontario Parole and Earned Release Board

Certificate of Parole/ Certificat de mise en liberté conditionnelle

Date(s) Issued/ Date d'émission	Warrant Expiry/ Expiration du mandat	Release Date/ Date de mise en liberté
	01/16/2008	09/26/2007

Supervision Service Sector/ Secteur de Service superviseur — Released from/Mise en liberté de

Central North Service Sector

Under the **Ministry of Correctional Services Act 1990**, and the regulations, the Ontario Parole and Earned Release Board releases:
/En vertu de la **Loi de 1990 sur le ministère des services correctionnels** et des réglements y afférents, la commission des libération conditionnelles et des mises en liberté méritées libère:

Last Name/ Nom de famille	First, Middle/ Prénom, deuxième	Client ID/ N° matricule	DOB/ Date de naissance	FPS No./ Numéro de SED

Under the following standard conditions/sous réserve du respect des conditions normales suivantes:

1) Remain within jurisdiction of the Board.
/Vous devez rester dans la jurisdiction de la Commission des libérations conditionnelles.
2) Keep the peace and be of good behaviour.
/Vous ne devez pas troubler l'ordre public et vous devez vous conduire convenablement.
3) Obtain the consent of the Board or the Parole Supervisor for any change of residence or employment.
/Vous devez obtenir l'autorisation de la commission ou de votre surveillant de libération conditionnelle si vous désirez changer d'emploi ou de résidence.
4) Report immediately upon release to your Parole Supervisor and local Police force. Report thereafter as required by your parole supervisor.
/Vous devez vous présenter au bureau de votre surveillant de libération conditionnelle et au poste de police immédiatement après votre libération. Et par après vous presenter tel que convenu avec votre surveillant de libération conditionnelle.
5) Refrain from associating with any person who is engaged in criminal activity or unless approved by the Parole Supervisor with any person who has a criminal record.
/Il vous est interdit de fréquenter des personnes impliquées dans des activités criminelles. D'autant plus, vous ne devez fréquenter des personnes ayant un casier judiciare, sans l'autorisation du surveillant de libération conditionnelle.
6) You must carry your parole certificate at all times and present it to any police officer or Parole Supervisor upon request.
/Vous devez porter votre certificat de libération conditionnelle en tout temps et le présenter, sur demande, à tous officier de police ou agent de probation.

Special Conditions/ Conditions spéciales

1. Upon release abide by your approved travel plan.
2. Abstain from the purchase, possession or consumption of alcohol or other intoxicating substances.
3. Not to enter or be found in any establishment whose primary source of business is the sale of alcohol.
4. Not to associate or hold any communication directly or indirectly with ____________ except within circumstances approved of by your Parole Officer in writing.
5. Abstain from owning, possessing or carrying any weapon as defined by the criminal code.
6. Continue to attend for and actively comply with any counselling program for anger management issues and substance use issues with North of Superior Community Health Program and provide written verification of same to your Parole Officer, or any such programming as may be recommended by your Parole Officer and provide proof of same to your Parole Officer.

According to Section 49 of the Regulations under the Ministry of Correctional Services Act, as a parolee you are required to submit a monthly report to your parole supervisor until your parole is completed.
/En vertu de la Loi sur le ministère des services correctionnels et selon l'article 49 des règlements, en tant que personne libérée, vous êtes tenu de soumettre un rapport mensuel à votre agent de surveillance jusqu'à l'expiration de la libération conditionnelle.

Upon Release you shall
/Lors de votre libérations vous devrez

Report immediately to a Parole Supervisor/ Lors de votre libération vous devrez vous présenter immédiatement à surveillant de libération
Reside at address/ Adresse d'habitation
Report to Police at/ Vous présenter au poste de police de

Parole Declaration/Déclaration de mise en liberté conditionnelle

I have carefully read or had read to me the conditions of this certificate. I understand the conditions and contents of this certificate of Parole. I accept my release and pledge myself honestly to comply with the conditions. I also understand that if I violate the conditions of my Parole, I may be returned to a correctional institution to serve the portion of my term of imprisonment, including any remission that remained unexpired at the time Parole was granted less the period of time spent on Parole.
/Je déclare avoir lu attentivement ce certificat ou en avoir reçu lecture. Je déclare voir lu attentivement ce certificat ou en avoir reçu lecture. Je comprends les conditions et la teneur de ce certificat de mise en liberté conditionnellle. J'accepte ma libération en ces termes et je promets en toute honnêteté d'observer ces conditions. Je sais également que, si je commets une infraction aux conditions stipulées pour ma libération conditionnelle, on peut me renvoyer dans un établissement corrrectionnel pour y purger le reste de ma peine d'emprisonnement, y compris toute réduction de peine, non encore purgée au moment où la libération conditionnelle m'a été accordée, moins la période de liberté conditionnelle.

Valid only when signed by Parolee/Ce certificat n'est valide que s'il est signé par la personne en liberté conditionnelle
Parolee's Signature/Signature de la personne en liberté conditionnelle

Date

Given in triplicate by the authority of the Ontario Parole and Earned Release Board.
/Établi en triple examplaire avec l'autorisation de la commission ontarienne des libérations conditionnelles et des mises en liberté méritées.
Vice Chair or Designate/Vice-Président ou mandataire

Signature — Date

DISTRIBUTION: Parolee (after signing)
Probation and Parole Office
Board Case File

REFERENCES

Bailey, S., and J. Bronskill. 2007. "Build Newer, Bigger Prisons and Scrap Early Release, Review Panel Urges." prisonjustice.ca. December 13. http://www.prisonjustice.ca/starkravenarticles/prison_panel_1207.html.

Birnie, L.H. 1990. *A Rock and a Hard Place: Inside Canada's Parole Board.* Toronto: Macmillan

Bonta, J., A. Harris, I. Zinger, and D. Carriere. 1996. *The Crown Files Research Project: A Study of Dangerous Offenders*. Ottawa: Solicitor General Canada. http://ww2.ps-sp.gc.ca/publications/corrections/pdf/199601_e.pdf

Bonta, J., I. Zinger, A. Harris, and D. Carriere. 1998. "The Dangerous Offender Provisions: Are They Targeting the Right Offenders?" *Canadian Journal of Criminology* 40(4): 377–400.

Campbell, D. 1997. "A Journalist Goes to Prison to See for Himself How Parole Boards Decide Which Convicts are Good Risks and Which Ones Are Not." *Ottawa Citizen*, November 3, A3.

CSC (Correctional Service of Canada) and National Parole Board. 2006. *National Joint Board of Investigation into the Release and Supervision of an Offender on Full Parole Charged with First-Degree Murder of a Parole Officer on October 7, 2004, in Yellowknife, Northwest Territories*. Ottawa. http://www.csc-scc.gc.ca/text/pblct/ci-report05-06/report-eng.pdf

Fauteux, G. 1956. *Report of a Committee Appointed to Inquire into the Principles and Procedures Followed in the Remission Service of the Department of Justice of Canada*. Ottawa: Queen's Printer.

Gibbs, W. 1999. "Reframing Parole." http://www.ciaj-icaj.ca/english/publications/DP1999/Gibbs.pdf

Grant, B.A. 1998. *Accelerated Parole Review: Were the Objectives Met?* Ottawa: Research Branch, Correctional Service of Canada. http://ww2.ps-sp.gc.ca/publications/corrections/ccra/accelerated_parole_review_e.asp

———. 1997. "Detention: Is It Meeting Its Goal?" *Forum on Corrections Research* 9(2): 19–24.

Grant, B.A., and S.L. Johnson. 1998. *Personal Development Temporary Absences*. Ottawa: Correctional Service of Canada. http://www.csc-scc.gc.ca/text/rsrch/reports/r65/r65_e.pdf

Grant, B.A., and W.A. Millson. 1998. *The Temporary Absence Program: A Descriptive Analysis*. Ottawa: Correctional Service of Canada. http://www.csc-scc.gc.ca/text/rsrch/reports/r66/r66_e.pdf

Greenspan, E., A. Matheson, and R. Davis. 1998. "Discipline and Parole." *Queen's Quarterly* 105(1): 9–27.

Houlahan, M. 2007. "Divining Future 'Hardest Job' for Parole Board." *New Zealand Herald* (July 24). http://www.nzherald.co.nz/section/1/story.cfm?c_id=1&objectiveid=10453550

Murphy, P.J., L. Johnsen, and J. Murphy. 2002. *Paroled for Life: Interviews with Parolees Serving Life Sentences*. Vancouver: New Star.

Naumetz, T. 2008. "Critics Accuse Day of 'Politicizing' Parole Board." *Winnipeg Sun*, June 30. http://www.winnipegsun.com

NPB (National Parole Board). 1994. *Parole: Balancing Public Safety and Personal Responsibility*. Ottawa: Solicitor General.

———. 2007. *Performance Monitoring Report, 2006–2007*. Ottawa. http:// www.npb-cnlc.gc.ca/reports/pdf/pmr_2006_2007/index-eng.htm

Public Safety Canada Portfolio Corrections Statistics Committee. 2007. *Corrections and Conditional Release Statistical Overview*. Ottawa. http://www.publicsafety.gc.ca/res/cor/rep/ccrso2007-eng.aspx

Purdy, C. 2005. "Lysyk Out on Parole: Disgraced Edmonton Banker Who Stole $16 million Now in Halfway House After Serving 14 Months." *Edmonton Journal*, December 6. http://www.canada.com

Sampson, R. (chair). 2007. *Report of the Correctional Service of Canada Review Panel*. Ottawa: Minister of Public Works and Government Services Canada. http://www.publicsafety.gc.ca/csc-scc/cscrpreport-eng.pdf

Solicitor General of Canada. 1998. *Sentence Calculation: How Does it Work?* Ottawa. http://www.ps-sp.gc.ca/publications/corrections/sentence_calcbook_how_e.asp

West-Smith, M., M.R. Progrebin, and E.D. Poole. 2000. "Denial of Parole: An Inmate Perspective." *Federal Probation* 64(2): 3–10.

WEBLINKS

Ontario Parole and Earned Release Board

http://www.operb.gov.on.ca
This site provides information on parole criteria and eligibility, the parole hearing process, victim participation in parole board decision making, and the mandate, organization, and history of the Board. Quick facts and statistics and a list of correctional institutions under the Board's four regions are also provided.

National Parole Board

http://www.npb-cnlc.gc.ca
Designed for victims, inmates due for parole, and the general public, this site contains news releases, reports and publications, information on the NPB's organization and decision-making process, policy manual updates, and links to various judicial, police, and correctional sites.

CHAPTER 9

REENTRY AND LIFE AFTER PRISON

CHAPTER OBJECTIVES

After reading this chapter you should be able to:

- *Describe reintegration as a process rather than as an event.*
- *Discuss what is meant by the pains of reentry.*
- *Describe the dual function of parole supervision and the views of offenders toward supervising parole officers.*
- *Provide examples of innovative programs for offenders reentering the community.*
- *Discuss the unique challenges faced by Aboriginal offenders, female offenders, mentally disordered offenders, and sex offenders on parole.*
- *Discuss the key issues that surround the practice of community notification.*
- *Describe the structure and dynamics of circles of support and accountability.*
- *Describe the procedures that apply when a parolee commits a new offence or violates the conditions of the parole certificate.*
- *Address the issue of the effectiveness of parole.*
- *Discuss the issues that surround Section 810 of the Criminal Code (judicial recognizance).*

KEY TERMS

Reintegration
Pains of reentry
Judicial recognizance
Community notification
Circles of support and accountability (COSAs)
Suspension of conditional release
Revocation of conditional release
Through care

PERSPECTIVE

An Ex-offender Reflects on Reentry

The moment offenders step off the bus they face several critical decisions. Where will they live, where will they be able to find a meal, where should they look for a job, how will they get to a job interview, and where can they earn enough money to pay for necessities? These returning inmates are also confronted with many details of personal business, such as obtaining identification cards and documents, making medical appointments, and working through the many everyday bureaucratic problems that occur during any transition. These choices prompt feelings of intense stress and worry over the logistics of their return to the outside world. To those who have had no control over any aspect of life for many years, each of these problems can be difficult. In accumulation, they can be overwhelming.

My own experience is a good example. Shortly after my release from prison to the halfway house, some friends took me to lunch at a local deli. The waiter came over to take our orders. Everyone else told him what they wanted, but I kept poring over the menu. My eyes raced over the columns of choices. I knew that I was supposed to order, but the number of options overwhelmed me. My friends sat in embarrassed silence. I was paralyzed. The waiter looked at me impatiently. I began to panic. How ridiculous that I wasn't able to do such a simple thing as order lunch. Finally, in desperation, I ordered the next item my eyes landed on, a turkey sandwich. I didn't even want it, but at least it put an end to this embarrassing incident.

For two years I hadn't been able to make any choices about what I ate. Now I was having a hard time making a simple choice that most people make every day. If I had this much difficulty after only a couple of years in prison, think how hard it is for those inmates who haven't made any choices for five, ten, or fifteen years. And what about those who didn't have the wonderful home, the loving family, the strong faith, and the good education that I had? They face a baffling array of options and little preparation. Is it any surprise that so many newly released prisoners make some bad choices and end up back in prison? If we do not prepare these inmates for their return to the community, the odds are great that their first incarceration will not be their last.

Source: Nolan 2005.

PERSPECTIVE

A Victim Reflects on Offender Reentry

Awakening: swollen eyelids opening to blurred vision. Through this blurred vision, I see tree branches far above me. My head feels foggy, my thoughts unclear. Where am I? What am I doing here? Intense pain begins to emanate from my head. I slowly lift my hand and touch my head. I feel something sticky, and what feels like a bird's nest, but in reality my fingers are intertwining in my hair. As I begin to grope about my head more and more, I feel something sharp and protruding. The rest of my body begins to awaken and starts to shake uncontrollably. Even though it is summer, I feel cold as if an ice storm has invaded my entire body. I reach out again, touching my body, and I realize I am naked. Slowly my eyesight becomes more focused. My thoughts and memory of what has happened hit me like a tidal wave. I've been raped, beaten, and left here. Tears begin to fall like hard rain, while at the same time my hand reaches out, grouping around for my clothes, anything to stop the cold shivers that rack my body. However, I could only find one piece of clothing and I am not sure what it is, nor is it enough to cover up my body.

Still clutching this material, I try to sit up, but the intense pain in my head makes this almost impossible. I sit still, not moving, trying to make the pain subside, as the realization of my situation begins to surface. My eyes feel swollen, and even when I do look around it is dark. Suddenly, a young man appears. In a shaky voice I cry out, "Help me, please help me, I've been raped." The look of shock registers immediately on his face as I stand there trying to cover up my body using the material I have in my hands. He then gives me some type of clothing and helps me put it on. He is joined by others, among them a young girl, who begins to give directions. I begin mumbling, calling out for my partner. In the background, people discuss their plan of action. Soon, waves of nausea begin to flood me and I struggle to move, knowing I am going to be sick. I begin to vomit. Just as the ambulance arrives, I hear the sound of birds chirping, announcing the coming of dawn.

Little did I know then that I had just stepped onto the path of victim/survivor. This path was full of obstacles that I had to face. Many times I was completely unaware of the challenges I would have to meet. Reflecting upon these times when I learned to overcome one challenge after another, drawing upon some inner strength I did not know I possessed. I now realize that these are the attributes of a survivor.

Now, eight years later, I have survived the experience of working with the criminal justice system to see my offender caught, tried, and sentenced. Today I am faced with yet another challenge, one which at the moment seems the most difficult to face: the reality of my offender's release. I began contemplating this event the moment the sentence was handed down. My thoughts went something like this: "Okay … I now have this many years to live my life. Better make the best of it." While this thought continues to dominate, the thought that follows is, "Let's not think about this right now, as I have so many years to be free from the constant fear of being stalked and possibly killed by this person." During this time I have worked hard, first of all, to make some sense of these events, recover from the trauma, and find a way to handle the fear that I face in my everyday life. I also have worked to find my new place in this world and answer the question, "What can I do to be of help, particularly to keep this kind of devastating, life-altering crime from happening to others?"

Source: Survivor of a kidnapping, sexual assault, and assault, in Seymour 2001, 1–2.

THE PROCESS OF REINTEGRATION

Reintegration is a process, not an event. It has been defined as "all activity and programming conducted to prepare an offender to return safely to the community as a law-abiding citizen" (Thurber 1998, 14). It begins with the treatment programs described in Chapter 7 and also includes the development of a release plan that sets out where the inmate will live, work, go to school, and, if required, participate in postrelease treatment programs (see Figure 9.1). The goal of reintegration is to avoid recidivism in the short term (i.e., until the warrant expiry date) as well as afterwards. When required, yet another goal is to address the interests of crime victims. Most inmates who reoffend do so within the first two years following release from a correctional institution.

To succeed, reintegration should involve continuity between institutional programs and the services an offender receives on conditional release in the community (Bumby et al. 2007; Burke 2008). The term "reintegration" should not be used too literally, as it suggests that before their incarceration, offenders had been successfully integrated into the community. Many inmates come from

Figure 9.1

The Reintegration Process for Federal Offenders

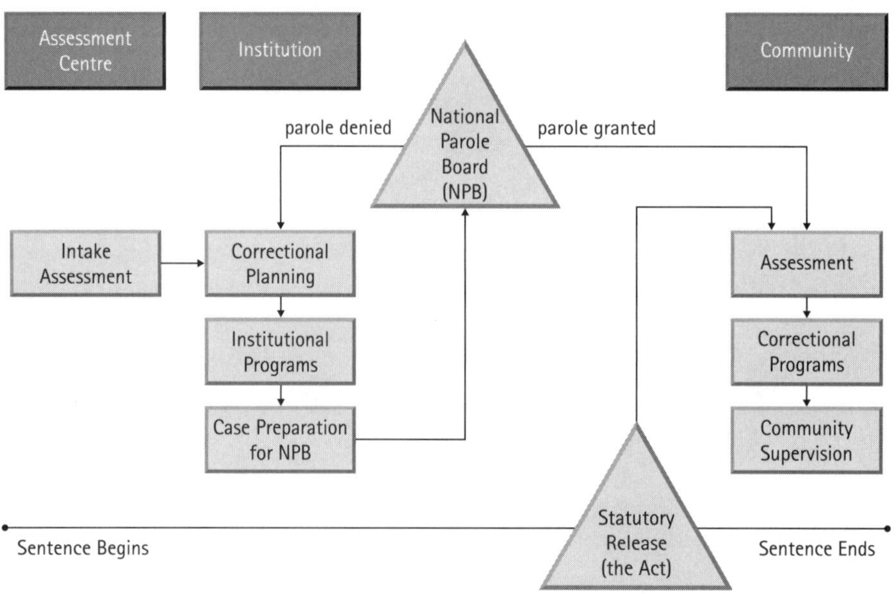

Source: Auditor General of Canada 1996, 30–31. Reproduced with permission of the Minister of Public Works and Government Service Canada, 2008.

marginalized backgrounds and have not acquired the attitudes and behaviours necessary to live as productive members of society (Griffiths, Dandurand, and Murdoch 2007).

THE PAINS OF REENTRY

> *Some of the struggles that people have is an identity problem, trying to identify with people who are out in the community who are lot different than people who you lived with in prison. Rules are different, your interactions with them are different, the way you act, the way you talk is different. (ex–dangerous offender, personal communication with author)*

In Chapter 6 the pains of imprisonment were identified and discussed. Similarly, offenders who are released from confinement experience **pains of reentry,** which highlights the irony of reintegration. That is, a sentence of imprisonment triggers a process whereby individuals are extracted from society and forced to adjust to a closed, structured, and artificial environment, one in which an antisocial value system predominates and inmates have little responsibility. Then, upon release, these same inmates are expected to resume life in the community and to hold prosocial values, exercise independence of thought and decision making, and display life skills that enable them to cope with the complexities of daily life in a fast-paced society. A transition this dramatic would challenge even the most gifted individual, and it is especially difficult for marginalized and socially isolated offenders who have been incarcerated for long periods. One long-term offender commented to the author: "The values, attitudes and behaviours that I learned inside were just the opposite of what I needed to make it in the free world."

Back on the Street

Inmates spend a considerable amount of time planning for, thinking about, and speaking with fellow inmates about freedom and life on the streets. Often, thoughts of release focus on the quick acquisition of long-denied commodities, such as heterosexual sex, fast food, and a cold beer. Life on the outside is everything prison is not: unpredictable, fast paced, filled with choices. As the release date approaches, however, this positive outlook may be replaced by feelings of anxiety and even fear. These emotions may be especially intense among inmates who have spent a lengthy time in confinement and/or who have failed on previous releases. Statements of bravado and an external display of optimism may conceal self-doubt and apprehension.

Imagine the difficulties you would encounter in adjusting to a law-abiding lifestyle in the community if you were a parolee with a grade nine education, a poor record of employment, tenuous or nonexistent family support, a substance-abuse problem, and few or no noncriminal friends. Unfortunately, a record of positive conduct inside a correctional institution, including completion of various treatment programs, may not adequately prepare an inmate for the challenges that await upon reentry into the community. The inmate may face social, economic, and personal challenges that make it difficult to avoid returning to criminal activity. Additional challenges may exist owing to mental illness, the presence of FASD, and substance abuse issues (Griffiths, Dandurand, and Murdoch 2007; Visher, Winterfield, and Coggeshall 2005).

Many of these factors may well have existed prior to the inmate's incarceration. Now add to them the "collateral effects" of confinement. These include the loss of personal relationships and social networks, the acquisition of self-defeating habits and attitudes, the loss of personal belongings, and a loss of the ability to maintain housing (Borzycki 2005).

Planning a day without the rigid timetable of prison routine can be a daunting task. A newly released offender can feel like the proverbial "stranger in a strange land"—embarrassed and inadequate, and convinced that every person on the street can tell at a mere glance that he or she has been in prison. In the words of a female parolee with a life sentence: "I didn't feel like I was back. I didn't feel like I belonged … I didn't feel part of this world anymore, I was still inside. In some respects, part of me will always be inside" (Murphy, Johnsen, and Murphy 2002, 166–67). Ironically, offenders may experience feelings of paranoia and fear for their safety upon reentering the community.

The stress of reentry may be especially acute for the state-raised offender (see Chapter 6). These individuals have very little experience living in the outside community, have few or no family ties, and—a key point—have no "stake" in the community. Their friends, identity, status, and power are all inside the correctional institution. Outside in the free community, there are no guarantees of status, of security, or of a routine that provides for one's basic needs. In such cases the pull of the institution may be greater than that of freedom on the streets. Close friendships are in danger of being lost, and there is often a sense that comrades are being abandoned. One long-term ex-offender told this author: "I have never had the intensity of friendships, the trust, the companionship, in the outside community that I had when I was incarcerated." These feelings may be especially acute when the soon-to-be-released inmate realizes that he or she has no friends on the outside who can be relied on for assistance, protection, and security. And it may be difficult for the inmate not to feel that he or she is abandoning close friends, confidants, and/or lovers inside.

One parolee, who had been incarcerated almost continuously from a young age for more than three decades, related an incident to this author that illustrates the anxiety and panic that ex-offenders may experience in completing tasks that people in the outside, free community take for granted. The situation occurred during his first trip to the grocery store soon after being released on day parole to live in a halfway house:

> *I wanted to buy some groceries, so I went to Safeway. I must have been in the store for hours. There were so many choices, I had no idea of what to put in my cart. Finally, my cart was full and I pushed it up to the checkout counter. The store was really crowded, and I was so focused on deciding what to buy that I hadn't given any thought to the price of the things I was putting in the cart. I think I had about $50 in my pocket. When the cashier rang up the total, it came to over $150. When she told me the total, I just froze. Everyone was looking at me. I stood there for what seemed like an eternity and then, without saying a word, ran out of the store. At the bus stop, my heart was racing and I was sweating. I never went back to that store. And, it was a long time before I went grocery shopping for more than one or two items.*

Even offenders who, prior to confinement, had relatively conventional lifestyles (with the exception of their lawbreaking) can find it hard to unlearn the automatic responses acquired in an environment where physical aggression is a survival skill. Compounding this, the ex-offender may miss the thrill and the rush of committing crimes. An ex-bank robber in the United States describes his experiences in Box 9.1.

There are more practical considerations as well. Criminal records disqualify people from some professions, including those that require being bonded (insured). Released offenders may not have suitable clothes for job interviews or job-specific gear such as steel-toed boots and special tools. Parolees may also experience job discrimination if employers are reluctant to hire them because of their prison record. As a result, they may be forced to lie about their criminal history when applying for jobs.

In an attempt to cope with the pains of reentry, the parolee may revert to high-risk behaviour, including heavy drinking, drug use, resuming friendships with former criminal associates, or spending time with old friends from prison. All the plans to go straight can crumble like a New Year's resolution in February. Though most will complete their period of conditional release without committing a new offence, many will be reconvicted of a criminal offence within three years of release.

BOX 9.1

Life After Hard Time

An accurate accounting is always a confusing business, so let's just say I robbed a lot of banks. The FBI estimated between 30 and 40. Even I lost count. But I do remember this: robbing banks was a cool thrill. And easy enough for any literate thug to commit.

A little-known fact: Stalin began his political life robbing the czar's banks. But unlike Uncle Joe, I didn't rob banks to help finance some great social cause. I robbed banks to support a lifestyle. I was the guy who always picked up the cheque and rented the limo for dinner at Circus and paid for all the trips to Vegas. I kept a Chinese tailor and several cars. I entered malls and left four hours later, six thousand dollars lighter. I was a hedonist. And popular, too.

On the morning of a robbery, I'd be naked in front of the bathroom's steamy mirror. I'd wipe off a circle big enough for me to stare at my wet image, at my dark sexy face, my collegiate haircut, the small scar on my left eyebrow, my dead eyes. I dared my hard self to flinch. My mouth opened slowly and murmurred an erotically morbid demand: "Don't return without fifty thousand dollars."

Stephen Crane describes a "delirium that encounters despair and death, and is heedless and blind to the odds." I knew that state. I'd surrender my fear of death to the bathroom mirror. Then, unafraid of consequences, I'd pick up my .357 Magnum, tuck it into the back of my trousers, draw a deep breath, then walk into those banks fully prepared for a final shootout with law enforcement if destiny decreed it.

But destiny never did.

I was arrested when a girlfriend informed on me. The FBI was waiting for me when I went to meet her at college. I was sitting outside the student union, sipping a cappuccino, reading the *Wall Street Journal*. The agents identified themselves. I leapt up and started swinging. It took eight men to subdue me.

I served seven years in prison—a biblical number. Seven dreary Christmases. Seven banal birthdays. The same inane banter on every prison tier for seven years. The tedium wore away the thug in me. I vowed never to return.

I was released six months ago. Adjustment is a bitch, especially with the recidivism statistics breathing down my neck. Close to 50 percent of all released inmates return to prison within three years.

If prison has its tedium, the world outside has its terrors. Part of my anxiety has to do with the reckless pace of the world. I am accustomed to the opposite, to the methodical tempo of prison life. Mindless rapidity startles me and leaves me feeling off balance.

On the day of my release, I got a check for $150 and was shown to the gate. The change of rhythm was startling. The friend who picked me up is a monk, the abbot of his monastery. But even this usually reverent man was a terror on the road. Charging ahead in fits and spurts, he wove maniacally through highway traffic, cutting off slower drivers.

And then there are the everyday humiliations an ex-convict must endure in order to remain free. Poverty is one of them. The cash I left prison with seemed like a mockery: I owned nothing but the clothes on my back, no change of underwear, no soap or toothbrush, no bed. The shame of living off handouts made me wake up one morning at three o'clock with the old temptation tugging at me. I wanted to say, "Fuck patience." I wanted to just go out and take mine.

The pitfalls for me are the everyday indignities the rest of you have learned to accept. The car that cuts me off on the freeway. The woman who barges into me while I wait in a grocery line. The obnoxious clerk at the Department of Motor Vehicles.

Or my devious neighbour.

Her. The one who substituted her clothes in my washing machine because she was in a hurry. I found my clothes, sopping wet, atop the rumbling machine I'd placed them in. If someone had done that to me in prison, I would have confronted him with a sharpened piece of bed spring and made him regret his insult, his foolish underestimation of me. Instead, in my role as a "free man," I returned to my apartment and suffered what Crane called the "rage of the baffled." I became mousy.

I don't presume to recall my violent past as halcyon days. But I know I never would have allowed myself to be treated like this when my mien included menace. The truth is that I wanted to walk next door and say, "Hey, you crazy bitch, don't ever touch my fucking clothes again or you'll find yourself spinning in that fucking machine." But I didn't play the thug.

It is, then, in the sting of everyday disrespect that I can vividly recall the thrills of my adventurous days when I loathed the future and abandoned caution. When the adrenaline sped through my veins as I drove away from a bank, laughing at the local cops racing past me in the opposite direction, toward the scene of the crime.

(continued)

I have a friend who used to suffer from severe manic depression. Grey, moody, Kafkaesque lows, hysterical highs. Now he tells me, with no trace of angst, that he manages his existence well in the boring hum of lithium normalcy. Yet he and I know that it's not just the highs and the lows the medicine has dulled: it is also his imagination. He went to the doctors for relief and was prescribed compulsory mediocrity.

I see sorrow in his tame liberation. Perhaps I see similarities in our freedoms. It's as if we have become slower versions of previous selves, lesser men.

I have had to learn to crawl to be free. It remains to be seen whether I can live without flying.

Source: Loya 1997. Reprinted with permission of the author.

Reintegration may be more difficult for certain categories of offenders. The special circumstances of Aboriginals, female offenders, the mentally disordered, sex offenders, and those inmates serving life sentences or sentences longer than 10 years will be discussed later in the chapter.

THE ROLE OF PAROLE SUPERVISION

Persons on conditional release are subject to differing levels of supervision by corrections officials. With some provincial temporary absences, this supervision can take the form of periodic telephone calls to verify the offender's presence at home. At the other end of the spectrum, supervision can include a requirement that the parolee reside in a community-based residential facility with 24-hour monitoring and attend frequent face-to-face meetings with a parole officer. This condition is often imposed on high-risk federal sex offenders who are on one-chance statutory release.

The Correctional Service of Canada (CSC) directly operates community correctional centres across the country and has contracts with private operators for beds in community residential centres. Federal inmates must apply to community residential centres and be accepted by centre staff. In every province/territory, there are parallel systems of residences, operated directly by the government or under contract with private operators. These facilities are collectively known as community-based residential facilities and are often referred to as halfway houses. There are also residential treatment centres and recovery

Community residential centre, suburban neighbourhood, Ontario

Courtesy of Addiction Services (Hasting and Prince Edward Counties) Inc.

houses that specialize in alcohol and substance abuse intervention. An ex-offender reflected on his time at a halfway house:

> *The halfway house gives the person a chance to look for a job without having to worry about where he is going to sleep tonight. It gives him an opportunity to take things a little bit slower, because if you just release him with nowhere to go, then everything happens so fast, and people get really discouraged, end up drinking a lot, or taking drugs, and going back to the old neighbourhood because it's a lot easier to do that than it is to find work, and find a place to live, and find money. I feel that being transferred from a medium-security institution, to a minimum-security institution, then out on day parole to a halfway house was good. It was a slow reentry back into the community, although it was sometimes really frustrating and hard to believe that it took so long; for me it still worked out. I was able to take it step-by-step. I was not forced into having to do anything real quick, and at the time when my full parole came along, I was actually well established in the community. I had made a lot of friends; I had acquired my own place to live, and all these things that in my past I didn't have. The reason I didn't*

> *have them is I didn't spend much time out (of prison), because I didn't feel I could ever get to where I wanted to be. (Personal communication with author)*

Offenders on parole are generally required to report regularly to a correctional agent such as a parole officer. All federal parolees are supervised by parole officers employed by or under contract to the CSC. By agreement, the CSC also supervises the provincial parolees released by the NPB. In two jurisdictions—Ontario and Quebec—provincial probation and parole officers provide supervision for offenders on parole as well as for many inmates on temporary absence. In provincial/territorial corrections, few distinctions are made between parole and probation, except with regard to provisions for enforcement. For example, the breach of a probation condition is a new offence, whereas the violation of a parole condition can (but does not always) lead to suspension of the release and a return of the parolee to custody.

The Dual Function of Parole Supervision

Like probation officers, parole officers have a dual role in their relations with clients. The first involves being a resource person and confidant to counter the pains of reentry. In this regard, the supportive activities of parole officers can include offering job search advice, referring clients for counselling, and advocating with welfare authorities on their behalf. The second role involves monitoring and enforcing parole conditions. These tasks often include contacting an employer to verify employment, running periodic checks to ensure continued employment, making home visits to verify residence or compliance with curfews, and conducting checks with the police and/or the staff at treatment programs.

Each parole officer has his or her own style of supervision. Some are more lenient and give the parolees assigned to them a longer "leash"; others are much stricter. The style of supervision also depends on the level of risk the parolee poses to the community. Ideally, a balance between the two roles is achieved, with more control/surveillance during the early phases of release and more assistance as the supervision period draws to an end. It is likely, however, that most parolees view their parole supervisor as more of a watcher than a helper. High-risk offenders, such as sex offenders, may be unlikely to disclose their urges to reoffend to their parole supervisor for fear of being returned to custody. A former parolee offered these observations on the dual role of parole officers:

> *I would like to see the parole officer become more of a helper than a policeman. If the parole officer is trying to wear two hats then he's not, or she's not, going to be as successful as a person who is wearing the one hat as*

> *being a helper. A helper could help you find work, or give you contacts so you would have an opportunity to get a job. So that when you were going to actually report to your parole officer and talk with them, there would be a lot more trust with that person. If the person is wearing two hats, it's very hard to really trust them. I think that communication is really important. If a person is having trouble in the community, then it's best to be able to talk to somebody, and the parole officer should be that person. Unfortunately, the parole officer is not that person, because you may say something to him that may create fear that you are going to reoffend or that you're going to do something that would require him to put you back in prison. So, sometimes you are not telling him everything that is going on in your life because if you did you wouldn't be out. (Personal communication with author)*

This perception was echoed by a long-term offender: "I felt basically that the whole entire parole system was not there for me, not there to assist me. They were more concerned about monitoring, about groups, about everything but seeing that I made it out there. No one was inviting me out to their place, to their families, or to go out and have dinner, or any social kind of thing" (Murphy, Johnsen, and Murphy 2002, 3).

There is evidence that many parole officers prioritize the enforcement role over social-work–oriented activities (Lynch 1998). The increasing emphasis on risk management in corrections (See Chapters 1 and 7) may transform the role of parole officers into one of monitoring and enforcing compliance with release conditions and periodically reassessing changes in risk and need. The paperwork burden of conducting these assessments and recording them in computerized, centralized databases has had a strong impact on the amount of time parole supervisors can spend in face-to-face contact with clients.

Intensity of Supervision

Not all offenders who are released into the community require the same level of supervision. The Community Intervention Scale (CIS) is used with every federal offender discharged on a conditional release and is readministered every six months to monitor any changes in the parolee's situation. The CIS classifies and rates the parolee in seven areas of need (academic/vocational, employment pattern, etc.). Using specific guidelines, each area is rated as being (1) an asset to community adjustment, (2) no current difficulties, (3) some need for improvement, and (4) considerable need for improvement. The parole officer then categorizes the offender into one of three need levels: low, medium, or high (Verbrugge et al. 2002).

The second part of the CIS is the criminal history risk rating. To achieve this rating, which is either low or high, the parole officer consults the offender's case record, including the Statistical Information on Recidivism Scale (discussed in Chapter 8).

When juxtaposed, these two ratings indicate the intensity of supervision required. For example, a low-risk offender with low needs requires only periodic supervision—about one contact per month. This allows parole officers to spend more time supervising high-risk and high-need offenders.

The activities of a CSC Team Supervision Unit that supervises high-risk offenders on statutory release in Metropolitan Toronto are described in Box 9.2.

Innovations in Community Assistance and Supervision

The London, Ontario, Community Parole Project

The objectives of the London Community Parole Project are to increase public involvement in the federal correctional process and to harness the talents of volunteers to assist parole officers. This program recruits qualified volunteers from the London area and trains them to perform a variety of community-based tasks for the CSC, including interviewing, report writing, and parole co-supervision. This project also uses circles of support with high-risk offenders who have reached warrant expiry (more on circles of support below).

The Community Adult Mentoring and Support Program (CAMS)

Operated by the Pacific Region of the CSC, the CAMS program was developed in collaboration with a church in Victoria. Following a thorough selection and screening process, volunteers undergo a 10-week training course.

The program's objective is to complement the work of parole officers and other community-based professionals by helping long-term offenders on statutory release cope with life in the community. Under the program, high-needs, high-risk offenders are matched with community mentors. A written document called a covenant sets out the expectations of the mentor and the offender and provides the framework for the relationship. The program appears to be a success: during the period 2001-05, only 3 of the 84 matches have ended as a result of new charges against the offender (Rankin 2005).

Reentry Courts

Reentry courts have been established in a number of American jurisdictions to provide judicial oversight of offenders released from prison (cf. Superior Court

BOX 9.2

The CSC Team Supervision Unit: A Night on the Town

CSC Parole Officers Sherri Rousell and Cathy Phillips buzz the apartment from the panel in the lobby; a woman's voice tells them to enter. They ride up the elevator and step out into a long corridor, at the end of which they see a woman. She's standing in an apartment doorway smiling and beckoning to them. It's not until they get closer that they see a man they know, Salvador, standing behind the smiling woman.

Salvador is not smiling. Salvador is standing silently with his head down and his arms folded, an expression of tight-lipped anger on his face. He doesn't acknowledge the two officers or look up at them. The woman, Salvador's wife, manages to make pleasant chit-chat with the two CSC officers and then bids them good evening and closes the door. There was no exchange between Sherri and Cathy and Salvador, but the two officers walk away satisfied. Their intent was to ensure that the Colombian immigrant is complying with his parole conditions, including a nightly curfew. A former cocaine trafficker with a history of narcotic-related and violent offences, Salvador must obey the imposed conditions or go back to prison. It's obvious to the officers that Salvador is not happy with this arrangement: he resents taking orders and being monitored, especially by two women.

This is just one of the stops that Sherri and Cathy will make during the late evening. They are part of a special team supervision unit (TSU) handling high-maintenance, often repeat offenders on statutory release in Metropolitan Toronto. Because of the volatile nature of these individuals, team members always work in pairs, manage smaller caseloads than most parole officers, and contact their "clients" more often than they would average parole cases. There are two teams in the TSU, based at the Keele Community Correctional Centre; they are headed by Director Shirley Hassard and Parole Supervisor Curtis Jackson. Members of the second unit are parole officers Paul Lay and Angela Beecher.

"The idea with team supervision units is stabilization," explains Curtis Jackson. "Guys come out of prison, we try to stabilize them. It requires intense supervision and we are held accountable for monitoring their behaviour. If they don't stabilize right away, they stay with us longer. Once we feel that they don't require such intensive supervision, we will transfer them to the jurisdiction of area offices."

Over the past 10 years, TSUs have proven to be highly effective. With increased monitoring, TSU officers can spot signs of deterioration in an offender's behaviour

(continued)

and quickly intervene. They identify factors that contribute to behaviour problems, provide access to counseling, and give practical advice that may head off trouble. "Some of these guys are fairly low functioning," says Curtis. "They have difficulty doing the things that most of us take for granted—finding a place to live, opening a bank account, managing their money. If we can teach them, for instance, not to blow all their money the first night out, then they won't immediately get into trouble looking for more."

Cathy and Sherri continue on their rounds, clocking mile after mile in their Corsica, heading east as far as Scarborough, then back in a big circle toward downtown. One night each week they spend five hours, usually from seven p.m. until midnight, checking to see that clients have made their curfews. During the week they may pick up the phone, drop in to an offender's workplace unannounced, or call a parolee in for an office interview to verify that he is complying with parole conditions. They reach the Sheppard and Warden area and knock on a townhouse door. A big fellow named Wayne appears barefoot, wearing a rumpled T-shirt and sweatpants. He's loud and abrupt with the officers; 16 years in Ontario's toughest maximum-security prisons for armed robbery and murder haven't smoothed his abrasive personality.

"Yeah, yeah, everything's okay," says Wayne. He's anxious to get out of the frosty air and get to bed. The officers let him go.

The next stop is Rick's place. Rick opens the door and Cathy and Sherri can see that he has guests in the living room, glued to an action adventure on the television. The officers say hi, how's it going; meanwhile they're sniffing the air and casting sharp looks over Rick's shoulder into the kitchen, scanning for evidence of drugs or alcohol. There are no liquor bottles or drug paraphernalia in sight, only a child's stuffed toy lying on the table. Sherri asks if she can step inside. She takes a few steps toward the living room to get a better look at what's going on. She asks to speak with Rick's girlfriend, Brenda, who is supposed to be supporting him until he can find a job. Brenda gets up from the couch, happy to oblige, and they have a quick word in the kitchen. Yes, still working at the video store. Satisfied, Sherri and Cathy wish Rick a good night and continue on their way.

Finally, around midnight, after all 14 visits have been completed, they drive back to the office at the Keele Community Correctional Centre, where they pick up a private vehicle and head home. It's late, and the paperwork can wait until morning.

Source: CSC 2001a.

of Delaware; http://courts.deleware.gov/Courts/Superior%20Court/?reentry.htm). These courts review the progress and problems of offenders, assist in the continuity of treatment from the institution to the community, monitor compliance with release conditions, and apply sanctions when offenders do not comply with treatment requirements. In reentry courts, judges actively involve themselves in the offender's transition from prison to the community, either by retaining jurisdiction over the offender from sentencing to warrant expiry or by assuming jurisdiction once the offender is released. Not enough research has been done to determine the effectiveness of reentry courts in reducing rates of recidivism (Farole 2003; Maruna and LeBel 2003).

Integrated Police/Parole Initiative

This program is a collaborative effort between the CSC and several police departments across the country (including the Regina Police Service and the Hamilton Police Service). It involves police officers being hired to work as Community Corrections Liaison Officers (CCLOs). These officers monitor the activities of high-risk/high-needs offenders in the community and liaise between police officers and parole officers.

SPECIAL OFFENDER POPULATIONS ON PAROLE

As noted earlier in the chapter, offenders vary in the specific types of problems they encounter on reentry. This disparity requires that correctional systems adapt policies and programs to meet the needs of special offender populations and to manage the risks they present.

Aboriginal Offenders

There are unique challenges to supervising Aboriginal offenders in the community. Recall that Aboriginal offenders are more likely than other offender groups to be admitted to federal institutions for revocation of parole or statutory release. Also, they have the highest rates of revocation for breach of conditions and breach of conditions with offence; they are also more likely to commit a violent offence while on conditional release (NPB 2007).

Systems of corrections recognize that Aboriginal communities should be encouraged to play a greater role in the reintegration of offenders. Section 81 of the Corrections and Conditional Release Act authorizes the federal government to enter into agreements with Aboriginal communities whereby the community will take over the "care and custody" of some Aboriginal inmates. Section 84 of that act states:

> *Where an inmate who is applying for parole has expressed an interest in being released to an aboriginal community, the Service shall, if the inmate consents, give the aboriginal community*
>
> *(a) adequate notice of the inmate's parole application; and*
>
> *(b) an opportunity to propose a plan for the inmate's release to, and integration into, the aboriginal community.*

In recent years a variety of community-based services and programs for offenders on conditional release have been developed in Aboriginal communities across the country. Many of these programs are rooted in traditional Aboriginal culture and spirituality and incorporate elements of the restorative/community justice initiatives discussed in Chapter 3. In addition, the CSC has established the Aboriginal Community Reintegration Program to enhance the role of Aboriginal communities in reintegrating Aboriginal federal offenders back into their communities.

There are specialized residential services for Aboriginals on conditional release, including these:

O-Chi-Chak-Ko-Sipi Healing Lodge. The CSC refers men (most of them Aboriginal) over the age of 18 to this lodge in Brandon, Manitoba. The program focuses on helping Aboriginal offenders through Aboriginal teachings. The offender's physical, mental, emotional, and spiritual well-being are addressed by elders, who provide guidance to program participants. The program follows traditional Aboriginal practices, including sweat lodges and sharing circles (http://www.csc-scc.gc.ca).

Circle of Eagles Lodge. In Vancouver, this 10-bed transition residence for Aboriginal men on release offers alcohol and drug counselling in individual and group sessions, including Alcoholics Anonymous meetings. Sweat lodges and talking circles are used to explore Aboriginal traditions and spirituality.

Regina House. This 35-bed facility for provincial and federal Aboriginal offenders offers treatment programs centred on relapse prevention and teachings of the Medicine Wheel.

Waseskun Healing Center. In Montreal, this 20-week residential program for Aboriginal men provides individual and group counselling as well as programs in life skills, conflict resolution, family systems awareness, and women's issues. Sweat lodges and talking circles are also offered (http://www.waseskun.net/).

An absence of evaluation studies makes it difficult to ascertain whether these programs work. The high rates of reoffending in this group suggest that much more work remains to be done to reintegrate Aboriginal offenders into the community.

Female Offenders

Female offenders, as a group, have greater needs in the areas of emotional stability, marital and family relations, academic/vocational skills, and employment. The relatively small population of federal female offenders and their geographic dispersal on release make it difficult to provide gender-specific health and residential services and programs.

For inmate-mothers, the challenges may include re-establishing contact with their children, finding suitable accommodation with sufficient space, and attempting to regain custody if the children have been placed in care during the mother's confinement. Especially when the inmate-mother is the sole caregiver, child protection authorities may require that the mother obtain stable employment and suitable accommodation before being allowed to reapply for custody. The frustrations that mothers may encounter upon release are reflected in the following comments of an ex-offender on parole in Ontario:

> *I took parole to get my kids back. Parole agreed to my present location, but now the Children's Aid Society is saying it's not suitable for the kids. I can't rent before I know whether I am going to get my kids, and I can't get them back until I rent. I can't get mother's allowance until I have my kids, and without it I can't rent. I never know what I have to do for who. There are just so many hoops to jump through. (in Wine 1992, 111)*

The CSC recognizes the need to provide gender-responsive programs for female offenders. To that end, it operates a variety of programs, including the Social Integration Program for Women, which involves group and individual sessions designed to help female offenders develop social integration plans. The program also provides women with community support workers to help them make contacts in the community.

Mentally Disordered Offenders

The mentally disordered parolee may require more assistance in reintegration. This is because mentally disordered offenders may be more at risk for experiencing social isolation and a co-occurring substance abuse disorder. They may also find it hard to arrange suitable housing and employment. Effective programs provide continuity of care from the institution to the community. Successful reintegration programs for mentally ill offenders do the following: stabilize the offender's illness, help the family provide support, enhance their ability to function independently, integrate treatment and case management, provide structure to the offender's daily life, and manage the offender's impulses (Chartier 2007; Griffiths, Dandurand, and Murdoch 2007).

In Newfoundland and Labrador, mentally ill offenders released into the community are managed by a multidisciplinary case management team composed of staff from the CSC, including a senior parole officer, a psychologist, a psychiatric nurse, and community mental-health professionals from Stella Burry Community Services (SBCS). SBCS provides one-on-one support services to help offenders strengthen their basic life skills (e.g., cooking, budgeting, shopping, medication management, and attending appointments). In Calgary, Robert's House is a 10-bed community residential facility that provides services for parolees with mental-health issues. The facility is operated by the CSC and the Canadian Mental Health Association (Chartier 2007).

Sex Offenders

No group of offenders has attracted more interest from the public, politicians, and correctional authorities than sex offenders. Their release from prison is often front-page news in the local press or even announced over the Internet (see Box 9.3). Correctional systems use a variety of techniques to manage the risks of this offender group. These techniques include treatment, drugs such as antiandrogens to reduce sex drive, community notification, registration, and supervision and monitoring strategies, including polygraph testing (Wilson et al. 2000). It is likely that the monitoring of sex offenders by means of GPS systems will become commonplace in the coming years (see Chapter 3). The successful reintegration of sex offenders may be assisted by relapse prevention programs (see Chapter 7).

The challenges that sex offenders face in avoiding situations that may lead to relapse are captured by the comments of an offender convicted of raping and killing a young girl. He is on parole for life:

> *Sometimes when I'm driving down the road and I see some well-developed 15-year-old and I think, "Oh yeah, she's cute," I kind of mentally give myself a slap and say, "Yeah, she's cute. Let her stay cute, you stupid bastard." I have to give myself the height of shit . . . I'm motivated by her memory not to do that sort of garbage. (Murphy, Johnsen, and Murphy 2002, 117)*

The CSC operates a high-risk offender program as well as a maintenance program for managing sex offenders on release in the community. The *high-risk offender program* is cognitive-behaviour oriented and includes individual and group counselling. Group therapy is used to address the four "F's" related to sexual offending: feelings, fantasy, future, and follow-through. This multidisciplinary program involves monthly case conference meetings attended by the supervising parole staff, treatment staff, and the program director. These case conferences provide an opportunity to discuss supervision of the offender and any concerns relating to the offender's no-contact orders, family relationships, employment, and attitude and behavior. Sex offenders who have admitted their guilt and who require lower intensity relapse prevention participate in the *maintenance program*. These offenders receive individual or group therapy designed to maintain their institutional treatment gains. Research findings suggest that there are lower rates of recidivism for sex offenders who are supervised via a case management approach and who are offered individualized treatment services in combination with an appropriate level of parole supervision (Wilson et al. 2000).

The federal government and several provinces (including B.C. and Ontario) have established sex offender registries to track high-risk sex offenders. Sex offenders must register 15 days prior to release into the community (or upon conviction if they receive a non-custodial sentence) and must then re-register annually as well as 15 days prior to any change of address. The register database includes information on the offender, such as their name, date of birth, current address, and identifying marks, as well as photographs. Offenders remain on the registry indefinitely unless they are acquitted on appeal or receive a pardon.

Judicial Recognizances for Sex Offenders

Federal sex offenders not released on either parole or statutory release remain in custody until warrant expiry. These offenders are then released "cold turkey" and are not obliged to inform law enforcement or correctional agencies of their location. One response to this problem is the use of community notification, which is discussed below. Another is the use of Section 810.1 of the Criminal Code to force the individual to enter into a **judicial recognizance,** often referred to in this context as a peace bond.

Judicial recognizance is most commonly used with pedophiles who have reached warrant expiry but who remain at a very high risk of offending against children under 16 years of age (Lussier, DesLauriers-Varin, and Ratel in press). This response is unusual as the applicant—who can be a police officer—need only have reasonable grounds to fear that the subject of the order may commit one of the designated offences in the near future. In other words, it is applied proactively for offences that *may* be committed rather than in reaction to offences that *have* been committed.

The application is heard in a provincial court, where the judge can order the subject to enter into a recognizance to comply with set conditions, which can include a prohibition from engaging in any activity that involves contact with persons under 16. For example, the subject would not be permitted to visit a daycare centre, schoolyard, playground, or any public park or swimming area where children are present or can reasonably be expected to be present. This order can be in effect for up to 12 months. A person who refuses to enter into the recognizance can be sent to prison for up to 12 months for the refusal, and an offender who violates a condition of the order commits an offence for which he is liable for up to two years in prison.

Section 810 raises the issue of how to balance the rights of ex-offenders with the need to protect the community. Share your views on the "At Issue 9.1: Should the Courts be Allowed to Impose Restrictions on Ex-offenders Under Section 810 of the Criminal Code?" presented at the end of the chapter.

VICTIM NOTIFICATION

As noted in Chapter 8, the victims of incarcerated offenders have the right to request that they be informed of the timing of the release. In some cases this information can help the victims take the necessary steps to ensure their safety. The large majority of crime victims are not harassed or threatened by offenders on conditional release; however, some victims are at great risk. It is in these cases that victim notification is most crucial, for both officially sanctioned releases and unauthorized absences from community supervision.

A victim's concerns about offender reentry may begin long before the offender is considered for release, perhaps even at the moment of sentencing. However, the process of addressing this issue is often one that is avoided, perhaps because of the emotional scars it reopens and the difficult work and planning it requires. Correctional agencies should address this issue with offenders through victim impact panels and focus groups, both with offenders who are incarcerated and those who have been released. Such groups would enable offenders to address questions like these: Do they fantasize about or plan to seek revenge against those they have harmed? In what way? What are their intentions toward their victims upon release? In developing these questions and establishing such panels and focus groups, it is imperative for correctional agencies to collaborate with victim service organizations.

Community Notification

The use of **community notification (CN)** when high-risk offenders are released into the community is a key component of various attempts to manage risk and protect the community. The premise of CN policies is that by warning potential victims, you are strengthening the community's ability to protect itself; offenders who know they are being watched will be deterred from reoffending (Zevitz 2006). In Canada, CN is possible because local police departments are always notified by the CSC of the impending arrival of federal parolees in their jurisdictions. Motivated in part by fear of exposure to lawsuits, most provinces have developed policies designed to facilitate police decision making with respect to the release of identifying offender information.

Decisions about CN are most often made by a committee. In Manitoba, the first province to establish a CN program, the police refer the cases of high-risk sex offenders to the Community Notification Advisory Committee, which comprises a private citizen, a specialist in medical/therapeutic interventions, and representatives from the RCMP, the police services of Winnipeg and Brandon, Manitoba Justice, Manitoba Corrections, and the CSC. The committee reviews all of the information about the offender—including criminal record, participation in treatment programs, the age and gender of past victims, proposed release plan or living arrangements, and support network—and then determines the type and scope of information to be released. The protocol also involves listing the designation with the Canadian Police Information Centre and notifying past victims of the release. The community notification process in Manitoba is illustrated in Figure 9.2.

Figure 9.2

Community Notification Process in the Province of Manitoba

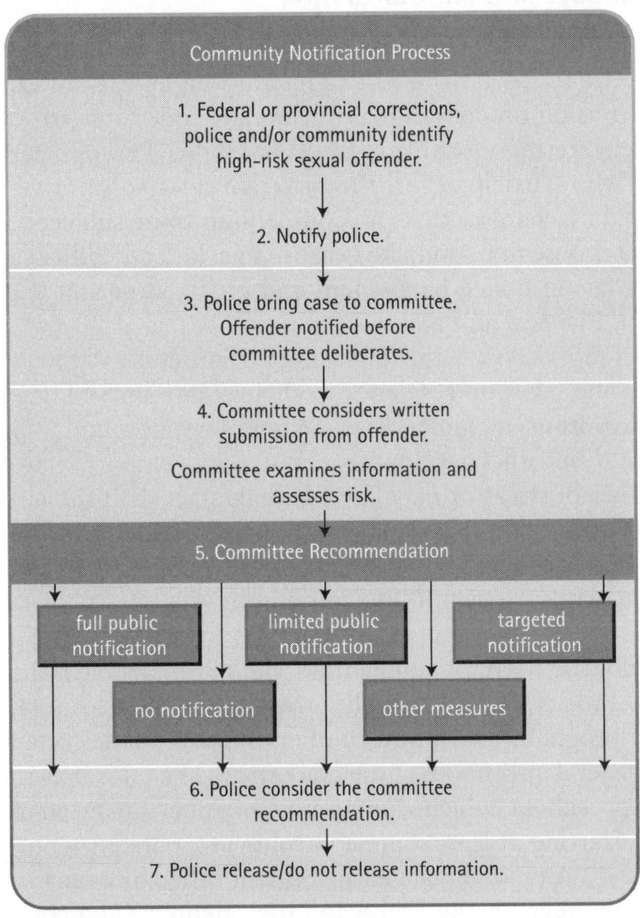

Source: Manitoba Justice. http://www.gov.mb.ca/justice/safe/cnac.html.
Reprinted by permission of Manitoba Justice.

There are several models of community notification, but all involve a public announcement, usually made by the police, that a high-risk offender has taken up residence in the area. CN can involve proactive measures, such as distribution of leaflets door to door, or it can be passive, involving posting the information on the Internet to be accessed by interested parties. In Canada, provincial authorities and police departments periodically place public warnings on their Internet sites. A community notification (with identifiers removed) from the Calgary Police Service is presented in Box 9.3. Contribute your opinion to "At Issue 9.2: Should the community be notified when a high-risk offender is released from prison?" presented at the end of the chapter.

Circles of Support and Accountability

Circles of support and accountability (COSAs) provide support for sex offenders who are released from federal institutions at warrant expiry or whose period of supervision on conditional release has ended due to warrant expiry. These offenders are the most likely targets of judicial recognizances and CN. Any offender who participates in the program does so on a voluntary basis; there is no legal mechanism that can compel him to be subject to monitoring. Offenders may choose to participate because they lack any other support system and/or wish to avoid police harassment and media attention (Cesaroni 2001, 91–92; Wilson, Picheca, and Prinzo 2005).

A circle of support is a team of five or six volunteers assigned to an offender to assist him as he takes up residence in their community. They help with all facets of reintegration, including housing, employment, budgeting and financial management, spiritual development, and moral support. The offender may call only in times of stress or may have daily contact with the circle members. Circle members can also mediate between the offender and the community, as suggested in the conceptual model in Figure 9.3. Mediation took place in the case of Joe, whose arrival in the community was the subject of a CN (see Box 9.4).

In Ontario, the Mennonite Central Committee operates the Community Reintegration Project (CRP), which provides the Circles of Support and Accountability program, which in turn offers support for sex offenders who are released from federal institutions at warrant expiry. The CRP uses a reintegrative/restorative approach in which community members play an active role in helping—and exerting at least some control over—persons who present a risk to the community. An individualized agreement called a covenant is negotiated between the volunteers in the group and the offender. The covenant sets out the roles and responsibilities of each party. For example, core volunteers in the group may agree to maintain the confidentiality of information about the

BOX 9.3

Community Notification Media Release
[Month, Day, Year]

The Calgary Police Service is issuing the following public information and warning in regards to the release of an inmate, in the interest of public safety.

John Doe is in the Calgary area having served a 9 year and 2 month Federal Prison term of incarceration for the following offences:

INVITATION TO SEXUAL TOUCHING WITH A CHILD UNDER 14 YEARS SEXUAL INTERFERENCE WITH A CHILD UNDER 14 YEARS SEXUAL ASSAULT

The public is warned that John Doe is an individual who has numerous convictions for sexual offences against young females. John Doe's pattern of sexual offending escalates under the influence of drugs and alcohol. John Doe is described as follows;

DOB: 1943/02/24
Weight: 88 kg
Height: 173 cm

Hair: Grey
Eyes: Brown
Complexion: Fair

John Doe was released to the Calgary area on [Month, Day, Year]

The Calgary Police Service is issuing this information and warning after careful deliberation and consideration of all related issues, including privacy concerns, in the belief that it is clearly in the public interest to inform the members of the community of the release of John Doe.

Members of the public are advised that the intent of the process is to enable members of the public to take suitable precautionary measures and not to embark on any form of vigilante action.

Photos are available from the Calgary Police Service, 133 - 6 Avenue S.E., Calgary, Alberta.

NOTE: This information is released under the authority of s.32 the *Freedom of Information and Protection of Privacy Act*, S.A. 2002 c .F - 25.

For further information, contact: Calgary Police Service
High Risk Offender Program
Phone: 266-1234

Figure 9.3

Conceptual Model of a Circle of Support: Relationships of the Circle within the Community

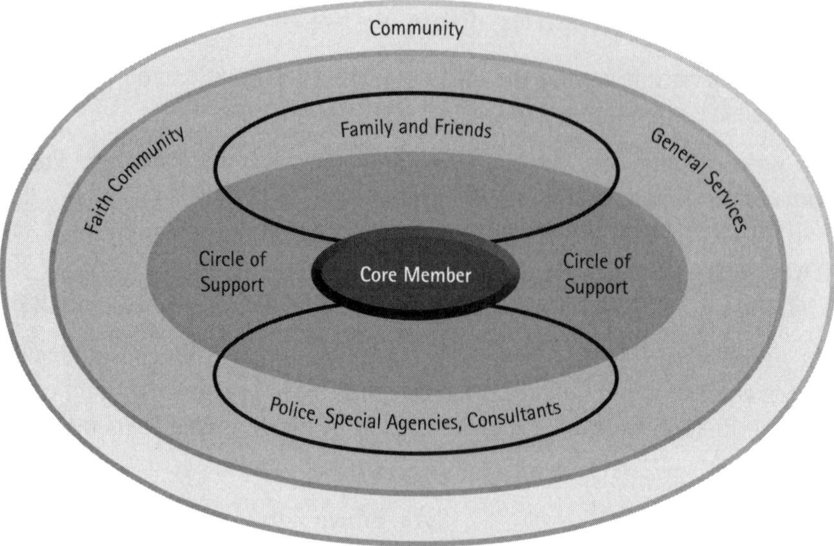

Source: Heise et al. 1996, 14. Reprinted by permission of Mennonite Central Committee Ontario.

BOX 9.4

Joe and His Circle of Support

It began with a telephone call. "Can you help me?" the caller asked. "I'm just out of prison, and the police have already been warning everyone that I am in town. Where am I going to find a quiet place to live?" Joe, 54, had been released at Warrant Expiry from prison after serving a 6-year sentence for sexual assault against a child. It was his 8th conviction.

Joe wanted to come to our city for several reasons. He knew us, he had met public resistance in another town when he attempted to settle there before his parole was [revoked], and he suspected that he could get help in relapse prevention. We agreed to help him find accommodation, help him to find a job, and try to build a Circle of friendship and support in his new city. We thought of people that we knew who could help him in each of these areas and who would be willing to work with us. We also agreed to make contact with the police.

The detectives, when we met with them, candidly said, "We don't want him here." Based on institutional reports, the police felt that Joe was likely to re-offend. There had been a lot of negative publicity recently about released prisoners re-offending, and they didn't want any of that kind of publicity for their department.

When Joe came to stay with us for the weekend while beginning the apartment search, the police quickly made his picture available to the media and warned the community of his presence among us.

The media descended upon us because we had been identified as providing support for Joe. Pickets of irate and concerned parents arrived in front of our home. After a number of angry and threatening phone calls, we finally bought a telephone answering machine.

The police mounted a plan of surveillance. They felt sure he would re-offend within a short period. They were concerned about the safety of the children in the neighbourhood, but they also wanted to ensure Joe's safety.

One of the neighbours had called the police and had a lengthy discussion with the detective. She later called to talk with me. Ann had small children and was very concerned for their safety and that of the many other children living in the area. After a discussion with her, and later with Joe, we agreed that he would meet with her to discuss her concerns. Lengthy negotiations ensued, finally resulting in a meeting proposed in a neutral site, and several other neighbours were invited to participate. The police detectives would also be present. They would be there not only as a resource, but as people who could add to the participants' feelings of security.

Joe, accompanied by two of his friends, was the first to arrive at the meeting and take a seat on the far side of the room. Soon the neighbours began to arrive. Then the detectives entered. The ground rules of the meeting were outlined. We would go around the circle to allow everyone an opportunity to share their first name and a particular concern they brought with them. We would have a statement from the neighbourhood group, followed by an opportunity for Joe to share, and from there we would move to addressing the issues presented. Only one person at a time would speak, and they would follow our direction and instructions for the orderly addressing of the issues. Before the end of the meeting, we would decide together what of this meeting would be appropriate to share with other people, outside of this meeting.

As we began to go around the circle, the first person began by saying how much she appreciated the willingness of Joe and his friends to attend such a meeting. Ann outlined the questions she had heard the others discussing with her. There was a long

(continued)

list of questions: they wanted to know what had happened, what the sentence was, what treatment he had obtained, and what treatment he planned to receive now that he was released. "From your experience, what is the best way to avoid the behaviour you were charged with?" "How do you plan to deal with the negative reactions and anger of some individuals in the community?"

Joe responded, outlining in general terms his offences. Appreciation was expressed for the constructive method the residents had chosen to address their concerns, which he acknowledged were understandable. He indicated that he had received some treatment while in the institution and was planning to arrange suitable community-based therapy and had indeed made arrangements for that already. He had also set up an accountability system through his Circle of Support, by which he had daily contact with us, and we were able to make inquiry as to his faithfulness to his commitments in specific relevant areas.

We talked, and the earlier tension in the room eased as we got on with the task of problem-solving around the various issues at hand. Though all the questions were not answered, by the end of the 2 1/2 hour meeting, there was a feeling of accomplishment and a readiness to move on.

Out of that meeting and others we had, some bridges were built. Neighbourhood residents, some of whom were vocally angry, began to see Joe as a person and recognized the difficulties with which he coped.

Throughout this time, Joe's Circle of Support met regularly with him. At least one of the Circle Members contacted him every day. After a year, we still talk to him daily. We took him to do his laundry, to shop for groceries and furnishings for his apartment.

The police have been partners with us in Joe's Circle of Support. Without the patient, humorous, understanding commitment of the detectives with whom we dealt most frequently, our efforts might not have reached this point. They came to our Circle meetings. They checked in with us frequently and we trusted their openness with us. Similarly, the police served as a buffer with the community, correcting rumours and diffusing problems.

Joe's life has settled into a comfortable pattern. He maintains a clean, comfortable apartment and has developed some close relationships. He is finding ways to spend his time and is slowly developing a small network of friends, although trust takes a long time.

Source: Heise et al. 1996, 5–7. Reprinted by permission of Mennonite Central Committee Ontario.

offender and to help the offender, while the core member (offender) may agree to develop a relapse prevention plan and to be open and honest in his communications with the group (Petrunik 2002).

Most volunteers in the CPR's Circles of Support and Accountability program are from the faith community; other participants include teachers, social workers, police officers, and local businesspeople. The positive view of the program held by offenders relates to the fact that it is operated by a private, philanthropic organization rather than by the CSC. This suggests that church-based organizations and community groups have a role to play in reintegration (see D'Amico 2007).

Research studies of the experiences of COSA participants (including offenders) and the impact of COSA on rates of reoffending by offender participants have found the following:

- Despite initial misgivings, offenders were grateful for the assistance, which they viewed as indispensable for their reintegration back into the community and to avoid reoffending.
- Agency representatives and professionals held the view that COSA increased offender accountability and responsibility as well as the focus on community safety.
- There was strong support among professionals and agency representatives for expanding COSA.
- Offenders participating in COSA had lower sexual and general recidivism rates than the offenders who did not participate in COSA and committed fewer severe sexual reoffences relative to the matched comparison group, which is important from a harm reduction perspective (Wilson, Picheca, and Prinzo, 2005).

FAILURE ON CONDITIONAL RELEASE: GOING BACK

It took me 34 years to get lucky, a lot of people don't get that opportunity, and they get really frustrated and they get really angry and down on themselves. They resort to alcohol and drugs, and that is sometimes why they are there in the first place, and then they just get out of control, they don't care about their life. They don't care if they get into trouble. When I look back in my life, going out on those mandatory supervision releases, I would be doing things like getting really drugged and getting high, and then hurting somebody. I think people, a lot of people, are doing that just because they don't have any positive things happening in their life, and they can't see a positive future. (ex-offender, personal communication with author)

Even the most institutionalized state-raised inmate does not leave a correctional institution with the intent of returning. And correctional systems have as a primary objective the reduction of recidivism among offenders released into the community. Statistics indicate that most federal offenders successfully complete conditional release and do not reoffend prior to warrant expiry. At the same time, offenders on *statutory* release are nearly seven times more likely to be convicted of a violent offence than offenders on full parole (Motiuk, Cousineau, and Gileno 2005; National Parole Board 2007). The outcome rates for provincial offenders indicate that there are very few revocations of parole resulting from the commission of a violent offence. Figures from Quebec indicate that 25 percent of offenders on parole had their conditional release revoked for violating a condition of their release certificate, while 5 percent committed a new offence (http://www.msp.gouv.qc.ca). In Ontario, 90 percent of parolees successfully completed their conditional release, 9 percent violated the conditions of their release certificate, and 1 percent committed a new offence (Ontario Parole and Earned Remission Board 2007).

A review of the release decisions of the two provincial boards reveals that the Ontario Board of Earned Remission and Parole grants parole in 26 percent of the cases it hears, whereas Quebec's provincial parole board grants parole in 48 percent of the cases it hears. Ontario's comparatively restrictive release policy may account for the high success rate of parolees in Ontario.

Unfortunately, as noted in Chapter 1, it is the handful of offenders who commit heinous crimes again who receive the attention of the media. It is they who often have a strong impact on corrections policies and practices—who encourage tougher sentencing laws and tighten the decision making of parole boards. The "silent majority" of offenders who successfully complete conditional release is invisible to the community. When asked about the connotations attached to the word "parolee," community residents tend to respond in one of two ways: "got out too soon," or "dangerous to the public." These responses reflect the fact, noted in Chapter 1, that most citizens get their information on crime, criminal justice, and corrections from the media.

Contrary to what media reports would have us believe, the rate of reconviction for violent offences for offenders under community supervision has declined over the past decade. The highest failure rate is among those offenders who were not granted parole but instead were released on statutory release by the CSC after serving two-thirds of their sentence. As a group, these offenders are at high risk to reoffend, which perhaps is one reason why they were not granted release on parole. Statistics also indicate that offenders released on day parole had significantly higher completion rates than offenders released on full parole or statutory release (CSC 2007; Public Safety Canada Portfolio Corrections Statistics Committee 2007).

Offenders who successfully complete their parole and go on to live law-abiding lives may apply for a pardon. Persons convicted of summary offences may apply for a pardon three years after completing their sentence; persons convicted of an indictable offence may apply five years after the end of their sentence.

Suspension of Conditional Release

Box 9.5 describes the execution of a Warrant of Suspension and Apprehension on a federal offender by a CSC Team Supervision Unit in Ontario.

Failing to abide by any of the set conditions, including committing a new criminal offence or failing to adhere to the conditions of the parole certificate, may result in a **suspension of conditional release.** This is a "limbo situation" during which the offender is placed in temporary detention in local custody. Parolees suspected of committing a new offence can be suspended as well, but most suspensions are for violations of conditions or to prevent the breach of a condition. When a parolee is suspended, two outcomes are possible: (1) the parole supervisor cancels the suspension and releases the person from custody, or (2) the case is referred back to the provincial parole board or the NPB for a hearing to determine whether there should be a **revocation of conditional release** (which usually means a transfer back to a federal correctional facility).

BOX 9.5

CSC Team Supervision Unit: Execution of a Warrant of Suspension and Apprehension

Jeff had violated the terms of his parole—missed his curfew, neglected to report in for several days—and now he's on the phone to Parole Officer Angela Beecher, sounding contrite and asking for her guidance. He admits he's been on a cocaine binge over the last few days and is, by his own description, "extremely messed up." Angela is surprised to hear from him; she figured he had gone on the run days ago. A warrant of suspension and apprehension had been issued the night before and the police are now on the lookout for Jeff. Once they find him, he'll have to go back to prison. Angela calmly speaks with Jeff. It's a touchy situation and she knows from experience

(continued)

that if she says the wrong thing, a man in Jeff's shaky condition might be tempted to disappear. Finally, she convinces him to meet her that same evening at his home.

As soon as she hangs up the phone, she contacts the Toronto Police Service, 42 Division, and requests backup. A meeting is quickly arranged. Officers from the Major Crimes Unit are gathered by the time Angela and Paul Lay, her coworker, arrive at 42 Division. They discuss how to apprehend Jeff if he is still at home when they arrive. It's necessary to somehow get Jeff out on the street so that they can make a legal arrest; without a search warrant, it's illegal to enter his home. They plan for possible scenarios: Jeff's not home when they arrive; Jeff panics and runs; Jeff pulls a gun, resists arrest, and tries to take Angela hostage. They decide that Angela and Paul should go to the door alone while police officers conceal themselves nearby, ready to move in. Angela and Paul will try to draw the offender out of his house and down the driveway, where their car will be parked.

On the way to Jeff's house, Angela calls to confirm that he's still there. She's relieved when she hears his voice and tells him she will be there soon. Angela and Paul pull up in front of the parolee's house with the plainclothes police officers not far behind. To their surprise, Jeff is outside waiting for them, a dishevelled and solitary figure at the edge of his driveway. Angela gets out of her car and has a few words with him. As they speak, Jeff sees men approaching from the corner of his eye. He immediately understands what is happening. He wavers momentarily, and Angela sees that his eyes have suddenly welled with tears, but he stands his ground. In a gentle voice, one officer asks Jeff if he knows why they are there. Jeff nods and offers no resistance. They lead him off to the waiting cruiser.

Later on, Paul and Angela go over the evening's events. "It couldn't have gone better," comments Paul. "I think Jeff knew what was going to happen and was ready for it. It was a perfect execution of a warrant; nobody was injured, safety wasn't compromised, and the rule of law was followed."

"Right now, I feel very happy about the way things were accomplished," says Angela. "However, I won't lie, early on I was apprehensive. At one point, I thought it was going to get out of hand, but given how the situation was dealt with, I'm pleased. I couldn't ask for a better resolution. It was a learning experience too. There's no written policy about what to do in a situation like this, so you have to improvise as you go along." She pauses for a moment, then continues. "The fact that Jeff phoned me this afternoon and was willing to cooperate, that told me he wanted help. So I did my best to get him the help he needs."

Source: CSC 2001b.

Those who violate parole by absconding become the subjects of arrest warrants. Their status is recorded in the Canadian Police Information Centre, a centralized, computer-based information system that is linked to municipal and provincial police forces and the RCMP. For these offenders, the sentence stops running until they are arrested. In Ontario, a Fugitive Apprehension Squad operates under the umbrella of the province's Criminal Intelligence Service, which coordinates the activities of municipal and regional police forces and the Ontario Provincial Police.

There is a specific rationale behind suspending a parolee for violating conditions. Release conditions are established in order to reduce or manage the risk of reoffending; thus a violation of these conditions might cause the parole board to reassess the original decision. In other words, if attendance at a treatment program is a release condition for a parolee, the parole board should be notified if the offender has dropped out of the program.

To suspend a release, a parole supervisor issues a warrant of apprehension and suspension of conditional release, which empowers the police to arrest the parolee and place him or her in the local lockup. Parole officers have considerable discretion in the use of suspensions. The law states that officers "may" suspend a parolee for violating a parole condition or when new offences are alleged. The number of cases in which technical violations occur or new offences are alleged but a suspension is not imposed is unknown.

As discussed earlier, a parole supervisor may suspend the conditional release for violations of conditions if there is reason to believe that the offender has committed or will commit a criminal offence. If the parole supervisor does not cancel the suspension, the case goes forward to a post suspension hearing before a parole board.

The parole board must then decide whether to (a) issue a warning letter to the parolee, or (b) issue a warrant of suspension that will result in the offender being apprehended and returned to prison to await a postsuspension hearing before the board.

Post-Suspension Hearing

Offenders who have had their conditional release suspended are returned to the correctional facility to await a post-suspension hearing before the parole board. Two key documents in the deliberations of the parole board are the report on the incident that triggered the suspension and the postsuspension report prepared by the supervising parole officer. These reports set out the circumstances surrounding the alleged violations of the conditional release or statutory release, consider the viability of the original release plan, and recommend whether the offender's release should be revoked, terminated, or reinstated.

During the postsuspension hearing the parole board has several options: (1) cancel the suspension, (2) revoke the release, or (3) terminate the release (for federal and Ontario provincial parolees). This last option is selected when there is a need to end the conditional release for reasons beyond the control of the individual offender, such as if the community residential facility where the offender has been living has burned down. If the board feels that this person cannot be on conditional release without a residency requirement, it will terminate the release until new accommodations can be secured.

In the federal system, two additional options are available: (1) issue a reprimand to the offender and cancel the suspension, or (2) cancel the suspension but order a delay in that cancellation for up to 30 days, so that it can only be imposed for a second or subsequent suspension. In neither case will the release be revoked. Most offenders whose releases are revoked have violated the general and/or specific conditions of their release certificate. This may include being in an unauthorized area, or making contact with prohibited persons.

The Effectiveness of Parole

Except to cite the fact that most offenders successfully complete parole, the effectiveness of parole as a correctional strategy has not been examined in Canada.

American researchers have found that Intensive Parole Supervision programs that include a treatment component in combination with surveillance result in higher success rates than intensive supervision programs that focus only on surveillance (Sherman et al. 1997). It also seems that offenders with less serious criminal records and less prior involvement in the criminal justice system are more responsive to the assistance and monitoring of parole officers, whereas offenders who have had extensive prior contact with the criminal justice system and who have committed more serious offences are little affected by the supervision and assistance of parole officers (Solomon et al. 2005).

The National Parole Board defines successful completion as "releases in which the offender remains under supervision in the community from release date until the end of the period of supervision (warrant expiry for full parole and statutory release) (2007, 147)." As noted above, most offenders successfully complete parole. If an ex-offender were to commit a new offence the day after the warrant expiry date, this would not be recorded as a failure.

The task of measuring the actual effectiveness of parole is complicated by the following factors:

- Many offenders (up to 85 percent in some provincial correctional institutions) do not apply for parole, but rather serve their time until release.

- Offenders on conditional release may be suspended and subsequently have their conditional release revoked for violations of the conditions of their release certificate and without having committed a new crime. This may include such minor incidents as having a beer with friends (thus violating the condition to abstain from alcohol and drug use).
- Most studies of conditional release follow offenders for only a short time following completion of their sentence.
- There is no measure of the offender's subsequent "quality of life," personal and family stability, substance use/abuse, or progress in addressing other need areas. The only criterion is whether the offender comes to the attention of the criminal justice system and is committed to custody.
- The most common measure of recidivism is "readmission"—that is, the number of offenders who reenter prison for a subsequent conviction who have been there before. Offenders who have moved to other jurisdictions or who have been deported to their home country are not counted.
- Even when an offender does not violate the conditions of a parole certificate or commit a new offence while on parole, this is not, in itself, an indication that parole supervision has been effective. Rather, the offender may have benefited from a supportive family, employer, or other life situation.

In recent years there has been an increasing focus on the reintegration of offenders into the community. Post-release programs designed to assist released prisoners and reduce re-offending are variously referred to as "'aftercare', 'transitional care', 'reentry', 'reentry support', 'reintegration or resettlement'" (Griffiths, Dandurand, and Murdock, 2007:3) and may involve the participation of justice personnel, NGOs, and community organizations and volunteers. This has resulted in a number jurisdictions, including several U.S. states and the UK to emphasize the concept "throughcare" in recognition of the fact that prisoners need to be prepared for release while incarcerated and that there should be continuity of treatment intervention from the prison to the community (see Griffiths, Dandurand, and Murdoch, 2007).

AT ISSUE

ISSUE 9.1: Should the courts be allowed to impose restrictions on ex-offenders under Section 810 of the Criminal Code?

Following is a case in which Section 810 was applied to an offender who had completed his sentence in custody and moved to another part of the country.

The Arrest of a Rapist under Section 810 of the Criminal Code

Thane Moore, a 43-year-old sex offender from Prince Edward Island, was arrested at Vancouver airport just hours after his release from prison. Moore, who referred to himself as a "walking time bomb," had been released from Dorchester Penitentiary earlier that day. He had served his entire 14-year sentence in custody after being found guilty of rape. NPB documents indicated that Moore was not rehabilitated and was at a high risk to reoffend.

After his release from custody, he left Atlantic Canada. The Vancouver Police High-Risk Offender Unit became aware of his intention to relocate in Vancouver, met him at the airport, arrested him, and took him into custody. A VPD spokesperson stated: "Our high-risk offender unit believes he poses a significant harm to the safety of adult females." Moore was arrested on a peace bond under Section 810 of the Criminal Code and was held in custody until a scheduled appearance before a judge, at which time the Vancouver police argued for the imposition of strict conditions to allow the police to monitor his activities. The judge imposed 17 separate restrictions on Moore and then released him to a halfway house in Vancouver. Among the conditions were that he report to the VPD Sex Offender Unit and a probation officer for a year; that he inform police of the model of car he was driving and his place of employment; that he not be alone in a car with a woman; that he not carry weapons, except roofing tools; and that he not contact certain families and the victim of his crime on PEI.

Moore signed a peace bond stating that he would not move to Whitehorse; a number of people had expressed fear that he might go there. He also agreed not to move to Dawson City after a public outcry in response to his originally stated intention to move there following release from custody. Moore was free to move anywhere else in Canada as long as he abided by the restrictions.

What do you think?

1. Does the use of Section 810 of the Criminal Code risk violating the rights of ex-offenders?
2. Should the police be allowed to arrest someone on the grounds that he or she may commit a crime after serving an entire sentence in custody?
3. Was Section 810 of the Criminal Code applied appropriately in this case?

Sources: CBC News 2007a, 2007b.

AT ISSUE

ISSUE 9.2: Should the community be notified when a high-risk offender is released from prison?

Community notification (CN) remains an intensely controversial issue. It is often framed as one of a balance of rights: the community to protection and the offender to privacy.

Proponents of CN make one key argument: that CN will alert the neighbourhood to a potential risk, thereby reducing the likelihood of another offence.

More specifically, they argue:

- Public safety overrides any expectation the offender has for privacy.
- Information on convictions is in the public domain.
- The protection of potential victims is an important goal for society.
- Offenders have forfeited the expectation of privacy by virtue of their offences and the risk they pose. Indeed, even those who are concerned about the civil rights of the identified offenders recognize the poor record of sex offender treatment and the high likelihood of recidivism.

Opponents of CN counter:

- There is no evidence that it is effective in reducing reoffending.
- It can engender an exaggerated sense of security, or conversely, it can increase public fear and paranoia.
- Vigilantism against identified offenders (and those who bear a resemblance to their pictures) is possible.
- The stress of CN could increase a sex offender's propensity to recidivate in much the same way that stress increases relapses among substance abusers.
- CN can make it difficult for some offenders to reintegrate into the community because they find it difficult to secure employment and/or accommodation.
- CN may unintentionally result in the displacement of offenders to criminogenic neighbourhoods.

The Research Evidence

There have been few studies (none of them Canadian) about the impact of CN on reoffending among high-risk offenders. Nor have there been any about whether CN improved feelings of personal safety in the community. In one American state, a study found no differences in the recidivism rates (commission of new offences and/or violations of release conditions) of male sex offenders (Zevitz 2006). A study that compared the perceptions of sex offenders with those of the general public as to the fairness of the CN law in that state found (not surprisingly) that sex offenders viewed the law as more unfair than did the general public; also, the sex offenders stated that they experienced more vigilantism than was publicly known and that notification had had a negative impact on their efforts to reintegrate into the community (Brannon et al. 2007).

Similarly, sex offenders who were required to register with the police in the community felt stigmatized and experienced difficulties in social relationships and in finding housing and employment (see Tewksbury 2005).

What do you think?

1. Would you want to be notified of the presence of a high-risk offender in your neighbourhood? Why or why not? If so, what would the knowledge cause you to do differently?
2. If you were notified that a high-risk offender was returning to your community, would you participate in a protest designed to force the offender to live elsewhere?
3. Does your province have a CN law? Check the statute books, because several do and more are planned. Check out the website of your local police. Many now have CN pages.
4. Do you think that CN breaches an individual's right to privacy?

Sources: Brannon et al. 2007; B.C. Civil Liberties Association 1996; Duwe and Donnay 2008; Kabat 1998; Schram and Millroy 1995.

KEY POINTS REVIEW

1. If it is to succeed, reintegration should involve continuity between the inmate's institutional programs and the services that person receives on conditional release in the community.
2. Incarceration has a number of collateral effects, which include the loss of personal relationships and social networks, the acquisition of self-defeating habits and attitudes, the loss of personal belongings, and the loss of the ability to maintain housing.
3. Persons on conditional release are subject to differing levels of supervision by corrections officials, ranging from periodic reporting, to electronic monitoring, to frequent face-to-face contacts with a parole officer.
4. Parole officers have a dual role in their relations with clients: they serve as resources and confidants while also monitoring those clients and enforcing conditional release conditions.
5. There are unique challenges in supervising Aboriginal offenders in the community. In recent years a variety of services and programs have been developed for Aboriginal offenders in their communities. These include specialized residential facilities.
6. Female offenders on conditional release have unique needs and face many challenges, including re-establishing contact with their children.

7. The general approach of correctional systems is to manage the risk of sex offenders on conditional release through drug therapy, community notification, registration, and various supervision and monitoring strategies.
8. Statistics indicate that most federal offenders successfully complete their conditional sentences and do not reoffend prior to warrant expiry.
9. The reconviction rate for violent offences for offenders under community supervision has declined in recent years.
10. A number of factors complicate attempts to assess the effectiveness of parole.

KEY TERM QUESTIONS

1. Define **reintegration** and its objectives.
2. What are the **pains of reentry** and how do they affect offenders on conditional release?
3. Describe the procedure of **judicial recognizance** for sex offenders and the issues this procedure raises.
4. Describe **community notification** and discuss the issues surrounding its use.
5. Describe **circles of support and accountability (COSAs),** how these circles operate, and what the research suggests regarding their effectiveness.
6. Define **suspension of conditional release** and **revocation of conditional release** and explain how these affect the status of an offender on conditional release.
7. What is meant by the term "*through care*" and what role does it play in offender re-entry?

REFERENCES

Auditor General of Canada. 1996. "Correctional Service of Canada—Reintegration of Offenders." *Report of the Auditor General to the House of Commons, Chapter 30*. Ottawa: Minister of Public Works and Government Services Canada. http://www.oag-bvg.gc.ca/internet/English/parl_oag_199611_30_e_5061.html

B.C. Civil Liberties Association. 1996. *BCCLA Privacy Positions: Community Notification Regarding Released Sex Offenders*. Vancouver.

Borzycki, M. 2005. *Interventions for Prisoners Returning to the Community*. Canberra: Australian Institute of Criminology. http://www.aic.gov.au/publications/reports/2005-03-prisoners.html

Brannon, Y.N., J.S. Levenson, T. Fortney, and J.N. Baker. 2007. "Attitudes About Community Notification: A Comparison of Sexual Offenders and the Non-Offending Public." *Sexual Abuse: A Journal of Research and Treatment* 19(4): 369–79.

Bumby, K., M. Carter, S. Gibel, L. Gilligan, and R. Stroker. 2007. *Increasing Public Safety Through Successful Offender Reentry: Evidence-Based and Emerging Practices in Corrections*. Washington: Center for Effective Public Policy and Bureau of Justice Assistance. http://www.ojp.usdoj.gov/BJA/pdf/SVORI_CEPP.pdf

Burke, P.B. 2008. *TPC Reentry Handbook: Implementing the NIC Transition for Prison to the Community Model*. Washington: National Institute of Corrections, U.S. Department of Justice. http://nicic.org/Downloads/PDF/Library/022669.pdf

CBC News. 2007a. "Convicted P.E.I. Rapist Arrested in Vancouver." September 15. http://www.cbc.ca/canada/british-columbia/story/2007/09/14/bc-rapist.html

———. 2007b. "Court Places Severe Restrictions on P.E.I. Rapist." September 17. http://origin.www.cbc.ca/canada/british-columbia/story/2007/09/17/bc-thane.html

Cesaroni, C. 2001. "Releasing Sex Offenders into the Community Through 'Circles of Support': A Means of Reintegrating the 'Worst of the Worst.'" *Journal of Offender Rehabilitation* 34(2): 85–98.

Chartier, G. 2007. "Addressing Mental Health Needs of Offenders." *Let's Talk* 32(1). http://www.csc-scc.gc.ca/text/pblct/lt-en/2007/32-1/pdf/32-1_e.pdf

CSC (Correctional Service of Canada). 2007. *Departmental Performance Report*. Ottawa: Treasury Board of Canada Secretariat. http://www.tbs-sct.gc.ca/dpr-rmr/2006-2007/inst/pen/pen00-eng.asp

———. 2001a. "CSC Team Supervision Unit: A Night on the Town." *Let's Talk* 26(2).

———. 2001b. "CSC Team Supervision Unit: Execution of a Warrant of Suspension and Apprehension." *Let's Talk* 26(2).

D'Amico, J. 2007. "'Ask and You Will Receive': Creating Faith-Based Programs for Former Inmates." *Corrections Today* 69(6): 78–82.

Duwe, G., and W. Donnay. 2008. "Impact of Megan's Law on Sex Offender Recidivism: The Minnesota Experience." *Criminology* 46(2): 411–46.

Farole, D.J. 2003. *The Harlem Parole Reentry Court Evaluation: Implementation and Preliminary Impacts*. New York: Center for Court Innovation. http://www.courtinnovation.org/_uploads/documents/harlemreentryeval.pdf

Griffiths, C.T., Y. Dandurand, and D. Murdoch. 2007. *The Social Reintegration of Offenders and Crime Prevention*. Ottawa: National Crime Prevention Centre, Public Safety Canada. http://www.publicsafety.gc.ca/res/cp/res/soc-reint-eng.aspx

Heise, E., L. Horne, H. Kirkegaard, H. Nigh, I.P Derry, and M. Yantzi. 1996. *Community Reintegration Project*. Toronto: Mennonite Central Committee.

Kabat, A.R. 1998. "Scarlet Letter Sex Offender Databases and Community Notification: Sacrificing Personal Privacy for a Symbol's Sake." *American Criminal Law Review* 35(2): 333–70.

Loya, J.S. 1997. "Life After Hard Time." http://www.joeloya.com/writing/htime.htm

Lussier, P., N. Deslauriers-Varin, and T. Ratel. 2008. "A Descriptive Profile of High-Risk Sex Offenders Under Intensive Supervision in the Province of British Columbia, Canada." *International Journal of Offender Therapy and Comparative Criminology*. In press.

Lynch, M. 1998. "Waste Managers? The New Penology, Crime Fighting, and Parole Agent Identity." *Law and Society Review* 32: 839–69.

Maruna, S., and T. LeBel. 2003. "Welcome Home? Examining the 'Reentry Court' from a Strengths-Based Perspective." *Western Criminology Review* 4(2): 91–107. http://wcr.sonoma.edu/v4n2/manuscripts/marunalebel.pdf

Motiuk, L., C. Cousineau, and J. Gileno. 2005. *The Safe Return of Offenders to the Community: Statistical Overview*. Ottawa: CSC. http://www.csc-scc.gc.ca/text/rsrch/safe_return2005/safe_return2005_e.pdf

Murphy, P.J., L. Johnsen, and J. Murphy. 2002. *Paroled for Life: Interviews with Parolees Serving Life Sentences.* Vancouver: New Star.

NPB (National Parole Board). 2007. *Performance Monitoring Report, 2006–2007*. Ottawa. http://www.npb-cnlc.gc.ca/reports/pdf/pmr_2006_2007/index-eng.htm

Nolan, P. 2005. "Prepared Statement presented to the Committee on the Judiciary, U.S. House of Representatives, November 3." http://www.justicefellowship.org/article.asp?ID=266

Nuffield, J. 1998. *Issues in Urban Corrections for Aboriginal People*. Ottawa: Solicitor General. http://ww2.ps-sp.gc.ca/publications/abor_corrections/199803b_e.pdf

Ontario Parole and Earned Remission Board. 2007. *2006–2007 Annual Report*. Toronto: Ministry of Community Safety and Correctional Services. http://www.operb.gov.on.ca/english/operb_annual_report.pdf

Petrunik, M.G. 2002. "Managing Unacceptable Risk: Sex Offenders, Community Response, and Social Policy in the United States and Canada." *International Journal of Offender Therapy and Comparative Criminology* 46(4): 483–511.

Public Safety Canada Portfolio Corrections Statistics Committee. 2007. *Corrections and Conditional Release Statistical Overview*. Ottawa. http://www.justicefellowship.org/article.asp?ID=266

Rankin, B. 2005. *Community Adult Mentoring and Support Program*. Ottawa: CSC. http://www.csc-scc.gc.ca/text/benevols/archive/2005/cams-eng.shtml

Schram, D.D. and C.D. Millroy. 1995. *Community Notification: A Study of Offender Characteristics and Recidivism*. Olympia: Washington State Institute for Public Policy.

Seymour, A.K. 2001. *The Victim's Role in Offender Reentry*. Washington: Office for Victims of Crime, U.S. Department of Justice. http://www.appa-net.org/resources/pubs/docs/VROR.pdf

Sherman, L.W., D. Gottfredson, D. MacKenzie, J. Eck, P. Reuter, and S. Bushway. 1997. *Preventing Crime: What Works, What Doesn't, What's Promising*. Washington: Office of Justice Programs, U.S. Department of Justice. http://www.ncjrs.gov/works

Solomon, A.L., V. Kachnowski, and A. Bhati. 2005. *Does Parole Work? Analyzing the Impact of Postprison Supervision on Rearrest Outcomes*. Washington: Urban Institute. http://www.urban.org/publications/311156.html

Tewksbury, R. 2005. "Collateral Consequences of Offender Registration." *Journal of Contemporary Criminal Justice* 21(1): 67–81.

Thurber, A. 1998. "Understanding Offender Reintegration." *Forum on Corrections Research* 10(1): 14–18.

Verbrugge, P., K. Nunes, S. Johnson, and K. Taylor. 2002. *Predictors of Revocation of Conditional Release Among Substance Abusing Women Offenders*. Ottawa: CSC. http://www.csc-scc.gc.ca/text/rsrch/reports/r133/r133_e.pdf

Visher, C.A., L. Winterfield, and M.B. Coggeshall. 2005. "Ex-offender Employment Programs and Recidivism: A Meta-analysis." *Journal of Experimental Criminology* 1(3): 295–315.

Wilson, R.J., J.E. Picheca, and M. Prinzo. 2005. *Circles of Support and Accountability: An Evaluation of the Pilot Project in South-Central Ontario*. Ottawa: CSC. http://www.csc-scc.gc.ca/text/rsrch/reports/r168/r168_e.pdf

Wilson, R.J., L. Stewart, T. Stirpe, M. Barrett, and J.E. Cripps. 2000. "Community-Based Sex Offender Management: Combining Parole Supervision and Treatment to Reduce Recidivism." *Canadian Journal of Criminology* 42(2): 177–88.

Wine, S. 1992. *A Motherhood Issue: The Impact of Criminal Justice System Involvement on Women and Their Children*. Ottawa: Solicitor General.

Zevitz, R.G. 2006. "Sex Offender Community Notification: Its Role in Recidivism and Offender Reintegration." *Criminal Justice Studies* 19(2): 193–208.

WEBLINKS

U.S. Department of Justice, Office of Justice Programs (Reentry)

http://www.reentry.gov
Contains information on reentry programs and evaluations.

Urban Institute Reentry Mapping Network

http://www.urban.org/reentry_mapping/index.cfm
Contains information on the Reentry Mapping Network, a partnership involving the Urban Institute and organizations in a number of American cities that involves mapping as well as analyzing and addressing the issues surrounding offender reentry. This site illustrates one of the more innovative approaches to offender reentry.

National Institute of Corrections—Prisoner Reentry

http://www.nationalinstituteofcorrections.gov/Library/017380
Provides information on a myriad of topics related to offender reentry, including publications, programs and links to the NCJRS Abstracts Database.

GLOSSARY OF KEY TERMS

accelerated parole review (APR): A process defined in the Corrections and Conditional Release Act in which some first-time federal offenders are fast-tracked for parole consideration. The intent is to expedite the release of inmates who have committed less serious offences.

aggressive precautions (against violence): Inmate strategies for avoiding violence and victimization, including developing a tough attitude, being physically strong, and keeping a weapon. See also *passive precautions.*

Auburn model (for prisons): A system that allowed prisoners to work and eat together during the day and provided housing in individual cells at night. A strict silent system, which forbade prisoners from communicating or even gesturing to one another, was enforced at all times. The Auburn system was the model upon which most prisons in the United States and Canada were patterned. See also *Pennsylvania model.*

Brown commission: An investigation into the treatment of prisoners in the Kingston Penitentiary that produced two reports (1848 and 1849). While the reports condemned the use of corporal punishment and emphasized the need to focus on the rehabilitation of offenders, the impact of the Brown commission on correctional reform was unclear, and the commission might best be viewed as a missed opportunity to reconsider the use of imprisonment.

Canadian Charter of Rights and Freedoms (1982): The primary law of the land that guarantees basic rights and freedoms for citizens (including those convicted of criminal offences) and includes sections on fundamental freedoms, legal rights, equity rights, and enforcement.

carceral corrections: That portion of systems of corrections relating to confinement in correctional institutions. Broadly defined, it includes sentencing judges, superintendents and wardens, inmates, correctional officers, program staff, volunteers, the offender's family, treatment professionals, health care providers, and spiritual advisers such as chaplains and Aboriginal Elders.

case management: The process by which identified needs and risks of inmates are matched with selected services and resources.

circle sentencing: A restorative justice strategy that involves a collaborative effort on the part of community residents (including the crime victim and the offender) and justice system personnel in order to reach a consensual decision through a process of reconciliation, restitution, and reparation.

circles of support and accountability: Community based forums that provide support for sex offenders who are released from correctional institutions at warrant expiry or whose period of supervision on conditional release has expired.

classical school: A perspective of crime and criminals set out in the writings of Cesare Beccaria and Jeremy Bentham in the 1700s. Among the basic tenets of this perspective are (1) criminal offenders exercise free will and engage in criminal behaviour as a consequence of rational choice, and (2) to be effective, punishment must be certain and must fit the crime.

classification: The process by which inmates are categorized through the use of various assessment instruments. Classification is used to determine the appropriate security level of the inmate and program placement.

cold turkey release: Discharge of an offender at the end of the sentence when no conditional release or supervision is possible. For federal offenders, this only occurs when statutory release is denied and the inmate serves the entire sentence in confinement. For provincial offenders, for whom cold turkey releases are far more common, this occurs when they have reached the two-thirds point in the sentence, if they have not lost any remission. However, if the sentencing judge orders probation to follow imprisonment, some provincial offenders will immediately begin a period of probation supervision.

community assessment: A document prepared by probation or parole officers for the parole board and containing information on the feasibility of the inmate-applicant's proposed community plan in terms of the level of supervision required and the availability of community resources.

community-based residential facilities (CRFs): Community-based facilities for federal offenders that are operated either directly by the government or by private contractors.

community correctional centres (CCCs): Community-based residential facilities operated by the Correctional Service of Canada.

community corrections: A generic term used to denote correctional programs that are delivered in community settings.

community notification: The practice, usually carried out by police agencies, of making a public announcement that a high-risk offender has taken up residence in an area.

conditional sentence: A sentence imposed on an offender who would otherwise be incarcerated for a period of less than two years but whose risk to the community is deemed by the court to be so low that the offender can serve the term at home, abiding by prescribed conditions and subject to imprisonment should the conditions be violated.

conservative correctional ideology: A perspective of criminality and corrections that focuses on free will and the lack of discipline as causes of crime and holds offenders responsible for their behaviour.

Constitution Act (1867): Formerly known as the British North America Act (1867), this legislation includes provisions that define the responsibilities of the federal and provincial governments in the area of criminal justice. The federal government is assigned the authority to enact criminal laws and procedures for processing criminal cases, while the provinces are assigned responsibility for the administration of justice.

continuum of correctional institutions: A term used to describe the differences in institutional environments among correctional institutions located at either ends of the security spectrum—maximum to minimum. While all correctional institutions are total institutions, some are more "total" than others.

correctional agenda (of correctional officers): The concept of correctional officers functioning as change agents and using their authority to assist inmates to cope with the problems of living in confinement.

correctional plan: A key component of the case management process that determines the offender's initial institution placement, specific training or work opportunities, and preparation for release.

corrections: The structures, policies, and programs that are delivered by governments, nonprofit agencies and organizations, and members of the general public to punish, treat, and supervise, in the community and in correctional institutions, persons convicted of criminal offences.

Corrections and Conditional Release Act: The primary legislation under which the federal system of corrections operates. The Act covers all facets of managing and supervising federal offenders.

Criminal Code: Federal legislation that sets out the criminal laws of Canada and the procedures for the administration of justice.

criminogenic risk factors: Risk/needs factors that contribute to a person's propensity to commit criminal offences, including the acceptance of antisocial values and substance-abuse problems. See also *dynamic risk factors*.

critical incident stress debriefing (CISD): A procedure for assisting correctional officers following a critical incident that includes debriefing by a trained intervenor, identifying the symptoms of stress, and providing the officer with stress-management strategies.

cross-gender staffing: The practice of staffing correctional institutions with both male and female officers. Most often discussed in terms of the issue of whether male correctional officers should work inside correctional facilities for women.

custodial agenda (of correctional officers): An historical conception of the role of correctional officers as "mindless and brutal" custodians who routinely use arbitrary and excessive force.

dangerous offender: A designation made by the judge after conviction (or up to six months later in some cases) that results in an indeterminate term of federal imprisonment. It is not commonly used and can be ordered only if the person poses such a clear danger to the community that preventive detention is justified. Dangerous offenders can be released by the National Parole Board only when they no longer constitute a danger to the community.

day parole: The authority granted by a parole board for inmates to be at large in order to prepare for full release (e.g., for job search) while returning at night to the institution or, more typically, to a community residential facility. Day parolees can seek full parole when they reach their parole eligibility dates.

deprivation theory (of inmate social system): An explanation which holds that the inmate social system develops as a consequence of inmates' attempts to mitigate the pains of imprisonment.

detention during the period of statutory release: A decision by the National Parole Board (after an application by the CSC) that a federal inmate be denied statutory release and be detained in the institution until warrant expiry.

differential amenability to treatment: The notion that, for a variety of reasons, not all inmates are receptive to treatment and/or require interventions tailored to meet their specific needs, abilities, and interests.

differential treatment availability: The recognition that within systems of corrections not all inmates have equal access to treatment programs.

differential treatment effectiveness: The requirement that, to be effective, treatment interventions must be multifaceted and matched to the specific needs of individual offenders.

diversion: Those programs that are designed to keep offenders from being processed further into the formal criminal justice system. May operate at the pre-charge, post-charge, or post-sentencing stage.

dynamic security: A variety of ongoing, meaningful interactions between staff and inmates, including officers making suggestions, assisting with problems, and speaking with inmates on a regular basis. See also *static security*.

electronic monitoring (EM): A correctional strategy that involves placing an offender under house arrest and then using electronic equipment to ensure that the conditions of supervision are fulfilled. May be used as either an alternative to confinement or following a term of incarceration in a provincial correctional facility.

expressive violence: Violence between inmates that is neither planned by the perpetrator nor deliberate. Rather, it is a result of specific problems that the inmate-initiator is experiencing, such as stress or difficulties in coping with life inside the institution.

full parole: The authority granted by a parole board for an inmate to be at large during the last part of his or her sentence. A term of full parole can begin as early as the one-third point in a sentence and will run until warrant expiry if not revoked. Provincial offenders on full parole give up their earned remission.

general deterrence: An objective of sentencing designed to deter others from engaging in criminal conduct.

importation theory (of inmate social system): An explanation that holds that the inmate social system develops as a consequence of pre-prison attitudes and behaviours that are brought by inmates into the institution.

inmate code: A key component of the inmate social system composed of a set of behavioural rules that govern interaction among the inmates and between inmates and correctional staff. Among the tenets of the code are (1) do your own time, (2) never rat on a con, (3) don't weaken, and (4) don't steal from cons.

inmate social system: See *inmate subculture*.

inmate subculture: The patterns of interaction and the relationships that exist among inmates confined in correctional institutions.

institutionalized: A term used to describe those inmates who have become so immersed in prison life (prisonized) that they are unable to function in the outside, free community.

instrumental violence: Violence between inmates that is the result of planned or deliberate action on the part of the inmate-perpetrator and most often used to gain status or to intimidate other inmates in order to secure illicit goods and services.

intermediate sanctions (also known as alternative sanctions or community sanctions): A term used to describe a wide variety of correctional programs that generally fall between traditional probation and incarceration (although specific initiatives may include either of these penalties as well).Includes fines, community service, day centres, home detention and electronic monitoring, intensive probation supervision and boot camps.

intensive supervision probation (ISP): An intermediate sanction (between the minimal supervision of traditional probation and incarceration) that generally includes reduced caseloads for probation officers, increased surveillance of probationers, treatment interventions, and efforts to ensure that probationers are employed.

interdiction strategies (for HIV/AIDS and infectious diseases): Efforts to reduce the use of illegal drugs and other high-risk behaviours, such as tattooing that include frequent searches, urinalysis programs, the use of drug dogs, ion scanners and video surveillance.

judicial determination: When a sentencing judge orders that a person being sentenced to a federal term must serve one-half of the sentence before being eligible to apply for parole. It is possible only for certain offences, specifically serious interpersonal offences and drug offences as specified in Schedule I and II of the Corrections and Conditional Release Act.

judicial recognizance: An order of the court, often referred to as a peace bond (section 810 of the Criminal Code), that requires the subject of the order to adhere to set conditions, such as avoiding places where children may be present. It is frequently used for high-risk sex offenders who reach warrant expiry.

judicial review (faint hope clause): A process authorized by section 745 of the Criminal Code whereby those serving life sentences for murder can, after serving 15 years, apply to a court and jury to have their period of parole ineligibility reduced.

liberal correctional ideology: A perspective on criminality and corrections that focuses on the role of poverty, racism, and social injustice as causes of crime and on the treatment and rehabilitation of offenders.

long-term offender: A designation under section 752 or 753 of the Criminal Code that requires the offender to spend a portion of time under supervision following the expiry of sentence. Long-term supervision orders may prescribe a period of supervision up to 10 years.

mature coping: A term coined by the criminologist Robert Johnson to describe a positive approach to adjusting to life inside correctional institutions. The three components of mature coping are (1) dealing with problems in a straightforward manner, (2) avoiding the use of deception and violence in addressing problems, and (3) being altruistic.

maximum-security institutions: Federal correctional facilities with a highly controlled institutional environment.

medical model of corrections: A perspective on corrections that emerged in the post–World War II period. The medical, or treatment, model held that the offender was ill—physically, mentally and/or socially—and criminal behaviour was a symptom of this illness. As in medicine, diagnosis and treatment were thought to ensure the effective rehabilitation of the offender.

medium-security institutions: Federal correctional facilities that have a less highly controlled institutional environment than maximum-security institutions and in which the inmates have more freedom of movement. These institutions generally have high-security perimeter fencing.

minimum-security institutions: Federal correctional facilities that allow unrestricted inmate movement, except during the night. These institutions generally have no perimeter fencing.

moral architecture: The term used to describe the design of the first penitentiary in Canada, the intent of which was to reflect the themes of order and morality.

mortification: A term coined by the sociologist Erving Goffman to describe the process by which new inmates are transformed from "free" citizens into inmates.

multi level institutions: Federal correctional institutions that contain one or more security levels (minimum, medium, maximum) in the same facility or on the same grounds.

need principle: The notion that, to be effective, treatment interventions must address the needs of inmates. The most amenable to treatment are the inmate's criminogenic needs, including substance abuse, relations with peers, and attitudes toward and experience with employment.

need (or dynamic) risk factors: Attributes of the inmate that can be altered through intervention, such as level of education and cognitive thinking abilities. Unlike static criminal history factors, dynamic factors can be changed (for the better or, if not addressed, for the worse).

net-widening: A potential, unanticipated consequence of diversion programs in which persons who would otherwise have been released outright by the police or not charged by Crown counsel are involved in the justice system.

niches (of inmates): The friendship networks among inmates in correctional institutions. These networks may be based on previous associations, shared ethnicity or culture (e.g., Aboriginal), or length of sentence (e.g., lifers).

NIMBY (Not In My Back Yard)/NOTE (Not Over There Either) syndrome: Terms used to describe the resistance of community residents and neighbourhoods to efforts of systems of corrections to locate programming and residences for offenders in the community.

noncarceral corrections: That portion of systems of corrections relating to supervision, control, and the provision of services for offenders in non-institutional settings. Broadly defined, it includes sentencing judges, probation officers, probationers, staff of not-for-profit organizations such as the John Howard Society, parole board members, parole officers, offenders released from confinement on parole, and staff in community halfway houses.

normative code of behaviour (of correctional officers): The behavioural rules that guide interaction and contribute to solidarity among correctional officers.

pains of imprisonment: The deprivations experienced by inmates confined in correctional institutions, including the loss of autonomy, privacy, security, and freedom of movement and association.

pains of reentry: The difficulties that inmates released from correctional institutions encounter in attempting to adjust to life in the outside, free community.

passive precautions (against violence): Inmate strategies for avoiding violence and victimization, including spending time in cells and avoiding certain areas of the institution. Generally used by older, socially isolated inmates serving long sentences. See also *aggressive precautions*.

Pennsylvania model (for prisons): A separate and silent system in which prisoners were completely isolated from one another, including being kept out of eyesight of one another. Inmates ate, worked, and slept in separate cells. The Pennsylvania system became the model for prisons in Europe, South America, and Asia. See also *Auburn model.*

pillory: A solid wood frame punctured with holes through which the head and hands of the offender were placed. This punishment device was used in Lower Canada until 1842.

positivist school: A perspective of crime and criminals set out in the writings of Cesare Lombroso, Enrico Ferri, and Raffaelo Garofalo in the 1800s. A basic tenet of this perspective is that criminal behaviour is determined by biological, psychological, physiological, and/or sociological factors that can be studied and understood by application of the scientific method.

post-traumatic stress disorder (PTSD): An extreme form of *critical incident stress* that includes nightmares, hypervigilance, intrusive thoughts, and other forms of psychological distress.

pre-sentence report (PSR): A document prepared by probation officers for the sentencing judge that contains information on the convicted offender, including sociobiographical information, offence history, and risk assessments. May also include a sentence recommendation, which is not binding on the judge.

prevention strategies (for HIV/AIDS and infectious diseases): Efforts to prevent and reduce high-risk behaviour among inmates and to reduce the levels of infection that include condoms, lubricants, dental dams, and bleach kits for needles (although not needles).

prisonization: A term coined by the criminologist Donald Clemmer in 1940 to describe the process by which new inmates are socialized into the norms, values, and culture of the prison.

probation: A sentence imposed on an offender by a judge in the criminal court that provides for supervision of the offender in the community by a probation officer. All probation orders contain *mandatory conditions* that the offender must adhere to and may also contain *additional conditions* tailored to meet the specific needs and requirements of the individual probationer.

program drift: The extent to which a treatment program as delivered has moved away from the original model, with a potential impact on program effectiveness.

program fidelity: The extent to which a treatment program is delivered in accordance with the original program design.

radical correctional ideology: A perspective of criminality and corrections that views the capitalist system, exploitation, and the gap between rich and poor as the causes of crime and systems of corrections as instruments of repression of the lower classes. Highlights the role of economics and politics in the administration of justice and the response to offenders.

recidivism rates: The traditional method used to determine success in correctional treatment. The number of offenders who, once released from confinement, are returned to prison either for a technical violation of a condition of their parole (or statutory release) or for the commission of a new offence.

reintegration: The process whereby an inmate is prepared for and released into the community after serving time in prison.

remission/discharge: Available to provincial inmates who have served two-thirds of their sentence. Often referred to as cold turkey release and there is no supervision by a parole officer.

responsivity principle: The notion that treatment interventions must be matched to the learning styles and abilities of individual inmates.

restorative justice: An approach to the administration of justice based on the principle that criminal behaviour injures not only the victim, but communities and offenders as well. A key feature of the restorative justice approach is the attempt not only to address the specific criminal behaviour of the offender but also to broaden the focus to consider the needs of the victims and the community.

revocation of conditional release: A decision by a releasing authority, such as a parole board, made in connection with an offender whose release has been suspended. When a release is revoked, the offender begins to serve the sentence on the inside again. A re-application to the parole board would then be necessary before another parole release would be granted.

risk principle: The notion that treatment interventions have a greater chance of success when they are matched with the risk level of the offender. Research studies suggest that high-risk inmates are more likely to benefit from intensive treatment programs than low-risk inmates.

social (or argot) roles: The various roles in the inmate social system, including "square john," "right guy," "rat," and "politician." These roles are based on the inmate's friendship networks, sentence length, current and previous offences, and extent of participation in illegal activities such as gambling and drug distribution.

Special Handling Unit (SHU): A federal correctional facility that houses inmates who pose such a high risk to inmates and staff that they cannot be confined in maximum-security institutions.

specific deterrence: An objective of sentencing designed to deter the offender from future criminal conduct.

Staff Application, Recruitment, and Training Program (START): The training program for provincial correctional officers in Ontario, consisting of three components: (1) admission process, (2) pre-employment training, and (3) institutional orientation.

state-raised offenders: Inmates who have spent the majority of their adult (and perhaps youth) lives confined in correctional facilities and, as a consequence, may have neither the skills nor ability to function in the outside, free community. For these offenders, prison is "home."

static risk factors: The offender's criminal history, including prior convictions, seriousness of prior offences, and whether the offender successfully completed previous periods of supervision in the community. These variables predict the likelihood of recidivism but are not amenable to change.

static security: Fixed security apparatus in a correctional institution, including perimeter fencing, video surveillance, alarms and fixed security posts wherein correctional officers are assigned to and remain in a specific area, such as a control room. See also *dynamic security*.

status degradation ceremonies: The processing of offenders into correctional institutions whereby the offender is psychologically and materially stripped of possessions that identify him or her as a member of the "free society."

statutory release: A type of conditional release that allows incarcerated federal offenders to be released at the two-thirds point of their sentence and to serve the remaining one-third under the supervision of a parole officer in the community.

suspension of conditional release: A process typically initiated by a parole supervisor (but sometimes directly by the parole board) in which an offender's release is suspended and he or she is taken back into local custody to await a further decision. In most cases, the parole board will reconsider the case, and may release the inmate or revoke the release. A decision to revoke the release would result in the person returning to federal or provincial/territorial custody.

temporary absence: A type of conditional release that allows an inmate to participate in community activities, including employment and education, while residing in a minimum-security facility or a halfway house.

total institution: A term coined by the sociologist Erving Goffman to describe prisons, mental hospitals, and other facilities characterized by a highly structured environment in which all movements of the inmates/patients are controlled 24 hours a day by staff.

two-year rule: The division of correctional responsibility between the federal and provincial governments whereby those offenders who receive sentences of two years or longer fall under the jurisdiction of the federal government, while those offenders receiving sentences of two years less a day are the responsibility of provincial correctional authorities.

throughcare: The notion that there should be continuity between institutional treatment and programs and community-based services for offenders.

COPYRIGHT ACKNOWLEDGEMENTS

Grateful acknowledgement is made to the copyright holders who granted permission to use previously published material. Where it was not possible to provide acknowledgement in the chapters, provision is made on this page, which constitutes an extension of the copyright page.

Fig. 1.2, p. 8: © Source: Public Safety Canada Website (www.ps-sp.gc.ca), URL: http://www.ps-sp.gc.ca/csc-scc/cscrpreport-eng.pdf, Correctional Service of Canada. 2008. Reproduced with the permission of the Minister of Public Works and Government Services Canada, 2008; **Fig. 1.3, p. 9:** © Source: Public Safety Canada Website (www.ps-sp.gc.ca), URL: http://www.publicsafety.gc.ca/res/cor/rep/_fl/CCRSO_2007-eng.pdf, Correctional Service of Canada. 2008. Reproduced with the permission of the Minister of Public Works and Government Services Canada, 2008; **Box 2.2, p. 61:** © 1966 Canadian Criminal Justice Association (www.ccja-acjp.ca/en/). Reprinted by permission of University of Toronto Press Incorporated www.utpjournals.com; **Box 2.3, p. 64–65:** © Source: Crime and Punishment - A Pictorial history, Part III, Volume 10, Number 11, page 5, June 15, 1985, Correctional Service of Canada. 2008. Reproduced with the permission of the Minister of Public Works and Government Services Canada, 2008; **Box 2.4, p. 65:** © Source: Crime and Punishment - A Pictorial history, Part III, Volume 10, Number 11, page 5, June 15, 1985, Correctional Service of Canada. 2008. Reproduced with the permission of the Minister of Public Works and Government Services Canada, 2008; **Box 3.1, p. 88:** Source: Church Council on Justice and Corrections 1996, 89; **Fig. 3.2, p. 106:** Marshall, T.F. (1999). Restorative Justice: An Overview. Home Office Occasional Paper 48. London: Home Office; **Box 3.6, p. 114–115:** Reprinted by permission of Church Council on Justice and Corrections (www.ccjc.ca/ccjc@ccjc.ca); **Box 4.4, p. 143–144:** © Queen's Printer for Ontario, 2004. Reproduced with permission; **Box 5.1, p. 175–176:** © Queen's Printer for Ontario, 2006. Reproduced with permission; **Box 6.1, p. 207:** © Source: Correctional Service of Canada Website (www.csc-scc.gc.ca), URL: http://www.csc-scc.gc.ca/text/prgrm/abinit/know/5-eng.shtml, Correctional Service of Canada. 2008. Reproduced with the permission of the Minister of Public Works and Government Services Canada, 2008; **Box 6.3, p. 213:** McGraw-Hill makes no representations or warranties as to the accuracy of any information contained in the McGraw-Hill Material, including any warranties of merchantability or fitness for a particular purpose. In no event shall McGraw-Hill have any liability to any party for special, incidental, tort, or consequential damages arising out of or in connection with the McGraw-Hill Material.; **Fig. 7.1, p. 254:** © Source: Public Safety Canada Website (www.ps-sp.gc.ca), URL: http://www.ps-sp.gc.ca/csc-scc/cscrpreport-eng.pdf, Correctional Service of Canada. 2008. Reproduced with the permission of the Minister of Public Works and Government Services Canada, 2008; **Box 7.1 p. 256:** © Source: Public Safety Canada Website (www.ps-sp.gc.ca), URL: http://ww2.ps-sp.gc.ca/publications/corrections/pdf/Static-99-coding-Rules_e.pdf, Correctional Service of Canada. 2008. Reproduced with the permission of the Minister of Public Works and Government Services Canada, 2008; **Box 8.1, p. 305–306:** Reproduced with the permission of the National Parole Board; **Fig. 8.1, p. 303:** Sentencing Milestones (Fixed Sentences) for Federal Offenders, Report of the Correctional Service of Canada Review Panel: A Roadmap to Strengthening Public Safety, http://www.publicsafety.gc.ca/csc-scc/cscrpreport-eng.pdf Reproduced with the permission of the Minister of Public Works and Government Services, [2008]; **Box 9.2, p. 355–356:** © Source: Correctional Service of Canada Website (www.csc-scc.gc.ca), URL: http://internet/text/pblct/letstalk/2001/no2/26no2_e.pdf, Correctional Service of Canada. 2008. Reproduced with the permission of the

Minister of Public Works and Government Services Canada, 2008; **Box 9.5, p. 371–372:** © Source: Correctional Service of Canada Website (www.csc-scc.gc.ca), URL: http://internet/text/pblct/letstalk/2001/no2/26no2_e.pdf, Correctional Service of Canada. 2008. Reproduced with the permission of the Minister of Public Works and Government Services Canada, 2008.

INDEX